D1551602

THE TEXT OF THE APOSTOLOS IN
ATHANASIUS OF ALEXANDRIA

Society of Biblical Literature

The New Testament in the Greek Fathers

Edited by
Roderic L. Mullen

Number 8

THE TEXT OF THE APOSTOLOS IN
ATHANASIUS OF ALEXANDRIA

Gerald J. Donker

THE TEXT OF THE APOSTOLOS IN
ATHANASIUS OF ALEXANDRIA

Gerald J. Donker

Society of Biblical Literature
Atlanta

BS
1938
.D67
2011

THE TEXT OF THE APOSTOLOS IN ATHANASIUS OF ALEXANDRIA

Copyright © 2011 by the Society of Biblical Literature

All rights reserved. No part of this work may be reproduced or transmitted in any form or by any means, electronic or mechanical, including photocopying and recording, or by means of any information storage or retrieval system, except as may be expressly permitted by the 1976 Copyright Act or in writing from the publisher. Requests for permission should be addressed in writing to the Rights and Permissions Office, Society of Biblical Literature, 825 Houston Mill Road, Atlanta, GA 30329, USA.

Library of Congress Cataloging-in-Publication Data

Donker, Gerald J.
    The text of the Apostolos in Athanasius of Alexandria / by Gerald J. Donker.
        p. cm. — (Society of Biblical Literature New Testament and the Greek fathers ; no. 9)
    Includes bibliographical references (p.   ) and index.
    ISBN 978-1-58983-550-4 (pbk. : alk. paper) — ISBN 978-1-58983-551-1 (electronic format)
    1. Orthodox Eastern Church. Apostolos. 2. Athanasius, Saint, Patriarch of Alexandria, d. 373. 3. Orthodox Eastern Church—Liturgy—Texts—History and criticism. I. Title.
    BX375.A65D66 2011
    225.6'6—dc22
                                        2011016328

Printed on acid-free, recycled paper conforming to
ANSI/NISO Z39.48–1992 (R1997) and ISO 9706:1994

CONTENTS

Series Editor's Foreword

Athanasius of Alexandria stands as one of the great figures among patristic writers, important not only as a theologian and bishop but also as a witness to the developing canon of the New Testament. His quotations from the Apostolos have much to teach us about the state of the text in fourth-century Egypt. Because the quotations derive from detailed theological and controversial works and from several of Athanasius' letters setting forth his positions, contexts in which patristic authors are generally believed to have taken special care with their biblical references, they have added value as witnesses to the nature of the New Testament text current in his day.

The Society of Biblical Literature's series entitled The New Testament in the Greek Fathers has often presented ground-breaking works in the analysis of patristic references. With the publication in this series of Gerald Donker's study on the text of the Apostolos according to Athanasius, the analysis of patristic witnesses to the New Testament has taken a significant methodological leap ahead. For some years the present editor has believed that the New Testament textual data can more easily be understood if it is displayed in more than two dimensions, and the figures in Donker's work now demonstrate some of the potential of a more spatially-oriented display of the results derived from patristic material. We are, therefore, proud to present a much more detailed analysis of patristic references than has been possible heretofore in this series and also to be able to present the supporting data online. Insofar as the author received his doctorate in Australia and now teaches in Africa, this is also the first time that a work in this series has been both written and prepared for press by an author outside of North America.

One of the advantages of studying patristic references to the New Testament is that scholars can gain an understanding of the text over time. Various earlier works in this series on the texts used by Clement of Alexandria, Origen and Didymus have also focused on Alexandria. Now, with the addition of a study of Athanasius, our picture of the New Testament as known and used in that city becomes yet clearer. While the classic notion of text-types has been challenged recently, the ability to identify and visually represent textual streams perduring over some centuries adds greatly to our understanding both of the text itself, broadly construed, and of the community that produced and transmitted it. In that light, the present work demonstrates that the Athanasian text may be seen as standing within the Alexandrian textual stream, though not always at the center of it.

It will be noted that the present volume, number 8 in the series, appears some years later than volume 9. The work necessary to prepare a manuscript for the press can be time consuming, and the dissertation originally scheduled to appear as number 8 in the series has not as yet become available for publication.

It is to be hoped that in future more scholars will be able to present the results of their work in this series.

Roderic L. Mullen,
Editor, The New Testament in the Greek Fathers

AUTHOR'S PREFACE

The journey from my initial interest in New Testament text-critical issues during undergraduate theological studies in the early 90's to the completion of a doctoral research project and this subsequent monograph has been somewhat convoluted, spanning a little over two decades. My first exposure to and interest in textual criticism of the New Testament was as a result of attending some lectures given by Gordon Fee, the original editor of the SBLNTGF series, during a visit he made to Australia in 1990. After completing a BTh in 1994 I was involved in pastoral ministry, further study to complete an MA and, alongside my wife and (then) two small daughters, preparing for missions work in Africa. We arrived in Sudan in late 1999 and lived there for 6 and a half years while I taught at Nile Theological College in Khartoum. During these years my interest in text-critical research was somewhat muted but not forgotten. Events in Sudan following the 2005 Comprehensive Peace Agreement between North and South provided the opportune time to finally pursue doctoral studies and after some initial enquiries I eventually narrowed my research interest to the New Testament in the Greek Fathers and particularly Athanasius of Alexandria (our mutual connection from having lived in Africa a not inconsiderable factor). This monograph, which presents a slightly revised version of a PhD thesis submitted and accepted at Macquarie University, Sydney, Australia in October 2009 is the culmination of that journey.

This journey however has not been undertaken alone and while the writing of a thesis and subsequent editing for presentation in a revised form such as this may sometimes be a lonely task it can never be considered an isolated endeavour. Many people have provided inspiration, encouragement and practical help to enable completion. While the list is ultimately too long, I would like here to acknowledge some especially: Ted Woods for suggesting I contact Macquarie University as a suitable location in Australia to conduct my research. Alanna Nobbs, Head of the Department of Ancient History, Macquarie University who was helpful and encouraging from the outset. Grateful appreciation goes to my Doctoral Supervisors: Don Barker who provided judicious oversight and guidance throughout the whole process and Stephen Llewelyn whose advice was particularly helpful in the latter stages of compilation and editing. Special thanks are due to Tim Finney without whose inspiration, concerning the use of multivariate analysis, this project would not have found focus and final form. He willingly made available his computer programs for use in my analysis. Our ongoing dialogue has also helped refine my approach. I am grateful for his indications that this contact has been mutually beneficial.

A number of individuals and institutions were involved in providing other resources: Rod Mullen for supplying a number of manuscript resources, the Ancient Biblical Manuscript Centre, Claremont, California for providing microfilms of manuscripts, and the Institut für Neutestamentliche Textforschung in Münster, Germany where I was able to access some microfilms that were otherwise difficult to obtain. Klaus Wachtel, Ulrich Schmid and other staff there were most welcoming and helpful. Special thanks are due to the Society for the Study of Early Christianity at Macquarie University and Tyndale House for arranging a visit to Cambridge in 2009. The Warden, Peter Williams and staff provided a congenial atmosphere for concentrated writing and completion of a number of chapters. I have appreciated the encouragement of James Libby, another fellow scholar utilizing three-dimensional multivariate analysis in biblical studies. Julian Leslie of the Statistics Department, Macquarie University gave valuable advice concerning statistical aspects that have been integrated into the methodology outlined herein. Greg Baker was most helpful in providing his programming expertise for the Python script which enabled me to produce the initial output data. Peter Costigan gave willing and specific help in understanding the intricacies of technical German. Carlingford Baptist Church, Sydney was a supportive and stimulating church home during the years 2006-2009 when most of the research and writing was undertaken

A few comments concerning the presentation of the data are in order. There are a significant number of tables and figures associated with the analysis presented in this study. All tables and figures specifically referred to in the text are presented immediately or as close as possible to the relevant references or (where noted) located in the Appendices. Refer to the Lists of Tables and Figures following for further details. Since most of the data analysis and output was completed using computing facilities the electronic source data and output files associated with this study have been made available and can be accessed online from the SBL website: http://www.sbl-site.org/assets/pdfs/pubs/Donker/Athanasius.zip. Other tables not specifically referred to in the text have been relegated to a supporting document: *Addenda to the Book. Donker-Apostolos in Athanasius* which is available as a PDF document within the .zip file located on the website. The *Addenda* also contains information related to the installation and use of various programs and scripts used in this study.

Finally, to my children Bethany, Jessica and Nathan and my wife Kathryn especially, I give thanks for their willingness to accept my absence during long hours of research and writing. Their understanding enables all my efforts. Thanks also be to God, the three in one, who is the inspiration and ultimate focus of the Apostolos.

Gerald J. Donker
Melut, Southern Sudan
May 2011

LIST OF ABBREVIATIONS

ABMC	American Biblical Manuscript Centre (Claremont, California)
AJT	*American Journal of Theology*
AJA	*American Journal of Archaeology*
ANTF	Arbeiten zur neutestamentlichen Textforschung
AW	Athanasius Werke (Series; de Gruyter)
BJRL	*Bulletin of the John Rylands University Library of Manchester*
CBGM	Coherence Based Genealogical Method
CPG	*Clavis patrum graecorum*
HSCP	*Harvard Studies in Classical Philology*
HTR	*Harvard Theological Review*
INTF	Institut für neutestamentliche Textforschung (Münster, Germany)
JBL	*Journal of Biblical Literature*
JP	*Journal of Philology*
JTS	*Journal of Theological Studies*
LCV	Lower Critical Value
LXX	Septuagint (the Greek OT)
MDS	Multi-Dimensional Scaling
NA²⁷	Nestle-Aland Greek New Testament, 27th ed.
NovT	*Novum Testamentum*
NPNF	Nicene and Post Nicene Fathers
NTS	*New Testament Studies*
NTTS	New Testament Tools and Studies
PG	Patrologia Cursus Completus: Series Graeca
PO	Patrologia orientalis
RBL	*Review of Biblical Literature*
SBL	Society of Biblical Literature
SBLDS	Society of Biblical Literature Dissertation Series
SBLMS	Society of Biblical Literature Monograph Series
SBLNTGF	Society of Biblical Literature The New Testament in the Greek Fathers
SC	Sources chrétiennes
SD	Studies and Documents
SacEr	*Sacris erudiri*
StPatr	Studia Patristica
TR	Textus Receptus (Stephanus, 1550)
TS	Texts and Studies
TS	*Theological Studies*
UCV	Upper Critical Value
UBS⁴	United Bible Societies Greek New Testament, 4th ed.
VC	*Vigiliae Christianae*

LIST OF TABLES

TABLES IN THE TEXT

TABLES IN THE APPENDICES

List of Figures

FIGURES IN THE TEXT

FIGURES IN APPENDIX B

INTRODUCTION

Within the field of New Testament textual-criticism the evidence of patristic citations, particularly those of the Greek Fathers, has been traditionally seen as the 'third class' of witness after the Greek manuscripts and versions.[1] This may indeed be an unfortunate historical anomaly since the distinct advantage of the Fathers is that they can be 'located' both chronologically and geographically. Therefore they have the potential to supply valuable evidence as 'fixed' points of reference which can help elucidate the complex history of the New Testament text.[2] The nature of patristic citations as a hitherto under utilized resource can be attributed to the difficulty and effort required to extract reliable data from the writings of the Fathers. References to the New Testament vary from accurate citations to loose adaptations to remote allusions and care needs to be taken when attempting to accurately reconstruct a Father's New Testament text.[3]

---

[1] Bruce Manning Metzger, *The Text of the New Testament: Its Transmission, Corruption and Restoration* (2d ed.; Oxford: Clarendon, 1968), 36.

[2] Fee notes that when "properly evaluated" the evidence of the Fathers can be of "primary importance". Gordon D. Fee, "The Use of the Greek Fathers for New Testament Textual Criticism," in *The Text of the New Testament in Contemporary Research: Essays on the Status Quaestionis* (SD 46; Grand Rapids: Eerdmans, 1995), 191; See also M. Jack Suggs, "The Use of Patristic Evidence in the Search for a Primitive New Testament Text," *NTS* 4 (1957-8); Robert Pierce Casey, "The Patristic Evidence for the Text of the New Testament," in *New Testament Manuscript Studies* (ed. Merrill M. Parvis and Allen P. Wikgren; Chicago: University of Chicago Press, 1950), 69. In the Editor's Foreword of the 2008 addition to the Society of Biblical Literature New Testament in the Greek Fathers (SBLNTGF) series, Holmes states; "In contrast to the earliest New Testament manuscripts, which can often be dated only rather generally and about whose geographical providence frequently nothing is known, citations of the New Testament by Christian writers of late antiquity can be located, often with some degree of precision, with respect to both time and space." Carl P. Cosaert, *The Text of the Gospels in Clement of Alexandria* (SBLNTGF 9; Atlanta: Society of Biblical Literature, 2008), ix; also Michael W. Holmes, "The Case for Reasoned Ecclecticism," in *Rethinking New Testament Textual Criticism* (ed. David A. Black; Grand Rapids: Baker Academic, 2002), 97.

[3] A further issue is the generally fragmentary nature of a Father's biblical text, coming as it does from often scattered quotations of only one verse or just part of a verse, found within the Father's writings. Major exceptions to this are commentaries written by the Fathers on portions of Scripture in which extended passages of the text are quoted, though these are relatively rare. Origen for example wrote commentaries on a number of Old and New Testament books. See Bart D. Ehrman, Gordon D. Fee and Michael W. Holmes, *The Text of the Fourth Gospel in the Writings of Origen* (SBLNTGF 3; Atlanta: Scholars Press, 1992), 18-19, 31-35. There are also minor 'exceptions' in the form of quotations that encompass a number of verses together though even these too must

Over the last few decades it has become increasingly clear that, despite the difficulties, the evidence of the Fathers is worthy of further research and has led to calls for more effort to be expended in this area.[4] Having been described as "one of the most imposing figures in all ecclesiastical history and the most outstanding of all Alexandrian bishops", it may seem surprising that the fourth century Greek Church Father, Athanasius of Alexandria has not received more attention as a pivotal witness to an early form of the New Testament text.[5] Apart from the plethora of studies on Athanasius' theology and ecclesiology, only relatively few have focussed on his use of the Scriptures from a text-critical perspective.[6] The most directly relevant study is that of Brogan's unpublished

---

be considered only fragmentary. For example Athanasius cites Heb 2:1–3 (46 words), 2:14–3:2 (103 words), Phil 2:8–11 (47 words).

[4] See Fee, "Use of the Greek Fathers," 199–200; Kurt Aland and Barbara Aland, *The Text of the New Testament: An Introduction to the Critical Editions and to the Theory and Practice of Modern Textual Criticism* (trans. Erroll F. Rhodes; 2d ed.; Grand Rapids: Eerdmans, 1989), 173. The fruit of these calls has been especially realised in the publication of a number of significant volumes in the Society of Biblical Literature New Testament in the Greek Fathers (SBLNTGF) series.

[5] Johannes Quasten, *Patrology* (4 vols.; Utrecht: Spectrum Publishers, 1960), 3:20. Athanasius' status as one of the four great Fathers of the Eastern Church clearly establishes his importance for theology, church history and ecclesiology. Up to approximately the beginning of the twentieth century the hagiographical attitude towards Athanasius was almost unbounded; he was seen as essentially the singlehanded defender of the true church during the theological controversies of the fourth century. But with the rise of critical scholarship the attitude toward Athanasius was almost reversed with studies such as those by Seeck, Schwartz, Bell and Barnes in particular portraying him as a "violent tyrant" and the equivalent of a modern gangster. Barnes, for example, states that "Athanasius may often disregard or pervert the truth, but he is a subtler and more skilful liar than Schwartz realised." See Timothy D. Barnes, *Athanasius and Constantius: Theology and Politics in the Constantinian Empire* (Cambridge, Mass.: Harvard University Press, 1993), 3; also James D. Ernest, *The Bible in Athanasius of Alexandria* (The Bible in Ancient Christianity 2; Boston: Brill, 2004), 2–3; See also Eduard Schwartz, *Zur Geschichte des Athanasius* (vol. 3 of *Gesammelte Schriften*; Berlin: de Gruyter, 1959); Harold Idris Bell, ed. *Jews and Christians in Egypt: The Jewish Troubles in Alexandria and the Athanasian Controversy* (London: Oxford University Press, 1924). With the recognition that both these perspectives may have fallen victim to the 'flaw of the excluded middle', a more balanced view has since been achieved in recent studies such as those by Arnold who claimed that some of the earlier critical studies misconstrued the evidence of the papyri. Duane W. H. Arnold, *The Early Episcopal Career of Athanasius of Alexandria* (Christianity and Judaism in Antiquity 6; Notre Dame, Indiana: University of Notre Dame Press, 1991), 11–23.

[6] The following bibliographies provide information on a wide range of Athanasian research: Christel Butterweck, Athanasius von Alexandrien: Bibliographie (Abhandlungen der Nordhein-Westfälischen Akademie der Wissenschaften 90. Opladen: Westdeutscher Verlag, 1995); Charles Kannengiesser, "The Athanasian decade 1974–84: A Bibliographical Report," *TS* 46 (1985); Johan Leemans, "Thirteen Years of Athanasius Research (1985–1998): A Survey and Bibliography," *SacEr* 39 (2000). Only a few of the studies conducted on the biblical text of Athanasius within the last half-century can properly be classed as text-critical and even then, in the case of both Nordberg and Zervopoulos' studies, are hampered by a number of methodological deficiencies. Refer to Henric Nordberg, "On the Bible Text of St. Athanasius," *Arctos* 3 (1962): 119–141; Gerassimos Zervopoulos, "The Gospels-Text of Athanasius" (Ph.D. diss., Boston University, 1955). The deficiencies of Nordberg's study are discussed in Chapter 2. Ernest's recent study on the Bible text of Athanasius is not text-critical but rhetorical and exegetical. Refer to the following footnote for bibliographic details concerning the closest relevant study by Brogan which also includes a critique of Zervopoulos' study.

dissertation on the Gospels text of Athanasius.[7] However the results of Brogan's research on the Gospels cannot be reliably assumed for describing the character of Athanasius' text in the remainder of the New Testament which is here referred to as the Apostolos.[8] Careful work on patristic sources over the last quarter of a century has highlighted the potential presence of 'mixed' texts.[9] Indeed failure to take such factors into account in some previous studies has led to faulty conclusions as has been ably demonstrated by Fee.[10] For this reason a lacuna has existed until now within text-critical research concerning the Apostolos of Athanasius. With this study on Athanasius' text of the Apostolos, a chapter in the analysis of Patristic New Testament texts can be drawn to a close.

This study has another related focus by seeking to advance discussion concerning methodology. The combination of a quantitative and group profile analyses has been used almost exclusively in studies on the texts of the Fathers for more than two decades.[11] While this methodology has been utilised successfully

---

[7] John Jay Brogan, "The Text of the Gospels in the Writings of Athanasius" (Ph.D. diss., Department of Religion, Duke University, 1997). Brogan discusses in detail the deficiencies of Zervopolous' study since it focuses, as he does, specifically on the text of the Gospels. Ibid., 57–77.

[8] The 'Apostolos' refers to the contents of the New Testament apart from (sans) the Gospels. The meaning of the term is derived from its usage by Basil of Caesarea in his work *On the Holy Spirit*, 27 where he states, "We do not content ourselves with what was reported in the Apostolos and in the Gospels, but, both before and after reading them , we add other doctrines, received from oral teaching and carrying much weight in the mystery." Quoted by Carroll D. Osburn, *The Text of the Apostolos in Epiphanius of Salamis* (SBLNTGF 6; Atlanta: Society of Biblical Literature, 2004), 1.

[9] E.g., Codex Alexandrinus (A 02) witnesses to a Byzantine text-type in the Gospels but an Alexandrian text-type in Acts, the Pauline and Catholic Epistles and Revelation and Codex Angelicus (L 020) witnesses to an Alexandrian text in the Gospels but a Byzantine text in the Pauline Epistles. See J. Harold Greenlee, *Introduction to New Testament Textual Criticism* (Grand Rapids: Eerdmans, 1964), 39, 117–118. Fee notes that Codex W makes a "distinct change from a Neutral to a Byzantine type of text at Luke 5:12 and is Western in Mark 1:1–5:30". See Gordon D. Fee, "Codex Sinaiticus in the Gospel of John: A Contribution to Methodology in Establishing Textual Relationships," in *Studies in the Theory and Method of New Testament Textual Criticism* (SD 45; Grand Rapids: Eerdmans, 1993). There are various reasons why this might have occurred. For example, though a Father may predominantly use a form of text common to one particular location, he may also have had access to and used other text-types as a result of travel or permanent relocation and hence the need to analyse carefully the data gathered. Origen for example began his career in Alexandria but subsequently relocated to Caesarea. Ehrman, Fee and Holmes, *Text of the Fourth Gospel*, 8–9; Cf. Fee, "Use of the Greek Fathers," 193. For an introduction and discussion of text-types refer to Metzger, *Text of the New Testament*, 169ff; also Greenlee, *New Testament Textual Criticism*, 86ff.

[10] Fee, "Text of John in Origen and Cyril," 302ff.

[11] See Ernest C. Colwell and Ernest W. Tune, "The Quantitative Relationships Between MS Text-Types," in *Biblical and Patristic Studies in Memory of Robert Pierce Casey* (ed. J. Neville Birdsall and Robert W. Thompson; Frieburg im Breisgau: Herder, 1963), 25–32; Ernest C. Colwell, "Method in Classifying and Evaluating Variant Readings," in *Studies in Methodology in Textual Criticism of the New Testament* (NTTS 9; Leiden: Brill, 1969), 96–105; Bart D. Ehrman, "Methodological Developments in the Analysis and Classification of New Testament Documentary Evidence," *NovT* 29, no. 1 (1987); Bart D. Ehrman, "The Use of Group Profiles for the Classification of New Testament Documentary Evidence," *JBL* 106, no. 3 (1987). The monograph in the SBLNTGF series by Cosaert was published in 2008. Cosaert, *Text of the Gospels in Clement*. The previous studies in the series are (in order of publication); Bart D. Ehrman, *Didymus the Blind and the Text of the Gospels* (SBLNTGF

in that time, it cannot be assumed there is no room for improvement or that no weaknesses are evident. Indeed, certain deficiencies have been identified by various scholars who have applied the methodology in numerous analyses of texts of the Fathers or critiqued its use. For example, in one of the more recent studies in the SBLNTGF series, *The Text of the Apostolos in Epiphanius of Salamis*, Osburn notes difficulties in how certain categories of readings are obtained in the Comprehensive Profile Method and concludes with the comment, "Clearly, a revision to the method is necessary to provide accurate data."[12]

Meanwhile, in the last few decades there have been significant developments in potentially advanced alternative methodologies which utilise computer technology. A particularly suitable methodological 'toolset' referred to as 'multivariate' analysis and specifically the technique of 'multidimensional scaling' which produces useful graphical output can be successfully applied to text-critical analysis of the New Testament in the Greek Fathers.[13] This study conducts a text-critical analysis on the Apostolos of Athanasius utilizing the 'traditional' methodology of a quantitative analysis and a Comprehensive Profile Method as well as the proposed alternative of multivariate analysis and specifically multidimensional scaling.

Since a Father's biblical text can be located both geographically and chronologically, we can place it within an appropriate historical context. In so doing we are able to examine the relationship and role of people, places and events in terms of the transmission history of the text.[14]

Therefore in Chapter 1 a brief outline of Athanasius' life along with a review on the influence of his educational background and hermeneutical outlook will

---

1; Atlanta: Scholars Press, 1986); James A. Brooks, *The New Testament Text of Gregory of Nyssa* (SBLNTGF 2; Atlanta: Scholars Press, 1991); Ehrman, Fee and Holmes, *Text of the Fourth Gospel*; Darrell D. Hannah, *The Text of 1 Corinthians in the Writings of Origen* (SBLNTGF 4; Atlanta: Scholars Press, 1997); Roderic L. Mullen, *The New Testament Text of Cyril of Jerusalem* (SBLNTGF 7; Atlanta: Scholars Press, 1997); Jean-François Racine, *The Text of Matthew in the Writings of Basil of Caesarea* (SBLNTGF 5; Atlanta: Society of Biblical Literature, 2004); Osburn, *Text of the Apostolos in Epiphanius*.

[12] Osburn, *Text of the Apostolos in Epiphanius*, 181–183; Mullen had earlier discovered similar difficulties and modified his use of the Group Profile Method to circumvent the problem; Mullen, *Text of Cyril*, 378; Cosaert also provided an "Adjusted Group Profile Analysis"; Cosaert, *Text of the Gospels in Clement*, 276, 300 ff; See Broman for a perceptive critique of the 'traditional' methodology; Vincent Broman, *TC: A Journal of Biblical Textual Criticism* 2 (1997): n.p. [cited 12th April 2007]. Online: http://ros etta.reltech.org /TC/vol02/ Mullen1997rev.html. See also Wasserman's review of Osburn's monograph; Tommy Wasserman, review of Carroll D. Osburn, *The Text of Apostolos in Epiphanius of Salamis*, *Review of Biblical Literature* [http://www. bookreviews.org] (2005).

[13] Multivariate analysis, and specifically the technique of multidimensional scaling, has previously been applied in a study on the Greek text of the epistle to the Hebrews in an unpublished dissertation by Finney. See Timothy J. Finney, "The Ancient Witnesses of the Epistle to the Hebrews: A computer-assisted analysis of the papyrus and uncial manuscripts of προς εβραιους" (Ph.D. diss., Murdoch University, 1999).

[14] Brogan's analysis of the Gospels text of Athanasius is particularly insightful here as he (Brogan) was able to demonstrate that the historico-political context in which Athanasius found himself influenced both his use of the biblical text and his role in its transmission. Brogan, "Text of the Gospels," 292ff.

provide an appropriate context for the discussion which follows, concerning the writings from which his quotations of the Apostolos are drawn.[15] In Chapter 2 an overview of the Alexandrian text-type is provided as the context for a review of previous studies on the text of Athanasius. Then the schema used to classify Athanasius' quotations of the Apostolos is discussed, followed by an explanation of the arrangement of the textual data and apparatus which appear in Chapter 3. In Chapter 4 the methodology used in the analysis of the textual data is discussed. This includes reviews of both a quantitative and group profile analysis commonly used in studies on the texts of the Fathers as well as an introduction to, and explanation of, multivariate analysis. In Chapters 5, 6 and 7 a quantitative, group profile and multivariate analysis of Athanasius' text of the Apostolos are presented. A final conclusion is then presented in Chapter 8.

---

[15] Despite his importance for ecclesial history no definitive modern biography of Athanasius has yet been published in English. Though see Annick Martin, *Athanase d'Alexandrie et l'Eglise d'Egypte au IVe siècle : (328–373)* (Rome: Ecole Française de Rome, 1996). See also Thomas G. Weinandy, *Athanasius: A Theological Introduction* (Aldershot, England: Ashgate, 2007), 1; Henric Nordberg, *Athanasius and the Emperor* (Helsinki: Helsingfors, 1963), 7. For brief biographies of Athanasius see, Khaled Anatolios, *Athanasius* (London: Routledge, 2004), 1–33; Alvyn Pettersen, *Athanasius* (London: Geoffrey Chapman, 1995); Quasten, *Patrology*; Arnold, *The Early Episcopal Career of Athanasius of Alexandria*; Charles Kannengiesser, *Arius and Athanasius: Two Alexandrian Theologians* (Hampshire: Variorum, 1991); Justo L. Gonzalez, *A History of Christian Thought* (3 vols.; Nashville: Abingdon, 1970).

1
ATHANASIUS OF ALEXANDRIA AND HIS WRITINGS

THE LIFE OF ATHANASIUS

Athanasius was born in Alexandria sometime between 295–298 C.E.[1] The circumstances of his early years are rather obscure with conflicting traditions describing his family background as either prosperous with Athanasius being "the son of a principal woman, a worshipper of idols, who was very rich" or otherwise "coming from a humble family" from Alexandria.[2] Regardless, he showed

---

[1] It is not possible to be more precise concerning the birth date of Athanasius as there is conflicting evidence. The Coptic *Encomium of Athanasius* states that Athanasius was 33 at the time of his consecration as bishop in 328 indicating a date of 295 C.E. See O. von Lemm, *Koptische Fragmente zur Patriarchengeschichte Alexandriens* (St.-Pétersbourg: Académie Impériale des sciences, 1888), 20, frag. P.5 (text); 36 (translation and discussion). Also see Tito Orlandi, ed. *Testi Copti: 1) Encomio de Atanasio. 2) Vita di Atanasio; Edizione critica, Traduzione e commento di Tito Orlandi. Testi e documenti per lo studio dell'antichità.* (Milano: Istituto Editoriale Cisilpano, 1968), 26–27; Anatolios, *Athanasius*, 243, n.8. Those who adopt this date include; Berthold Altaner, *Patrology* (trans. Hilda C. Graef; Freiburg: Herder, 1960), 312; Quasten, *Patrology*, 20. On the other hand, a passage in the *Festal Index* 3 refers to the accusation brought against Athanasius on the occasion of his election to the episcopate to the effect that he was "too young" (below the required canonical age of 30), therefore suggesting a date closer to 298 C.E. As Brogan notes, this charge could have been simply a fabrication of his opponents. Brogan, "Text of the Gospels," 6, n. 6; also see Archibald Robertson, ed. *Select Writings and Letters of Athanasius, Bishop of Alexandria* (NPNF[2] 4:xiv, n.1). Nevertheless, there must have been some room for doubt concerning his age otherwise the challenge could have been too easily dismissed. For further discussion concerning the birth date of Athanasius refer to Brogan, "Text of the Gospels," 6, n. 6.

[2] The first quotation is taken from the Arabic *History of the Patriarchs of Alexandria* by the tenth century Egyptian Bishop 'Severus' (Sawirus). See Sawirus ibn 'al-Muqaffa', *History of the Patriarchs of the Coptic Church of Alexandria* (PO 2; Paris: Firmin-Didot, 1904); quoted also by Anatolios, *Athanasius*, 3. Most likely this tradition is the source for Robertson's comment that "His [Athanasius'] parents, according to later writers, were of high rank and wealthy" though this cannot be verified since Robertson provides no reference to support his statement. Robertson (NPNF[2] 4:xiv). Anatolios indicates that the question of the historical veracity of all the details of the account from Sawirus is an open one. On the other hand, certain features of the story can be seen to have correspondences to other direct evidence. For example, his (Augustine's) lineage from "pagan" parents (which could be the case for both streams of tradition) may go part way in explaining his concern to explicate the theme of Christianity vs "the Greeks" in his first major doctrinal work, *Oratio contra Gentes*. See Anatolios, *Athanasius*, 3. For the second quote see Barnes, *Athanasius and Constantius*, 10; also see Brogan, "Text of the Gospels," 7. Brogan suggests that

early acumen and came to the attention of Alexander, Bishop of Alexandria who appointed him a deacon in 319. As Alexander's secretary, Athanasius attended the Council of Nicaea in 325 which was of such significance that it came to define his theology concerning the full divinity of the Son. Following the death of Alexander in 328 and in accordance with his dying wishes, Athanasius was appointed bishop in his stead, though his ordination was not without controversy, being opposed by both the Meletian party and Arian sympathizers.[3] It was the Arians, whom Athanasius in his writings refers to as the "Ario-maniacs" who would prove to be the greatest challenge throughout his long tenure as bishop, though in the end it was Athanasius who came out the victor.[4]

---

earlier traditions also indicated that his parents were "wealthy *Christians*" [italics mine] though none of his cited sources explicitly make this claim. The account from the Egyptian Bishop Severus does state that both Athanasius and his mother were baptised in conformity with the religion of "the Galileans", his father apparently having died when Athanasius was quite young – "he was an orphan on the [his] father's side". Sawirus then goes on to state that "after a time she [Athanasius' mother] died and Athanasius remained like a son with the Father Alexander". As such it could be interpreted that his mother, at least for a time, was a "wealthy Christian". See Sawirus, *History*, 407–408; also see Brogan, "Text of the Gospels," 7. Concerning Athanasius' father, Robertson refers to a statement from Athanasius in his second letter to Lucifer (*Epistula II. ad Luciferum*) that "I have not been able to see even the parents whom I have", indicating possibly that his father was still alive at this time. Robertson (*NPNF*[2] 4:562, n. 6). But Robertson points out some difficulties concerning this statement; 1) Athanasius by this time was over 60 years old. 2) About 6 years later Athanasius supposedly hid for four months (according to Socr. iv. 13) in his father's tomb during the time of Valens. A further difficulty is that *Clavis Patrum Graecorum* classifies *Epistula ii ad Luciferum* as "Spurious" so the weight of its testimony must be substantially discounted. Maurice Geerard, ed., *Clavis Patrum Graecorum* (5 vols.; Turnhout: Brepols, 1974–1987), 2:42. Kannengiesser has presented another intriguing possibility concerning Athanasius' ancestry when he refers to a presentation by G. H. Bebawi at the September 1983 *Ninth International Patristics Conference* held at Oxford, England. Bebawi argued that a late Coptic narrative transmitted in an Arabic fragment located Athanasius' birthplace in Upper Egypt and Athanasius as the son of a Coptic, partly non-Christian family. Charles Kannengiesser, "Athanasius of Alexandria vs. Arius: The Alexandrian Crisis," in *The Roots of Egyptian Christianity* (eds. Birger A. Pearson and James E. Goehring; Philadelphia: Fortress, 1986), 211.

[3] In his *Prolegomena*, Robertson recounts that Alexander, on his death-bed, called for Athanasius (though another deacon by that name came forward) and said to him, "You think to escape, but it cannot be." (Sozom ii. 17.) Robertson (*NPNF*[2] 4:xxi). Athanasius' history of contention with both the Meletians and the Arians has been well documented elsewhere. Refer to Anatolios, *Athanasius*, 20ff. As noted earlier (n. 1) one of the initial claims of his opponents was that he was below the required age (of 30) to be ordained as a deacon. Further claims were that he had paid bribes to orchestrate his episcopal election or that he had forcibly arranged his appointment by compelling two bishops to consecrate him in the Church of Dionysius. See Weinandy, *Athanasius*, 3; Robertson (*NPNF*[2] 4:103, n. 5).

[4] For major treatments on Arianism see Robert C. Gregg, ed. *Arianism: Historical and Theological Reassesments* (Patristic Monograph Series 11; Cambridge, Mass.: The Philadelphia Patristic Foundation, 1985); Rowan Williams, *Arius: Heresy and Tradition* (Grand Rapids: Eerdmans, 2002). For a more succinct summary see Charles Kannengiesser, ed. *Handbook of Patristic Exegesis* (The Bible in Ancient Christianity; ed. D. Jeffrey Bingham; Leiden: Brill, 2006), 684 ff; Kannengiesser, "Athanasius of Alexandria vs. Arius: The Alexandrian Crisis."; see also T. E. Pollard, "The Exegesis of Scripture and the Arian Controversy," *BJRL* 41 (1959); David M. Gwynn, *The Eusebians: The polemic of Athanasius of Alexandria and the construction of the 'Arian controversy'* (Oxford: Oxford University Press, 2007).

However, early in his ministry this conclusion was far from certain when, following his ordination, the Meletians and Arians fomented dissension and charged Athanasius with various offences including murder of the Meletian bishop Arsenius. Athanasius was able to easily refute the charge before the emperor Constantine by presenting Arsenius in person and very much alive and so the emperor dismissed the charges.[5] Nevertheless intense opposition continued and Athanasius, despite protestations of innocence, was unable to decisively refute a further accusation that he was conspiring to withhold grain shipments bound for Constantinople and so was exiled by the emperor to Trier (Gaul) in 335.[6]

This was the first of numerous exiles which taken together equated to more than seventeen years out of his forty-five year ministry.[7] The death of Constantine in 337 and a subsequent edict by his three sons (Constantine II, Constantius II and Constans) permitting all exiled bishops to return to their sees allowed Athanasius to return to Alexandria in November of that year. His enemies however, were still active and as a result of old charges renewed and new ones added he was again deposed at a synod in Antioch (338–339) attended by the emperor Constantius II. His second exile from April 339 until October 346 saw him in Rome, Milan, Trier, Sardica, Naissus and Aquileia.[8] A rival bishop, Gregory of Cappodocia was installed in Alexandria, but following the death of Gregory and a successful reconciliatory meeting with Constantius II, Athanasius was permitted to return to his church.

Then followed ten years of productive ministry in Alexandria, though political developments gradually made the situation for him more difficult. Constantius consolidated his power after the death of his brother Constans in 350 and began to assert his anti-Nicene policies more vigorously. His growing opposition to Athanasius, who championed Nicene theology, became more intense. In February 356 an attack by the troops of the *dux Syrianus* was made upon a church where Athanasius was worshipping, but he escaped and was forced

---

[5] Anatolios, *Athanasius*, 13.

[6] Athanasius protested that he had neither the means nor the power to hold up the grain shipments. Regardless of the truth of the matter, Athanasius' opponents had managed to strike a raw nerve and their charges were upheld. Robertson (*NPNF*[2] 4:xl, 105); Weinandy, *Athanasius*, 3; see also Michael J. Hollerich, "The Alexandrian Bishops and the Grain Trade: Ecclesiastical Commerce in Late Roman Egypt," *Journal of the Economic and Social History of the Orient* 25, no. 2 (1982): 190; H. A. Drake, "Athanasius' First Exile," *Greek, Roman and Byzantine Studies* 27, no. 2 (1986: Summer): 202–203.

[7] Little wonder then that the contentious nature of Athanasius' ministry has led to the oft quoted appraisal–Athanasius *contra mundum*. For clarity the dates for all (5) of Athanasius' exiles are listed here: (July 335–November 337 in Trier); (April 339–October 346 in Rome, Milan, Trier, Sardica, Naissus, Aquileia); (February 356–February 362 in the deserts of Upper and Lower Egypt); (October 362–February 364 in Upper Egypt); (October 365–February 366 in the desert region outside of Alexandria).

[8] Sardica (now Sofia, Bulgaria) was the site of a Council convened by emperor Constans in 343.

into his third exile, living amongst the eremitic monks in the Egyptian desert.[9] His time in the desert allowed Athanasius to focus on writing and he became a prolific author producing numerous apologies such as *Apologia ad Constantium*, *Apologia de fuga sua*, *Historia Arianorum* as well as his famous hagiographical *Vita Antonii*.[10] Constantius II died in 360 and his cousin Julian became emperor. Julian allowed all exiled bishops to return to their Sees and so Athanasius returned to Alexandria in February 362. His return was short lived however, as Julian rejected Christianity and attempted to revive the ancient pagan religions. Julian then revised his earlier decree by allowing exiled bishops permission to return to their home countries but not to resume ministry.

Athanasius in particular, due to his continuing theological and ecclesiastical importance and influence as the champion of Nicaea, again became the focus of imperial opposition when he held a Synod at Alexandria in 362 in an attempt to reconcile the semi-Arian and orthodox parties and was ordered not only to leave his church but Egypt as well.[11] He was therefore exiled for a fourth time from October 362 until February 364 though he did not leave Egypt but spent this time amongst the monks in the Upper desert region. Following the death of Julian in 363, Athanasius was able to return to Alexandria.[12] The new emperor Jovian proved to be friendly to Athanasius though this was short lived as Jovian died soon after in 364, whereupon he was succeeded by Valentinian who appointed his brother Valens as governor of the East. Valens was opposed to the theological position represented by Nicaea and ordered all Nicene bishops into exile. Athanasius at first refused but was again attacked while worshipping in the Church of Dionysius and managed to escape only at the last minute.[13] He fled to the desert outside of Alexandria for his fifth and final exile in October 365. Valens relented following political pressure to maintain stability in Egypt and permitted Athanasius to return in February 366. Athanasius then spent his remaining years of fruitful ministry in relative peace and died on 2 May 373.

ATHANASIUS' EDUCATION

In his useful discussion on the nature of Athanasius' education, Brogan suggests that Athanasius was most probably educated in the catechetical school of Alexandria though the *History of the Patriarchs of the Coptic Church of Alexandria* indicates that Alexander himself gave Athanasius a basic grounding in literature and contemporary philosophy as well as more comprehensive training in

---

[9] See Anatolios, *Athanasius*, 26

[10] See the later discussion concerning dating of the various writings of Athanasius.

[11] Julian's intent was to weaken the Christian powerbase by exacerbating discord and dissension among them and Athanasius' efforts as a peace-maker were antithetical to the emperor's policy. Quasten, *Patrology*, 21.

[12] Brogan indicates February 363 as the date for the return of Athanasius from his fourth exile. Brogan, "Text of the Gospels," 19. The correct date is February 364.

[13] See Anatolios, *Athanasius*, 32.

Scripture and the theological tradition of Alexandria.[14] Brogan quotes from Gregory of Nazianzus' panegyric of Athanasius (ca. 380) since it provides an important insight into the nature of Athanasius' education and the impact that education had on his writings. Gregory states that, "He was brought up from the first in religious habits and practices, after a brief study of literature and philosophy, so that he might not be utterly unskilled in such subjects, or ignorant of matters which he had determined to despise." (*Oratio* 21.6)[15] After a review of the available evidence concerning Athanasius' early education and a consideration of the focus of a typical secondary education in Alexandria, Brogan concludes that Athanasius had only a rudimentary knowledge of classical authors and his rhetorical skills were also basic but adequate.[16] Athanasius also provides no evidence that he had imbibed the strong Alexandrian philological and text-critical tradition, most likely because in his limited secondary education, which focussed mainly on set pieces of classical literature, he was never exposed to the relevant techniques to any substantial degree and hence never developed such skills and personal interest.

Where Athanasius shines however is in his study of Scripture itself, the focus of the famous 'Alexandrian School' where Athanasius was a pupil. Robertson notes that, "But from early years another element had taken a first place in his training and in his interest. It was in the Holy Scriptures that his martyr teachers had instructed him, and in the Scriptures his mind and writings are saturated. Ignorant of Hebrew and only rarely appealing to other Greek versions... his knowledge of the Old Testament is limited to the Septuagint. But of it, as well as of the New Testament, he has an astonishing command".[17] Gregory of Nazianzus (ca. 330–389 C.E.) expresses unbounded admiration in his panegyric when he lauds Athanasius' grasp of Scripture; "From meditating on every book of the Old and New Testament, with a depth such as none else has applied even to one of them he grew rich in contemplation, rich in splendor of life, combining them in

---

[14] See Brogan, "Text of the Gospels," 8ff. Sawirus states that it was Alexander "who educated him [Athanasius] quietly in every branch of learning. And Athanasius learnt the gospels by heart, and read the divine scriptures, and when he was fully grown, Alexander ordained him deacon, and made him his scribe, and he became as though he were the interpreter of the aforesaid Father, and a minister of the word which he wished to utter." Sawirus , *History*, 408. It is entirely possible that Athanasius was educated in the catechetical school and (within that context) was also personally tutored by Alexander.

[15] See Brogan, "Text of the Gospels," 9. Also Charles Gordon Brown and James Edward Swallow eds. *Select Orations of Saint Gregory Nazianzen* (*NPNF²*, 7:270).

[16] See Brogan, "Text of the Gospels," 6–18. Brogan's conclusions are largely based on Grant's reconstruction concerning theological education in Alexandria; Robert M. Grant, "Theological Education at Alexandria," in *The Roots of Egyptian Christianity* (eds. Birger A. Pearson and James E. Goehring; Philadelphia: Fortress, 1986). For an analysis of Athanasius' rhetorical method see George Christopher Stead, "Rhetorical Method in Athanasius," *VC* 30 (1976): 125ff.

[17] Robertson (*NPNF²* 4:xiv). Coasert argues that to refer to the Alexandrian School as a catechetical training institution is incorrect at the time of Clement but allows that it may be applicable in the "more developed stage of the church hierarchy in the Alexandria after Clement had already left the city." See Cosaert, *Text of the Gospels in Clement*, 7.

wondrous sort by that golden bond which few can weave".[18] Athanasius' writings are saturated in scriptural quotations and these point strongly to the centrality of Scripture in his education. It is likely that he memorised large portions of scripture and this aspect bears directly on the methodology he used when quoting scripture in his writings.[19]

Nordberg claims that it is "obvious" that Athanasius' method was to cite the verses or portions of scripture he wished to discuss by transcribing them directly from his biblical exemplar prior to developing his argumentation concerning the passages quoted.[20] However, this is open to question. Certainly this is one possible scenario but the claim that it is "obvious" appears too ambitious. The process of transcribing the biblical text from an exemplar may not have necessarily occurred as a prior step but rather took place during the writing of his tracts.[21] More likely Athanasius' substantial memorization of Scripture allowed him to quote at will whether or not his biblical exemplar was available and easily accessible. This is all the more likely since Athanasius generally quotes short passages and only rarely, as noted earlier, extended passages that contain a number of verses.

The accuracy of these longer quotations suggest that on such occasions he had access to an exemplar that provided the opportunity for direct transcription though even here it is not beyond the range of possibility that he is again simply quoting from memory. As Brogan notes, the impression that Athanasius generally quoted from memory rather than transcribed directly from an exemplar also makes it more likely that the characteristic of his text-type remained generally consistent despite his numerous exiles being the provenance for a good number of his writings. This is because he would be more prone to quote from a familiar text than to adopt the readings of different text-types that might have been available to him in various locations during his forced travels.[22]

---

[18] Brown and Swallow (*NPNF*[2] 7:270). So thoroughly has Athanasius imbibed Scripture that his writings are replete not only with specific quotes and interpretations of the biblical text but his basic narrative is also steeped in biblical language and imagery. In such a context there is a greater burden to delineate more carefully the genuine biblical quotations within his writings.

[19] So Brogan concludes. "Text of the Gospels," 17.

[20] Nordberg provides no further justification for this claim. Nordberg, "Bible Text of St. Athanasius," 121.

[21] This is not to suggest that Athanasius would not at least have had in mind a clear conception of the various disputed or contentious passages which he intended to discuss prior to developing the structure of his arguments.

[22] Brogan claimed that in his review of the Gospels data he found no variability across Athanasius' writings that might otherwise suggest Athanasius had used different text-types at various stages throughout his career. Brogan, "Text of the Gospels," 20, n. 30. Athanasius' apparent disinterest in philological concerns makes it more likely he would avoid the potential complication of such issues in his writings by maintaining a preference for his own familiar text. Ernest makes reference to "development across Athanasius' writings" but has in mind here the issue of theological development throughout Athanasius' career as well as his ability to use different approaches (genre) for his writings dependant on various contexts (rhetorical settings) in which he found himself. Ernest, *The Bible in Athanasius*, 14.

The above discussion leads to the conclusion that Athanasius' rudimentary classical and (lack of) philological training meant that these aspects were not significant or influential factors in the development of his writings. While he does make some references to classical authors, they are rare and form no major component of his writings. Philological concerns and related text-critical comments, so evident in earlier Alexandrian Fathers, are conspicuous by their absence in Athanasius' writings. We find almost no discussion or argumentation concerning preferences for certain wording over against others and none for the 'correct' or 'incorrect' nature of various readings.[23] Rather, his training and immersion in Scripture became the decisive element that shaped his writings, wherein biblical quotations along with their interpretation and elucidation constitute a significant component of the overall content.

ATHANASIUS' HERMENEUTICS

While classical and philological aspects of his educational background cannot be considered significant influences in his writings, Athanasius' hermeneutical approach is certainly more important, coming as it does out of his ministerial focus and ecclesiastical context. Indeed it was the centrality of his pastoral concerns that formed the primary motivation for Athanasius to write.[24] An earlier generation liked to claim that Athanasius had eschewed the unashamedly Alexandrian tradition of allegorical exegesis in favour of the Antiochene emphasis on a literal interpretation. Pollard mitigates this somewhat by describing Athanasius as a 'moderate literalist' over against the 'extreme literalist' tendencies of the Arians since Athanasius does occasionally betray the influence of an Alexandrian allegorical tradition.[25]

---

[23] Brogan, "Text of the Gospels," 16.

[24] Weinandy argues that the primary theological motivation for Athanasius was soteriological. Weinandy, *Athanasius*, vii. Ernest notes that "the exposition of a central *pastoral* concern in Athanasius' anti-Arian dogmatic writings is well established and crucial to understanding those works." [emphasis his]. Ernest, *The Bible in Athanasius*, 3. Commenting on the pastoral imperative as the primary motivation for Athanasius' writings, Robertson states that; "Athanasius was not an author by choice. With the exception of the early apologetic tracts [*Against the Heathen* and *The Incarnation of the Word*] all the writings that he has left were drawn from him by the stress of theological controversy or by the necessities of his work as a Christian Pastor." Robertson (*NPNF*[2] 4:lxvi).

[25] Pollard, "The Exegesis of Scripture and the Arian Controversy," 419. Athanasius' approach is clearly in contradistinction to the (earlier) allegorical methodology of Origen (ca. 185–254 C.E.) which was the "single most significant influence" on Patristic biblical interpretation in Alexandria and elsewhere. See Joseph W. Trigg, *Biblical Interpretation* (Message of the Fathers of the Church 9; Wilmington: Michael Glazier, 1988), 26. Athanasius' rejection of the allegorical method in favour of a literal one, probably under the influence of Alexander and Peter before him, makes all the more surprising his appointment of Didymus the Blind (313–398 C.E.) to lead the Alexandrian catechetical school since Didymus faithfully perpetuated Origen's allegorical method to the extent that both their works were condemned together in 553 at the Second Council of Constantinople. See Ehrman, *Didymus*, 17; Trigg, *Biblical Interpretation*, 27.

It is also generally acknowledged that Athanasius was not an exegete though Ernest agrees with this verdict only "insofar as 'exegesis' implies deliberate exposition of continuous biblical text".[26] Ernest goes on to note that while the *Clavis Patrum Graecorum* does include a category of *Exegetica*, the writings listed there are mostly spurious.[27] Even the possible major exception that could be classified as exegetical, the *Expositiones in psalmos*, is generally now seen as inauthentic.[28] To say that Athanasius was not an exegete as the word is commonly understood does not mean that he fails to use exegetical principles. Rather his exegesis is subsumed by his hermeneutical imperative. As Ernest notes, "Athanasius is more fundamentally a pastor than a theologian."[29]

Therefore while Athanasius does engage in dogmatic-polemical and historical-polemical argumentation, it is his pastoral motivation which is central. Indeed a danger is that because the dogmatic-polemical aspect dominates in some of Athanasius' major works such as the *Orationes contra Arianos III* it tends to tip the scale away from a more balanced perspective of his pastoral approach that may be evident in other non-polemical works such as *Vita Antonii*.[30]

What then are the implications for the character of the Apostolos text as found in Athanasius' writings? One has already been mentioned; Athanasius does not engage in exegetical discourse on extended passages of scripture.[31] We

---

[26] See Ernest, *The Bible in Athanasius*, 6. Ernest quotes Simonetti who explains that "Athanasius only holds marginal interest for us, because he himself took little interest in exegesis." Manlio Simonetti, *Biblical Interpretation in the Early Church: An Historical Introduction to Patristic Exegesis* (trans. John A. Hughes; Edinburgh: T&T Clark, 1994), 77. Margerie introduces Athanasius with the statement that while he is famous as the heroic defender of Nicaea he "is less known as an exegete." Bertrand de Margerie, *An Introduction to the History of Exegesis* (3 vols.; Petersham, Mass.: Saint Bede's, 1993), 1:117. Though it is acknowledged that Athanasius did not write commentaries (see note below) it would appear that he had read them since he knew the relevant technical terms such ἀλληγορεῖν and τύπος. See Ernest, *The Bible in Athanasius*, 19, referring to the observation of Stead; George Christopher Stead, "Athanasius als Exeget," in *Christliche Exegese zwischen Nicaea und Chalcedon* (eds. J. van Oort and U. Wickert; Kampen: Kok Pharos, 1992), 174–184.

[27] Geerard (*CPG* 2:28–31).

[28] See Ernest for a fuller discussion concerning the consensus of opinion against the Athanasian authorship of *Expositiones in psalmos*. Ernest, *The Bible in Athanasius*, 9, n. 26.

[29] Ibid., 11. In an apparent attempt to rehabilitate Athanasius' reputation concerning his exegetical competency, Ernest states, "If Athanasius is not an exegete in the usual sense of that word, he is nevertheless a significant interpreter of scripture." Ibid., 38. For further discussion on Athanasius' theology see E. P. Meijering, *Orthodoxy and Platonism in Athanasius: Synthesis or Antithesis?* (Leiden: Brill, 1974). For a review of the intersection of theology and Scripture for Athanasius in soteriology see John R. Meyer, "Athanasius' use of Paul in his Doctrine of Salvation," *VC* 52, no. 2 (May, 1998).

[30] Ernest, *The Bible in Athanasius*, 9. Ernest also makes reference here to the unpublished dissertation of Hermann Josef Sieben, "Studien zur Psalterbenutzung des Athanasius von Alexandrien im Rahmen seiner Schriftauffassung und Schriftlesung" (Ph.D. diss., Institut Catholique zu Paris, 1968), 6–7.

[31] This means that the recovered text of the Apostolos of Athanasius will remain at best fragmentary and therefore a representative sample of the larger population which (in the case of this present study) is the complete Apostolos text. This is one of the difficulties inherent in trying to recover the texts of the Fathers. Quasten notes that "No ancient author ever mentions that Athanasius wrote commentaries on any part of the New Testament." Quasten, *Patrology*, 39.

are therefore unable to recover long contiguous sections of the Apostolos text from Athanasius' writings. Rather, in his dogmatic-polemical writings at least, he is generally responding to what he perceives as the false theological interpretation of his opponents concerning various scattered passages and isolated verses of scripture. For example, in the case of the *Orationes contra Arianos III* referred to earlier, Athanasius' method was twofold. First he responds to various writings in the *Thalia* attributed to Arius (256–336 C.E.) and also to selections from the *Syntagma* of Asterius (d. ca. 341).[32] He refutes the heretical doctrines of these writings and what he considered the false interpretation of the Arianists concerning certain biblical references in both the Old and New Testaments.

Then secondly he provides instead an orthodox Christological interpretation of the same scriptural references.[33] Some texts are given extensive consideration such as Proverbs 8:22 and in the case of the Apostolos, Philippians chapter 2 and Hebrews chapter 2, since they specifically contain Christological formulations. Generally however, scattered references are introduced as supporting evidence without accompanying exegetical comments on the basis that the otherwise isolated verses form together a cohesion that elucidates the general teaching of the whole which Athanasius refers to as the 'scope' (σκοπός) of Scripture.[34] Further, the 'occasional' nature of Athanasius' writings dictate the selection of Apostolos passages such that concentrations of quotations can be observed from certain epistles while there is a dearth of references from others.[35] For example, Athanasius quotes Phil 2:6 fifteen times, 2:7 twenty-two times and Heb 3:2 seventeen times but Philemon and 2 John not at all. This however, is not atypical of the type of New Testament textual data found in the writings of other Greek Fathers. Osburn's study on the Apostolos text of Epiphanius of Salamis also found concentrations such as Titus 2:11–14, but scarce references for other epistles such as Philemon (two quotations for only one verse) and just two quotations for 2 John.[36]

---

[32] Charles Kannengiesser, "Athanasius of Alexandria, *Three Orations Against the Arians*: A Reappraisal" *Studia Patristica* 18, no. 3 (1982): 981–95; Quasten, *Patrology*, 26. For an analysis of the contents of the Thalia against which Athanasius responded see George Christopher Stead, "The 'Thalia' of Arius and the Testimony of Athanasius," *JTS* 29 (1978): 22ff.

[33] Kannengiesser, "*Three Orations*: A Reappraisal": 981–995.

[34] Ernest claims that while the concept of 'scope' cannot really be considered an element of Athanasius' exegesis, it is indeed an important criterion in his hermeneutics. Ernest, *The Bible in Athanasius*, 8; See also Pollard, "Exegesis of Scripture," 423. See also Ernest's earlier discussion on Athanasius' concept of the 'scope' of Scripture; Ernest, James D., "Athanasius of Alexandria: The Scope of Scripture in Polemical and Pastoral Context," *VC* 47 (1993): 342ff.

[35] The use of the appellation 'occasional' indicates that the writings of Athanasius, especially the dogmatic-polemical and historico-polemical writings are *responses* to various theological and ecclesiastical controversies and as such these controversies set the agenda and essentially dictate the subject matter that is addressed. This is not so much the case in *Vita Antonii*, though one might argue that the promotion of an ascetic ideal in this writing was in response to an ecclesiastical context that was responsible, at least in part, for setting the agenda.

[36] Osburn, *Text of the Apostolos in Epiphanius*, 157–158, 70. Concerning Athanasius' quotations of the Gospels, Brogan notes that; "Amazingly, only one clear reference to the Gospel of Mark could be identified in Athanasius' writings." Brogan, "Text of the Gospels," 199. Clearly

THE WRITINGS OF ATHANASIUS

In seeking to extract quotations of the biblical text from writings of the Fathers, a number of important conventions must be applied in order to obtain reliable data. The first requirement is that only authentic writings of a Father should be used since it is clear that there are often writings attributed to a Father but which, upon critical investigation, are shown to be inauthentic. Much as one might wish it otherwise, the scholarly consensus on this matter is not always unanimous and in such cases a decision must be made concerning a disputed writing's authenticity or otherwise based on all the evidence available to date.[37] The second requirement is that the only authentic writings considered are those for which critical editions are available. This requirement has come out of the recognition that the failure to utilise critical editions in earlier textual studies of the Fathers has led to deficiencies in the results obtained, both in the unreliability of the data and in the subsequent analysis.[38] As Brogan notes, "The use of critical editions helps to filter out later scribal corruptions and provide a text closer to Athanasius' original wording."[39]

The following writings of Athanasius are available in critical editions and discussion of their date, provenance and arguments for authenticity are provided where necessary. While a number of ordering schemes may be used for the

---

then Athanasius is not concerned to provide proportionally balanced quotations across the New Testament corpora.

[37] In determining which writings to utilise in this present study, *CPG* was consulted along with the major patrologies as well as the list of writings accepted and rejected by Brogan. In two specific cases a digression was made from Brogan's list of rejections. The first case concerns the disputed authenticity of *Orationes contra Arianos III*. The second case concerns the writing, *Historia Arianorum*. Both will be discussed in the text.

[38] Brogan provides an extended discussion on the problems inherent in Zervopoulos' study on the Gospels text of Athanasius precisely as it relates to the two requirements noted above. Brogan's conclusion is that Zervopoulos' uncritical acceptance of certain writings as being genuinely Athanasian but which were otherwise generally considered as dubious or spurious "seriously damages the results of his textual study." Zervopoulos had used Migne's edition of Patrologiae Cursus Completus, Series Graeca *(PG)* which, as Brogan notes, is unfortunately not reliable. Brogan, "Text of the Gospels," 61–62. Fee had also previously raised such issues in his landmark survey concerning the use of Greek Patristic citations. See Gordon D. Fee, "The Use of Greek Patristic Citations in New Testament Textual Criticism: The State of the Question," in *Studies in the Theory and Method of New Testament of New Testament Textual Criticism* (SD 45; Grand Rapids: Eerdmans, 1993), 344–359; See also Fee, "Use of the Greek Fathers," 193. Winstedt provides a representative list of examples concerning the "untrustworthiness" of Montfaucon's edition as regards both biblical and patristic quotations. See E. O. Winstedt, "Notes from Cosmas Indicopleustes," *JTS* 6 (1905): 284; E. O. Winstedt, "A further note on Cosmas," *JTS* 7 (1906): 626. The policy of only using critical editions has direct relevance not only for the form of the edited text but also for the first requirement [that all writings be authentic] by eliminating from contention most of the spurious or dubious writings for which Athanasian authorship is claimed or that have been traditionally associated with him but which scholarly investigation has determined are not authentic. This is not always the case and some important exceptions will be discussed below.

[39] Brogan, "Text of the Gospels," 63.

presentation of the writings, for example chronologically or by genre, they are listed here in the order shown in *Clavis Patrum Graecorum II*.[40]

The critical edition of Thomson[41] contains: *Oratio contra gentes* while the critical edition of Kannengiesser[42] contains: *Oratio de incarnatione Verbi*. These two writings are here considered together since they essentially form two parts of a single composition.[43] In *Oratio contra gentes* Athanasius refutes the folly of pagan mythologies, worship and beliefs and especially the immorality and folly of idolatry and polytheism. As the only valid and reasonable alternative he proposes the monotheism of the Christian faith. The second writing, *Oratio de incarnatione Verbi* follows on from the previous treatise by delineating the corruption of human nature and the subsequent necessity of restoration only through the incarnation which is primarily expressed in the death and resurrection of Christ.[44] Christianity is then defended against the objections of both Jews and Greeks by a classic exposition of the doctrine of Redemption.

An important element to note concerning arguments for the dating of these writings is that there is no elucidation on the relationship of Jesus as the 'Divine Word' to 'God the Father' and strongly suggests that *Oratio contra gentes* at least was first drafted before the outbreak of the Arian controversy in 319 C.E.[45] This however, locates it very early in Athanasius' career with the question being raised as to whether someone as young as Athanasius (at the time 20–23 years old) would have been capable of such mature theological formulations; consequently

---

[40] A consensus on a chronological scheme based on the date of the writings would be difficult to obtain since a number of these dates remain contentious. See the following discussion in the text for details. While Athanasius' writings may be classified by genre, there is again no consistent agreement concerning these categories. Quasten discusses the writings of Athanasius using the categories of: 1) Apologetic and Dogmatic Writings, 2) Spurious Dogmatic Writings, 3) Historico-Polemical Writings, 4) Exegetical Writings, 5) Ascetical Writings, 6) Letters. See Quasten, *Patrology*, 24–66. *CPG* on the other hand categorises Athanasius' writings as: *Apologetica, Exegetica, Ascetica, Fragmenta Varia, Dubia, Appendix* and *Spuria*, though the majority of authentic writings are listed first and not under any of the above classifications. See Geerard (*CPG* 2:12–60); Fee, "Use of the Greek Fathers," 195. Geerard assigns an identification number to each writing, whether considered authentic or spurious/dubious/inauthentic as well as providing a title which may conveniently serve to standardise nomenclature (as suggested by Fee) and which are adopted for this study.

[41] Robert W. Thomson, ed. *Athanasius: Contra Gentes and De Incarnatione* (Oxford: Clarendon, 1971); See also Luigi Leone, ed. *Sancti Athanasii, Archiepiscopi Alexandriae: Contra Gentes-Introduzione, Testo Critico, Traduzione* (Collana di Studi Greci 43; Napoli: Libreria Scientifica Editrice, 1965).

[42] Charles Kannengiesser, ed. *Athanase d'Alexandrie: Sur l'incarnation du Verbe: Introduction, Texte Critique, Traduction Notes et Index* (SC 199; Paris: Editions du Cerf, 1973); See also Thomson ed. *Athanasius: Contra Gentes and De Incarnatione*, 134–276.

[43] See Quasten, *Patrology*, 24–25; Robertson (*NPNF²* 4:1).

[44] Athanasius also refers to their inter-dependant status by connecting them at the beginning of the *Oratio de incarnation Verbi* when he states; "Whereas on what precedes we have drawn out...a sufficient account of the error of the heathen concerning idols, and of the worship of idols." Robertson (*NPNF²* 4:36).

[45] See ibid., 4:lxiii. Lorimer also sees echoes of Aristotle's *De Mundo* in *Contra Gentes*. See W. L. Lorimer, "Critical notes on Athanasius," *JTS* 40 (1939): 37.

later dates have been suggested.[46] Kannengiesser proposed a mediatorial solution by suggesting that while *Oratio contra gentes* may indeed represent an early draft, it was only finally paired with the *Oratio de incarnatione Verbi* at a later date, during his first exile in Trier (335–337).[47] In the mid-twentieth century a shorter recension of *Oratio de incarnatione Verbi* was discovered and published. However, it is generally considered that the Long Recension is the original and the Short Recension from (later) fourth century Antioch.[48]

The critical edition of Metzler[49] contains: *Epistula ad episcopos Aegypti et Libyae*. This historical-polemical letter to the bishops of Egypt and Libya was written in 356, just at the beginning of his third exile after having been expelled by Syrianus. In it Athanasius warns the hierarchy of the church against the attempts of the heretics to substitute another Creed for the Nicene.[50] The two critical editions (1998 and 2000) of Metzler and Kyriakos[51] contain: *Orationes contra*

---

[46] Weinandy suggests a date sometime after 325, introducing this opinion with the innocuous phrase "It is thought..." though by whom is not indicated. Weinandy, *Athanasius*, 3. Anatolios posits a dating of between 328–335 though he does so only tentatively and provides no justification for this option. Anatolios, *Athanasius*, 12; so also Ernest, *The Bible in Athanasius*, 45. Schwartz, taking over the opinion of Opitz, posits the date for *Oratio de incarnation Verbi* in the first exile (335–337). See Charles Kannengiesser, "The Dating of Athanasius' Double Apology and Three Treatises Against the Arians," *ZAC* 10, no. 1 (2006): 21; see also Quasten, *Patrology*, 25–26. Nordberg postulated a much later date of 362/363 but this view has received little support. See Henric Nordberg, "A Reconsideration of the Date of St. Athanasius' *Contra Gentes* and *De Incarnatione*," (StPatr 3; Berlin: Akademie Verlag, 1961), 262–266; also Henric Nordberg, *Athanasius' Tractates Contra Gentes and De Incarnatione; An attempt at Redating* (Helsinki: Helsingfors, 1961). Stead suggests that if Athanasius had indeed written ἡ φίλαρχος (as Stead claims) rather than Alexander when he was "little more than 20 years" of age, then he would also have been capable of writing *Oratio contra gentes* and *Oratio de incarnatione Verbi* a year or two earlier. See George Christopher Stead, "Athanasius' Earliest Written Work," *JTS* 39 (1988): 91. Van Winden also supports an early dating. See J. C. M. van Winden, "On the Date of Athanasius' Apologetical Treatises " *VC* 29 (1975): 294.

[47] Kannengiesser, "Dating of Athanasius' Double Apology and Three Treatises," 23; see also the summary in Appendix D of Ernest, *The Bible in Athanasius*, 423–424.

[48] Casey however concluded that the Short Recension "may plausibly be attributed to Athanasius himself or to one of his immediate circle." George Jeremiah Ryan and Robert Pierce Casey eds., *De incarnatione verbi Dei: Part 1. The Long Recension Manuscripts by George Jeremiah Ryan; Part 2. The Short Recension by Robert Pierce Casey* (SD 14; London: Christophers, 1945–1946). See also Quasten, *Patrology*, 25.

[49] Metzler, Karin, Dirk U. Hansen and Kyriakos Savvidis, eds., *Athanasius Werke: Die Dogmatischen Schriften-Epistula ad Episcopos, Aegypti et Libyae* (vol. (Band) 1, Teil 1, Lieferung 1; Berlin: de Gruyter, 1996).

[50] The dating and provenance for this letter is firm. See Robertson (*NPNF*[2] 4:222).

[51] Karin Metzler and Kyriakos Savvidis, eds., *Athanasius Werke: Die Dogmatischen Schriften - Orationes I et II Contra Arianos* (vol. (Band) 1, Teil 1, Lieferung 2; Berlin: de Gruyter, 1998); Karin Metzler and Kyriakos Savvidis, eds., *Athanasius Werke: Die Dogmatischen Schriften-Oratio III Contra Arianos* (vol. (Band) 1, Teil 1, Lieferung 3; Berlin: de Gruyter, 2000). When Brogan was working on his dissertation no critical editions of the *Orationes contra Arianos III* were available so he used instead Kannengiesser's "collations of the leading manuscripts of *Orationes I–II contra Arianos*." See Brogan, "Text of the Gospels," 65, n. 30. Since the completion of Brogan's dissertation more critical editions of Athanasius' writings have become available, especially in the *Athanasius Werke* series. The writings for which critical editions are now available that have been published since the completion of Brogans' dissertation (or too late for him to incorporate) are: *Epistula ad episcopos Aegypti et Libyae, Vita Antonii, Epistula ad Ioannem et Antiochum presb., Epistula ad*

Arianos III. The three *Orationes* take pride of place in the Athanasian corpora as his chief dogmatic works in which, as noted earlier, he refutes the theological heterodoxy of the Arians while defending the classic Nicene ὁμοούσιον theology concerning the nature of Christ.[52] One characteristic of the *Orationes Contra Arianos III* that is particularly relevant for the present study is the disproportionately high concentration of biblical references they contain compared with other groups of writings of Athanasius.

Ernest provides tabular data for various groups of Athanasius' writings and shows that words of scripture account for approximately 15% of the total content of the *Orationes Contra Arianos III* which is nearly double that found in other groups.[53] An earlier consensus had assigned the date for the writing of the *Orationes* to the time of Athanasius' third exile while he was with the monks in the Egyptian desert (356–362).[54] A challenge to this traditional dating has however become the basis for much discussion and some disagreement.[55] The primary cause is Athanasius' own statement in *Orationes I contra Arianos 1* where he refers to the Arian heresy as one "which has now risen as a harbinger of Antichrist... since she has already seduced certain of the foolish".[56] It seemed doubtful that this could be said in the mid-late 50's of a heresy which had existed since the time of Alexander and Nicaea more than twenty years earlier and so an earlier date of around 338/9 has been suggested.[57] On the other hand in *Epistula ad monachos*, generally considered to have been written in 358, Athanasius refers to the *Orationes contra Arianos III* in such a way as to indicate their contemporary provenance rather than to a work produced twenty years before.

Kannengiesser's analysis of Athanasius' writings led him to deny a late date for *Epistula ad monachos* and to postulate that Athanasius had first drafted a

---

Palladium, Epistula ad Dracontium, Epistula ad Afros, Tomus ad Antiochenos, Epistula ad Jovianum, Epistula Joviani ad Athanasium and *Petitiones Arianorum*. Refer to the bibliographic data of the relevant critical edition for details of publication date. It is worthwhile clarifying here that the designation *Orationes contra Arianos III* in CPG refers to the three dogmatic treatises that together constitute the *Orationes*. Where necessary, and especially in the Text and Apparatus, reference will be made to the individual treatises by the designations; *Oratio I, II* or *III contra Arianos* (in abbreviation *Or. I, II* or *III c. Ar.*)

[52] For discussion on the ὁμοούσιον theological formula see Robertson (*NPNF*[2] 4:xxx).

[53] The 'groups' of Athanasius' writings that Ernest considers are: Apologetic, Dogmatic-Polemical, Historical-Polemical and Pastoral. See Ernest, *The Bible in Athanasius*, 67, 114, 207, 275 ; see also Claudio Zamagni, review of James D. Ernest, *The Bible in Athanasius of Alexandria. RBL* 8 (2006), 569–573.

[54] Kannengiesser notes that Montfaucon's dating of the *Orationes* to the period of Athanasius' third exile "had become a three-centuries-old *opinio communis*." Kannengiesser, "Dating of Athanasius' Double Apology and Three Treatises," 26; also William Bright, *The Orations of Saint Athanasius against the Arians according to the Benedictine Text, with an account of His Life* (trans. William Bright; Oxford: Clarendon Press, 1873).

[55] Robertson posits a date of between 356–360 for the *Orationes Contra Arianos I–III*. Robertson (*NPNF*[2] 4:303); see also Quasten, *Patrology*, 26.

[56] Metzler and Savvidis eds. *Athanasius Werke: Die Dogmatischen Schriften–Orationes I et II Contra Arianos*; for English translation see Robertson (*NPNF*[2] 4:306).

[57] Quasten, *Patrology*, 27. See also Kannengiesser, "Dating of Athanasius' Double Apology," 22, n. 14.

Orationes contra Arianos (about 340) that was shortly afterwards (342–343) redacted and enlarged to become the *Orationes contra Arianos III*.[58] Kannengiesser has recently reconsidered these dates and suggests, if somewhat more tentatively than before, that in his amended reconstruction the writing and editing process occurred between 337–342.[59] While this scenario seems plausible, its acceptance has not been complete.[60] Nevertheless, allowing for the earlier dating suggests a maximum twenty-five year period (337–362) for the writing of the *Orationes* sometime between Athanasius' first and third exile.

Of more concern is Kannengiesser's doubt about the authenticity of *Oratio III contra Arianos*. One of the foremost Athanasian scholars for more than a quarter of a century, he regarded *Orationes I–II contra Arianos* as genuine but for a long time held doubts that Athanasius had written *Oratio III contra Arianos*, claiming instead that it had been written by Athanasius' young protégé Apollinarius of Laodicea.[61] His main reason for taking this position was the perceived differences of structure and style in *Oratio III contra Arianos* when compared to the first two *Orationes*. Kannengiesser however, remained almost alone on this issue, though his arguments were persuasive enough for Brogan to exclude *Oratio III contra Arianos* from his textual analysis of the Gospels.[62] Ernest addressed the issue in his research and in an appendix noted the chorus refuting Kannengiesser's exclusion of *Oratio III contra Arianos* as a genuine Athanasian writing.[63] While acknowledging that some stylistic differences may exist, numerous studies have suggested viable solutions which nonetheless maintain Athanasian authorship. Stead for example concluded that Kannengiesser had only demonstrated that *Oratio III contra Arianos* is different from *Oratio I–II contra Arianos*, not that it was inauthentic and that it is simply a later work while Abramowski argued for

---

[58] Kannengiesser, "*Three Orations*: A Reappraisal": 981–995.

[59] Kannengiesser, "Dating of Athanasius' Double Apology," 33.

[60] For example Ernest still holds to the later traditional date of Athanasius' third exile. See Ernest, *The Bible in Athanasius*, 430.

[61] Kannengiesser, "*Three Orations*: A Reappraisal".

[62] Brogan accepted the *Orationes I–II contra Arianos* as genuine works of Athanasius but rejected *Oratio III contra Arianos*, though, on his own admission, entirely due to the influence of Kannengiesser. Brogan, "Text of the Gospels," 59, n. 2. Since much of the debate on this issue occurred prior to Brogan's dissertation it is surprising that he makes no particular references to the dissenting voices, though he does acknowledge that most scholars "still affirm its authenticity". In his dissertation Brogan indicated his intention to undertake a future comparison of the data derived from *Oratio III contra Arianos* with his conclusions concerning the *Orationes I–II contra Arianos* to determine textual affinity or otherwise. Ibid., 61–62, n.15. In private email communication (dated 12th Dec. 2006) he indicated that he had undertaken such a study but that the results were as yet only "preliminary" and required "much more work". Indeed it may be that such a study would prove indeterminate since even Ernest noted some slight differences (e.g., frequency of hapax) between his data derived from *Oratio I–II contra Arianos* and *Oratio III contra Arianos*. Ernest, *The Bible in Athanasius*, 430. This however cannot necessarily be taken to imply difference of authorship. There is now almost no scholarly doubt that the writing *Oratio IV contra Arianos* listed as 'Spurious' in *CPG (2230, PG 26, 468–525)* is inauthentic and Brogan rightly criticizes Zervopoulos for having used it. See Brogan, "Text of the Gospels," 58–59; also Geerard, *CPG*, 42; Quasten, *Patrology*, 27.

[63] Ernest, *The Bible in Athanasius*, 429–430; Appendix G.

a different provenance for the writing of *Oratio III contra Arianos*.[64] The arguments supporting Athanasian authorship of *Oratio III contra Arianos* appear to have prevailed since at the close of his appendix on the matter Ernest notes that Kannengiesser himself, at the 2003 Oxford Conference, "stated in a presentation that he was no longer prepared to deny Athanasian authorship of CA III [*Oratio III contra Arianos*]."[65] With the claim for non-Athanasian authorship of *Or. III c. Ar.* essentially abandoned by this admission, the present study will therefore include *Or. III c. Ar.* as an authentic work for the analysis of Athanasius' Apostolos text.

Critical editions are also available for *Epistula ad Epictetum*,[66] *Vita Antonii*,[67] *Epistulae festales: Fragmenta apud Cosman Indicopleustam*[68] and *Epistula xxxix*.[69] The letter *Epistula ad Epictetum* is a response to Bishop Epictetus of Corinth concerning some questions of theology that had been raised in his diocese. The date for this writing is unknown, though most likely it was late in Athanasius' career. With the treatise *Vita Antonii* Athanasius created a new genre of hagiographical ascetic literature. Considered the most important document of early monasticism, it was composed about 357 not long after the death of Antony in 356 in response to a request from the desert monks and was influential in introducing monasticism to the West.[70] The *Epistulae festales* consists of fragments of Greek

---

[64] George Christopher Stead, review of C. Kannengiesser, "*Athanase d'Alexandrie, évêque et écrivain*", *JTS* 36 (1985): 220–229. Abramowski held that the Council of Serdica in 343 was the context for the writing of CA III. Luise Abramowski, "Die dritte Arianerrede des Athanasius: Eusebianer und Arianer und das westliche Serdicense," *ZAC* 102, no. 3 (1991): 389.

[65] This backdown came after Kannengiesser had been "moved" by the adverse scholarly argumentation. Ernest, *The Bible in Athanasius*, 430. In his subsequent 2006 article on the dating of Athanasius' Double Apology and Three Treatises Against the Arians Kannengiesser stated: "Did Athanasius write a third Contra Arianos? Initially, my answer to this question was negative, based on a lexical and redactional analysis of the present Contra Arianos III. After the recent contributions of Luise Abramowski and Markus Vinzent my answer now is a carefully qualified "yes". Indeed Athanasius himself has to be considered responsible for what we call the third Oratio contra Arianos. Between 1974 and 1991 I had denied that authorship because of the pastoral style of a narrative argumentation and the inner cohesion explicitly emphasized in Contra Arianos I–II, but which I found missing in Contra Arianos III. My attention was also galvanized by the more systematic abstractness and the lexical peculiarities in Contra Arianos III. In the meantime the responses of friends and critics, such as Christopher Stead and E.P. Meijering convinced me that I had over-reacted: my perception of these data was largely unfounded. But since my failed attempt has prompted an unprecedented attention to Contra Arianos III over the past thirty years, my present retractatio becomes easier." Kannengiesser, "Dating of Athanasius' Double Apology," 30.

[66] Georgius Ludwig, ed., *Athanasii Epistula ad Epictetum* (Jenae: Typis H. Pohle, 1911). See Quasten for general descriptions of many of the writings noted here.

[67] G. J. M. Bartelink, ed., *Athanase d'Alexandrie: Vie d'Antoine–Introduction, texte critique, traduction, notes et Index* (SC 400; Paris: Editions du Cerf, 1994).

[68] E. O. Winstedt, ed., *The Christian Topography of Cosmas Indicopleustes* (Cambridge: Cambridge University Press, 1909); See also Wanda Wolska-Conus, ed., *Cosmas indicopleustes: topographie chrétienne* (SC 197; Paris: Editions du Cerf, 1973).

[69] P.-P. Joannou, ed., *Fonti. Fasciolo ix. Discipline générale antique (ii-ix s.)* (*Les canon des pères grecs*; Rome: Tipographia Italo-Orientale "S.Nilo", 1963), 71–76. See also Ernest, *The Bible in Athanasius*, 336 ff.

[70] Barnard claims a more precise dating for this writing as "late in 357 or early in 358, which

text of various Athanasian Festal Letters preserved in the writings of Cosmas Indicopleustes. *Epistula xxxix* from the year 367 C.E. is well known for its listing of the canon of Scripture. The letter is not complete since the beginning is missing and numerous other lacunae are evident.

The critical edition of Halkin[71] contains *Epistula I ad Orsisium, Epistula II ad Orsisium* and *Narratio Athanasii*. The critical edition of Joannou[72] contains *Epistula ad Amun* and *Epistula ad Rufinianum*. *Epistula ad Amun* was written sometime before 356 to an eremitic monk Amun in order to settle the conscience of some overzealous monks concerning the uncleanness or otherwise of "involuntary thoughts" and natural bodily "secretions of the belly".[73] *Epistula ad Rufinianum*, written not long after 362, is Athanasius' reply to Rufianus concerning how to deal with former Arian sympathizers who wished to be readmitted to the church.

The critical edition of Opitz[74] contains *De decretis Nicaenae synodi, De sententia Dionysii, Apologia de fuga sua, Apologia contra Arianos (=Apologia secunda), Epistula encyclica, Epistula ad Serapionem de morte Arii, Epistula ad monachos, Historia Arianorum* and *De synodis Arimini in Italia et Seleucia in Isauria*. *De decretis Nicaenae synodi* is generally considered to have been written sometime in the years 351–355 and is a defence of the Nicene formulation which the Arians claimed used the non-scriptural terms ἐκ τῆς οὐσίας and ὁμοούσιος. *De sententia Dionysii*, a later addition is Athanasius' refutation against the claim of the Arians that certain passages in Dionysius could be favorably interpreted to support their own theology. In *Apologia de fuga sua*, written in 357, Athanasius provides a defence against claims of cowardice when he fled into his third exile. He cites for justification the examples in Scripture of a number of saints as well as of Christ himself. *Apologia contra Arianos (=Apologia secunda)* was written sometime after his return from his second exile in 346 and most likely in 351 (but not 357 contra Quasten since this would put it into his third exile which is too late).[75] In it Athanasius refutes the more personal charges against him made by

---

would fit in with the external evidence." See L. W. Barnard, "The Date of S. Athanasius' 'Vita Antonii'," *VC* 28 (1974): 175; for a critique of Barnard see B. R. Brennan, "Dating Athanasius' 'Vita Antonii'," *VC* 30 (1976): 54; also see David Brakke, *Athanasius and the politics of asceticism* (Baltimore: John Hopkins University, 1998), 13; A. Louth, "St. Athanasius and the Greek 'Life of Antony'," *JTS* 39 (1988), 504–509.

[71] Francisci Halkin, ed., *Sancti Pachomii Vitae Graecae* (*Subsidia Hagiographica*; Bruxelles: Société des Bollandistes, 1932). Orsisius was an abbot in Tabenne, Upper Egypt. *Epistula I ad Orsisium* is dated to 363 CE and *Epistula II ad Orsisium* to the following year. See Robertson (*NPNF*² 4:569).

[72] Joannou ed., *Fonti. Fasciolo ix. Discipline générale antique (ii–ix s.)*, Ep. ad Amun., 63–71 and Ep. ad Rufin., 76–80. See Quasten, *Patrology*, 64; Robertson (*NPNF*² 4:556).

[73] Quasten indicates the date 356 but *NPNF*² prefers 354. See Quasten, *Patrology*, 64.

[74] Hans Georg Opitz, ed., *Athanasius Werke: Die "Apologien"–De decretis Nicaenae synodi, De sententia Dionysii, Apologia de fuga sua, Apologia contra Arianos, Epistula encyclica, Epistula ad Serapionem de morte Arii, Epistula ad monachos, Historia Arianorum, De syodis Arimini in Italia et Seleucia in Isauria*. (vol. (Band) 2, Lieferung 1–7; Berlin: de Gruyter, 1934–1935).

[75] Jones claims that while written earlier, Athanasius revised *Apologia contra Arianos* some time after 370. A. H. M. Jones, "The Date of the 'Apologia Contra Arianos' of Athanasius," *JTS* 5 (1954).

the Arians (the Eusebian party) and the Meletians which related to events before the year 332 as well as outlining the various judicial investigations which proved his innocence.

The *Epistula encyclica* was written in 339 and appeals to the Catholic Bishops to unite with him against Gregory who had recently usurped Athanasius' position in Alexandria.[76] He also details the violent actions of the *dux* who had seized churches and given them over to the Arians. In *Epistula ad Serapionem de morte Arii*, written about 358, Athanasius gives an account of the death of Arius to Bishop Serapion. In *Epistula ad monachos* (357–358) Athanasius instructs the monks to beware since some Arians are visiting the monasteries with the intention of deceiving the "simple". Athanasius wrote *Historia Arianorum* in 358 in response to a request from the monks with whom he was residing during his third exile. In it he attacks the emperor Constantius as an enemy of Christ, since he had sided with Arius who was admitted back into communion at the Synod of Jerusalem (335).

Brogan chose not to include *Historia Arianorum* after Kannengiesser, in private correspondence, expressed doubt about the authenticity of this writing, attributing it to a secretary of Athanasius.[77] It is however included without reservation in Opitz's critical edition and doubts concerning its authenticity, based mainly on the use of Athanasius' name in the third person throughout the writing, seem at best tentative. Ernest concludes that, "It seems safe to treat the *History of the Arians* as authentic."[78] Therefore this writing is included as authentic.

De synodis Arimini in Italia et Seleucia in Isauria, written in 359, is more in the form of a report than a letter since it deals with the history of the two synods of Ariminum and Seleucia which were held that same year. Other parts include a history of the Arian creeds as well as an appeal to semi-Arians who apparently misunderstood certain terms used in the Nicene formula. The critical edition of Brennecke[79] contains *Apologia ad Constantium, Epistula ad Ioannem et Antiochum presb., Epistula ad Palladium, Epistula ad Dracontium, Epistula*

---

[76] See Gwynn, *The Eusebians*, 20–21, 51ff.

[77] Brogan, "Text of the Gospels," 59–60, n. 9.

[78] Ernest, *The Bible in Athanasius*, 243. The withdrawal of Kannengiesser's earlier objection to *Orationes III contra Arianos* (refer to the previous discussion concerning that writing) would also tend to mitigate the objection here. Brogan appears to disclose the somewhat tenuous and ambivalent nature of his own decision by stating that "Whether included or not, the Gospel references from *Historia Arianorum* would not have a significant impact on the textual analysis since they are so few in number." See Brogan, "Text of the Gospels," 60, n. 9. The present study contains 11 quotations from *Historia Arianorum* but only 2 are responsible for significant variants (1 Tim 1:4, 3:2).

[79] Brennecke, Hans Christof, et al. eds. *Athanasius Werke: Die "Apologien"-Apologia ad Constantium, Epistula ad Joannem et Antiochum, Epistula ad Palladium, Epistula ad Dracontium, Epistula ad Afros, Tomus ad Antiochenos, Epistula ad Jovianum, Epistula Joviani ad Athanasium, Petitiones Arianorum* (vol. (Band) 2, Lieferung 8; Berlin: de Gruyter, 2006), 279–280; See also Jan M. Szymusiak, ed., *Athanase d'Alexandrie: deux apologies, à l'empereur Constance et apologie pour sa fuite–Introduction, texte critique, traduction et notes* (SC 56; Paris: Editions du Cerf, 1987). Brogan used the critical edition of Szymusiak for *Apologia ad Constantium* since that was the only edition available to him at the time of writing his dissertation. The *Epistula ad Ioannem et Antiochum presb.* and *Epistula ad Palladium* are both concise letters written in the winter of 371–372.

ad Afros, Tomus ad Antiochenos, Epistula ad Jovianum, Epistula Joviani ad Athanasium and *Petitiones Arianorum*. The *Apologia ad Constantium* was written not long after Athanasius began his third exile (so around 356–357). In it he provides a defence against a number of specific charges that Constantius had brought against him. One charge was that Athanasius had poisoned the mind of Constans against his brother Constantius and another that he had sided with Magnentius, the general who had killed Constans and subsequently fought (and lost) against Constantius. It appears that at first Athanasius had intended to present the defence in person before Constantius, but by the close of the writing it is clear that he had given up on this idea. There is also no indication that it was even read by Constantius and if it was, it appears to have had no positive effect.

In the *Epistula ad Dracontium*, written in 354–355, Athanasius urges the abbot Dracontius to accept nomination to the episcopate and not to refuse on the basis that it would endanger his personal spiritual health as others were apparently advising. The letter appears to have been successful since Dracontius is present at the synod of Alexandria in 362 as the bishop of Hermupolis Parva. Athanasius wrote *Epistula ad Afros* on behalf of ninety bishops of Egypt and Libya present at the Alexandrian synod of 369 warning the church hierarchy of Western Africa not to accept the decisions of the synod of Ariminum which was being championed by the Arians as a final solution to their arguments with the supporters of Nicaea.

The letter *Tomus ad Antiochenos* was written in the name of the Alexandrian synod of 362 shortly after Athanasius' return from his third exile and is concerned with a peaceful settlement of previous unrest at Antioch and recommends procedures for the reintegration of repentant former Arian sympathizers. The *Epistula ad Jovianum* is an exposition of faith requested by the emperor Jovian and commissioned by the Alexandrian synod of 363 C.E.

Table 1: List of Athanasius' Writings Considered Authentic and Having Critical Editions Available.

Writings of Athanasius considered authentic and having critical editions available	Abbreviated Title used in Text and Apparatus	CPG #
Oratio contra gentes	Or. c. gentes	2090
Oratio de Incarnatione Verbi	Or. de Inc. Verb.	2091
Epistula ad episcopos Aegypti et Libyae	Ep. ad ep. Aeg. et Lib.	2092
Orationes contra Arianos III	Or. I c. Ar., Or. II c. Ar. Or. III c. Ar.	2093
Epistula ad Epictetum	Ep. ad Epic.	2095
Vita Antonii	Vita Ant.	2101
Epistulae festales: Fragmenta apud Cosman Indicopleustam	Ep. Cosm. Indic.	2102 (1)
Epistula xxxix	Ep. xxxix	2102 (2)
Epistula I ad Orsisium	Ep. i ad Orsis.	2103
Epistula II ad Orsisium	Ep. ii ad Orsis.	2104
Narratio Athanasii	Narr. Ath.	2105
Epistula ad Amun	Ep. ad Amun	2106
Epistula ad Rufinianum	Ep. ad Rufin.	2107
De decretis Nicaenae synodi	De decretis	2120
De sententia Dionysii	De sent. Dion.	2121
Apologia de fuga sua	Apol. de fuga	2122
Apologia contra Arianos (= Apologia secunda)	Apol. c. Ar.	2123
Epistula encyclica	Ep. encycl.	2124
Epistula ad Serapionem de morte Arii	Ep. ad Ser.	2125
Epistula ad monachos	Ep. ad monach.	2126
Historia Arianorum	Hist. Arian.	2127
De synodis Arimini in Italia et Seleucia in Isauria	De Syn.	2128
Apologia ad Constantium imperatorum	Ap. ad Const.	2129
Epistula ad Ioannem et Antiochum presb.	Ep. ad Ioan. et Ant.	2130
Epistula ad Palladium	Ep. ad Pall.	2131
Epistula ad Dracontium	Ep. ad Drac.	2132
Epistula ad episcopos Afros	Ep. ad Afros	2133
Tomus ad Antiochenos	Tom. ad Ant.	2134
Epistula ad Jovianum	Ep. ad Jov.	2135
Epistula Joviani ad Athanasium	Ep. Jov. ad Ath.	2136
Petitiones Arianorum	Pet. Arian.	2137

THE MANUSCRIPT TRADITION OF ATHANASIUS' WRITINGS

In comparison with the relative paucity of the manuscript sources for the writings of Clement, the extant manuscript tradition for Athanasius' writings are a veritable 'embarrassment of riches'.[80] It has been well analyzed over the period of the last century, despite the complexity which the abundance of extant manuscripts brings, beginning with the first attempts by Wallis in 1902 to reconstruct the mutual relations and history of the manuscripts that were known to him at the time.[81] Many more manuscripts have been added since culminating in the most recent iteration of the resultant stemmata being those presented in the Athanasius Werke series, especially in the editions published during the last decade.[82] Within the manuscript tradition a number of specific compilations or collections of Athanasius' writings have been recognized.[83]

For the apologetic writings three compilations are listed in the Athanasius Werke series as *a*-Sammlung, *x*-Sammlung and *y*-Sammlung along with a more generally labelled *b*-Tradition. Further, these collections overlap for a number of Athanasius' writings.[84] For example, *Tomus ad Antiochenus* is included in the *a* and *y* compilations and the *b*-Tradition. This means that the stemmata look quite different depending on which collection of writings is being considered, since different manuscripts are involved. Codex R (Parisinus gr. 474, s. XI) is included in the stemmata for both the dogmatic and apologetic writings but another equally important manuscript, Codex S (Parisinus Coislinianus gr. 45 (133), s. XII) is included only in the stemma for the dogmatic writings since it does not contain any apologetic works.[85] While subsequent editions in the AW

---

[80] Cosaert notes as far from ideal the fact that "the sole authority for each of Clement's extant writings is ultimately dependant upon a single manuscript". See Cosaert, *Text of the Gospels in Clement*, 14.

[81] F. Wallis, "On Some Mss of the Writings of St. Athanasius: Part 1," *JTS* 3 (1902); F. Wallis, "On Some Mss of the Writings of St. Athanasius: Part 2," *JTS* 3 (1902); See also K. Lake, "Some further notes on the mss of the writings of St Athanasius," *JTS* 5 (1904). Conybeare investigated the manuscripts of the Armenian Version and notes that "these mss of the version are themselves older than the Greek mss hitherto used for the Greek text." See Fred C. Conybeare, "On the Sources of the Text of S. Athanasius," *JP* 24, no. 48 (1896): 284.

[82] For example Wallis discussed fourteen manuscripts whereas the reconstruction of the stemma for the manuscript tradition for Or. III c. Ar. alone in the Athanasius Werke edition includes forty manuscripts, not including hypothesised Vorlage. See Metzler and Savvidis, *Oratio III Contra Arianos*, 277. Altogether more than one hundred and ninety manuscripts are listed in the first AW edition for Athanasius' dogmatic writings. See Metzler, Hanson and Savvidis, *Epistula ad Episcopos*, xi–xvii.

[83] Casey investigated the order of treatises in the manuscripts as a means for determining genealogy. See Robert Pierce Casey, "Greek Manuscripts of Athanasian Corpora," *ZNW* 30 (1931): 50ff; also Kirsopp Lake and Robert Pierce Casey, "The Text of the De Virginitate of Athanasius," *HTR* 19, no. 2 (1926): 176–177. Though outside the scope of this study, Casey also discusses the order of writings listed in Armenian manuscripts of Athanasius. Robert Pierce Casey, "Armenian Manuscripts of St. Athanasius of Alexandria," *HTR* 24, no. 1 (Jan., 1931).

[84] See Brennecke, Heil and von Stockhausen, *Die "Apologien"*, xix.

[85] The Athanasian writings included in the manuscripts vary widely. Codex R contains twenty-nine Athanasian treatises besides other non-Athanasian works, whereas three minor

series demonstrate that the stemmata have undergone a process of refinement it is clear that in the case of the dogmatic writings, which constitute a substantial proportion of Athanasius' works, there are two main traditions that diverge very early designated as the *RS* and *x* traditions.[86]

The main manuscripts in the *RS* tradition understandably include the codices R and S noted earlier. Codex 57 (Parisinus gr. 475, s. XVI) is considered a descendent of S as is Codex 56 (Londinensis Musei Britannici Harleianus 5579, a. 1320/21). Codex b[3] (Genevensis gr. 29 tom. III (now 892), s. XVI) is descended from Codex 56. In the *x* tradition, two of the main groups are one composed of Codex L (Londinensis Burneianus 46, s. XII) and descendants; codex 46 (Monacensis gr. 26, a. 1548), codex 47 (Cantabrigiensis (Trinity College B 9.8) gr. 204, s. XV/XVI) and codex b[1] (Genevensis gr. 29 tom. I (now 890), s. XVI), and a group which includes Codex B (Basiliensis gr. A III 4, s. XIII) with its descendants; codex 48 (Vindobonensis theol. Gr. 2, s. XV) and codex 50 (Oxonensis (Th. Roe) 29 (olim 275), a. 1410). The B group is considered to descend from a B/A Vorlage which is descended from the *x-Hyparchetype* while L is directly descended from the *x-Hyparchetype*.[87] A well developed genealogy of the extant manuscripts, with their synchronic and diachronic range, constitute an excellent resource for producing quality critical editions of Athanasius' writings upon which this analysis of his text of the Apostolos is based.

---

codices, Laura B20, Laura B58 and Laura Gamma 106, contain only three writings, *Contra Gentes*, *De Incarnatione* and *Disputatio contra Arium*. See Wallis, "Some Mss: Part 1," 98–99; also Lake, "Some Further Notes," 114. Another factor is the presence of recensions within the manuscripts for a number of Athanasius' writings, particularly in the apologetic writings. Four recensions are noted in the Apologetic writings designated; *a*-Rezension, *b*-Rezension, *x*-Rezension and *y*-Rezension. See Brennecke, Heil and von Stockhausen, *Die "Apologien"*, xx–xxviii.

[86] These major manuscript textual streams (traditions) are not to be confused with the *b*-Tradition collection. Compare the earlier to later versions of the stemmata presented in the various editions of the AW series. See Metzler, Hansen and Savvidis, *Epistula ad Episcopos*, 8; also Metzler and Savvidis, *Orationes I et II Contra Arianos*, 89; Metzler and Savvidis, *Oratio III Contra Arianos*, 277; See also the reviews by Stuart George Hall, review of Karin Metzler, ed., *Athanasius Werke*. I/i. *Die dogmatischen Schriften. 2. Lieferung. Orationes I et II Contra Arianos. JTS* 51, no. 1 (2000); Stuart George Hall, review of Karin Metzler, ed., *Athanasius Werke*. I/i. *Die dogmatischen Schriften. 3. Lieferung. Oratio III Contra Arianos. JTS* 53, no. 1 (2002): esp. 333.

[87] See Metzler and Savvidis, *Oratio III Contra Arianos*, 265–275.

2

ATHANASIUS AND THE TEXT OF THE APOSTOLOS

THE ALEXANDRIAN TEXT: OVERVIEW AND CLASSIFICATION

A primary aim of the present study is 'locating' Athanasius' text of the Apostolos within the various text-type categories. Ehrman claims that "it is not enough to conclude that 'Athanasius is therefore an Alexandrian witness'. Of *course* [emphasis his] he is an Alexandrian witness; he lived in Alexandria."[1] Nevertheless, this assumption must be tested and verified on the basis of reliable data. In order to more accurately delineate Athanasius' text of the Apostolos within the classification of text-types and specifically the Alexandrian tradition, it is necessary to consider the nature and development of that tradition and how it has been perceived within the text-critical endeavour.[2]

Brogan notes that text critics advocate two major theories concerning the history of the New Testament text in Alexandria: 1) The Alexandrian text represents a recension of the New Testament made in Alexandria sometime between the 2nd–4th centuries; 2) The Alexandrian text represents a carefully preserved textual tradition that is not a recension.[3] A recension is understood to be a specific editorial exercise whereby text critical methodology is applied ostensibly to 'improve' the text in order to render a more faithful representation of the 'original'.[4] Rather than provide a general history of the Alexandrian text which is available elsewhere, it will suffice to consider here various relevant aspects of the two major

---

[1] Bart D. Ehrman, "The Use of the Church Fathers in New Testament Textual Criticism," in *The Bible as Book: The Transmission of the Greek Text* (eds. McKendrick and O'Sullivan; London: The British Library, 2003), 158.

[2] Specifically related to this is an analysis of the similarities and differences of Athanasius' text of the Apostolos from the text of other recognised Alexandrian manuscripts which will in turn provide further evidence for the development of the Alexandrian text during the fourth century.

[3] Brogan, "Text of the Gospels," 33 ff.

[4] This is not the only meaning that has been applied to the term 'recension'. Metzger notes that "Semler was the first to apply the term recension to groups of New Testament witnesses (*Hermeneutische Vorbereitung*, iii [1] [Halle, 1765]). Properly, a recension is the result of deliberate critical work by an editor; it is, however, often used in a loose sense as synonymous with *family*." Bruce Manning Metzger and Bart D. Ehrman, *The Text of the New Testament: Its Transmission, Corruption and Restoration* (New York, Oxford: Oxford University Press, 2005), 161, n. 58.

positions.[5] In regards to the first, that the Alexandrian text represents a recension, it should be noted that this view has had distinguished support from such textual scholars as Semler (1725–1791) and Griesbach (1745–1812) who posited that the recension stemmed from Origen. Hug (1765–1846) on the other hand attributed the Alexandrian (or Egyptian) recension to Heyschius who supposedly revised a form of the κοινὴ ἔκδοσις (*vulgaris editio*) which was very similar to the text found in Codex Cantabrigiensis (D).

The view of an Alexandrian recension prevalent toward the end of the 18th century was however, challenged by the alternative theory proffered by Westcott and Hort and explained in their *Introduction to the New Testament in the Original Greek* published in 1881.[6] In the *Introduction* Hort argued for a separation between an Alexandrian and what he referred to as a 'Neutral' text. As Martini points out, however, the term 'Neutral' as intended by Hort does not refer to *another text type* as distinct from the Alexandrian and also present in Egypt (or elsewhere for that matter) nor is it to be associated with certain manuscripts since its primary characteristic is not positive but negative.[7] That is to say the term 'Neutral' "applies to those variants which cannot be characterized *either* [emphasis his] as Syrian *or* as Alexandrian *or* as Western." Rather the 'Neutral' text represents a relatively pure line of descent from the original but since it is not a text type in its own right 'Neutral' readings can be found in any of the other text types though they are found predominantly in old Alexandrian manuscripts. This however, as Hort points out, is simply a result of historical accident since the only manuscripts surviving from the first centuries happen to come from Egypt. Concerning the Alexandrian text-type itself, Hort postulated that it had its origin possibly as early as the 2nd century and not as a recension but rather as a philologically motivated trend towards the use of 'literary' Greek in the transcription of the manuscripts.[8]

Subsequent text-critical scholarship responded to Hort's construction in various ways. While the implications of the designation 'Neutral' in the minds of many text critics caused them to both castigate and reject the term, the idea of a close association of 'Neutral' readings with the old Alexandrian manuscripts was attractive and led to the perception of a 'proto-Alexandrian' text-type which is best represented in the early Alexandrian manuscripts as distinct from a 'later-Alexandrian' text-type which continued to be regarded as the product of specific recensional activity.[9] This view eventually came to assume the dominant position

---

[5] For example see Fee, "The Myth of Early Textual Recension in Alexandria."; Carlo M. Martini, "Is There a Late Alexandrian Text of the Gospels?" *NTS* 24 (1977–78).

[6] Brooke Foss Westcott and Fenton John Anthony Hort, *The New Testament in the Original Greek* (2 vols.; London: Macmillan and Co., 1881, 1882).

[7] Martini, "Late Alexandrian Text," 288. Nevertheless Westcott and Hort did consider the 'Neutral' text to be best represented in the two great codices, B and ℵ. See Westcott and Hort, *New Testament*, 210ff.

[8] Westcott and Hort, *New Testament*, 130 ff; See also Martini, "Is There a Late Alexandrian Text of the Gospels?," 288.

[9] Martini, "Late Alexandrian Text," 288.

to the extent that Metzger continued to reflect this general consensus when dividing the Alexandrian witnesses into two groups, designating the following manuscripts as Proto-Alexandrian: $\mathfrak{P}^{45}$ (in Acts) $\mathfrak{P}^{56}$ $\mathfrak{P}^{66}$ $\mathfrak{P}^{75}$ ℵ B Sahidic (in part), Clement of Alexandria, Origen (in part), and most of the papyrus fragments with Pauline text; and Later Alexandrian (in the Apostolos): Acts: $\mathfrak{P}^{50}$ A (C) Ψ 33 81 104 326 1739; Pauline Epistles: A (C) H^p I Ψ 33 81 104 326 1739; Catholic Epistles: $\mathfrak{P}^{20}$ $\mathfrak{P}^{23}$ A (C) Ψ 33 81 104 326 1739; Revelation: A (C) 1006 1611 1854 2053 2344; less good $\mathfrak{P}^{47}$ ℵ.[10]

With the discovery, publication and subsequent analysis of the Chester Beatty and Bodmer biblical papyrus from Egypt, any support for the idea of an Alexandrian recension was effectively removed. Though they were initially interpreted as supporting the idea of a recension, it eventually became clear that since $\mathfrak{P}^{75}$ in particular contained a text very similar to B and since this text existed in Egypt in the second century, the text of B cannot be attributed to a (later) Heyschian recension.[11] This reading of the evidence was further confirmed by Fee's study of $\mathfrak{P}^{75}$, $\mathfrak{P}^{66}$ and Origen where he conclusively demonstrated that "the concept of a scholarly recension of the NT text in Alexandria either in the fourth century *or* the second century, either as a created or a carefully edited text, is a myth... an analysis of the textual character of $\mathfrak{P}^{75}$ B *when compared with other manuscript traditions* indicates that there is little evidence of recensional activity of any kind taking place in this text-type."[12] Rather, "These MSS seem to represent a 'relatively pure' form of preservation of a 'relatively pure' line of descent from the original text."[13] Martini also rejected the idea of a late Alexandrian recension and suggested as an alternative reconstruction that the later Alexandrian text is better understood as an early "slight correction" of the old "pre-recensional" or so called Proto-Alexandrian text and that these two streams of tradition existed in Alexandria side by side from a very early period.[14]

---

[10] Metzger, *Text of the New Testament*, 216.

[11] See Brogan, "Text of the Gospels," 46.

[12] Fee, "The Myth of Early Textual Recension in Alexandria," 272.

[13] Ibid., 272. Despite the evidence amassed by Fee, Brogan claims that Fee's arguments against the recensional character of the $\mathfrak{P}^{75}$ B text "are not completely convincing." For example Brogan argues that "the fact that neither $\mathfrak{P}^{66}$ nor Origen could have created a recension does not preclude the possibility that someone else was involved in such philological pursuits" or "the fact that $\mathfrak{P}^{75}$ does not exhibit recensional activities says absolutely nothing about whether the ancestor of $\mathfrak{P}^{75}$ was a recension." Brogan, "Text of the Gospels," 48. Brogan, however, provides no alternative evidence to support these arguments. He rightly points out a more significant weakness in Fee's reconstruction; his classifications of the Alexandrian witnesses, since he divides them into not just two, but four groups with two levels of "primary" 'Neutrals' (level one consisting of $\mathfrak{P}^{75}$ B and Origen and level two consisting of $\mathfrak{P}^{66}$ C) and two levels of "secondary" 'Neutrals' (level one consisting of L 33 and Cyril and level two consisting of Ψ 579 892 1241 A) but without a clear elucidation of how these classifications are defined. Indeed the danger is that such classifications become so fragmentary that the terms begin to lose all meaning. As Ehrman succinctly points out "The idea of a 'secondary Neutral' witness is bizarre in the extreme!" Ehrman, *Didymus*, 265.

[14] Martini, "Late Alexandrian Text," 295. Martini was essentially reviving the Hortian reconstruction but whereas Hort suggested the Alexandrian text had developed over a long period, Martini's important alteration is to propose the revision to the old Alexandrian occurred at a very

As a result of his study of the Gospels text of Didymus the Blind, Ehrman came to question the accuracy and veracity of the categories, 'Proto'-Alexandrian and 'Later'-Alexandrian witnesses as popularized by Metzger and others.[15] Ehrman demonstrated from a Quantitative analysis that Didymus' text in the Gospels shows overall agreement with the Early/Proto-Alexandrian witnesses whereas the group profile analysis showed Didymus to be more closely aligned to the Late-Alexandrian witnesses.[16] Ehrman suggested that the Alexandrian subgroups would be better labelled as 'Primary Alexandrian' and 'Secondary Alexandrian'.[17] Brogan adopted this suggestion and concluded that Athanasius' text of the Gospels "agrees most closely with the Secondary Alexandrian group".[18]

Brogan also claimed that the analysis of Athanasius' text of the Gospels was of direct relevance in helping to answer one important question on the nature of the Secondary Alexandrian witnesses; whether these witnesses "represent a very early revision of the 'pure line' of text that existed side by side with that 'pure line' in Alexandria, or whether the 'Secondary Alexandrians' represent independent corruptions of the pure line that were made at various times[?]"[19] From analysis of Athanasius' text of the Gospels, Brogan concluded that the latter explanation is more likely. Brogan's conclusions for the Gospels text of Athanasius provide a convenient direct point of comparison when evaluating and analyzing Athanasius' text of the Apostolos in the present study.

Brogan's dissertation is most relevant for the present study, though a number of earlier works should be noted. Their focus is more general since Nordberg analyzed the whole of the biblical text of Athanasius while Zervopoulos and Metzler analyzed the whole of his New Testament text.[20] What becomes evident however is the range of different conclusions reached by these authors.

---

early stage. See also Brogan, "Text of the Gospels," 51–52.

[15] Metzger, *Text of the New Testament*, 216.

[16] A quantitative analysis is used by text-critics to determine the general affinity of any particular text or manuscript within broad documentary groupings and sub-groupings on the basis of textual consanguinity. See Ehrman, "Methodological Developments."

[17] Ehrman claims that the advantage of these terms is that they imply "nothing about the overall superiority or the unrevised character of this text". Ehrman, *Didymus*, 265–266.

[18] Brogan, "Text of the Gospels," 428.

[19] Ibid., 55. Another aspect of Brogan's study on the Gospels text of Athanasius was a consideration of the extent to which Athanasius "corrupted" his biblical text; that is, to what extent he was directly responsible for introducing unique readings into the textual tradition which were primarily motivated by his theological convictions. Brogan concluded that Athanasius did occasionally 'corrupt' his text by omissions, grammatical changes and word substitutions. See ibid., 261ff; See also Ehrman, Bart D., *The Orthodox Corruption of Scripture: The Effect of Early Christological Controversies on the Text of the New Testament* (New York. Oxford: Oxford University Press, 1993); also Epp, Eldon Jay, "The Multivalence of the Term "Original Text" in New Testament Textual Criticism," *HTR* 92, no. 3 (1999): 258ff. For the factors involved in scribal alterations in the textual tradition, including doctrinal motives, see Royce, James R., "Scribal Tendencies in the Transmission of the Text of the New Testament," in *The Text of the New Testament in Contemporary Research: Essays on the Status Questionis* (SD 46; Grand Rapids: Eerdmans, 1995), 240.

[20] Metzler also considered Athanasius' text of the Septuagint.

PREVIOUS STUDIES

Henric Nordberg: Nordberg's 1962 article on the Bible text of Athanasius makes reference to Gwatkin's "very superficial investigation" of the biblical quotations of Athanasius that led him to make a brief statement about Athanasius' text-type affinity.[21] Even the use of the term 'investigation' would seem to inflate the importance of Gwatkin's conclusion since all he does is to claim that in the Old Testament, Athanasius' text, "at least in his *c. Gentes...* is nearer to the Vatican than to the Alexandrine text."[22] This hardly constitutes a comprehensive textual study and it would be presumptuous to apply these conclusions to the New Testament text. Indeed, Brogan's study on the Gospels text concluded otherwise and the analysis in the present study will show that Gwatkin's view is not upheld in the case of the Apostolos.[23] Nordberg concluded, on the basis of his own study, that Athanasius used two different text-types during his career; an A text-type represented primarily by Codex Alexandrinus (A 02) which was predominant during his ministry in Alexandria and a B text-type represented primarily by Codex Vaticanus (B 03) which came to the fore during his numerous exiles, but particularly in his fourth exile under Julian.[24]

A number of factors serve to weaken the force of these rather tentative findings. The first is Nordberg's use of the unfortunately unreliable edition of Migne (PG) for some of Athanasius' writings including the *Orationes contra Arianos I–III*. His hypothesis was also dependant on a specific chronological order for Athanasius' writings and primarily on a very late dating for *Oratio conra gentes* and *Oration de Incarnatione Verbi*, since it was in these two writings particularly that Nordberg claimed to detect a strong B text. His postulation of a late date (362–363) for these writings has not met with any acceptance and therefore weakens his argument significantly.[25] A further complication is that Codex A has a mixed text-type alignment in the New Testament, being Byzantine in the Gospels but Alexandrian (alongside MS B) in the Apostolos, a factor ignored by Nordberg, and a juxtaposition of these witnesses as representing differing text-types in that latter part of the New Testament is therefore rendered superfluous. For these reasons Nordberg's claims as they relate to the Apostolos must be discounted.[26]

---

[21] See Nordberg, "Bible Text of St. Athanasius," 120.

[22] Henry Melvill Gwatkin, *Studies of Arianism* (Cambridge: Deighton, Bell and Co., 1900), 73.

[23] For example Brogan's Quantitative analysis in the Gospels shows that Athanasius is more closely aligned with Ψ (77.0%), ℵ (71.1%), 892 (70.2%)—all three being Secondary Alexandrian, before B (67.6%)—a Primary Alexandrian. See Brogan, "Text of the Gospels," 221. Refer to Chapter 5 for the quantitative analysis results for the Apostolos of Athanasius. Brogan also refers to Nordberg's article and in Chapter 1 of his thesis indicates his intention to discuss its "shortcomings" in Chapter 3. However there is no mention of Nordberg's article in that chapter. See ibid., 1, 57–77.

[24] See Nordberg, "Bible Text of St. Athanasius," 123.

[25] Refer to the earlier discussion in Chapter 1 concerning the dating of these two works.

[26] Nordberg only provides samples of the data on which the analysis is based and no final results of a quantitative analysis. Only general statements are provided such as, "The B text dominates over the A text." Nordberg, "On the Bible Text of St. Athanasius." This is insufficient as

Gerassimos Zervopoulos: One of the few studies to focus specifically on the New Testament text of Athanasius was written just over a half-century ago by Zervopoulos.[27] It was however restricted only to the text of the Gospels which made it of specific interest to Brogan but as a result is only of peripheral importance to the present study. Brogan provided an extensive critique of Zervopoulos' work in his own study on the Gospels text of Athanasius in which he notes a number of significant shortcomings that diminished the significance of Zervopoulos' results.[28] First, Brogan notes that Zervopoulos included a number of writings attributed to Athanasius of which the authenticity is highly questionable and lacking a scholarly consensus.[29] Another serious deficiency was the use of Migne's edition of *Patrologiae Cursus Completus, Series Graece* (PG) for the text of Athanasius' writings.[30] The unreliable nature of this edition has already been noted.[31] A further issue, particularly related to the nature of the Gospels text, was Zervopoulos' use of citations identified as coming from one Gospel but which could have equally come from a parallel passage in another Gospel therefore increasing the possibility of misidentification of quotation sources. Related to this was the incorrect use of harmonizations and conflations of Gospel citations. Zervopoulos' presentation and classification of the textual data was also deficient.

Brogan notes that Zervopoulos' data was "plagued with mistakes" as well as being "marred by some minor weaknesses that make it difficult for a reader to reconstruct the evidence" in order to verify his conclusions.[32] Another weakness concerns his methodology since Zervopoulos collated Athanasius' quotations against the Textus Receptus, a procedure that is now well discredited in contemporary text-critical analysis.[33] The deficiencies that plagued Zervopoulos' study

---

evidence for proof of his claims. Despite the paucity of data presentation Nordberg finally concludes that Athanasius employed no less than "four Bible manuscripts", by which he means four distinct text-types. However again only a small sample of the data used to support this claim is provided. See ibid., 137. This again serves to underline the necessity of a comprehensive analysis with all the data presented before any firm conclusions can be drawn.

[27]   Zervopoulos, "The Gospels-Text of Athanasius."

[28]   See Brogan, "Text of the Gospels," 57ff.

[29]   Most prominent was Zervopoulos' inclusion of *Orationes IV contra Arianos* even though it has been recognised for a long time that it cannot be from the hand of Athanasius. See R. P. C. Hanson, "The Source and Significance of the Fourth 'Oratio contra Arianos' attributed to Athanasius," *VC* 42 (1988): 257–266.

[30]   J.-P. Migne, ed., PG (Paris: Migne, 1863).

[31]   See the discussion in Chapter 1. In his *General Introduction* Zervopoulos states "The principal subject of my thesis is based on Migne's "Patrologia" which up to this day is the most complete available source of Athnasius' printed writings." See Zervopoulos, "The Gospels-Text of Athanasius," v. This was despite the availability of Opitz's edition in the Athanasius Werke series. Zervopoulos apparently referred to this critical edition but elected not to use it after claiming to have found "only 4 variants" against PG in sixty quotations. Ibid., 206. Yet, as Brogan notes, "even this amount of difference could significantly alter the statistical data." See Brogan, "Text of the Gospels," 63.

[32]   See Brogan, "Text of the Gospels," 69–70.

[33]   See Zervopoulos, "The Gospels-Text of Athanasius," 84. Note the fuller discussion on this issue below.

can be avoided by the application of a rigorous methodology now commonly adopted in more recent studies in the texts of the Fathers such as using only recognized authentic writings in modern critical editions with full presentation of the data and all manuscript witnesses collated against each other.

Karin Metzler: Another textual study published approximately the same time as the completion of Brogan's dissertation was Metzler's *Welchen Bibeltext benutzte Athanasius im Exil?*[34] She included an extensive critique of both Nordberg and Zervopoulos' studies noting many of the shortcomings already mentioned but also observing that while using the same data they had arrived at essentially opposite conclusions.[35] This underlines for Metzler the necessity of a well developed and clear methodology to enable trustworthy results. Being unconvinced by Nordberg's conclusion that Athanasius used different texts in Alexandria and in exile, Metzler's aim was to re-test this hypothesis. However rather than undertaking an extensive analysis incorporating all of Athanasius' authentic writings, Metzler utilised only *Epistula ad episcopos Aegypti et Libyae* to represent Athanasius' Alexandrian writings (i.e. text-type) and compared it with Vita Antonii along with *Orationes contra Arianos I* and *III* which represent his exilic phase.[36] Her conclusion was that Athanasius' text-type changes between *Orationes contra Arianos I* and *Orationes contra Arianos III* but this only consti- tutes a change within the Alexandrian text-type and therefore excludes the idea that Athanasius used different text-types between his Alexandrian ministry and numerous exiles. Metzler indicates that even these conclusions are somewhat tentative and far from certain. While utilizing a quantitative analysis, Metzler's selective use of only a few authentic writings mean that its relevance for the pres- ent study is limited.[37]

CLASSIFICATION OF ATHANASIUS' QUOTATIONS OF THE APOSTOLOS

Of consideration here is the type of data that can be extracted from the writings of Athanasius or for that matter the writings of any of the Fathers. A review of Athanasius' texts makes it clear that he refers to the New Testament text in various ways. Sometimes he provides clear indication that what he says is a direct quotation from Scripture. For example he might say "Paul (has) written in his Epistle to the Romans" (ὁ Παῦλος ἐν τῇ πρὸς Ῥωμαίους … γράφων) or "for as the Apostle has written" (ὡς γὰρ ὁ Ἀπόστολος ἔγραψεν) or "for the Apostle says" (Φησὶ γὰρ ὁ Ἀπόστολος).[38] At other times he simply says "for it is written"

---

[34] See Metzler, Karin, *Welchen Bibeltexte Benutzte Athanasius im Exil?* (Opladen: Westdeutscher Verlag, 1997).
[35] Ibid., 9ff.
[36] Ibid., 10.
[37] Metzler provides an extensive set of tables containing the data for the quantitative analysis. Ibid., 84–113.
[38] Athanasius uses the term 'Apostle' to refer to Peter the disciple of Jesus as well as of Paul the Apostle.

(γέγραπται γάρ) or "says Scripture" (φησὶν ἡ Γραφὴ). On other occasions there is no explicit indication that what is being quoted is based on or drawn from Scripture, but rather the pattern of words alone provides the clue. Therefore, some method of classification is required which will allow, to the greatest extent possible, a determination as to what text of the Apostolos Athanasius actually used.

In discussions concerning methodology for text-critical studies of the Church Fathers, Fee suggested that the three categories of Citation, Adaptation and Allusion be used.[39] This scheme was subsequently adopted by other patristic scholars doing research in the Greek Fathers.[40] Fee initially defined these terms in the following way; "Allusion: Reference to the *content* of a biblical passage in which *verbal* correspondence to the NT Greek text is so remote as to offer no value for the reconstruction of that text. Adaptation: Reference to a biblical passage, which has clear *verbal* correspondence to the Greek NT, but which has been adapted to fit the Father's discussion and/or syntax. Citation: Those places where a Father is consciously trying to cite, either from memory or by copying, the very words of the biblical text."[41] However, in a later study on Origen the definitions had been modified somewhat to; Citation [C]: "a verbally exact quotation of the biblical text"; Adaptation [Ad]: "a quotation that has been somewhat modified (syntactically or materially) in light of the context of Origen's discussion"; Allusion [All]: "a clear echo of a passage which nonetheless lacks a sustained verbal agreement."[42] Brogan noted the change in definitions particularly as regards Citations and especially the "enormous" difficulty with the first definition when "trying to establish the intent lying behind the church Father's citation techniques."[43] In a later study on the Gospels text of Didymus, Ehrman

---

[39] See Fee, "Text of John in the *Jerusalem Bible*," 340; also Fee, "Text of John in Origen and Cyril," 304.

[40] See Ehrman, *Didymus*; also Brooks, *New Testament Text of Gregory*; Brogan, "Text of the Gospels,". In one of the most recent studies to be added to the Society of Biblical Literature's, The New Testament in the Greek Fathers series, Osburn has added a fourth category of 'Reminiscence'. Osburn, *Text of the Apostolos in Epiphanius*, 28, esp. n. 30; Ernest, *The Bible in Athanasius*, 40.

[41] Fee, "Text of John in Origen and Cyril," 304.

[42] Ehrman, Fee and Holmes, *Fourth Gospel in Origen*, 22.

[43] Brogan, "Text of the Gospels," 73–74, n.45. Ernest was aware of the categories of Citation, Adaptation and Allusion used by text-critics but also noted some "grade deflation" in the definition of those terms between the first suggestion for their use by Fee and their subsequent use by Fee, Ehrman and Holmes in their study of Origen's text of the Fourth Gospel. See Ernest, *The Bible in Athanasius*, 29 n.91. There is also the issue of a subjective element in classifying various texts into these categories which can potentially lead to variations in both the data sets and subsequent analysis. The main difficulty lies in the differentiation between these classifications which more correctly represent relative points along a continuum than strictly autonomous categories. Cf Ehrman, *Didymus*, 13. This subjective element has been noted by other scholars working with the New Testament text in the Greek Fathers. Osburn claims that "it is not easy to decide when an adaptation is useful for establishing a father's text, nor is it easy to determine when an allusion is to be included in the assessment. Osburn, *Text of the Apostolos in Epiphanius*, 28. Brogan notes that despite this subjective element the categories are "a helpful and necessary tool for weighing the evidence." Brogan, "Text of the Gospels," 74.

avoided the problem of intentionality by utilizing the categories of Citation, Adaptation and Allusion but classifying the biblical quotations in each category with respect to their degree of correspondence or conformity to the NT source.[44] An alternative classification system used by Ernest includes the categories of Citation, Quotation, Allusion, Reminiscence and Locution. Ernest defines his terms as follows: Quotation: "Where the Athanasian text corresponds entirely (for very brief instances) or largely (for longer instances) with the biblical text"; Citation: "marked with formulas that indicate direct discourse together with an explicit or implicit cue that what is being quoted is the Bible."; Allusion: "used for instances where Athanasius's wording points at Scripture without formally citing it."; Reminiscence: "Where the correspondence is looser but still identifiably with a specific biblical text".[45] While some of the terms are identical, the definitions applied to these terms indicate that some differences exist and hence they are not synonymous in application. A comparison between these two classification systems can be approximated by adopting Ehrman's suggestion that the various categories be viewed as relative points along a continuum ranging from exact citation to distant allusion as follows:[46]

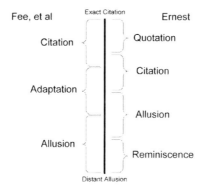

This comparison begs the question as to the degree of correspondence between the two classification systems. Even allowing for variation in the use of terms, the differences between cited instances of Scripture from the lists of Ernest and the present study are not inconsequential. This may best be illustrated by a comparison of the source data in the present study with Ernest's tables of

---

[44]   Ehrman, *Didymus*, 12–13. This approach would initially appear to be in danger of a form of 'circularity'. That is, the Father's text is classified according to its affinity to a specific New Testament text (e.g. Nestle-Aland/United Bible Societies Greek New Testament) or range of textual tradition before it is collated against that same textual tradition to determine its affinity. Therefore the method appears to pre-empt the result. Ehrman recognised that such an approach "appears problematic" but claims that in practice it is "not difficult to distinguish between a faint allusion and a precise citation." ibid., 12–13. This viewpoint has been adequately confirmed in the present analysis on the basis of a comparison with UBS[4]. Kurt Aland, et al. eds., *The Greek New Testament* (4th ed.; Stuttgart: United Bible Societies, 1993); see also Kurt Aland, et al. eds., *Nestle-Aland Novum Testamentum Graece* (27th ed.; Stuttgart: Deutsche Bibelgesellschaft, 1994).

[45]   Ernest, *The Bible in Athanasius*, 39–40.

[46]   Ehrman, *Didymus*, 13.

references to the book of Acts.[47] From a total of 116 references there are 75 differences for a disagreement of 65%.[48] The differences are not as great as first appears since, for example, Ernest includes a number of quotations of just one word even though they are not New Testament hapax legomena. These have not been included in the Apostolos data presented here.

Since Ernest's focus is not specifically text-critical, his criterion is more inclusive of accepting even remote reminiscences. The main difficulty, however, is that Ernest does not reproduce the texts for the references he quotes so as to permit direct comparison with the references in the present study and hence it is not possible to verify Ernest's source data and statistics. This serves to demonstrate that care must be taken in the choice of classification system and underscores the need for full presentation of the data. This also precludes use of the otherwise convenient and extensive list of references for the Apostolos which Ernest provides in (his) Appendix B, since without the actual text his references and classifications cannot be adequately verified.[49] Within this study the three categories of Citation, Adaptation and Allusion will be adopted. This also permits direct comparison with the results of similar textual studies that have utilised the same classification system for quotations of the New Testament in the writings of the Greek Fathers.[50]

ATHANASIUS' CITATION HABITS

From the brief discussion on Athanasius' education and hermeneutics in Chapter 1 and from his introductory formulae as noted on pp. 35–36 above, it appears that Athanasius generally cited from memory rather than transcribing directly from an exemplar. Brogan notes that this has two contrasting effects; "On the one hand it increases the number of alterations to the 'parent' text [the text Athanasius memorized] ... On the other hand citation from memory has a stabilizing effect on the textual character of the citations."[51] That this is the case for Athanasius can be seen from a review of the text as presented in Chapter 3

---

[47]   Ernest, *The Bible in Athanasius*, 404–406.

[48]   Refer to Appendix D, References for the book of Acts: Ernest-Donker.

[49]   Ernest, *The Bible in Athanasius*, Appendix B, 406–417. This situation recalls the urgent plea of Fee that *all* the relevant data concerning a Father's New Testament text should be presented. Fee, "Text of John in Origen and Cyril," 301. Another weakness is that Ernest includes as quotations of the biblical text, references where Athanasius refers to the writings of his opponents which include quotations from scripture. However these must be disallowed as it cannot be determined conclusively that Athanasius in such cases either quotes his own text directly (or from memory) rather than quoting verbatim from the writings of his opponents.

[50]   The procedure for the present research is: a) Analysis of Athanasius' writings to identify all instances where he quotes from the Apostolos. b) Compare the various quotations identified with an eclectic Greek New Testament text (NA[27]) to determine their degree of verbal correspondence with the biblical text and therefore the most appropriate category into which they may be classified. In practice the majority of quotations can be classified with a reasonable degree of confidence when using verbal correspondence as the basis of evaluation.

[51]   Brogan, "Text of the Gospels," 17–18.

following, especially where Athanasius has quoted the same references multiple times such as for Phil 2:6, 2:7 and Heb 3:2. A corollary to Athanasius' tendency to cite from memory is that the majority of his citations are short passages, with extended quotations being the exception rather than the rule. Further, Athanasius rarely exhibits any philological concerns such as preference for a certain form of wording over against others and he never discusses text-critical issues such as 'correct' or 'incorrect' word substitutions.[52] Therefore an evaluation of Athanasius' use of Scripture must be predominantly based on the quotations themselves rather than on extraneous (and in this case essentially absent) philological and text-critical comments and to this text we now turn.

ATHANASIUS' TEXT OF THE APOSTOLOS

The following chapter lists all the quotations of the Apostolos contained in Athanasius' writings (as discussed in Chapter 1) collated against a range of selected New Testament manuscript witnesses. Since the data may be presented in various ways, an explanation of the layout used here is required. An earlier method of presenting a Father's text was simply to list all textual variants from the *Textus Receptus*. The weakness of this system was that "other scholars did not have direct access to the full NT text of the Father."[53] A later refinement was to list all textual variants as found in a group of selected representative witnesses in passages quoted by the Father. However, as Ehrman noted, though the advantage of such a presentation is brevity while still allowing the reader to see the textual alignments in all variants and correspondingly points of disagreement, the weakness of such a system is that points of agreement cannot readily be seen.[54] The reader is prevented from seeing just how extensively the Father *agrees* with any specific witness. It may be, for example, that a variant involves substitution of one or two words or a change of case while the points of agreement extend for whole verses and passages. A further weakness, as with the first method, is that the reader is required to reconstruct the Father's text should they wish to consult the original data used to determine the variants. Therefore, more recent studies on the New Testament text of the Greek Fathers have followed Fee's recommendation that the *full* data of the Father's text be reproduced by listing all the biblical Citations, Adaptations and Allusions along with a critical apparatus showing all variants of the Father's text against the selected witnesses.[55] This format will be used to present the data in the following chapter.

---

[52] Ibid., 16. Refer also to the earlier discussion on pp. 12–13.

[53] Fee, "Use of the Greek Fathers," 198.

[54] Ehrman, *Didymus*, 30–31.

[55] Fee, "Text of John in Origen and Cyril," 301–304. Even the study on the New Testament text of Gregory of Nyssa by Brooks which is part of the SBLNTGF series has some weakness in data presentation. While providing a reconstructed text he still does not present all instances of Citations, Adaptations and Allusions in full, requiring the reader to determine these quotations from the critical apparatus. Brooks, *New Testament Text of Gregory*, 15.

Each biblical reference is listed by book (or epistle), chapter and verse. Then follows the text of the Apostolos reproduced from the writings of Athanasius. This varies from whole verses to part of a verse only. Then below the text is indicated the source of the quotation from the writings of Athanasius. In general the quotation is identified by chapter alone or chapter and section number but where this varies the particular scheme can be readily determined by reference to the relevant critical edition. Next the reference is classified as a Citation [C], Adaptation [Ad] or Allusion [All], with the various quotations presented in that classification order. Where any text is part of a longer uninterrupted reference consisting of multiple verses, this is indicated by the symbol + placed at the end of one verse and the beginning of the next.[56]

All Athanasius' quotations of the Apostolos have been reproduced. However where he quotes the exact same text numerous times the text has been reproduced only once and then below the text are listed the details of all locations where these quotations are found. Only identical instances of the same classification type are grouped together (i.e. Citations, Adaptations or Allusions).[57] An exception to the above is where the text, even though identical to another quotation, is part of a reference containing multiple verses. In such cases the references are kept separate so as to allow the contiguous text to be readily identified. Words such as conjunctions, that do not strictly form part of the actual reference but are found within Athanasius' text and help to provide context, will appear in brackets.

Where there are multiple Citations for a verse which are not identical in form and order of the text, then the Citation marked with a double asterisk ** is used as the basis for collation. A single asterisk * is used to indicate Adaptations or Allusions that provide evidence for a significant variant. Sometimes Athanasius quotes from the writings of his opponents and included in the quotation is a reference to the biblical text. In such cases these indirect quotations have not been used since it cannot be determined with any confidence whether Athanasius utilised his own biblical text or quoted strictly verbatim from his opponents' writings. In a few cases, due to the differences between Citations, it has been necessary to attempt a reconstruction of Athanasius' textual *Vorlage* on the basis of the available evidence. This reconstructed text is used as the basis for collation and is indicated by the preceding word TEXT in capitals.

---

[56] e.g. See Phil 2:5–11 in *Or. I c. Ar.* 40.

[57] Differences of punctuation in the critical edition of Athanasius' writings (e.g. commas within the text or capitalisation at the beginning of sentences) have been ignored and treated as identical references. In only a few instances is this the case.

THE CRITICAL APPARATUS

Variants determined from the collation of Athanasius' text against the range of New Testament manuscripts are separated from the references of a verse by a short indented dividing line. The basis for collation is as follows: When the reference to a verse includes a single Citation, whether or not Adaptations and/or Allusions are also present, collation will be made against the Citation. In cases where there are multiple Citations and the texts conform exactly, then all the Citations collectively form the basis of the collation.[58] Genetically insignificant variants will not be collated. These include movable nu, itacism, nonsense readings and other minor spelling differences including orthographic variations in proper names.[59] Manuscripts that have significant lacuna and hence where reliable collation has not been possible will be noted with the symbol "Lac." Where part of the text is lacunose in any particular manuscript the symbol "inc." (*incipit* = beginning with) followed by a Greek word will show where the manuscript witness begins and the symbol "expl." (*explicit* = ending with) followed by a Greek word will show where that witness ends.

The apparatus explicitly cites all selected manuscripts in every variation unit except for manuscripts that are lacunose in which case they will be specifically noted and listed at the beginning of the apparatus. This arrangement avoids the use of the siglum "rell" (= reliqui, i.e., all the rest) and allows all the manuscripts that support a particular reading to be seen at a glance and also aids in compiling and cross-checking the relevant data matrices compiled from the significant variants. A variant is defined as genetically significant when it has at least two different readings which are each supported by at least two manuscripts.[60] This definition has been generally adopted in all studies that have appeared in the SBLNTGF series with the exception of Osburn who defined significant variants as those "in which the reading of Epiphanius and at least one other reading have valid support from at least *three* Greek manuscripts used as control witnesses." [emphasis mine][61] Osburn adopts this definition after noting the comment of Hort that

---

[58] In some instances different Citations provide unique text while also overlapping with common text or else provide adjoining sections or isolated parts of the verse with no overlap.

[59] Ehrman, *Didymus*, 34. Colwell argued that "Singular readings should not be included in any *apparatus criticus*. They belong to special studies." See Ernest C. Colwell, "Method in Evaluating Scribal Habits: A Study of P⁴⁵, P⁶⁶, P⁷⁵," in *Studies in Methodology in Textual Criticism of the New Testament* (NTTS 9; Leiden: Brill, 1969), 123; See also George D. Kilpatrick, "Atticism and the Text of the Greek New Testament," in *Neutestamentliche Aufsatze* (eds. J. Blinzler, O. Kuss and F. Mussner; Regensburg, 1963).

[60] Epp, summarises Colwell and Tune's original definition of a variation unit as "a segment of text containing 'at least two variant forms' consisting of 'elements of expression in the Greek text which regularly exist together,' each supported by at least two Greek manuscripts." Eldon Jay Epp, "It's All about Variants: A Variant Conscious Approach to New Testament Textual Criticism," *HTR* 100, no. 3 (2007): 277; see also Ernest C. Colwell and Ernest W. Tune, "Method in Classifying and Evaluating Variant Readings," in *Studies in Methodology in Textual Criticism of the New Testament* (NTTS 9; Leiden: E. J. Brill, 1969), 97–99.

[61] Osburn, *Text of the Apostolos in Epiphanius*, 41. Osburn also notes that Richards suggests

"with three MSS in agreement, the statistical probability of independent scribal error decreases radically in comparison with agreement of only two witnesses."[62] However the result of increasing the number of manuscripts required to qualify a variant as significant is to (potentially) dramatically *decrease* the number of significant variants used for the sample base upon which the statistical probabilities are determined and thus to inadvertently *increase* the statistical uncertainty, a valid criticism raised by Wasserman of Osburn's approach.[63] Therefore in this study the original definition as outlined earlier has been maintained.

These significant variants are presented in order as they appear in the relevant Citation and are preceded by a point, a numeral identifying that particular variant and a right closing parenthesis. Then are listed the various readings, preceded by an identifying numeral and a point. This nomenclature, which allows all significant variants and readings within the Apostolos to be uniquely identified, is also used throughout the tables and charts in the analysis chapters as well as the various appendices and provides a convenient method for collation, cross checking and verification. For example, Acts 2:22 contains two significant variants, the first of which is identified as .1) with 4 readings (1–4 respectively). The unique identification for reading 4 of this variant is: Acts.2.22.1.4. The second variant has 3 readings, so the unique identification for the third reading of this variant is: Acts.2.22.2.3.[64]

Below and following the significant variation units are the non-significant (singular) variants listed in order as they appear in the text. These variants consist of one reading attested by the majority of manuscript witnesses with alternative readings each attested by only a single witness. In these variants the reading attested by Athanasius always appears to the left of the square bracket]. All other readings are placed to the right of the bracket. The manuscript witnesses are listed in the order: papyri, majuscules and minuscules. A superscript asterisk (*) directly following the notation for a manuscript indicates the "first hand" (i.e. the original reading). A superscript letter 'c' (^{c}) is used to indicate a corrected reading of that particular manuscript witness.[65]

The following table (Table 2) lists the representative New Testament manuscript witnesses cited in the apparatus and used as the basis for collation against

---

no less than four witnesses. W. Larry Richards, *The Classification of the Greek Manuscripts of the Johannine Epistles* (SBLDS 35; Missoula: Scholars Press, 1977), 35ff.

[62]   Westcott and Hort, *New Testament*, 46.

[63]   See Tommy Wasserman, review of Carroll D. Osburn, *The Text of the Apostolos in Epiphanius of Salamis*, *RBL* 6 (2005). The real tension here is between the quality of variation units versus the number of units obtained and as such an acceptable compromise must be determined.

[64]   Note that the unique identifier for each significant *reading* always contains a set of numerals consisting of four sections separated by points. The numerals in the first two sections identify the chapter and verse (respectively) of the relevant book or epistle. The third section identifies the number of the significant variant and the fourth section identifies the number of (one of) the individual readings associated with the variant. The reading supported by Athanasius is always the first reading.

[65]   No distinction is made between the various correctors of any specific manuscript witness (e.g., א or B).

Athanasius' text of the Apostolos. The witnesses are listed according to commonly accepted text-types.[66]

Table 2: Textual Witnesses Cited in the Apparatus

Genre	Text Type and Sub-type	Manuscript Witnesses
Acts	Alexandrian	
	Primary[67]	$\mathfrak{P}^{74}$ ℵ B
	Secondary[68]	A C ψ 81 1175 (Family 1739= 630 945 1704 1739 1891)
	Byzantine[69]	H L P 049 1073 1352
	Western[70]	D E 383(13:1–22:30) 614
Pauline Epistles	Alexandrian	
	Primary[71]	$\mathfrak{P}^{46}$ ℵ B 1739
	Secondary[72]	ℵ^c A C P ψ 33 104
	Byzantine[73]	K L 049 223 876 2423
	Western	D F G
Catholic Ep's	Alexandrian[74]	$\mathfrak{P}^{72}$ ℵ A B C ψ 33 323 1739
	Byzantine[75]	L 049 105 201 325 1022 1424 2423
Revelation[76]	Older Primary	A C Oecumenius
	Older Secondary	ℵ
	Later Andreas	P Andreas
	Later Koine	046

---

[66] See Metzger and Ehrman, *Text of the New Testament*, 305–313; also Greenlee, *New Testament Textual Criticism*, 117–118. The witnesses are identified according to their traditional sigla as found in Kurt Aland, *Kurzgefasste Liste der griechischen Handschriften des Neuen Testaments* (ANTF 1; Berlin: de Gruyter, 1994); also J. K. Elliott, *A Bibliography of Greek New Testament Manuscripts* (Cambridge: Cambridge University Press, 2000). While the *Text und Textwert* volumes from the INTF in Munster use very different methods and approaches for grouping manuscripts there does not appear to be anything in their groupings that would call the analysis as utilised here into question.

[67] For MS $\mathfrak{P}^{74}$ see Rudolf Kasser, *Papyrus Bodmer XVII: Actes des Apôtres, Epîtres de Jacques, Pierre, Jean et Jude* (Cologny, 1961); also Reuben Joseph Swanson, ed., *New Testament Greek Manuscripts: Acts. Variant Readings Arranged in Horizontal Lines Against Codex Vaticanus* (Wheaton: Tyndale House, 1998). For MS ℵ see Kirsopp Lake and Helen Lake, *Codex Sinaiticus Petropolitanus* (Oxford: Clarendon Press, 1911). For MS B see βιβλια, τα ιερα, *Novum Testamentum e Codice Vaticano Graeco 1209 (Codex B): tertia vice phototypice expressum.* (In Civitate Vaticana: Ex Bibliotheca Apostolica Vaticana, 1968).

[68] For MS A see Frederic George Kenyon, ed., *The Codex Alexandrinus in Reduced Photographic Fascimile: New Testament and the Clementine Epistles* (London: British Museum, 1909). For MS C see Eduardus H. Hansell, ed., *Novum Testamentum Graece: Antiquissimorum codicum textus in ordine parallelo dispositi, accedit collatio codicis Sinaitici* (3 vols.; Oxford: Oxford University, 1864). For MS Ψ see Athos, Lavra, B' 52 (Gregory-Aland Ψ 044), (ABMC), Claremont, California. For MS 81 see London, Brit. Libr., Add. 20003; Alexandria, Bibl. Patriarch., 59 (Gregory-Aland 81), (ABMC),

Claremont, California. For MS 1175 see *Patmos, Joannu, 16* (Gregory-Aland 1175), (INTF), Münster, Germany. For Family 1739 MSS see *Roma, Bibl. Vatic., Ottob. Gr. 298* (Gregory-Aland 630), (INTF), Münster, Germany; *Athos, Dionysiu, 124 (37)* (Gregory-Aland 945), (ABMC), Claremont, California; *Athos, Kutlumusiu, 356* (Gregory-Aland 1704), (INTF), Münster, Germany; *Jerusalem, Orthod. Patriarchat, Saba, 107; St. Petersburg, Ross. Nac. Bibl., Gr. 317* (Gregory-Aland 1891), (ABMC), Claremont, California; for MS 1739 see W. J. Elliott, "An Examination of Von Soden's IB² Group of Manuscripts" (MA Thesis, University of Birmingham, Dept. of Theology, 1969).

⁶⁹ For MS H see *Modena, Bibl. Estense, α. V. 6.3 (G. 196)* (Gregory-Aland H 014), (ABMC), Claremont, California; also Henry A. Sanders, "New Manuscripts of the Bible from Egypt," *American Journal of Archaeology* 12, no. 1 (Jan.–Mar., 1908). For MS L see *Roma, Bibl. Angelica, 39* (Gregory-Aland L 020), (ABMC), Claremont, California; also William Henry Paine Hatch, *The Principal Uncial Manuscripts of the New Testament* (Chigaco: The University of Chicago Press, 1939), XLVIII. For MS P (025)(Acts) see Constantinus Tischendorf, ed., *Apocalypsis et Actus Apostolorum: Duobus Codicibus Palimpsestis, Altero Porphryii Episcopi* (*Monumenta Sacra Inedita (Nova collectio)*; Leipzig: J. C Hindrichs, 1869). For MS 049 see *Athos, Lavra, A' 88* (Gregory-Aland 049), (ABMC), Claremont, California. For MS 1073 see *Athos, Lavra, A' 51* (Gregory-Aland 1073), (INTF), Münster, Germany. For MS 1352 see *Jerusalem, Orthod. Patriarchat, Stavru 94* (Gregory-Aland 1352), (ABMC), Claremont, California.

⁷⁰ For MSS D and E see Hansell, *Novum Testamentum Graece*; also for MS D see *Codex Bezae Cantabrigiensis Quattor Evangelia et Actus Apostolorum complectens Graece et Latine Sumptibus Academiae phototypice repraesentatus* (Cambridge: Cambridge University Press, 1899); D. C. Parker, *Codex Bezae: An early Christian manuscript and its text* (Cambridge: Cambridge University Press, 1992); Frederick Henry A. Scrivener, ed., *Bezae Codex Cantabrigiensis* (Cambridge; Deighton, Bell & Co., 1864). For MSS 383 and 614 see A.V. Valentine-Richards, ed., *The Text of Acts in Codex 614 (Tisch. 137) and its Allies* (Cambridge: Cambridge University Press, 1934).

⁷¹ For MS 𝔓⁴⁶ see Frederic George Kenyon, *The Chester Beatty Biblical Papyri, fasc. 3, supp. 3.1, Pauline Epistles, Text* (London: Emery Walker Limited, 1936); Frederic George Kenyon, *The Chester Beatty Biblical Papyri, fasc. 3, supp. 3.2, Pauline Epistles, Plates* (London: Emery Walker Limited, 1937); also Philip W. Comfort and David P. Barrett, *The Text of the Earliest New Testament Greek Manuscripts: A Corrected, Enlarged Edition of The Earliest New Testament Manuscripts* (Wheaton: Tyndale House, 2001), 203ff; K. Junack, E. Güting, U. Nimtz and K. Witte, eds., *Das Neue Testament Auf Papyrus: Die Paulinischen Briefe. Teil 1: Röm., 1 Kor., 2 Kor.* (ANTF 12; Berlin: de Gruyter, 1989).

⁷² For MS P (025) (Paulines) see Constantinus Tischendorf, ed., *Epistulae Pauli et Catholicae: fere integrae ex Libro Porphryii Episcopi Palimpsesto* (*Monumenta Sacra Inedita (Nova collectio)*; Leipzig: J. C Hindrichs, 1865). For MS 33 see *Paris, Bibl. Nat. Gr. 14* (Gregory-Aland 33), (ABMC), Claremont, California. Also see Constantinus Tischendorf, ed., *Novum Testamentum Graece* (Octava Critica Maior ed.; 2 vols.; Leipzig: Giesecke & Devrient, 1869–1872). For MS 104 see *London, Brit. Libr., Harley 5537* (Gregory-Aland 104), (ABMC), Claremont, California. Ms 33 has not been used as a witness in Acts since Geer concluded that it is Byzantine in the first eleven chapters and then Alexandrian thereafter. Geer, Thomas C., Jr., "The Two Faces of Codex 33 in Acts," *NovT* 31, no. 1 (1989).

⁷³ For MS K see Tischendorf, *Novum Testamentum Graece*. For MSS 223, 876, 2423 see Kenneth Willis Clark, *Eight American Praxapostoloi* (Chicago: University of Chicago Press, 1941). For MS F see Frederick Henry A. Scrivener, *An Exact Transcript of the Codex Augiensis* (Cambridge: Deighton, Bell & Co., 1859). For MS G see Alexander Reichardt, ed., *Der Codex Boernerianus: Der Briefe Des Apostels Paulus* (Leipzig: Karl W. Hiersemann, 1909).

⁷⁴ For MS 𝔓⁷² see Michael Testuz, ed., *Papyrus Bodmer VII–IX* (Cologny-Geneva: Bibliotheca Bodmeriana, 1959). For MS 323 see Elliott, "Von Soden's IB² Group"; also W. J. Elliott, "The Relationship between Mss 322 and 323 of the Greek New Testament," *JTS* 18 (1967).

⁷⁵ For MS 105 see *Oxford, Bodl. Libr., Auct. T. inf 1.10* (Gregory-Aland 105), (INTF), Münster, Germany. For MS 201 see *London, Brit. Lib., m Butler 2, Ms 11,387* (Gregory-Aland 201), (ABMC), Claremont, California. See also Frederick Henry A. Scrivener, *A Full and Exact Collation of About*

The editions used as the primary sources for witnesses are listed in the Bibliography section; Biblical Text: Manuscripts, Editions and Collations. Family 1739 witnesses are identified as a unique group in Acts since specific comments concerning this group will be made in the multivariate analysis in Chapter 7. Most of the witnesses have been chosen because they have also been used as representatives for the various textual groups in previous studies on the texts of the Fathers and particularly where such studies have analyzed all or part of the Apostolos. The four relevant studies are those by Brooks, Hannah, Mullen and Osburn.[77] Utilizing the same witnesses as much as possible allows for direct comparison with the results of these studies. Witnesses were also chosen where they were used by Brogan in his study on the Gospels text of Athanasius.[78]

Though it has been common to utilise the TR and the modern critical edition UBS[3/4] as extra witnesses in some of the earlier studies in the NTGF series, they have not been included here since they do not represent any specific early manuscript witness but are rather eclectic representatives of the Byzantine and Primary Alexandrian text-types respectively. Without their inclusion a direct comparison of extant manuscript witnesses is maintained.[79]

A number of the witnesses were cited from microfilms provided by the Ancient Biblical Manuscript Centre (ABMC) in Claremont, California; H (014), L (020), Ψ (044), 049, 33, 81, 104, 201, 945, 1352, 1424 and 1891. A number of other microfilms were accessed at the *Institut für Neutestamentliche Textforschung* (*INTF*) in Münster Germany; 105, 325, 630, 1073, 1175 and 1704. The two manuscript witnesses F and G require specific comment. It has long been recognized that these two manuscripts share a special relationship with each other and that in the Pauline epistles their readings are virtually identical.[80] If their exclusive

---

Twenty Greek Manuscripts of The Holy Gospels, (Hitherto Unexamined), Deposited in the British Museum, The Archiepiscopal Library at Lambeth, &c. with a Critical Introduction. (Cambridge: John W. Parker & Son, 1853), xliv. For MS 325 see *Oxford, Bodl. Libr., Auct E. 5.9* (Gregory-Aland 325), (INTF), Münster, Germany. For MS 1022 see Clark, *Eight American Praxapostoloi.* For MS 1424 see *Chicago/Ill., Jesuit-Krauss-McCormick Libr., Gruber Ms. 152* (Gregory-Aland 1424), (ABMC), Claremont, California.

[76] For Oecumenius and Andreas see Josef Schmid, *Studien zur Geschichte des griechischen Apokalypse-Textes* (3 vols.; Munich: Karl Zink Verlag, 1955–1956). For MS 046 see Hansell, *Novum Testamentum Graece.*

[77] Brooks, *Text of Gregory*; Hannah, *Text of 1 Corinthians in Origen*; Mullen, *Text of Cyril*; Osburn, *Text of the Apostolos in Epiphanius.*

[78] See Brogan, "Text of the Gospels," 83–85.

[79] Broman also rejects the use of these critical editions as witnesses. In regards to their inclusion in Mullen's study, he comments "Unfortunately, UBS[3] and the TR are included among these control witnesses, even though they are modern productions of mixed origin." Broman, review of Mullen, n.p. Racine, in one of the more recent studies in the SBLNTGF series, has also chosen not to include these critical editions in his analysis. See Racine, *Text of Matthew in Basil*, 34–35.

[80] William Henry Paine Hatch, "On the Relationship of Codex Augiensis and Codex Boernerianus of the Pauline Epistles," *HSCP* 60 (1951); Scrivener, *Exact Transcript of Codex Augiensis*; also William Benjamin Smith, "The Pauline Manuscripts F and G: A Text-Critical Study. Part 1," *AJT* 7, no. 3 (1903); William Benjamin Smith, "The Pauline Manuscripts F and G: A Text-Critical Study. Part 2," *AJT* 7, no. 4 (1903).

agreements together against all other witnesses were to be included as significant they would add another forty-nine variation units to the total in the Pauline Epistles which would greatly inflate the proportional agreement of all the other witnesses with each other. Therefore these agreements have not been included.[81]

Table 3: Summary of Abbreviations and Sigla Used in the Text and Apparatus

[Ad]	Adaptation
[Ad]*	Adaptation that attests a reading in a significant variant
[All]	Allusion
[All]*	Allusion that attests a reading in a significant variant
[C]	Citation
ᶜ	Superscript letter 'c' indicates a correction to the manuscript
Lac.	Lacunose: Indicates that a verse or portion of a verse is missing from the following cited manuscripts
TEXT	Indicates the reconstructed text used as the basis for collation
*	Superscript asterisk indicates the original reading (first hand) of a corrected manuscript
+	Indicates that the verse is part of a continuous quotation. If found at the beginning of a quotation it indicates that the relevant verse continues without interruption from the preceding verse. If found at the end of a quotation it indicates that the quotation continues without interruption into the following verse
( )	Parenthesis indicate that: a) the word/s so enclosed are not strictly part of the citation of a verse but are contextually related; b) the manuscript so enclosed in the list of lacunose witnesses is partially lacunose for this verse
[ ]	Used in the list of lacunose witnesses to enclose the Greek word that explicitly begins (inc.) or ends (expl.) the extant text in a particular manuscript
⸻	Short indented dividing line used to separate the Critical Apparatus from the textual data

---

[81] Brooks did not include the exclusive agreements of F and G in his study on the New Testament text of Gregory of Nyssa though Mullen did in his study of Cyril of Jerusalem. See Brooks, *New Testament Text of Gregory*, 19; also Mullen, *Text of Cyril*, 208, 212–213, 216–217.

3

THE APOSTOLOS OF ATHANASIUS: TEXT AND APPARATUS

ACTS

Acts 1:1

πεποίηκέ τε καὶ ἐδίδαξεν
Ep. ad ep. Aeg. et Lib. 1.2 [Ad]

———————

Lac. 𝔓⁷⁴ L P

———————

Acts 1:7

οὐχ ὑμῶν ἐστι γνῶναι χρόνους ἢ καιροὺς, οὓς ὁ πατὴρ ἔθετο ἐν τῇ ἰδίᾳ
ἐξουσίᾳ
Or. III c. Ar. 48 [C]

οὐχ ὑμῶν ἐστι γνῶναι χρόνους ἢ καιροὺς, οὓς ὁ πατὴρ ἔθετο ἐν τῇ ἰδίᾳ
ἐξουσίᾳ +
Or. III c. Ar. 48 [C]

ὑμῶν οὐκ ἔστι γνῶναι
Or. III c. Ar. 48 [Ad]

οὐκ ἔστιν ὑμῶν γνῶναι
Or. III c. Ar. 49 [Ad]

———————

Lac. 𝔓⁷⁴ L P

———————

Acts 1:8

+ ἀλλὰ λήψεσθε δύναμιν
Or. III c. Ar. 48 [C]

Lac. 𝔓⁷⁴ [expl. αλλα], L P

.1)   1. λήψεσθε Ath Bc[1] H Ψ 049 81 614 630 945 1073 1175 1352
              1704 1739 1891
        2. λήμψεσθε ℵ² A B* C D E

Acts 1:18

καὶ πρηνὴς γενόμενος ἐλάκησε μέσος
Ep. ad ep. Aeg. et Lib. 18.27 [C]

πρηνὴς γενόμενος ἐλάκησε μέσος
Ep. ad Ser. 3 [C]

ἐξεχύθη γοῦν, (ὡς γέγραπται) κατὰ τὸν Ἰούδαν, τοῖς σπλάγχνοις
Hist. Arian. 57 [All]

Lac. 𝔓⁷⁴ L P 1891

ελακησε Ath ℵ A B C D E H Ψ 049 81 614 630 945 1073 1175 1352 1704
    1739] ελακκησε 630

Acts 2:22

ἄνδρες Ἰσραηλῖται, ἀκούσατε τοὺς λόγους τούτους· Ἰησοῦν τὸν Ναζωραῖον
ἄνδρα ἀπὸ τοῦ θεοῦ ἀποδεδειγμένον εἰς ὑμᾶς δυνάμεσι, καὶ τέρασι, καὶ
σημείοις, οἷς ἐποίησε δι' αὐτοῦ ὁ θεὸς ἐν μέσῳ ὑμῶν, καθὼς αὐτοὶ οἴδατε
Or. II c. Ar. 12 [C]**

ἄνδρες Ἰσραηλῖται, ἀκούσατε τοὺς λόγους τούτους· Ἰησοῦν τὸν Ναζωραῖον,
ἄνδρα ἀποδεδειγμένον ἀπὸ τοῦ θεοῦ εἰς ὑμᾶς δυνάμεσι καὶ τέρασι καὶ
σημείοις, οἷς ἐποίησεν ὁ θεὸς δι' αὐτοῦ ἐν μέσῳ ὑμῶν, καθὼς οἴδατε +
De sent. Dion. 7 [C]

ἐποίησε σημείων καὶ τεράτων
Or. II c. Ar. 16 [All]

Lac. (𝔓⁷⁴) L

---

[1] Correction is by partial erasure of μ
[2] -θαι.

.1)   1. απο του θεου αποδεδειγμενον Ath A Dᶜ E H P Ψ 049 614 1073
        1352 1891
      2. αποδεδειγμενον απο του θεου ℵ B C 630 945 1175 1704 1739
      3. απο του θεου δεδοκιμασμενον D*
      4. αποδεδεγμενον απο του θεου 81

.2)   1. αυτοι Ath 𝔓⁷⁴ ℵ A B C* D 81 1175 1739 1891
      2. υμεις παντες E
      3. και αυτοι Cᶜ H P Ψ 049 614 630 945 1073 1352 1704

οις Ath ℵ A B C Dc E H P Ψ 049 81 614 630 945 1073   1175 1352 1704
        1739 1891] οσα D*
δι αυτου ο θεος Ath ℵ A B D H P Ψ 049 81 614 630 945 1073 1175 1352
        1704 1739 1891] δι αυτου θεος C; ο θεος δι αυτου E
και τερασι Ath ℵ A B C D E H P Ψ 049 81 614 945 1073 1175 1352 1704
        1739 1891] omit 630

Acts 2:23
+ τοῦτον τῇ ὡρισμένῃ βουλῇ καὶ προγνώσει τοῦ θεοῦ ἔκδοτον διὰ χειρὸς
ἀνόμων προσπήξαντες ἀνείλατε
De sent. Dion. 7 [C]

Lac. L

.1)   1. εκδοτον Ath 𝔓⁷⁴ ℵ A B C 81 1739 1891
      2. εκδοτον λαβοντες D E H P Ψ 049 614 630 945 1073 1175 1352
        1704

.2)   1. χειρος Ath 𝔓⁷⁴ ℵ A B C D Ψ 81 945 1175 1704 1739 1891
      2. χειρων E H P 049 614 630 1073 1352

.3)   1. ανειλατε Ath 𝔓⁷⁴ ℵ A B C D E H P Ψ 049 81 1073
      2. ανειλετε 614 630 945 1175 1352 1704 1739 1891

Acts 2:24
ὃν ὁ θεὸς ἀνέστησε, λύσας τὰς ὠδῖνας τοῦ θανάτου, καθότι οὐκ ἦν
δυνατὸν κρατεῖσθαι αὐτὸν ὑπ' αὐτοῦ
Or. I c. Ar. 44 [C]

Ἐκεῖνος δὲ ὁ πάλαι τῷ θανάτῳ πονηρῶς ἐναλλόμενος διάβολος, λυθεισῶν
αὐτοῦ τῶν ὠδίνων
Or. de Inc. Verb. 27.3 [All]

δυνατὸν οὐκ ἦν κρατεῖσθαι αὐτὸν ὑπὸ τοῦ θανάτου
Or. I c. Ar. 44 [All]

κεκράτηται ὑπὸ τοῦ θανάτου
Or. I c. Ar. 44 [All]

κρατεῖσθαι ὑπὸ τοῦ θανάτου
Or. II c. Ar. 16 [All]

———————

Lac. L

λυσας Ath 𝔓⁷⁴ ℵ A C D H P Ψ 049 81 614 630 945 1073 1175 1352 1704
    1739 1891] λυσας δι αυτου E
θανατου Ath 𝔓⁷⁴ ℵ A C E H P Ψ 049 81 614 630 945 1073 1175 1352 1704
    1739 1891] αδου D

———————

Acts 2:36

πᾶς οἶκος Ἰσραὴλ, ὅτι καὶ κύριον αὐτὸν καὶ χριστὸν ἐποίησεν ὁ θεὸς τοῦτον τὸν Ἰησοῦν, ὃν ὑμεῖς ἐσταυρώσατε³
Or. I c. Ar. 53 [C]

ὃν ὑμεῖς ἐσταυρώσατε
Or. II c. Ar. 16 [C]

κύριον καὶ χριστὸν αὐτὸν ἐποίησε
Or. II c. Ar. 1 [Ad]

κύριον καὶ χριστὸν ἐποίησε τοῦτον τὸν Ἰησοῦν, ὃν ὑμεῖς ἐσταυρώσατε
Or. II c. Ar. 11 [Ad]

Κύριον καὶ Χριστὸν αὐτὸν ἐποίησεν
Or. II c. Ar. 12 [Ad]

ἐποίησεν αὐτὸν κύριον, καὶ χριστὸν
Or. II c. Ar. 14 [Ad]; Or. II c. Ar. 16 [Ad]

ἀσφαλῶς γινωσκέτω πᾶς οἶκος Ἰσραὴλ, ὅτι οὗτος ὁ Ἰησοῦς
Or. II c. Ar. 16 [Ad]

κύριον αὐτὸν ἐποίησε καὶ χριστὸν
Or. II c. Ar. 17 [Ad]

———————

³ 81 and 945 contract εσταυρωσατε to εστρωσατε.

Lac. (𝔓⁷⁴) L

.1) 1. οικος Ath 𝔓⁷⁴ ℵ A B E H P Ψ 049 81 614 630 945 1175 1352
          1704 1739 1891
      2. ο οικος C D 1073

.2) 1. κυριον αυτον και χριστον Ath 𝔓⁷⁴ ℵ A B C Dc Ψ 630 945
          1175 1704 1739 1891
      2. κυριον και χριστον αυτον E H P 049 81 614 1073 1352
      3. κυριον και χριστον D*

.3) 1. εποιησεν ο θεος Ath ℵ B Ψ 81 1073
      2. ο θεος εποιησεν 𝔓⁷⁴ A C D E H P 049 614 630 945 1175 1352
          1704 1739 1891

τον Ιησουν Ath ℵ A B C Dc E H P Ψ 049 81 614 630 945 1073 1175 1352
1704 1739 1891] Ιησουν D*

Acts 3:12
ἰδίᾳ δυνάμει
Or. III c. Ar. 2 [C]

Lac. 𝔓⁷⁴ L

Acts 3:15
χορηγὸν ζωῆς
Or. II c. Ar. 16 [All]

οὗτος ἀρχηγὸς τῆς ζωῆς ἐστιν
De sent. Dion 8 [All]

Lac. L

Acts 4:4
πεντακισχίλιοι
Or. III c. Ar. 20 [All]

Lac. C L

Acts 4:10

ὃν ὑμεῖς ἐσταυρώσατε
Or. II c. Ar. 16 [C]

ἐν τῷ ὀνόματι Ἰησοῦ Χριστοῦ τοῦ Ναζωραίου, ὃν ὑμεῖς ἐσταυρώσατε[4],
ὃν ὁ θεὸς ἤγειρεν ἐκ νεκρῶν, ἐν τούτῳ οὗτος παρέστηκεν ἐνώπιον ὑμῶν
ὑγιής
De sent. Dion. 7 [C]

γνωστὸν (οὖν) ἔστω ὑμῖν
Or. I c. Ar. 53 [Ad]

ἵν' ἐν τῷ ὀνόματι Ἰησοῦ
Or. II c. Ar. 16 [Ad]

Lac. C L 81

υμων υγιης Ath ℵ A B C D H P Ψ 049 81 614 630 945 1073 1175 1352 1704
        1739 1891] υμων σημερον υγιης και εν αλλω ουδενι E

Acts 4:32

οἵτινες ὡς εἷς ἐτύγχανον ὄντες
Or. III c. Ar. 20 [All]

Lac. (𝔓[74]) C L 81

Acts 4:35

καὶ ἐτίθουν[5] παρὰ τοὺς πόδας τῶν ἀποστόλων
Vita Ant. 2.2 [C]

Lac. C L 81

Acts 5:29

Πειθαρχεῖν δεῖ Θεῷ μᾶλλον ἢ ἀνθρώποις
Or. III c. Ar. 57 [C]

---

[4] 945 contracts εσταυρωσατε to εστρωσατε
[5] The use of the imperfect active instead of the aorist and παρα (not προς) indicates that the quote is from Acts 4:35 rather than 4:37.

Lac. C L 81

δει Ath 𝔓⁷⁴ ℵ A B D E H P Ψ 049 614 630 945 1073 1175 1352 1739 1891]
    omit 1704

Acts 7:50

ἡ χείρ μου ἐποίησε ταῦτα πάντα
Or. II c. Ar. 71 [C]

Lac. L

.1)   1. ταυτα παντα Ath ℵ B H Ψ 049 81 614 630 945 1175 1704 1739
        1891
    2. παντα ταυτα 𝔓⁷⁴ A C D E P 1073 1352

Acts 7:56

ἰδοὺ θεωρῶ τοὺς οὐρανοὺς διηνοιγμένους καὶ τὸν υἱὸν τοῦ ἀνθρώπου ἐκ
δεξιῶν ἑστῶτα τοῦ θεοῦ
De sent. Dion. 7 [C]

Lac. L

.1)   1. διηνοιγμενους Ath ℵ A Bᶜ C 81 630 945 1175   1704 1739 1891
    2. ανεωγμενους 𝔓⁷⁴ D⁶ E H P Ψ 049 614 1073 1352
    3. διηνυγμενους B*

.2)   1. ανθρωπου Ath ℵ A B C D E H P Ψ 049 81 630 945 1073 1175
        1352 1704 1739 1891
    2. θεου 𝔓⁷⁴ 614

.3)   1. εκ δεξιων εστωτα Ath 𝔓⁷⁴ ℵᶜ B D H P Ψ 049 81 614 630 945
        1073 1352 1704 1739 1891
    2. εστωτα εκ δεξιων ℵ* A C E 1175

Acts 8:10

ἡ δύναμις τοῦ Θεοῦ
Vita Ant. 40.1 [All]

---

[6] D has been corrected from ηνεωγ- to ανεωγ-.

Lac. ($\mathfrak{P}^{74}$) L

_____

Acts 8:20

σὺν σοὶ εἴη εἰς ἀπώλειαν
Vita Ant. 11.4 [C]

σὺν ὑμῖν εἴη εἰς ἀπώλειαν
Or. III c. Ar. 65 [Ad]

_____

.1)   1. ειη Ath $\mathfrak{P}^{74}$ ℵ A B C D E H L P Ψ 81 630 945 1073 1175 1352
                 1704 1739 1891
             2. omit 049 614

_____

Acts 8:27

Αἰθιοπίας εὐνοῦχος
Hist. Arian. 38 [Ad]

_____

Acts 8:32

ὡς πρόβατον ἐπὶ σφαγὴν ἤχθη, καὶ ὡς ἀμνὸς ἐναντίον τοῦ κείροντος
αὐτὸν ἄφωνος, οὕτως οὐκ ἀνοίγει τὸ στόμα αὐτοῦ +
Or. de Inc. Verb. 34.2 [C]

ὡς πρόβατον ἐπὶ σφαγὴν ἤχθη
Or. I c. Ar. 54 [C]

_____

Lac. ($\mathfrak{P}^{74}$) D

.1)   1. κειροντος Ath B P 81 630 945 1073ᶜ 1352 1704 1739 1891
             2. κειραντος $\mathfrak{P}^{74}$ ℵ A C E H L Ψ 049 614 1073* 1175

_____

Acts 8:33

+ ἐν τῇ ταπεινώσει αὐτοῦ ἡ κρίσις αὐτοῦ ἤρθη
Or. de Inc. Verb. 34.2 [C]

_____

Lac. ($\mathfrak{P}^{74}$) D

.1)   1. ταπεινωσει αυτου Ath C E H L P Ψ 049 81 614 630 945 1073
                 1175 1352 1704 1891
             2. ταπεινωσει $\mathfrak{P}^{74}$ ℵ A B 1739

Acts 8:34

δέομαί σου, περὶ τίνος ὁ προφήτης λέγει; περὶ ἑαυτοῦ, ἢ περὶ ἑτέρου τινός;
Or. I c. Ar. 54 [C]

Lac. D

.1)   1. λεγει Ath B*
         2. λεγει τουτο 𝔓⁷⁴ ℵ A Bᶜ C E H L P Ψ 049 81 614 630 945 1073 1175 1352 1704 1739 1891

.2)   1. ετερου τινος Ath 𝔓⁷⁴ ℵ A B C H L P 049 81 614 630 945 1073 1175 1352 1704 1739 1891
         2. τινος ετερου E Ψ

σου Ath 𝔓⁷⁴ ℵ A B C E H L P 049 81 630 945 1073 1175 1352 1704 1739 1891] κυριε Ψ
εαυτου Ath 𝔓⁷⁴ ℵ A B C E L P Ψ 049 81 630 945 1073 1175 1352 1704 1739 1891] αυτοῦ H

Acts 9.4

Σαῦλε[7], τί με διώκεις;
Or. II c. Ar. 80 [C]

Lac. (𝔓⁷⁴)

Acts 10.12

τετραπόδων καὶ ἑρπετῶν
Vita Ant. 51.5 [All]

Acts 10:26

κἀγὼ ἄνθρωπός εἰμι
Or. II c. Ar. 23 [Ad]

ἄνθρωπός εἰμι κἀγὼ ὥσπερ καὶ σύ
Vita Ant. 48.2 [All]

[7] There are extensive orthographic variations for the proper name here, e.g., Σαουλ for Σαυλε but these are not counted as variants.

Acts 10:38

ὡς ἔχρισεν αὐτὸν ὁ θεὸς πνεύματι ἁγίῳ
Or. I c. Ar. 47 [C]

.1)   1. πνευματι αγιω Ath 𝔓⁷⁴ ℵ A B C E H L P Ψ 049 81 614 630
              945 1073 1175 1352 1704 1739 1891
        2. αγιω πνευματι D
        3. εν πνευματι αγιω E L

ως Ath 𝔓⁷⁴ ℵ A B C E H L P Ψ 049 81 630 945 1073 1175 1352 1704 1739
    1891] ον D; ος 614
αυτον Ath 𝔓⁷⁴ ℵ A B C E H L P Ψ 049 81 614 630 945 1073 1175 1352 1704
    1739 1891] omit D

Acts 13:22

μεταστήσας ὁ θεὸς τὸν Σαοὺλ ἤγειρε τὸν Δαυὶδ εἰς βασιλέα, ᾧ καὶ εἶπε
μαρτυρήσας· εὗρον Δαυὶδ τὸν τοῦ Ἰεσσαὶ ἄνδρα κατὰ τὴν καρδίαν μου, ὃς
ποιήσει τὰ θελήματά μου +
De sent. Dion 7 [C]

.1)   1. τον Δαυιδ Ath
        2. τον (Δαυιδ)⁸ αὐτοις 𝔓⁷⁴ ℵ A B 1175
        3. αυτοις τον (Δαυιδ) C E H L P Ψ 049 81 383 614 630 945 1073
               1352 1704 1739 1891
        4. (Δαυιδ) αυτοις D

.2)   1. ανδρα Ath 𝔓⁷⁴ ℵ A C D H L P Ψ 049 81 383 614 630 945
               1073 1175 1352 1704 1739 1891
        2. omit B E

μεταστησας ο θεος τον Σαουλ Ath] μεταστήσας αὐτον 𝔓⁷⁴ ℵ A B C D E
    H L P Ψ 049 81 383 614 630 945 1073 1175 1352 1704 1739 1891
τον του Ιεσσαι Ath 𝔓⁷⁴ ℵ A B C E H L P Ψ 049 81 383 614 630 945 1073
    1175 1352 1704 1739 1891] τον υιον Ιεσσαι D
κατα την καρδιαν μου, ος Ath 𝔓⁷⁴ ℵ A B C D H L P Ψ 049 81 383 614 630
    945 1073 1175 1352 1704 1739 1891] omit E
ποιησει Ath] ποιησει παντα 𝔓⁷⁴ ℵ A B C D E H L P Ψ 049 81 383 614 630
    945 1073 1175 1352 1704 1739 1891

---

⁸ Also Δαυειδ

Acts 13:23
+ τούτου ὁ θεὸς ἀπὸ τοῦ σπέρματος κατ᾽ ἐπαγγελίαν ἤγαγε τῷ Ἰσραὴλ
σωτῆρα Ἰησοῦν
De sent. Dion. 7 [C]

.1)   1. ηγαγε Ath 𝔓⁷⁴ ℵ A B E H L P Ψ 049 81 383 1073 1175 1352
       2. ηγειρεν C D 614 630 945 1704 1891
       3. omit 1739

.2)   1. σωτηρα Ιησουν Ath ℵ A B C E P Ψ 81 614 630 945 1175 1704
          1739 1891
       2. σωτηρα τον Ιησουν D
       3. σωτηριαν 𝔓⁷⁴ H L 049 1073 1352
       4. σωτηρα 383

τουτου ο θεος απο του σπερματος Ath 𝔓⁷⁴ ℵ A B C E H L P Ψ 049 81 383
    614 630 945 1073 1175 1352 1704 1739 1891] ο θεος ουν απο του
    σπερματος αυτου D
τω Ισραηλ Ath 𝔓⁷⁴ ℵ A B C D E H L P Ψ 049 383 614 630 945 1073 1352
    1704 1739 1891] omit 81; τον Ισραηλ 1175

Acts 13:32
τοὺς πατέρας ἐπαγγελίας
De decretis 2 [Ad]*

.1)   1. πατερας Ath 𝔓⁷⁴ ℵ A B C H L P Ψ 049 81 383 614 630 945 1073
          1175 1352 1704 1739 1891
       2. πατερας ημων D E

επαγγελια(ς) (γενομενην) Ath 𝔓⁷⁴ ℵ A C E H L P Ψ 049 81 383 614 630
    945 1073 1175 1352 1704 1739 1891] γενομενην επαγγελιαν D

Acts 13:36
προσετέθη (καὶ αὐτὸς) πρὸς τοὺς πατέρας αὐτοῦ
Ep. ad ep. Aeg. et Lib. 21.18 [C]

προσετεθη Ath 𝔓⁷⁴ ℵ A B C D E H L P Ψ 049 81 383 614 630 945 1073
    1352 1704 1739 1891] ετεθη 1175

πρὸς τοὺς Ath 𝔓⁷⁴ ℵ A B D E H L P Ψ 049 81 383 614 630 945 1073 1175
1352 1704 1739 1891] πρὸς C⁹

Acts 14:15

καὶ ἡμεῖς ὁμοιοπαθεῖς ἐσμεν ὑμῖν ἄνθρωποι, εὐαγγελιζόμενοι ὑμᾶς ἀπὸ
τῶν ματαίων ἐπιστρέφειν ἐπὶ θεὸν ζῶντα, ὃς ἐποίησε τὸν οὐρανὸν καὶ τὴν
γῆν καὶ τὴν θάλασσαν καὶ πάντα τὰ ἐν αὐτοῖς +
Or. c. gentes 35.22-30 [C]

.1)   1. και ημεις Ath 𝔓⁷⁴ ℵ A B C E H L P Ψ 81 383 614 630 945
1073 1352 1704 1739 1891
2. ημεις D 049 1175

.2)   1. εσμεν υμιν Ath 𝔓⁷⁴ ℵ A B D E L P 049 81 630 945 1073
1352(vid) 1704 1891
2. υμιν εσμεν C Ψ 383 614 1175 1739
3. εσμεν H

.3)   1. απο Ath Ψ 614
2. απο τουτων 𝔓⁷⁴ ℵ A B C D E H L P 049 81 383 630 945 1073
1175 1352 1704 1739 1891

.4)   1. επιστρεφειν Ath 𝔓⁷⁴ ℵ A B C H L P 049 81 383 630 945 1073
1175 1352 1704 1739 1891
2. επιστρεψηται D
3. επιστρεφητε E
4. τουτων επιστρεφειν Ψ 614

.5)   1. θεον Ath 𝔓⁷⁴ ℵ A B C Dc E Ψ 81 630 945 1175 1704 1739
1891
2. τον θεον D* H L P 049 383 614 1073 1352

.6)   1. ζωντα Ath 𝔓⁷⁴ ℵc A B C D E Ψ 81 630 945 1175 1704 1739 1891
2. τον ζωντα ℵ* H L P 049 383 614 1073 1352

ομοιοπαθεις Ath 𝔓⁷⁴ ℵ A B C Dc E H L P Ψ 049 81 383 614 630 945 1073
1352 1704 1739 1891] ομοιοπαηθεις D*
υμας Ath 𝔓⁷⁴ ℵ A B C H L P Ψ 049 81 630 945 1073 1175 1704 1739 1891]
υμιν τον θεον οπως D; υμας ινα E

---

⁹ Swanson shows τους in MS C but in Hansell it is missing, as in Tischendorf. NA²⁸ shows it
missing. See Swanson, *Greek Manuscripts: Acts*; Hansell, *Novum Testamentum Graece*; Tischendorf,
Novum Testamentum Graece; also Luc Herren, *New Testament Transcripts Prototype* (University
of Münster–Institute for New Testament Textual Research, 2003–2006); available from http://
nttranscripts.uni-muenster.de/AnaServer?NTtranscripts+0+start.anv.

ος εποιησε Ath 𝔓⁷⁴ ℵ A B C E H L P Ψ 049 81 383 614 630 945 1073 1175
   1352 1739 1891] τον ποιησαντα D; omit 1704
τον ουρανον και την γην και την θαλασσαν και παντα τα Ath 𝔓⁷⁴ ℵ A B
   C D E H L P Ψ 049 81 630 945 1073 1175 1739 1891] omit 1704

Acts 14:16
   + ὃς ἐν ταῖς παρῳχημέναις γενεαῖς εἴασε πάντα τὰ ἔθνη πορεύεσθαι ταῖς
   ὁδοῖς αὐτῶν +
   Or. c. gentes 35.22-30 [C]

ταις^sec Ath 𝔓⁷⁴ ℵ A B C D E H P Ψ 049 81 383 614 630 945 1073 1175 1352
   1704 1739 1891] τοις L

Acts 14:17
   + καίτοι γε οὐκ ἀμάρτυρον ἑαυτὸν ἀφῆκεν ἀγαθουργῶν, οὐρανόθεν ἡμῖν
   ὑετοὺς διδοὺς καὶ καιροὺς καρποφόρους, ἐμπιπλῶν τροφῆς καὶ εὐφροσύ-
   νης τὰς καρδίας ἡμῶν
   Or. c. gentes 35.22-30 [C]

.1)   1. καιτοι Ath 𝔓⁷⁴ ℵ A B C H L P Ψ 049 81 383 614 630 945
         1073 1175 1352 1704 1739 1891
      2. και D E

.2)   1. γε Ath ℵ D E H L P Ψ 049 81c 383 614 630 1073 1352
      2. omit 𝔓⁷⁴ A B C 81* 945 1175 1704 1739 1891

.3)   1. εαυτον αφηκεν Ath 𝔓⁷⁴ ℵ^c C H P Ψ 049 81 383 614 630 945
         1073 1175 1352 1704 1739
      2. αυτον αφηκεν ℵ* A B E
      3. αφηκεν εαυτον D
      4. εαυτον ηφηκεν L
      5. ετον αφηκεν 1891

.4)   1. αγαθουργων Ath 𝔓⁷⁴ ℵ A B C Ψ 81 630 945 1175 1704 1739
         1891
      2. αγαθοποιων D E L P 049 383 614 1073 1352
      3. αγαθοπων II

.5)   1. ημιν Ath ℵ* B C D E H L P 049 383 614 630 945 1073 1175 1352
         1704 1739 1891
      2. omit 𝔓⁷⁴ ℵ^c A Ψ 81

.6) 1. υετους διδους Ath B C D E H L P 049 614 1073 1175 1352
2. διδους υετους 𝔓⁷⁴ ℵ A Ψ 81 383 630 945 1704 1739 1891

αμαρτυρον Ath 𝔓⁷⁴ ℵ A B D E H L P Ψ 049 81 383 614 630 945 1073 1175
1352 1704 1739] αμαρτυραν C
και ευφροσυνης Ath 𝔓⁷⁴ ℵ A B C D E H L P 049 81 383 614 630 945 1073
1175 1352 1704 1739] omit Ψ

Acts 15:36
χρεία δὲ ἦν ἡ διὰ τοὺς ἀδελφοὺς ἐπίσκεψις
Vita Ant. 15.1 [All]

Acts 17:26
ἐκ τοῦ ἑνὸς
Or. III c. Ar. 18 [All]

Lac. (𝔓⁷⁴)

Acts 17:28
ἐν αὐτῷ ζῶμεν, καὶ κινούμεθα, καὶ ἐσμεν
Or. III c. Ar. 1 [C]; De decretis 20 [C]

τοῦ γὰρ καὶ γένος ἐσμὲν
De Syn. 39 [C]

καὶ τὰ πάντα ὑπ' αὐτοῦ κινεῖται καὶ ἐν αὐτῷ ζωοποιεῖται
Or. de Inc. Verb. 1.1 [All]

Lac. C 81

.1) 1. του Ath 𝔓⁷⁴ ℵ A B E H L P Ψ 049 630 945 1073 1175 1352 1704
1739 1891
2. τουτου D 383
3. τουτο 614

Acts 17:29
γένος τοῦ θεοῦ ὑπάρχομεν
Ep. ad Amun 65 [Ad]

Lac. C 81

_____

Acts 17:30

τοὺς μὲν οὖν χρόνους τῆς ἀγνοίας ὑπεριδὼν ὁ θεὸς τὰ νῦν παραγγέλλει τοῖς ἀνθρώποις, πάντας πανταχοῦ μετανοεῖν +
De sent. Dion. 7 [C]

_____

Lac. C 81

.1) 1. παραγγελλει Ath 𝔓⁷⁴ ℵᶜ A D E H L P Ψ 049 383 614 630 945
       1073 1175 1352 1704 1739 1891
     2. απαγγελλει ℵ* B

.2) 1. παντας Ath 𝔓⁷⁴ ℵ A B Dᶜ E 1175
     2. ινα παντες D*
     3. πασι II L P Ψ 049 383 614 630 945 1073 1352 1704 1739 1891

τους μεν ουν χρονους Ath ℵ A B D H L P Ψ 049 383 614 630 945 1073
     1175 1352 1704 1739 1891] τους χρονους μεν ουν E; τους μεν
     χρονους 𝔓⁷⁴
υπεριδων Ath 𝔓⁷⁴ ℵ A B Dᶜ E H L P Ψ 049 383 614 630 945 1073 1175
     1352 1704 1739] ταυτης περιδων D*; τα της περιδων 1891

_____

Acts 17:31

+ καθότι ἔστησεν ἡμέραν, ἐν ᾗ μέλλει κρίνειν τὴν οἰκουμένην ἐν δικαιοσύνη, ἐν ἀνδρὶ ᾧ ὥρισε, πίστιν παρασχὼν πᾶσιν, ἀναστήσας αὐτὸν ἐκ νεκρῶν
De sent.Dion. 7 [C]

_____

Lac. (𝔓⁷⁴) C 81

.1) 1. καθοτι Ath 𝔓⁷⁴ ℵ A B D E P Ψ 383 614 630 945 1175 1704 1739
       1891
     2. διοτι H L 049 1073 1352

εν η μελλει Ath 𝔓⁷⁴ ℵ A B E H L P Ψ 049 383 614 630 945 1073 1175 1352
     1704 1739 1891] omit D
εν ανδρι Ath 𝔓⁷⁴ ℵ A B D E H L P Ψ 049 383 614 630 945 1073 1175 1352
     1704 1739 1891] ανδρι Ιησου D

_____

Acts 23:11

εἰς Ῥώμην δεῖ ὑμᾶς μαρτυρῆσαι
Apol. de fuga 18.20 [Ad]

Lac. D

Acts 24:19

ἔδει τοὺς ἀπὸ τῆς Ἀσίας Ἰουδαίους ἐπὶ σοῦ παρεῖναι καὶ κατηγορεῖν, εἴ τι
ἔχοιεν
Apol. c. Ar. 82 [Ad]

Lac. D

Acts 25:11

(Παῦλος) ἐπικαλούμενος Καίσαρα
Apol. de fuaga 17.9 [Ad]

(ὡς ὁ Ἀπόστολος) ἐπεκαλέσατο τότε τὸν Καίσαρα
Apol. ad Const. 12.1 [All]

Lac. D

Acts 25:16

οὐκ ἔστιν ἔθος Ῥωμαίοις χαρίζεσθαί τινα ἄνθρωπον, πρὶν ἢ ὁ
κατηγορούμενος κατὰ πρόσωπον ἔχοι τοὺς κατηγόρους τόπον τε
ἀπολογίας λάβοι περὶ τοῦ ἐγκλήματος
Apol. c. Ar. 82 [C]

Lac. D

.1)   1. τινα Ath 𝔓⁷⁴ ℵ A B E H L P Ψ 049 81 614 1073 1175 1352
       2. τινι C 630 945¹⁰ 1704 1739 1891

.2)   1. ανθρωπον Ath 𝔓⁷⁴ ℵ A B C E Ψ 81 630 945 1175 1704 1739 1891
       2. ανθρωπον εις απολειαν H L P 049 614 1073 1352

---

[10] Swanson shows incorrectly as τινα. Swanson, *Greek Manuscripts: Acts*. Klaus Witte notes
the correction: See http://www-user.uni-bremen.de/~wie/texte/Swanson-Acts-945.txt.

.3)   1. κατα προσωπον εχοι Ath 𝔓⁷⁴ A B C E H L P Ψ 049 81 630 945
         1073 1175 1704 1739 1891
      2. εχοι κατα προσωπον ℵ
      3. κατα προσωπον εχει 614 1352

.4)   1. τε Ath 𝔓⁷⁴ ℵ A C H L P Ψ 049 81 630 945 1073 1175 1352 1704
         1739 1891
      2. δε B E 614

.5)   1. εγκληματος Ath ℵ A B H L P Ψ 049 81 614 630 945 1073
         1175 1352 1704 1739 1891
      2. ενκληματος 𝔓⁷⁴ C E

χαριζεσθαι Ath 𝔓⁷⁴ ℵ A B E H L P Ψ 049 81ᶜ 614 630 945 1175 1352 1704
   1739 1891] χαριζζεσθαι 81*; χαρισασθαι 1073
λαβοι Ath 𝔓⁷⁴ℵ A B C E H L P Ψ 049 81 614 630 945 1073 1175 1704 1739
   1891] λαβη 1352

Acts 26:14
   κέντρα λακτίζοντες
   De decretis 1 [Ad]

   Lac. D

Acts 26:26
   ἐν γωνίᾳ
   Or. de Inc. Verb. [C]

   Lac. C D 1704

   γωνια Ath 𝔓⁷⁴ ℵ A B E L P Ψ 049 81 614 630 945 1073 1175 1352 1739
   1891] γωνι H

PAULINE EPISTLES

Rom 1:1

    ἀφωρισμένος ἀπόστολος εἰς εὐαγγέλιον +
    Or. II c. Ar. 54 [C][11]

    ἀπόστολος τοῦ εὐαγγελίου γέγονεν +
    Ep. ad ep. Aeg. et Lib. 4.3-4 [Ad]

    ———————

    Lac. 𝔓⁴⁶ C D F G

    αφωρισμενος αποστολος Ath] αποστολος αφωρισμενος ℵ A B K L P Ψ
        049 33 104 223 876 1739 2423
    ευαγγελιον Ath] ευαγγελιον θεου ℵ A B K L P Ψ 049 33 104 223 876 1739
        2423

    ———————

Rom 1:2

    + οὗ προεπηγγείλατο διὰ τῶν προφητῶν αὐτοῦ ἐν γραφαῖς ἁγίαις
    Ep. ad ep. Aeg. et Lib. 4.3-4 [C]

    + ὃ προεπηγγείλατο ὁ Κύριος διὰ τῶν προφητῶν
    Or. II c. Ar. 54 [Ad]

    ———————

    Lac. 𝔓⁴⁶ C D F G

    ου Ath] ο ℵ A B K L P Ψ 049 33 104 223 876 1739 2423
    αυτου Ath ℵ A B K L P Ψ 049 104 223 876 1739 2423] omit 33

    ———————

Rom 1:12

    παράκλησις διὰ τῆς ἐν ἀλλήλοις πίστεως
    Vita Ant. 54.7 [All]

    ———————

    Lac. 𝔓⁴⁶ F

    ———————

Rom 1:19

    γνωστὸν τοῦ θεοῦ φανερόν ἐστιν ἐν αὐτοῖς. ὁ θεὸς γὰρ αὐτοῖς ἐφανέρωσε
    +
    Or. II c. Ar. 81 [C]

---

[11] This is a case in which a Citation in one verse is directly connected with an Adaptation in the next verse. The situation for the second quotation is exactly reversed. It can be deduced from such examples that, within extended passages, Athanasius quotes with varying accuracy.

διότι τὸ γνωστὸν τοῦ θεοῦ φανερόν ἐστι ἐν αὐτοῖς· ὁ θεὸς γὰρ αὐτοῖς ἐφανέρωσε +
Or. II c. Ar. 78 [C]

Lac. 𝔓⁴⁶ F

.1)   1. διοτι Ath ℵ A B C K L P Ψ 049 33 104 223 876 1739 2423
       2. οτι D G

.2)   1. ο θεος γαρ Ath ℵ A B C D* G Ψ 33 223 1739 2423
       2. ο γαρ θεος Dᶜ K L P 049 104 876

Rom 1:20

τὰ γὰρ ἀόρατα αὐτοῦ ἀπὸ κτίσεως κόσμου τοῖς ποιήμασι νοούμενα καθορᾶται
Or. c. gentes 35.20-21 [C]

+ τὰ γὰρ ἀόρατα αὐτοῦ ἀπὸ κτίσεως κόσμου, τοῖς ποιήμασι νοούμενα καθορᾶται, ἥ τε ἀίδιος αὐτοῦ δύναμις καὶ θειότης, εἰς τὸ εἶναι αὐτοὺς ἀναπολογήτους +
Or. II c. Ar. 81 [C]

+ τὰ γὰρ ἀόρατα αὐτοῦ ἀπὸ κτίσεως κόσμου τοῖς ποιήμασι νοούμενα καθορᾶται
Or. II c. Ar. 78 [C]

τὰ γὰρ ἀόρατα αὐτοῦ ἀπὸ κτίσεως κόσμου τοῖς ποιήμασι νοούμενα καθορᾶται, ἥ τε ἀίδιος αὐτοῦ δύναμις καὶ θειότης
Or. I c. Ar. 11 [C]; Or. II c. Ar. 37 [C]

ἀπὸ κτίσεως κόσμου
Or. II c. Ar. 32 [C]

ἥ τε (γὰρ) ἀίδιος αὐτοῦ δύναμις καὶ θειότης
Des Syn. 49 [C]

τά τε ἀόρατα αὐτοῦ ἀπὸ κτίσεως κόσμου, τοῖς ποιήμασι νοούμενα, καθορᾶται
Or. II c. Ar. 19 [Ad]

κακῶν ἐφευρεταὶ
Or. I c. Ar. 4 [Ad]

τοῦ Χριστοῦ δύναμιν καὶ θεότητα
Or. de Inc. Verb. 32.2 [All]

ἤ τε ἀίδιος αὐτοῦ δύναμις καὶ θειότης
Or. I c. Ar. 12 [All]

Ἀπὸ δὲ τῆς φαινομένης κτίσεως τοῦ κόσμου τὰ ἀόρατα αὐτοῦ τοῖς ποιήμασι νοούμενα καθορῶμεν
 Or. II c. Ar. 49 [All]

Lac. 𝔓⁴⁶ F

νοουμενα Ath ℵ A B C Dᶜ G K L P Ψ 049 33 104 223 876 1739 2423]
      νοουμεν D*

Rom 1:21

Ἐματαιώθησαν ἐν τοῖς διαλογισμοῖς αὐτῶν, καὶ ἐσκοτίσθη ἡ ἀσύνετος
αὐτῶν καρδία +
Or. c. gentes 19.11-17 [C]

+ διότι, γνόντες τὸν Θεὸν, οὐχ ὡς Θεὸν ἐδόξασαν ἀλλ ⬚
Or. II c. Ar. 81 [C]

Lac. 𝔓⁴⁶ F

.1)   1. αυτων καρδια Ath ℵ A B C Dᶜ K L P Ψ 049 33 104 223 876 1739
             2423
        2. καρδια αυτων D* G

εδοξασαν Ath] εδοξασαν η ευχαριστησαν ℵ A B C D G K L P Ψ 049 33
      104 223 876 1739 2423

Rom 1:22

+ φάσκοντες εἶναι σοφοί, ἐμωράνθησαν +
Or. c. gentes 19.11-17 [C]

Φάσκοντες εἶναι σοφοί, ἐμωράνθησαν
Or. II c. Ar. 81 [C]

φάσκοντές τε εἶναι Χριστιανοὶ +
Or. I c. Ar. 22 [All]

Lac. 𝔓⁴⁶ F

Rom 1:23

+ καὶ ἤλλαξαν τὴν δόξαν τοῦ ἀφθάρτου Θεοῦ ἐν ὁμοιώματι εἰκόνος φθαρτοῦ ἀνθρώπου, καὶ πετεινῶν καὶ τετραπόδων καὶ ἑρπετῶν +
Or. c. gentes 19.11-17 [C]

ἐν ὁμοιώματι εἰκόνος φθαρτοῦ ἀνθρώπου
Or. I c. Ar. 2 [C]

+ ἀλλάσσουσι τὴν τοῦ Θεοῦ εἰκόνα ἐν ὁμοιώματι εἰκόνος φθαρτῶν
ἀνθρώπων
Or. I c. Ar. 22 [Ad]

σέβειν τετράποδα, καὶ ἑρπετά, καὶ ἀνθρώπων εἰκόνας
Vita Ant. 74.5 [Ad]

τετράποδα καὶ ἑρπετά
Vita Ant. 74.7 [Ad]

καὶ διὰ τοῦτο σέβειν τετράποδα, καὶ ἑρπετά, καὶ ἀνθρώπων εἰκόνας
Vita Ant. 74.5 [All]

Lac. 𝔓⁴⁶ F

ηλλαξαν Ath ℵ A B C D G L P Ψ 049 33 104 223 876 1739 2423] ηλλαξα-
ντο K

Rom 1:24
+ διὸ καὶ παρέδωκεν αὐτοὺς ὁ Θεὸς
Or. c. gentes 19.11-17 [C]

Lac 𝔓⁴⁶ F

.1)   1. διο και¹² παρεδωκεν Ath D G K L P Ψ 049 223 876 2423
       2. διο παρεδωκεν ℵ A B C 33 104 1739

---

¹² While the addition/omission of και and other conjunctions at the beginning of a quotation
are not normally considered as significant, in this case the quotation is a continuation from the
previous verse and hence the variant here is considered as significant.

Rom 1:25

τῇ κτίσει παρὰ τὸν κτίσαντα
Or. de Inc. Verb. 11.4 [C]

ἐλάτρευσαν τῇ κτίσει παρὰ τὸν κτίσαντα θεόν
Ep. ad ep. Aeg. et Lib. 13.17 [C]

ἐλατρεύσαμεν τῇ κτίσει παρὰ σὲ τὸν κτίσαντα
Hist. Arian. 80 [C]

τὴν κτίσιν παρὰ τὸν κτίσαντα δοξάζοντες
Or. c. gentes 8.29-30 [Ad]

τῇ κτίσει παρὰ τὸν κτίσαντα λατρεύοντες
Or. c. gentes 47.18-19 [Ad]

λατρεύοντες τῇ κτίσει παρὰ τὸν κτίσαντα
Ep. ad ep. Aeg. et Lib. 4.18 [Ad]

λατρεύοντες τῇ κτίσει παρὰ τὸν κτίσαντα θεόν
Vita Ant. [Ad]

ἐλάτρευσαν τῇ κτίσει παρὰ τὸν κτίσαντα τὰ πάντα, ὅς ἐστιν εὐλογητὸς
εἰς τοὺς αἰῶνας, ἀμήν
Or. II c. Ar. 81 [All]

τῇ κτίσει (δουλεύοντες) παρὰ τὸν κτίσαντα
Or. II c. Ar. 14 [All]

ἀλλὰ τῇ κτίσει λατρεύετε παρὰ τὸν τὰ πάντα κτίσαντα Θεόν
Vita Ant. 76.2 [All]

Lac. 𝔓⁴⁶ F

θεον Ath] omit ℵ A B C D G K L P Ψ 049 33 104 223 876 1739 2423

Rom 1:26

αἵ τε γὰρ θήλειαι αὐτῶν μετήλλαξαν τὴν φυσικὴν χρῆσιν εἰς τὴν παρὰ
φύσιν +
Or. c. gentes 26.9-13 [C]

αἵ τε γὰρ θήλειαι αὐτῶν μετήλλαξαν τὴν φυσικὴν χρῆσιν εἰς τὴν παρὰ φύσιν +
Or. de Inc. Verb. 5.5 [C]

εἰς πάθη ἀτιμίας
Or. c. gentes 19.17 [C]

Lac. 𝔓⁴⁶ F

.1)   1. φυσιν Ath ℵ A B C K L P Ψ 049 33 104 223 876 1739 2423
        2. φυσιν χρησιν D G

θηλειαι Ath ℵ A B C D G K Lᶜ P Ψ 049 33 104 223 876 1739 2423] θηλει
        L*
χρησιν Ath ℵ A B C G K L P Ψ 049 33 104 223 876 1739 2423] κτισιν D

Rom 1:27
        + ὁμοίως δὲ καὶ οἱ ἄρρενες, ἀφέντες τὴν φυσικὴν χρῆσιν τῆς θηλείας,
        ἐξεκαύθησαν ἐν τῇ ὀρέξει αὐτῶν εἰς ἀλλήλους, ἄρρενες ἐν ἄρσεσι τὴν
        ἀσχημοσύνην κατεργαζόμενοι
        Or. c. gentes 26.9-13 [C]

        + ὁμοίως δὲ καὶ οἱ ἄρρενες, ἀφέντες τὴν φυσικὴν χρῆσιν τῆς θηλείας,
        ἐξεκαύθησαν ἐν τῇ ὀρέξει αὐτῶν εἰς ἀλλήλους, ἄρρενες ἐν ἄρσεσι τὴν
        ἀσχημοσύνην κατεργαζόμενοι, καὶ τὴν ἀντιμισθίαν ἣν ἔδει τῆς πλάνης
        αὐτῶν ἐν ἑαυτοῖς ἀπολαμβάνοντες
        Or. de Inc. Verb. 5.5 [C]

Lac. 𝔓⁴⁶ F

.1)   1. δε Ath A D* G P Ψ 33 104 1739
        2. τε ℵ B Dᶜ K L 049ᶜ 2423
        3. omit C 049* 223 876

.2)   1. αρρενεςᵖʳⁱ Ath ℵ A C K L P Ψ 049 33 104 223 876
        2. αρσενες B D G 1739 2423

.3)   1. αρρενεςˢᵉᶜ Ath ℵ A C 33 1739
        2. αρσενες B D G K L P Ψ 049 104 223 876 2423

.4)   1. αρσεσι Ath B C D G K L P Ψ 049 104 223 876 2423
        2. αρρεσι ℵ A 33 1739

.5)   1. εν εαυτοις Ath ℵ A C D G L P Ψ 049 33 104ᶜ 223 876 1739
          2423*
          2. εν αυτοις B K 104*
          3. εαυτοις 2423ᶜ

χρησιν Ath ℵ A B C D G K L P Ψ 049 104 223 876 1739 2423] φυσιν 33
εξεκαυθησαν Ath ℵ A B C D G K L P Ψ 049 33 104 223 876 1729 2423*]
          εξεκαθησαν 2423ᶜ
απολαμβανοντες Ath ℵ A B C D K L P Ψ 049 33 104 223 876 1739 2423]
          αντειλαμβανοντες G

Rom 2:5

ὅσην ἑαυτοῖς ἐθησαύρισαν ὀργὴν
De Syn. 2 [All]

Lac. 𝔓⁴⁶ F

Rom 2:13

καὶ ποιητὰς (ὁ ἀπόστολος εἶπε) νόμου
De sent. Dion. 20 [All]

ποιητὰς νόμου καὶ κρίσεως καὶ δικαιοσύνης (λέγουσα)
De sent. Dion. 21 [All]

Lac. 𝔓⁴⁶ F

Rom 2:24

οὐαὶ δι᾽ οὓς τὸ ὄνομά μου βλασφημεῖται ἐν τοῖς ἔθνεσι
De Syn. 2 [Ad]

Lac. 𝔓⁴⁶ C F G P

Rom 3:29

ἢ Ἰουδαίων μόνων ὁ θεός, οὐχὶ καὶ ἐθνῶν; ναὶ καὶ ἐθνῶν +
De. Syn. 28.1 [C]

Lac. 𝔓⁴⁶

.1)   1. ουχι Ath ℵ A B C D K 104 1739
        2. ουχε F G
        3. ουχι δε L P Ψ 049 33 223 876 2423

μονων ο θεος Ath] ο θεος μονον ℵ A B C F G K L P Ψ 049 33 104 223 876
    1739 2423; ο θεος μονος D

Rom 3:30
    + ἐπείπερ εἷς ὁ θεός, ὃς δικαιώσει περιτομὴν ἐκ πίστεως καὶ ἀκροβυστίαν
    διὰ πίστεως
    De Syn. 28.1 [C]

Lac. 𝔓⁴⁶

.1)   1. επειπερ Ath ℵᶜ D* F G L P Ψ 049 33 104 223 876 2423
        2. ειπερ ℵ* A B C Dᶜ 1739
        3. επειδηπερ K

ο θεος Ath ℵ A B C Dᶜ F G K L P Ψ 049 33 104 223 876 1739 2423] θεος
    D*
δια πιστεωςˢᵉᶜ Ath] δια της πιστεως ℵ A B C D F G K L P Ψ 049 33 223
    876 1739 2423; εκ πιστεως 104

Rom 4:17
    καλῶν τὰ μὴ ὄντα εἰς τὸ εἶναι
    De decretis 11 [All]

Lac. 𝔓⁴⁶

Rom 5:3
    ἡ θλίψις ὑπομονὴν κατεργάζεται +
    Apol. de fuga 21.19-21 [C]

Lac. 𝔓⁴⁶

Rom 5:4
    + ἡ δὲ ὑπομονὴ δοκιμήν, ἡ δὲ δοκιμὴ ἐλπίδα +
    Apol. de fuga 21.19-21 [C]

Lac. 𝔓⁴⁶

δοκιμην Ath ℵ A B C D F G K L P Ψ 049 104 223 876 1739 2423] δικαιω-
συνην 33

Rom 5:5
+ ἡ δὲ ἐλπὶς οὐ καταισχύνει
Apol. de fuga 21.19-21 [C]

Lac. 𝔓⁴⁶

Rom 5:12
διὰ τῆς ἁμαρτίας ὁ θάνατος εἰσῆλθεν εἰς τὸν κόσμον
Or. I c. Ar. 51 [Ad]*

εἰς πάντας τοὺς ἀνθρώπους
Or. I c. Ar. 51 [Ad]

Lac. 𝔓⁴⁶

ο θανατος Ath ℵ A B C D K L P Ψ 049 33 104 223 876 1739 2423]
θανατος F G

Rom 5:14
ἐβασίλευσεν ὁ θάνατος ἀπὸ Ἀδὰμ μέχρι Μωσέως¹³, καὶ ἐπὶ τοὺς μὴ
ἁμαρτήσαντας, ἐπὶ τῷ ὁμοιώματι τῆς παραβάσεως Ἀδάμ
Or. III c. Ar. 33 [C]

ἀπὸ Ἀδὰμ μέχρι Μωϋσέως ὁ θάνατος ἐβασίλευσεν
Or. I c. Ar. 59 [Ad]

τὸν θάνατον εἶχον βασιλεύοντα
Or. I c. Ar. 44 [All]

Lac. 𝔓⁴⁶

---

¹³ While this form does not appear in the New Testament it is commonly used in the Fathers.
Cf. G. W. H. Lampe, ed., *A Patristic Greek Lexicon* (Oxford: Clarendon Press, 1961), 895.

μεχρι Ath ℵ A B C D F G K L P Ψ 049 33 104 876 1739 2423] αχρι 223

και Ath ℵ A B C D F G K L P Ψ 049 33 104 223 876 1739ᶜ 2423] omit
1739*

μη Ath ℵ A B C D F G K L P Ψ 049 33 104 223 876 1739ᶜ 2423] omit 1739*

επιˢᵉᶜ Ath ℵ A C D F G K L P Ψ 049 33 104 223 876 1739 2423] εν B

Rom 5:21

βασιλευούσης ἐν αὐτοῖς ἁμαρτίας
Or. II c. Ar. 52 [All]

ἡ ἁμαρτία τῆς σαρκὸς ἐβασίλευσεν
Or. II c. Ar. 56 [All]

Rom 6:18

ἐλευθερωθέντες ἀπὸ τῆς ἁμαρτίας
Or. I c. Ar. 48 [C]

ἐλεύθεροι μὲν ἀπὸ τῆς ἁμαρτίας
Or. I c. Ar. 69 [Ad]

Lac. 𝔓⁴⁶

.1)   1. απο Ath
       2. δε απο ℵᶜ A B D F G K L P Ψ 049 33 104 223 876 1739 2423
       3. οὐν απο ℵ* C

Rom 7:12

ὁ νόμος ἅγιος καὶ ἡ ἐντολὴ ἁγία καὶ δικαία καὶ ἀγαθή
De Syn. 45 [C]

Lac. 𝔓⁴⁶

Rom 7:14

ὁ νόμος πνευματικός ἐστι
De Syn. 45 [C]

Rom 8:3

τὸ γὰρ ἀδύνατον τοῦ νόμου, ἐν ᾧ ἠσθένει διὰ τῆς σαρκὸς, ὁ θεὸς τὸν ἑαυτοῦ υἱὸν πέμψας ἐν ὁμοιώματι σαρκὸς ἁμαρτίας, καὶ περὶ ἁμαρτίας κατέκρινε τὴν ἁμαρτίαν ἐν τῇ σαρκί +
Or. II c. Ar. 55 [C]**

τὸ ἀδύνατον τοῦ νόμου, ἐν ᾧ ἠσθένει διὰ τῆς σαρκὸς, ὁ θεὸς τὸν ἑαυτοῦ υἱὸν πέμψας ἐν ὁμοιώματι σαρκὸς ἁμαρτίας, καὶ περὶ ἁμαρτίας κατέκρινε τὴν ἁμαρτίαν ἐν τῇ σαρκὶ
Or. I c. Ar. 60 [C]

τὸ γὰρ ἀδύνατον τοῦ νόμου, ἐν ᾧ ἠσθένει
De Syn. 45 [C]

ἁμαρτίαν κατακρίναντος ἐν τῇ σαρκὶ +
Vita Ant. 7.1 [Ad]

τὴν μὲν ἁμαρτίαν ἐν αὐτῇ κατακρίνῃ
Or. I c. Ar. 51 [All]

Lac. 𝔓⁴⁶, (33)

εαυτου Ath ℵ* A B C D G K L P Ψ 049 104 223 876 1739 2423] αυτου ℵᶜ; ευαυτου F
πεμψας Ath ℵ A B C D G K L P Ψ 049 104 223 876 1739 2423] πεμφψας F

Rom 8:4

+ ἵνα τὸ δικαίωμα πληρωθῇ ἐν ἡμῖν, τοῖς μὴ κατὰ σάρκα περιπατοῦσιν, ἀλλὰ κατὰ πνεῦμα
Or. II c. Ar. 55 [C]

+ ἵνα τὸ δικαίωμα τοῦ νόμου πληρωθῇ ἐν ἡμῖν, τοῖς μὴ κατὰ σάρκα περιπατοῦσιν, ἀλλὰ κατὰ πνεῦμα
Vita Ant. 7.1 [C]**

μηκέτι κατὰ σάρκα περιπατεῖν, ἀλλὰ κατὰ πνεῦμα
Or. I c. Ar. 60 [Ad]

τὸ δικαίωμα τοῦ νόμου πληροῦν
Or. I c. Ar. 51 [All]

Lac. 𝔓⁴⁶, (33)

νομου Ath ℵA B C D F G K L P Ψ 049 104 223 1739 2423] θεου 876

Rom 8:9
ἡμεῖς δὲ οὐκ ἐσμὲν ἐν σαρκὶ, ἀλλ᾽ ἐν πνεύματι, εἴπερ πνεῦμα θεοῦ οἰκεῖ ἐν ἡμῖν
Or. I c. Ar. 51 [C]

ἡμεῖς οὐκ ἐσμὲν ἐν σαρκὶ, ἀλλ᾽ ἐν πνεύματι
Or. I c. Ar. 60 [C]

Lac. 𝔓⁴⁶

εσμεν Ath] εστε ℵ A B C D F G K L P Ψ 049 33 104 223 876 1739 2423

Rom 8:15
οὐ γὰρ ἐλάβομεν πνεῦμα δουλείας πάλιν εἰς φόβον
Ep. ad ep. Aeg. et Lib. 20.17-18 [Ad]

Lac. 𝔓⁴⁶

Rom 8:18
Οὐ γὰρ ἄξια τὰ παθήματα τοῦ νῦν καιροῦ πρὸς τὴν μέλλουσαν ἀποκαλυφθῆναι εἰς ἡμᾶς δόξαν
Vit Ant. 17.1 [C]

αποκαλυφθηναι εις ημας δοξαν Ath] δοξαν αποκαλυφθηναι εις ημας 𝔓⁴⁶
      ℵ A B C D K L P Ψ 049 33 104 223 876 1739 2423; δοξαν αποκα-
      λυψθηναι εις ημας F G

Rom 8:19
ἀπεκδεχομένη τὴν ἀποκάλυψιν τῶν τέκνων τοῦ θεοῦ
Or. II c. Ar. 63 [Ad]*

Lac. (𝔓⁴⁶) [expl. υἱῶν]¹⁴, (104)

---

¹⁴ θεου is conjecturally transcribed by Kenyon as *nomina sacra* here in 𝔓⁴⁶ though these two

απεκδεχεται (Ath) ℵ A B C D F G K L P Ψ 049ᶜ 33 104 223 876 1739 2423]
   εκδεχεται 049*
του Ath ℵ A B C D K L P Ψ 049 33 104 223 876 1739 2423] omit F G

Rom 8:21

ἐλευθερωθήσεταί (ποτε) ἀπὸ τῆς δουλείας τῆς φθορᾶς εἰς τὴν ἐλευθερίαν
τῆς δόξης τῶν τέκνων τοῦ Θεοῦ
Or. II c. Ar. 63 [C]

ἐλευθερωθέντες ἀπὸ τῆς φθορᾶς
Or. III c. Ar. 40 [All]

τῇ δουλείᾳ τῆς φθορᾶς
Or. II c. Ar. 14 [Ad]

ἐλευθερώσας τε τὸ γένος ἡμῶν ἀπὸ τῆς δουλείας τῆς φθορᾶς
Apol. ad Const. 33.1 [Ad]

ἡμῖν εἰς τὸ ἐλευθερωθῆναι ἀπὸ τῆς δουλείας τῆς φθορᾶς
Or. II c. Ar. 72 [All]

Lac. ($\mathfrak{P}^{46}$) [φθορᾶ]ς, [τέκνω]ν

ελευθεριαν Ath ℵ A B C D G K L P Ψ 049 33 104 223 876 1739 2423]
   ελευθεραν F

Rom 8:22

ἡ κτίσις συστενάζει καὶ συνωδίνει[15]
Or. II c. Ar. 45 [C]

τῆς κτίσεως πάσης συστεναζούσης
Or. II c. Ar. 72 [All]

.1)   1. συστεναζει Ath ℵ A Bᶜ [16] C Dᶜ K L P Ψ 049 223 876 1739 2423
       2. συνστεναζει[17] $\mathfrak{P}^{46}$ B* D* F G 33 104

---

words at the beginning of the line are lacunose. In the following collations all *nomina sacra*
will be transcribed in full.

[15] $\mathfrak{P}^{46}$ has συνωδεινει. However, this is a clear case of itacism and is not considered to be a
significant variant. All further cases of itacism will be ignored.

[16] According to NA²⁸. Herren, *New Testament Transcripts Prototype*. However the image of the
manuscript shows no such erasure/correction.

[17] Since there is a lacuna in $\mathfrak{P}^{46}$ for the first part of this word, Kenyon has provided a conjectural
reconstruction as follows: συνστ]εναζει. Kenyon, *Pauline Epistles, Text*. NA²⁸ notes this as the form

συνωδινει Ath 𝔓⁴⁶ ℵ A B C D K L P Ψ 049 33 104 223 876 1739 2423]
οδυνει F G

___

Rom 8:26
ἀλαλήτους στεναγμοὺς τοῦ πνεύματος
Or. II c. Ar. 14 [All]

___

Lac. 𝔓⁴⁶

___

Rom 8:28
συνεργεῖ ὁ θεὸς εἰς τὸ ἀγαθόν
Vita Ant. 19.1 [C]

   .1)   1. συνεργει ο θεος Ath 𝔓⁴⁶ A B
             2. συνεργει ℵ C D F G K L P Ψ 049 33 104 223 876 1739 2423

   .2)   1. το αγαθον Ath L 049
             2. αγαθον 𝔓⁴⁶ ℵ A B C D F G K P Ψ 33 104 223 876 1739 2423

___

Rom 8:29
πρωτότοκος μὲν ἐν πολλοῖς ἀδελφοῖς
Or. II c. Ar. 63 [C]

πρωτότοκος ἐν πολλοῖς ἀδελφοῖς
Tom. ad Ant. 7.2 [C]**

πρωτότοκος ἀδελφῶν
Or. II c. Ar. 75 [All]

___

πρωτοτοκος Ath] πρωτοτοκον 𝔓⁴⁶ ℵ A B C D F G K L P Ψ 049 33 104 223
   876 1739 2423

___

Rom 8:32
ὃς οὐκ ἐφείσατο τοῦ ἰδίου υἱοῦ, ἀλλ᾿ ὑπὲρ ἡμῶν πάντων παρέδωκεν αὐτόν
Vita Ant. 14.7 [Ad]

___

Rom 8:35
τίς ἡμᾶς χωρίσει ἀπὸ τῆς ἀγάπης τοῦ Χριστοῦ
Or. III c. Ar. 25 [C]**

___

of the first hand in B. Herren, *New Testament Transcripts Prototype*. It is possible that Kenyon was here influenced by the original reading of B.

χωρίσει ἀπὸ τῆς ἀγάπης τοῦ Χριστοῦ
Vita Ant. 9.2 [C]

οὐδέν με χωρίσει ἀπὸ τῆς ἀγάπης τοῦ Χριστοῦ[18]
Vita Ant. 40.5 [C]

χωρίσει τῆς ἀγάπης τοῦ Χριστοῦ
Ep. ad ep. Aeg. et Lib. 20.15 [Ad]

οὐδὲν ἡμᾶς χωρίσει ἀπὸ τῆς ἀγάπης τοῦ Χριστοῦ
De decretis 20 [Ad]

οὐδὲν γὰρ ἡμᾶς χωρίσει ἀπὸ τῆς ἀγάπης τοῦ Χριστοῦ
Apol. de fuga 20.34-35 [Ad]

οὐδὲν ἡμᾶς χωρίσει ἀπὸ τῆς ἀγάπης τοῦ Χριστοῦ
Hist. Arian. 1 [Ad]

———————

Lac. (𝔓[46]) inc. ημας… expl. αγαπης, (A) P

τις Ath ℵ A B C D K L Ψ 049 33 104 223 876 1739 2423] τις ουν F G
Χριστου Ath C D F G K L Ψ 049 33 104 223 876 1739 2423] θεου ℵ; θεου
της εν Χριστω Ιησου B

———————

Rom 8:37
ἀλλ᾽ ἐν τούτοις πᾶσιν ὑπερνικῶμεν
Apol. de fuga 20.34 [C]

ἐν τούτοις πᾶσιν ὑπερνικῶμεν
Ep. ad Drac. 3.2 [C]

———————

Lac. P

———————

Rom 9:5
ἐπὶ πάντων[19]
Or. de Inc. Verb. 55.2 [C]

———————

[18] This reference is not from Rom 8:39 as suggested by Bartelink. Bartelink, *Vie d'Antoine*.

[19] While επι παντων is also found in Eph 4:6, this reference from Athanasius is more likely from Rom 9:5 since here the focus is Christ the Saviour, whereas in Eph 4:6 the focus is God the Father. Athanasius in this quote refers specifically to Christ the Saviour and powerful God the Word.

ἐξ ὧν ὁ Χριστὸς[20] τὸ κατὰ σάρκα, ὁ ὢν ἐπὶ πάντων θεὸς εἰς τοὺς αἰῶνας εὐλογητὸς
Or. I c. Ar. 11 [C]

Ὁ ὢν ἐπὶ πάντων Θεὸς εὐλογητὸς εἰς τοὺς αἰῶνας. Ἀμήν.
Or. I c. Ar. 24 [C]

ἐξ ὧν ὁ Χριστὸς τὸ κατὰ σάρκα, ὁ ὢν ἐπὶ πάντων θεὸς εὐλογητὸς εἰς τοὺς αἰῶνας ἀμήν
Ep. ad Epic. 10.6-7 [C]**

ἐπὶ πάντων εὐλογημένος εἰς τοὺς αἰῶνας
Or. I c. Ar. 10 [Ad]

Lac. (𝔓[46]) σαρ[κα ο ων] [αιωνας], P

το κατα Ath ℵ A B Cᶜ D K L Ψ 049 33 104 223 876 1739 2423] ο κατα 𝔓[46];
    κατα F G; τα κατα C*

Rom 9:13
τὸν μὲν Ἰακὼβ ἠγάπησε, τὸν δὲ Ἡσαῦ ἐμίσησε
Or. I c. Ar. 52 [Ad]
Lac. C, (33)

Rom 9:19
τῷ βουλήματι αὐτοῦ τίς ἀνθέστηκεν
Or. II c. Ar. 29 [C]

τῷ βουλήματι αὐτοῦ οὐδεὶς ἀνθέστηκε
Or. II c. Ar. 24 [Ad]

Lac. C

βουληματι Ath 𝔓[46] ℵ A B D F G K L P Ψ 049 33 104 223 1739 2423]
    θεληματι 876

Rom 9:20
ἢ πῶς ἐρεῖ τὸ πλάσμα τῷ κεραμεῖ, τί με οὕτως ἐποίησας
Or. I c. Ar. 29 [Ad]*

---

[20] Written as nomina sacra in 𝔓[46] as also θεος.

Lac. ($\mathfrak{P}^{46}$) [inc. πλάσμα...expl. τί], C

κεραμει Ath] πλασαντι $\mathfrak{P}^{46}$ ℵ A B D F G K L P Ψ 049 33 104 223 876 1739
    2423
ουτως εποιησας Ath] εποιησας ουτως $\mathfrak{P}^{46}$ ℵ A B F G K L P Ψ 049 33 104
    223 876 1739 2423; επλασας ουτως D

Rom 9:32
    προσέκοψαν τῷ λίθῳ τοῦ προσκόμματος[21]
    Or. III c. Ar. 28 [C]

    προσκόψει τῷ λίθῳ τοῦ προσκόμματος
    De decretis 17 [Ad]

Lac. C

.1)   1. τω Ath $\mathfrak{P}^{46}$ ℵ* A D* F G
        2. γαρ τω ℵ^c B D^c K L P Ψ 049 33 104 223 876 1739 2423

προσεκοψαν Ath $\mathfrak{P}^{46}$ ℵ^c A B D K L P Ψ 049 33 104 223 876 1739 2423]
    προσεκοψεν ℵ*; προσεκοφαν F G[22]

Rom 9:33
    λίθον ἐν Σιὼν προσκόμματος
    Ep. ad Afros 5.2 [C]

Lac. $\mathfrak{P}^{46}$, C

λίθον εν Σιων προσκομματος Ath] εν Σιων λιθον προσκομματος ℵ A B D
    F G K L P Ψ 049 104 223 876 1739 2423; εν Σιων λιθον ακρογονι-
    αιον εν τημον και λιθον προσκομματος 33

---

[21] This verse is partially lacunose in $\mathfrak{P}^{46}$ and has been conjecturally reconstructed by Kenyon.
Due to the arrangement of the lacuna the last two extant lines of the ms. (fol. 13ᵛ.) are shown here
in full:
    οτι ουκ εκ [πιστεως αλλ ως εξ εργων προσεκο
    ψαν τω λιθω [
[22] Swanson incorrectly notes G as reading προσεκοψαν though the formation of φ and ψ are
easy to distinguish in the manuscript.

Rom 10:8

Τὸ ῥῆμα τῆς πίστεως ἐντὸς τῆς καρδίας σοῦ ἐστιν
Or. c. gentes 30.7-8 [All][23]

Lac. C

Rom 10:18

εἰς πᾶσαν τὴν γῆν ἐξῆλθεν[24]
Or. I c. Ar. 59 [C]

Lac. K

Rom 10:20

ἐμφανὴς ἐγενόμην τοῖς ἐμὲ μὴ ζητοῦσιν, εὑρέθην τοῖς ἐμὲ μὴ ἐπερωτῶσιν
Or. de Inc. Verb. 38.1 [Ad]*

Lac. K

.1)   1. εγενομην τοις Ath 𝔓⁴⁶ ℵ A C Dᶜ F G L P Ψ 049 33 104 223 876
          1739 2423
       2. εγενομην εν τοις B D*

.2)   1. ευρεθην τοις Ath ℵ A C Dᶜ L P Ψ 049 33 104 223 876 1739 2423
       2. ευρεθη εν τοις 𝔓⁴⁶ B D* F G

εμφανης Ath 𝔓⁴⁶ ℵ A B C D L P Ψ 049 33 104 223 876 1739 2423]
    ενφανης F G
μη ζητουσιν Ath 𝔓⁴⁶ ℵ A B C D F G L P Ψ 33 104 223 876 1739 2423]
    ζητουσιν 049

Rom 10:21

ἐξεπέτασα τὰς χεῖράς μου πρὸς λαὸν ἀπειθοῦντα καὶ ἀντιλέγοντα
Or. de Inc. Verb. 38.1 [C]
Lac. (33) K

προς Ath 𝔓⁴⁶ ℵ A B C F G L P Ψ 049 33 104 223 876 1739 2423] επι D

---

[23] Cf. also Deut 30:14. i.e., καὶ Μωυσῆς ἐδίδασκε λεγων. Athanasius here is quoting from both Deut 30:14 and Rom 10:8 and conflating the quote. See Edward Maunde Thompson, *An Introduction to Greek and Latin Palaeography* (New York: Lenox Hill, 1912), 82-83.

[24] Also found in Ps 18 [19]:5.

και αντιλεγοντα Ath 𝔓⁴⁶ ℵ A B C Dᶜ L P Ψ 049 33 104 223 876 1739 2423]
και λεγοντα D*; omit F G

Rom 11:29

Ἀμεταμέλητα γὰρ τὰ χαρίσματα τοῦ Θεοῦ καὶ ἡ χάρις τῆς κλήσεως
Or. III c. Ar. 25 [Ad]

Lac. K P

Rom 11:34

τίς γὰρ ἔγνω νοῦν κυρίου, ἢ τίς σύμβουλος αὐτοῦ ἐγένετο
Or. I c. Ar. 29 [C]; Or. III c. Ar. 43 [C]

Lac. 𝔓⁴⁶ C K P

κυρίου Ath ℵ A B Dᶜ F G L Ψ 049 33 104 223 876 1739 2423] θεου D*

Rom 11:36

καὶ δι' αὐτοῦ δὲ καὶ εἰς αὐτὸν τὰ πάντα
Or. c. gentes 46.51 [Ad]

Lac. C K P

Rom 12:3

παρ' ὃ δεῖ φρονεῖν
Or. III c. Ar. 28 [C]; Or. I c. Ar. 2 [C]

Lac. (𝔓⁴⁶) [o], C K

παρ ο δει φρονειν Ath 𝔓⁴⁶ ℵ A B D L P Ψ 049 33 104 223 876 1739 2423]
omit F G

Rom 12:4

ἑνὸς σώματος πολλὰ μέλη
Or. II c. Ar. 48 [Ad]*

Lac. C K

.1)   1. πολλα μελη Ath 𝔓⁴⁶ ℵ B D F G
           2. μελη πολλα A L P Ψ 049 33 104 223 876 1739 2423

Rom 12:10
    τῇ τιμῇ προηγεῖσθαι
    Vita Ant. 67.1 [All]

    Lac. K

Rom 12:12
    καὶ χαιρέτω ἀεὶ ἡ ψυχὴ τῇ ἐλπίδι
    Vita Ant. 42.8 [All]

    Lac. K

Rom 12:15
    κλαίειν μετὰ κλαιόντων
    Ep. encycl. 6 [C]

    Lac. C K (33)

Rom 14:14
    οἶδα γὰρ καὶ πέπεισμαι
    Ep. ad ep. Aeg. et Lib. 23.18 [C]

    Lac. 𝔓⁴⁶ K

Rom 15:5
    τὸ αὐτὸ φρονεῖν²⁵
    Ep. ad Afros 10.1 [C]

    Lac. 𝔓⁴⁶ K

---

²⁵ This phrase is also found in Phil 4:2 but the similar context of Athanasius' writing with Rom 15:5 indentifies that reference as the source of Athanasius' quotation.

Rom 15:12

Ἔσται (γάρ, φησίν) ἡ ῥίζα τοῦ Ἰεσσαί, καὶ ὁ ἀνιστάμενος ἄρχειν ἐθνῶν, ἐπ᾽ αὐτῷ ἔθνη ἐλπιοῦσι
Or. de Inc. Verb. 35.6 [C]

Lac. (C) K

του Ath ℵ A B C D F G L P Ψ 049 33 104 223 876 1739 2423] omit 𝔓⁴⁶
ανισταμενος Ath A B C D F G L P Ψ 049 33 104 223 876 1739 2423]
        ανιστανομενος ℵ; νιστανομενος 𝔓⁴⁶
εθνων Ath 𝔓⁴⁶ ℵ A B C D G L P Ψ 049 33 104 223 876 1739 2423] εθων F

Rom 15:16

ἁγιάζει τοὺς πάντας τῷ Πνεύματι
Or. I c. Ar. 48 [All]

Lac. K

Rom 15:19

ὥστε ἀπὸ Ἰερουσαλὴμ μέχρι τοῦ Ἰλλυρικοῦ, πληρῶσαι τὸ εὐαγγέλιον
Apol. de fuga 20.38-40 [C]

μέχρι τοῦ Ἰλλυρικοῦ κηρύττειν
Ep. ad Drac. 4.5 [Ad]

.1)   1. απο Ιερουσαλημ μεχρι του Ιλλυρικου πληρωσαι Ath
       2. με απο Ιερουσαλημ και κυκλω μεχρι του Ιλλυρικου
          πεπληρωκεναι 𝔓⁴⁶ ℵ A B C P Ψ 049 33 104 223 876 1739
          2423
       3. με απο Ιερουσαλημ κυκλω μεχρι του Ιλλυρικου πεπληρωκεναι
          L
       4. πεπληρωθησαι απο Ιερουσαλημ μεχρι του Ιλλυρικου και κυκλω
          D F G

---

[26] The final line has been conjecturally reconstructed (plausibly) by Kenyon.

1 Cor 1:4

Εὐχαριστῶ (γὰρ, φησὶν ὁ Ἀπόστολος γράφων Κορινθίοις,) τῷ Θεῷ μου πάντοτε περὶ ὑμῶν ἐπὶ τῇ χάριτι τοῦ Θεοῦ τῇ δοθείσῃ ὑμῖν ἐν Χριστῷ Ἰησοῦ
Or. III c. Ar. 13 [C]

Lac. 𝔓⁴⁶ [inc. επὶ], K

.1)   1. μου Ath ℵᶜ A C D F G L P Ψ 049 33 104 223 876 1739 2423
         2. omit ℵ* B

1 Cor 1:10

τὸ αὐτὸ λέγοντες
Or. III c. Ar. 21 [Ad]

τὸ αὐτὸ λέγειν
Ep. ad Afros 10.1 [Ad]

τὸ αὐτὸ λέγειν
De Syn. 54 [Ad]

Lac. K

1 Cor 1:17

οὐκ ἐν σοφίᾳ λόγων Ἑλληνικῶν
Vita Ant. 78.1 [All]

Lac. K

1 Cor 1:21

ἐπειδὴ γὰρ ἐν τῇ σοφίᾳ τοῦ θεοῦ οὐκ ἔγνω ὁ κόσμος διὰ τῆς σοφίας τὸν θεόν, εὐδόκησεν ὁ θεὸς διὰ τῆς μωρίας τοῦ κηρύγματος σῶσαι τοὺς πιστεύοντας
Or. de Inc. Verb. 15.1 [C]**

ἐπειδὴ ἐν τῇ σοφίᾳ τοῦ θεοῦ οὐκ ἔγνω ὁ κόσμος διὰ τῆς σοφίας τὸν θεόν, ηὐδόκησεν ὁ θεὸς διὰ τῆς μωρίας τοῦ κηρύγματος σῶσαι τοὺς πιστεύοντας
Or. II c. Ar. 81 [C]

ἐπειδὴ γὰρ, ἐν τῇ σοφίᾳ τοῦ θεοῦ οὐκ ἔγνω ὁ κόσμος διὰ τῆς σοφίας
τὸν θεὸν, ἀλλ᾽ ηὐδόκησε διὰ τῆς μωρίας τοῦ κηρύγματος σῶσαι τοὺς
πιστεύοντας
Or. II c. Ar. 16 [C]

ἐπειδήπερ ἐν τῇ σοφίᾳ τοῦ θεοῦ οὐκ ἔγνω ὁ κόσμος διὰ τῆς σοφίας τὸν
θεόν
Or. II c. Ar. 79 [C]

—————————

Lac. K

γαρ Ath 𝔓⁴⁶ ℵ A B C D L P Ψ 049 33 104 223 876 1739 2423] omit F G
θεου Ath ℵ A B C D F G L P Ψ 049 33 104 223 876 1739 2423] κοσμου²⁷
        𝔓⁴⁶
ο κοσμος Ath 𝔓⁴⁶ ℵ A B C D G L P Ψ 049 33 104 223 876 1739 2423]
        κοσμος F
ο θεος Ath 𝔓⁴⁶ ℵ A B C D L P Ψ 049 33 104 223 876 1739 2423] τω θεω F
        G
πιστευοντας Ath 𝔓⁴⁶ ℵ A B C D F G L P Ψ 049 33 104 223 876 1739 2423]
        πιστευσαντας L

—————————

1 Cor 1:22
ἦν Ἰουδαῖοι μὲν διαβάλλουσιν, Ἕλληνες δὲ χλευάζουσιν
Or. de Inc. Verb. 1.1 [All]

—————————

Lac. K

—————————

1 Cor 1:23
Ἰουδαίοις μὲν σκάνδαλόν ἐστιν, ἔθνεσι δὲ μωρία
De Syn. [C]

Ἰουδαίοις σκάνδαλόν μὲν
Or. III c. Ar. 30 [Ad]

σκάνδαλον νομίσει τὸν σταυρὸν, ὡς δὲ Ἕλλην μωρίαν
Or. III c. Ar. 35 [All]

—————————

Lac. 𝔓⁴⁶ ²⁸ K

———————————————

²⁷ Kenyon notes the error in his apparatus; κοσμου] sic per errorem pro θεου. Kenyon, *Pauline Epistles, Text*, 53.
²⁸ Osburn includes the witness of 𝔓⁴⁶ for ἔθνεσι following Kenyon's reconstruction, since

.1)   1. εθνεσι(ν) Ath ℵ A B C* D* F G L P Ψ 33 104
         2. Ελλησι Cᶜ Dᶜ 049 223 876 1739 2423

εστιν Ath] omit ℵ A C D F G L P Ψ 049 33 104 223 876 2423

---

1 Cor 1:24
θεοῦ δύναμις καὶ θεοῦ σοφία
Or. c. gentes 40.34-35 [Ad]

χριστὸς θεοῦ δύναμις καὶ θεοῦ σοφία
Ep. ad ep. Aeg. et Lib. 16.20 [Ad]; Or. I c. Ar. 11 [Ad]; Or. II c. Ar. 62 [Ad];
Or. III c. Ar. 51 [Ad]; De decretis 15 [Ad]; De sent. Dion. 25 [Ad]; De Syn.
34 [Ad]*

δύναμιν θεοῦ καὶ θεοῦ σοφίαν
Or. I c. Ar. 32 [Ad]; Or. I c. Ar. 37 [Ad]

χριστὸς δὲ θεοῦ δύναμις καὶ θεοῦ σοφία
Or. II c. Ar. 32 [Ad]
χριστὸς (γὰρ) θεοῦ δύναμις καὶ θεοῦ σοφία
Or. II c. Ar. 42 [Ad]

(ἡμῖν δὲ) χριστὸς θεοῦ δύναμις καὶ θεοῦ σοφία
Or. III c. Ar. 30 [Ad]

θεοῦ δύναμις καὶ θεοῦ σοφία
Or. III c. Ar. 48 [Ad]

χριστὸς (γὰρ) θεοῦ δύναμις
Or. III c. Ar. 63 [Ad]

δύναμις γάρ ἐστι τοῦ θεοῦ
Or. II c. Ar. 55 [All]

σοφίαν καὶ δύναμιν
De sent. Dion. 15 [All]

σοφία καὶ δύναμίς
De sent. Dion. 26 [All]

Lac. K

---

the last line of folio 39v, that includes this word, is lacunose. See Osburn, *Text of the Apostolos in Epiphanius*, 85.

.1)   1. Χριστος…δυναμις…σοφια Ath 𝔓46
         2. Χριστον…δυναμιν…σοφιαν ℵ A B C D F G L P Ψ 049 33 104
            223 876 1739 2423

---

1 Cor 1:25
   μωρὸν τοῦ θεοῦ
   Or. I c. Ar. 43 [C]

Lac. K

---

1 Cor 1:30
   δικαιοσύνη γένηται
   Or. I c. Ar. 41 [All]

   σοφία γεγέννηται
   De sent. Dion. 25 [All]

Lac. K

---

1 Cor 2:4
   ἐν πειθοῖ σοφίας λόγοις
   Or. III c. Ar. 2 [C]

   οὐκ ἐν πειθοῖ σοφίας Ἑλληνικῆς
   Vita Ant. 80.1 [Ad]

Lac. K

.1)   1. πειθοι σοφιας λογοις Ath
         2. πειθοις σοφιας 𝔓46 F G
         3. πειθοις ανθρωπινης σοφιας λογοις ℵc A C L P Ψ 049 104 876
            2423
         4. πειθοις σοφιας λογοις ℵ* B D 33 1739
         5. πειθοι ανθρωπινης σοφιας λογοις 223

---

1 Cor 2:8
   οὐκ ἂν τὸν κύριον τῆς δόξης ἐσταύρωσαν
   Or. de Inc. Verb. 53.4 [C]

   εἰ γὰρ ἔγνωσαν, οὐκ ἂν τὸν κύριον τῆς δόξης ἐσταύρωσαν
   Or. III c. Ar. 39 [C]

οὐκ ἂν τὸν κύριον τῆς δόξης
De decretis 13 [C]

εἰ γὰρ ἐγίνωσκον, οὐκ ἂν ἠσέβουν εἰς τὸν κύριον τῆς δόξης
Or. I c. Ar. 53 [Ad]

εἰ γὰρ ἐγίνωσκον, οὐκ ἂν τὸν κύριον τῆς δόξης
Or. III c. Ar. 1 [Ad]

κυρίου τῆς δόξης
Or. I c. Ar. 2 [Ad]

κύριος τῆς δόξης
Or. III c. Ar. 39 [Ad]

——————

Lac. (33) K

δοξης Ath ℵ A B C D Fᶜ G L P Ψ 049 104 223 876 1739 2423] δοξης
    αυτων 𝔓⁴⁶; δοξες F*

——————

1 Cor 2:9
ὀφθαλμὸς οὐκ εἶδε καὶ οὓς οὐκ ἤκουσε καὶ ἐπὶ καρδίαν ἀνθρώπου οὐκ
ἀνέβη, ἃ ἡτοίμασεν ὁ θεὸς τοῖς ἀγαπῶσιν αὐτὸν
Apol. c. Ar. 53 [C]

ἃ ὀφθαλμὸς οὐκ εἶδεν, οὐδὲ οὓς ἤκουσεν, οὐδὲ ἐπὶ καρδίαν ἀνθρώπων
ἀνέβη, ὅσα ἡτοίμασται τοῖς
Or. de Inc. Verb. 57.3 [Ad]

ἀγαπῶσι τὸν Θεὸν
Or. de Inc. Verb. 57.3 [Ad]

——————

Lac. (33) K

.1)   1. α Ath 𝔓⁴⁶ ℵ D F G L P Ψ 049 33 104 223 876 1739 2423
        2. οσα²⁹ A B C

ουκ Ath ℵ A B C D F G L P Ψ 049 33 104 223 876 1739 2423] ουχ 𝔓⁴⁶
ους Ath 𝔓⁴⁶ ℵ A B C D L P Ψ 049 33 104 223 876 1739 2423] ους ου F G

——————

²⁹ Though Athanasius appears to know of this variant reading (note the first Adaptation) his
citation does not include it and the collation is made on that basis.

1 Cor 2:16
>   τοῦ Χριστοῦ νοῦν ἔχων
>   De Syn. 39 [All]

Lac. K

---

1 Cor 3:10
>   ἕκαστος δὲ βλεπέτω, πῶς ἐποικοδομεῖ
>   Or. II c. Ar. 74 [C]

>   ἀρχιτέκτων σοφὸς
>   Or. II c. Ar. 77 [Ad]*

>   ἀρχιτέκτονες σοφοὶ
>   De sent. Dion. 8 [Ad]

Lac. F G K

αρχιτεκτων σοφος Ath] σοφος αρχιτεκτων 𝔓⁴⁶ ℵ A B C D L P Ψ 049 33
    104 223 876 1739 2423
εποικοδομει Ath 𝔓⁴⁶ ℵ A B C D L P Ψ 049 33 223 876 1739 2423] οικοδο-
    μει 104

---

1 Cor 3:11
>   θεμέλιον ἄλλον οὐδεὶς δύναται θεῖναι παρὰ τὸν κείμενον, ὅς ἐστιν Ἰησοῦς
>   Χριστός
>   Or. II c. Ar. 74 [C]

>   ἔχοντες τὸν θεμέλιον ἀσφαλῆ, ὅς ἐστιν Ἰησοῦς Χριστὸς ὁ Κύριος ἡμῶν
>   Ep. ad Ioan. et Ant. 2 [All]

Lac. F G K

θειναι παρα τον κειμενον Ath 𝔓⁴⁶ ℵ A B C D L P Ψ 049 104 223 876 1739
    2423] παρα τον κειμενον θειναι 33
Ιησους Χριστος Ath 𝔓⁴⁶ ℵ A B L P Ψ 049 33 104 223 876 1739 2423]
    Χριστος C*;Χριστος Ιησους Cᶜ D

---

1 Cor 3:12
    λίθοι τίμιοι
    Or. II c. Ar. 74 [All]

    ———————

    Lac. K

    ———————

1 Cor 3:16
    οὐκ οἴδατε, ὅτι ναὸς θεοῦ ἐστε, καὶ τὸ πνεῦμα τοῦ θεοῦ οἰκεῖ ἐν ὑμῖν
    Or. I c. Ar. 47 [C]

    οὐκ οἴδατε, ὅτι ναὸς θεοῦ ἐστε
    Or. I c. Ar. 16 [C]

    ———————

    Lac. (F) inc. οἰκεῖ, (G) inc. οἰκεῖ[30], K

    .1)   1. θεου[pri] Ath 𝔓[46] ℵ A B C D L P Ψ 049 33 223 1739 2423
            2. του θεου 104 876

    .2)   1. οικει εν υμιν Ath 𝔓[46] ℵ A C D F G L Ψ 049 104 223 876 2423
            2. εν υμιν οικει B P 33 1739

    ———————

1 Cor 3:20
    γινώσκων τοὺς διαλογισμοὺς τῶν ἀνθρώπων, ὅτι εἰσὶ μάταιοι
    Ep. ad ep. Aeg. et Lib. 9.21 [C]

    ———————

    Lac. K

    .1)   1. ανθρωπων Ath 33 876
            2. σοφων 𝔓[46] ℵ A B C D F G L P Ψ 049 104 223 1739 2423

    γινωσκων Ath] γινωσκει 𝔓[46] ℵ A B C D F G L P Ψ 049 33 104 223 876
           1739 2423

    ———————

1 Cor 4:1
    οἰκονόμοι μυστηρίων θεοῦ
    De sent. Dion. 8 [Ad]

---

[30] Note the close relationship between F and G here. See Hatch, "On the Relationship of Codex Augiensis and Codex Boernerianus."

οἰκονόμοι τῶν μυστηρίων
Ep. ad Drac. 8.1 [Ad]

οἰκονόμοι μυστηρίων θεοῦ
Ep. encycl. 1 [Ad]

_____

Lac. K

θεου Ath 𝔓⁴⁶ ℵ A B C D F G L P Ψ 049 33 104 223 876 1739 2423] του
    θεου F G

_____

1 Cor 4:6
ταῦτα δὲ μετεσχημάτισα εἰς ἐμαυτὸν καὶ Ἀπολλώ, ἵνα ἐν ἡμῖν μάθητε τὸ
μὴ ὑπὲρ ἃ γέγραπται φυσιοῦσθαι
Or. III c. Ar. 21 [C]

μετεσχημάτισα εἰς ἐμαυτὸν, ἵνα μάθητε
Vita Ant. 40.6 [Ad]

_____

Lac. (A) K

   .1)   1. ταυτα δε Ath
            2. ταυτα δε αδελφοι 𝔓⁴⁶ ℵᶜ B C D F G L P Ψ 33 104 223 1739 2423
            3. ταυτα αδελφοι ℵ* 049 876

   .2)   1. εις Ath 𝔓⁴⁶ ℵ B C D L P Ψ 049 33 104 223 1739 2423
            2. omit F G 876

   .3)   1. α Ath 𝔓⁴⁶ ℵ A B C P Ψ 33 104 1739
            2. ο D F G L 049 223 876 2423

   .4)   1. γεγραπται Ath 𝔓⁴⁶ℵ* A B C D F G Ψ 1739 2423
            2. γεγραπται φρονειν ℵᶜ L P 049 33 104 223 876

   .5)   1. φυσιουσθαι Ath
            2. ινα μη εις υπερ του ενος φυσιουσθαι 𝔓⁴⁶ ℵ A B C L P Ψ 049 33
               104 223 876 1739
            3. ινα εις υπερ του ενος φυσιουσθαι D
            4. ινα μη εις κατα του ενος φυσιουσθαι F G
            5. ινα μη εις υπερ του ενος μη φυσιουσθαι 2423

Ἀπολλω Ath] Ἀπολλω δι υμας 𝔓⁴⁶ ℵ A B C D F G L P Ψ 049 33 104 223
876 1739 2423

το Ath 𝔓⁴⁶ ℵ A B C D L P Ψ 049 33 104 223 876 1739 2423] omit F G

---

1 Cor 4:11

πεινᾶν καὶ διψᾶν³¹
Ep. ad Drac. 9.1 [All]

Lac. K

---

1 Cor 5:3

ὡς τῷ πνεύματι παρόντες
Apol. c. Ar. 47 [All]

Lac. K

1Cor 5:4

συναχθέντων³²
Ep. encycl. 2 [C]

σὺν τῇ δυνάμει τοῦ κυρίου ἡμῶν Ἰησοῦ Χριστοῦ
Ep. encycl. 2 [C]

καὶ τοῦ πνεύματος
Ep. encycl. 2 [Ad]

Lac. C K

.1)   1. ημων Ιησου Χριστου Ath Dᶜ F G L 049 104 223 876 2423
         2. Ιησοῦ 𝔓⁴⁶ P Ψ
         3. ημων Ιησου ℵ A B D*
         4. omit 33 1739

συναχθεντων Ath 𝔓⁴⁶ ℵ A B D F G L P Ψ 049 104 223 876 2423] omit 33³³

---

³¹ The words are found together in various conjugations in both Matt 5:6 and 1 Cor 4:11.
However Athanasius' references to Paul clearly allude to the reference in 1 Corinthians.

³² New Testament hapax in form.

³³ Omission due to homoioteleuton.

1 Cor 5:7

τὸ (γὰρ) πάσχα ἡμῶν ἐτύθη Χριστός
Ep. Cosm. Indic. XLII; 10.8 [C]

Lac. (𝔓⁴⁶) [expl. το], K

.1)   1. το πασχα ημων Ath ℵ* A B C* Dᶜ F G 33 1739
       2. το πασχα ημων υπερ ημων ℵᶜ Cᶜ L P Ψ 049 104 223 876 2423
       3. το πασχα ημων ετυθη D*

Χριστος Ath ℵ A B C D L P Ψ 049 33 104 223 876 1739 2423] ο Χριστος
F G

---

1 Cor 5:13

ἐξάρατε τὸν πονηρὸν ἐξ ὑμῶν αὐτῶν
Apol. c. Ar. 19 [C]

Lac. K 049

.1)   1. εξαρατε Ath ℵ A B C D* F G P Ψ 33 104
       2. εξαιρετε 𝔓⁴⁶ 1739
       3. εξαρειτε Dᶜ L 223 876 2423

---

1 Cor 6:10

λοίδοροι βασιλείαν Θεοῦ κληρονομήσουσιν
Apol. de fuga 1.12-13 [C]

Lac. F G K 049

.1)   1. θεου Ath 𝔓⁴⁶ ℵ A B C D L P Ψ 33 104 1739*
       2. θεου ου 223 876 1739ᶜ 2423

λοιδοροι Ath] λοιδοροι ουχ αρπαγες 𝔓⁴⁶ ℵ A B C D L P Ψ 33 104 223 876
1739 2423
βασιλειαν θεου Ath 𝔓⁴⁶ ℵ A B C L P Ψ 33 104 223 876 1739 2423] θεου
βασιλιαν D

---

1 Cor 6:12

πάντα ἔξεστιν, ἀλλ᾽ οὐ πάντα συμφέρει
Or. c. gentes 4.34-35 [C]

Lac. (𝔓⁴⁶) [inc. …στιν αλλ], F G K 049

παντα Ath] παντα μοι ℵ A B C D L P Ψ 33 104 223 876 1739 2423
συμφερει Ath ℵ A B C Dᶜ L P Ψ 33 104 223 876 1739 2423] συνφερει D*

1 Cor 6:19
      ναὸς τοῦ ἐν ἡμῖν οἰκοῦντος ἁγίου πνεύματος
      Or. II c. Ar. 74 [C]

Lac. 049

οικουντος Ath] omit 𝔓⁴⁶ ℵ A B C D F G K L P Ψ 33 104 223 876 1739
      2423
αγιου πνευματος Ath 𝔓⁴⁶ ℵ A C D F G K L P Ψ 33 104 223 876 1739 2423]
      πνευματος αγιου B

1 Cor 6:20
      δοξάζετε οὖν τὸν κύριον
      Vita Ant. 64.4 [All]

Lac. 049

1 Cor 7:27
      δέδεσαι γυναικί, μὴ ζήτει λύσιν
      Apol. c. Ar. 6 [C]

Lac. C 049

1 Cor 7:32
      ἵνα τῷ κυρίῳ αὐτοῦ ἀρέσῃ
      Vita Ant. 18.2 [All]

      καὶ ἀρέσκειν μὲν τῷ Κυρίῳ
      Vita Ant. 55.13 [All]

Lac. 049

_____

1 Cor 8:6

εἷς (γὰρ) θεὸς ὁ πατήρ, ἐξ οὗ τὰ πάντα, καὶ ἡμεῖς εἰς αὐτὸν, καὶ εἷς κύριος Ἰησοῦς Χριστὸς, δι' οὗ τὰ πάντα, καὶ ἡμεῖς δι' αὐτου
Or. I c. Ar. 19 [C]

εἷς κύριος Ἰησοῦς Χριστὸς, δι' οὗ τὰ πάντα, καὶ ἡμεῖς δι' αὐτοῦ
Or. II c. Ar. 31 [C]

εἷς κύριος Ἰησοῦς Χριστός
Or. III c. Ar. 4 [C]

εἷς κύριος Ἰησοῦς Χριστός, δι' οὗ τὰ πάντα καὶ ἡμεῖς δι' αὐτοῦ
De decretis 17 [C]

καὶ εἷς κύριος Ἰησοῦς Χριστός, δι' οὗ τὰ πάντα
De decretis 19 [C]

εἷς κύριος Ἰησοῦς Χριστός, δι' οὗ τὰ πάντα
De sent. Dion. 2 [C]; De Syn. 49 [C]

καὶ εἷς κύριος Ἰησοῦς Χριστός, δι' οὗ τὰ πάντα
De Syn. 35 [C]

εἷς κύριος Ἰησοῦς, δι' οὗ τὰ πάντα
Or. II c. Ar. 71 [Ad]

εἷς κύριος (ἦν), δι' οὗ τὰ πάντα
Or. III c. Ar. 39 [Ad]

δι' αὐτοῦ τὰ πάντα
Or. III c. Ar. 61 [Ad]

εἷς θεὸς ἐξ οὗ τὰ πάντα, καὶ εἷς κύριος Ἰησοῦς Χριστὸς δι' οὗ τὰ πάντα
De decretis 7 [Ad]

εἷς (γὰρ) θεὸς, ἐξ οὗ τὰ πάντα
Ep. ad Afros 5.4 [Ad]

εἷς θεὸς ἐξ οὗ τὰ πάντα
De decretis 19 [Ad]

εἷς θεός, ἐξ οὗ τὰ πάντα
De Syn. 35 [Ad]

_____

Lac. C 049

.1)   1. δι ου Ath 𝔓⁴⁶ ℵᶜ A D F G K L P Ψ 33 104 223 876 1739 2423
          2. δι ον ℵ* B

εις θεος Ath ℵᶜ A B D K L P Ψ 33 104 223 876 1739 2423] εις θεος και 𝔓⁴⁶;
          εις ℵ*; εις ο θεος F G
Ιησους Χριστος Ath 𝔓⁴⁶ ℵ A B D F G K L Ψ 33 104 223 876 1739 2423]
          Ιησους ο Χριστος P
τα πανταᵖʳⁱ Ath 𝔓⁴⁶ ℵ A B Dᶜ F G K L P Ψ 33 104 223 876 1739 2423]
          παντα D*

_____

1 Cor 8:8
          βρῶμα ἡμᾶς οὐ παραστήσει τῷ θεῷ
          Ep. ad Amun 66 [C]

_____

Lac. C K 049

.1)   1. παραστησει Ath 𝔓⁴⁶ ℵ* A B 33 1739
          2. παριστησιν ℵᶜ D L P Ψ 104 223 876 2423
          3. συνιστησιν F G

_____

1 Cor 9:16
          Οὐαὶ γάρ μοί ἐστιν, ἐὰν μὴ εὐαγγελίζωμαι
          Ep. ad Drac. 4.4 [C]

_____

Lac. 049

.1)   1. γαρ Ath 𝔓⁴⁶ ℵ* A B C D F G P 33 1739
          2. δε ℵᶜ K L Ψ 104 223 876 2423

.2)   1. ευαγγελίζωμαι Ath 𝔓⁴⁶ ℵ A K L P Ψ 33 104 223 876 1739 2423
          2. ευαγγελισωμαι B C D F G

εστιν Ath 𝔓⁴⁶ ℵ A B C D K L P Ψ 33 104 223 876 1739 2423] εσται F G

_____

1 Cor 9:22
          τοῖς ἀσθενοῦσιν ἀσθενὴς γίνεται, ἵνα τοὺς ἀσθενεῖς κερδήσῃ
          Ep. ad Pall. 5 [Ad]*

Lac. 049

.1)   1. ασθενουσιν ασθενης Ath
       2. ασθενεσιν ασθενης 𝔓⁴⁶ ℵ* A B 1739
       3. ασθενουσιν ως ασθενης D F G Ψ
       4. ασθενεσιν ως ασθενης ℵᶜ C K L P 33 104 223 876 2423

1 Cor 9:27
    ὑπεπίαζε τὸ σῶμα καὶ ἐδουλαγώγει
    Vita Ant. 7.4 [All]

    μᾶλλον τὸ σῶμα παρ' αὐτῆς δουλαγωγῆται
    Vita Ant. 45.6 [All]

    δουλαγωγεῖν τὸ σῶμα
    Vita Ant. 55.13 [All]

Lac. 049

1 Cor 10:3
    τῆς πνευματικῆς τροφῆς
    Vita Ant. 45.3 [All]

Lac. 049

1 Cor 10:13
    πιστὸς ὁ Θεὸς, ὃς οὐκ ἐάσει ὑμᾶς πειρασθῆναι ὑπὲρ ὃ δύνασθε
    Or. II c. Ar. 6 [C]

Lac. 049

.1)   1. εασει Ath 𝔓⁴⁶ ℵ A B C K L P Ψ 33 104 223 876 1739 2423
       2. αφησει D F G

    ο δυνασθε Ath 𝔓⁴⁶ ℵ A B C D K L P Ψ 33 104 223 876 1739 2423] ο ου
    δυνασθαι³⁴ F G

---

³⁴ The variant here is for the addition of ου rather than the itacism found in δυνασθε/
δυνασθαι

υμας πειρασθηναι Ath 𝔓⁴⁶ ℵ A C D F G K L P Ψ 33 104 223 876 1739
2423] πειρασθηναι υμας B

---

1 Cor 11:1
μιμηταὶ[35]
Or. III c. Ar. 10 [C]

Lac. 049

---

1 Cor 11:2
ἐπαινῶ δὲ ὑμᾶς, ὅτι πάντα μου μέμνησθε, καὶ καθὼς παρέδωκα ὑμῖν τὰς
παραδόσεις, οὕτω κατέχετε
Ep. ad Afros 10.4 [C]

Lac. 049

.1)   1. υμας Ath 𝔓⁴⁶ ℵ A B C P 1739
         2. υμας αδελφοι D F G K L Ψ 33 104 223 876 2423

.2)   1. ουτω Ath
         2. omit 𝔓⁴⁶ ℵ A B Dᶜ K L P Ψ 33 104 223 876 1739 2423
         3. μου D* F G
         4. ουτως C

καθως Ath 𝔓⁴⁶ ℵ A B C D K L P Ψ 33 104 223 876 1739 2423] καθως
        πανταχου F G
υμιν Ath 𝔓⁴⁶ ℵ A B C D K L P Ψ 33 104 223 876 1739 2423] τας F; omit G
και Ath 𝔓⁴⁶ ℵ Aᶜ B C D F G K L P Ψ 33 104 223 876 1739 2423] omit A*
παντα Ath 𝔓⁴⁶ ℵ A B C D F G K L Ψ 33 104 223 876 1739 2423] παντοτε P

---

1 Cor 11:3
κεφαλὴ δέ (, ὅ ἐστιν ἀρχή,) τοῦ Χριστοῦ ὁ θεός
De Syn. 27.1 [C]

κεφαλὴ γὰρ Χριστοῦ ὁ θεός
De Syn. 26.4 [Ad]

---

[35] While there are a number of verses that contain μιμηται (all in the Pauline Epistles), the immediate context makes it clear that here Athanasius has 1 Cor 11:1 in mind.

Lac. 049

.1)   1. του Χριστου Ath ℵ A B D 33
       2. Χριστου 𝔓⁴⁶ C F G K L P Ψ 104 223 876 1739 2423

θεος Ath 𝔓⁴⁶ ℵ A B D F G K L P Ψ 33 104 223 876 2423] χριστος C

---

1 Cor 11:7
εἰκὼν καὶ δόξα Θεοῦ[36]
Or. III c. Ar. 10 [C]; Ep. ad Afros 5.6 [C]

(ὁ μὲν ἀνὴρ) εἰκὼν καὶ δόξα Θεοῦ ὑπάρχει, ἡ δὲ γυνὴ δόξα ἀνδρός ἐστιν
Or. II c. Ar. 30 [Ad]

εἰκών ἐστιν ὁ ἄνθρωπος καὶ δόξα θεοῦ ὑπάρχει
De decretis 20 [Ad]

Lac. 049

---

1 Cor 11:9
οὐ γὰρ ἐκτίσθη (,φησὶν ἡ Γραφὴ,) ἀνὴρ διὰ τὴν γυναῖκα, ἀλλὰ γυνὴ διὰ
τὸν ἄνδρα
Or. II c. Ar. 30 [C]

Lac. 049

ου γαρ Ath] γαρ ουκ 𝔓⁴⁶ ℵ A B C D F G K L P Ψ 33 104 223 876 1739
       2423
ανδρα Ath ℵ A B C D F G K L P Ψ 33 104 223 876 1739 2423] ανθρωπον
       𝔓⁴⁶

---

1 Cor 12:10
διακρίνειν τὰ πνευματικὰ
Ep. ad ep. Aeg. et Lib. 4.32 [All]

χάρισμα διακρίσεως πνευμάτων
Ep. ad ep. Aeg. et Lib. 4.37 [All]

---

[36] Kenyon's transcription is in error concerning the nomina sacra for θεου. It records only the
θ with overscore but omits the upsilon. See Kenyon, *Pauline Epistles, Text*, 76.

διακρίσεως πνευμάτων
Vita Ant. 22.3 [All]; Vita Ant. 38.5 [All]; Vita Ant. 88.1 [All]

διάκρισιν τῶν πνευμάτων
Vita Ant. 44.1 [All]

Lac. 049

---

1 Cor 12:26
συμπάσχει πάντα τὰ μέλη
Ep. encycl. 6 [C]

ἵνα εἴτε πάσχει εἴτε χαίρει ἓν μέλος ἢ συμπάσχωμεν ἢ συγχαίρωμεν
ἀλλήλοις
De decretis 35 [All]

Lac. P 049

.1)   1. συμπασχει Ath B^c K L Ψ 104 223 876 1739 2423
       2. συνπασχει 𝔓^46 ℵ A B* C D^37 F G 33

---

1 Cor 14:25
ὄντως ὁ Θεὸς ἐν τούτοις ἐστί
Or. I c. Ar. 43 [All]

Lac. C P

---

1 Cor 14:33
οὐκ ἔστιν ἀκαταστασίας ἀλλ' εἰρήνης
Apol. c. Ar. 34 [C]

Lac. C P

.1)   1. ακαταστασιας Ath
       2. ακαταστασιας θεος 𝔓^46 F G
       3. ακαταστασιας ο θεος ℵ B D K L Ψ 049 33 104 223 876 1739
          2423

---

[37] Hansell incorrectly shows C and D as supporting the reading συμπασχει. Hansell, *Novum Testamentum Graece.*

4. ο θεος ακαταστασιας A

_____

1 Cor 15:3

ὃ καὶ παρέλαβεν, ὅτι Χριστὸς ἀπέθανεν ὑπὲρ τῶν ἁμαρτιῶν ἡμῶν κατὰ
τὰς γραφάς
Ep. ad Epic. 8.21-22 [C]

_____

Lac. C

παρελαβεν Ath] παρελαβον $\mathfrak{P}^{46}$ ℵ A B D F G K L P Ψ 049 33 104 223 876
    2423
αμαρτιων Ath $\mathfrak{P}^{46}$ ℵ A B D G K L P Ψ 049 33 104 223 876 1739 2423]
    αμαρτιων η F

_____

1 Cor 15:9

Οὐκ εἰμὶ ἱκανὸς καλεῖσθαι ἀπόστολος
Ep. ad Drac. 4.4 [C]

_____

Lac. C

_____

1 Cor 15:10

οὐκ ἐγὼ δέ, ἀλλ᾽ ἡ χάρις τοῦ θεοῦ ἡ σὺν ἐμοί
Vita Ant. 5.7 [C]

_____

Lac. C

.1)   1. η συν εμοι Ath ℵᶜ A Dᶜ K L P Ψ 049 33 104 223 876 2423
       2. η εις εμε $\mathfrak{P}^{46}$
       3. συν εμοι ℵ* B D* F G 1739

δε Ath ℵ A B D F G K L P Ψ 049 33 104 223 876 2423] δε μονος 1739

_____

1 Cor 15:20

ἐκ νεκρῶν ἀπαρχὴ τῶν κεκοιμημένων
Or. II c. Ar. 64 [C]

ἀπαρχὴ τῶν νεκρῶν
Or. II c. Ar. 75 [Ad]

———————

Lac. C

νεκρων Ath 𝔓⁴⁶ ℵ A B D K L P Ψ 049 33 104 223 1739 2423] των νεκρων
    F G; νεκρων εγηγερται 876
κεκοιμημενων Ath ℵ A B D F G K L P Ψ 049 33 104 223 876 2423]
    κεκοιμενων 𝔓⁴⁶

———————

1 Cor 15:21
    ἐπειδὴ γὰρ δι' ἀνθρώπου θάνατος, καὶ δι' ἀνθρώπου ἀνάστασις νεκρῶν +
    Or. de Inc. Verb. 10.5 [C]

    ἐπειδὴ δι' ἀνθρώπου ὁ³⁸ θάνατος, καὶ δι' ἀνθρώπου ἀνάστασις
    Or. II c. Ar. 55 [C]

———————

Lac. C (33)

———————

1 Cor 15:22
    + ὥσπερ γὰρ ἐν τῷ Ἀδὰμ πάντες ἀποθνήσκουσιν, οὕτως καὶ ἐν τῷ χριστῷ
    πάντες ζωοποιηθήσονται
    Or. de Inc. Verb. 10.5 [C]

    ἐν τῷ Ἀδὰμ ἀποθνήσκομεν, ἐν δὲ τῷ Χριστῷ πάντες ζωοποιούμεθα
    Or. I c. Ar. 59 [Ad]

    ἐν τῷ Ἀδὰμ ἀποθνήσκομεν
    Or. III c. Ar. 33 [Ad]

    πάντες ἐν τῷ Ἀδὰμ ἀποθνήσκομεν
    Or. III c. Ar. 33 [Ad]

    πάντες ζωοποιούμεθα
    Or. III c. Ar. 33 [Ad]

    ζωοποιήσῃ πάντας
    Or. I c. Ar. 44 [All]

———————

38 Though this can be considered a variant: θανατος Ath 𝔓⁴⁶ ℵ A B D* K 1739] ο θανατος Ath
Dᶜ F G L P Ψ 049 104 223 876 2423. Athanasius witnesses to both readings and therefore it is not
possible to determine which is quoted from his *Vorlage*.

Lac. C

.1)   1. ουτως Ath 𝔓⁴⁶ ℵ A B D F G L P Ψ 049 33 223 876 2423
         2. ουτω K 104 1739

_____

1 Cor 15:31
κaθ' ἡμέραν ἀποθνήσκω
Vita Ant. 19.2 [C]

ὡς καθ' ἡμέραν ἀποθνήσκοντας ζῆν
Vita Ant. 89.4 [All]

ὡς καθ' ἡμέραν ἀποθνήσκοντες ζήσατε
Vita Ant. [All]

_____

Lac. C

αποθνησκω Ath 𝔓⁴⁶ ℵ A B C D F G K L P Ψ 049 33 104 223 876 1739
         2423] omit 876

_____

1 Cor 15:32
φάγωμεν καὶ πίωμεν· αὔριον γὰρ ἀποθνήσκομεν
Hist. Arian. 79 [C]

_____

Lac. C

_____

1 Cor 15:33
φθείρουσιν ἤθη χρηστὰ ὁμιλίαι κακαί
De Syn. 39 [C]

_____

Lac. C

.1)   1. χρηστα Ath 𝔓⁴⁶ ℵ A B D F G K L P Ψ 049 33 104
         2. χρησθ 223 876 1739 2423

ηθη Ath 𝔓⁴⁶ ℵ A B D K L P Ψ 049 33 104 223 876 1739 2423] ηθηρ F G

_____

1 Cor 15:41

   ἀστὴρ δὲ ἀστέρος
   Or. I c. Ar. 57 [All]

   διαφέρει ἐν δόξῃ
   Or. I c. Ar. 57 [All]

   Ἀστὴρ γοῦν ἀστέρος ὑπερέχει δόξηι
   Or. II c. Ar. 20 [All]

   ἐν δόξῃ διαφέρειν αὐτῶν
   Or. II c. Ar. 23 [All]

   διαφέρουσι δὲ ἀλλήλων ἐν δόξῃ
   Or. II c. Ar. 49 [All]

   τῇ δόξῃ διαφέρῃ
   Or. III c. Ar. 64 [All]; Or. II c. Ar. 48 [All]

———————

1 Cor 15.42

   πάλιν δὲ φθαρτὸν ἀποθέμενοι τὸ σῶμα, ἄφθαρτον ἀπολαμβάνομεν αὐτό
   Vita Ant. 16.8 [All]

———————

1 Cor 15:45

   ὁ πρῶτος ἄνθρωπος Ἀδάμ
   Or. I c. Ar. 51 [C]

   τὸν πρῶτον ἄνθρωπον τὸν Ἀδάμ
   Ep. ad ep. Aeg. et Lib. 2.5-6 [Ad]

———————

   .1)   1. ανθρωπος Ath 𝔓⁴⁶ ℵ A C D F G L P Ψ 049 33 104 223 876 1739
        2423
        2. omit B K

   Αδαμ Ath 𝔓⁴⁶ ℵ A B C D F G K L P Ψ 049 33 223 876 1739 2423] omit
     104

———————

1 Cor 15:47

   ὁ δεύτερος ἄνθρωπος ἐξ οὐρανοῦ
   Or. I c. Ar. 44 [C]

ἐξ οὐρανοῦ[39]
Or. III c. Ar. 55 [C]

τὸν δεύτερον
Or. I c. Ar. 51 [Ad]

.1)   1. ανθρωπος Ath ℵ* B C D* F G 33 1739*
        2. ανθρωπος πνευματικος 𝔓[46]
        3. ανθρωπος ο κυριος ℵ[c] A D[c] K L P Ψ 049 104 223 876 1739[c] 2423

---

1 Cor 15:48
ἐπουράνιος[40]
Or. I c. Ar. 44 [C]

.1)   1. επουρανιος Ath ℵ A B C K L P Ψ 049 33 104 223 876 1739 2423
        2. ουρανιος 𝔓[46] D F G

---

1 Cor 15:53
δεῖ τὸ φθαρτὸν τοῦτο ἐνδύσασθαι ἀφθαρσίαν, καὶ τὸ θνητὸν τοῦτο ἐνδύσασθαι ἀθανασίαν +
Or. de Inc. Verb. 21.2 [C]

δεῖ τὸ φθαρτὸν τοῦτο ἐνδύσασθαι ἀφθαρσίαν καὶ τὸ θνητὸν τοῦτο
ἐνδύσασθαι ἀθανασίαν
Ep. ad Epic. 6.23-24 [C]

ἀφθαρσίαν ἐνδυσάμενοι
Or. II c. Ar. 69 [All]

.1)   1. δει το Ath 𝔓[46] ℵ
        2. δει γαρ τὸ A B C D K L P Ψ 049 33 104 223 876 1739 2423
        3. δει γαρ ο F G

τοῦτο[sec] Ath 𝔓[46] ℵ A B C D K L P Ψ 049 33 104 223 876 1739 2423] omit
F G

---

[39] Though there are numerous references to the phrase εξ ουρανου in the New Testament, only 1 Cor 15:47 clearly uses it to refer to Christ, the Second man over against the First man (Adam) who was from the earth. Cf Matt 21:25, 28:2; Mark 11:30, 11:31; Luke 3:22, 11:13, 11:16, 20:4, 20:5; John 1:32, 6:58; 2 Cor 5:2; Gal 1:8; 2 Pet 1:18.
[40] Biblical hapax in form.

1 Cor 15:54

+ ὅταν δὲ τὸ θνητὸν τοῦτο ἐνδύσηται ἀθανασίαν, τότε γενήσεται ὁ λόγος
ὁ γεγραμμένος· κατεπόθη ὁ θάνατος εἰς νῖκος +
Or. de Inc. Verb. 21.2 [C]

ἐνέδυσεν ἀφθαρσίαν
Or. de Inc. Verb. 9.2 [All]

.1)   1. οταν δε το θνητον τουτο ενδυσηται αθανασιαν Ath 𝔓⁴⁶ C*
        1739*
        2. οταν δε το θνητον τουτο ενδυσηται την αθανασιαν ℵ*
        3. οταν δε το θνητον τουτο ενδυσηται την αθανασιαν και το
        φθαρτον τουτο ενδυσηται αφθαρσιαν A
        4. οταν δε το φθαρτον τουτο ενδυσηται αφθαρσιαν και το θνητον
        τουτο ενδυσηται αθανασιαν ℵᶜ B Cᶜ D K L P Ψ 049 104 223
        876 1739ᶜ 2423
        5. omit F G¹¹
        6. οταν δε το φθαρτον τουτο ενδυσηται την αφθαρσιαν και το
        θνητον τουτο ενδυσηται την αθανασιαν 33

---

1 Cor 15:55

+ ποῦ σου, θάνατε, τὸ κέντρον;
Or. de Inc. Verb. 21.2 [C]

ποῦ σου, θάνατε, τὸ νῖκος; ποῦ σου, ᾅδη, τὸ κέντρον;
Or. de Inc. Verb. 27.4 [C]⁎⁎⁴²

.1)   1. που σου θανατε το νικος που σου αδη το κεντρον Ath 33 1739ᶜ
        2. που σου θανατε το νικος που σου θανατε το κεντρον 𝔓⁴⁶ ℵ* B C
        1739*
        3. που σου θανατε το κεντρον που σου αδη το νικος ℵᶜ A K L P Ψ
        049 104 223 876 2423
        4. που σου, θανατε το κεντρον που σου θανατε το νικος D F G

---

1 Cor 16:22

οὐ φιλεῖ τὸν κύριον, ἤτω ἀνάθεμα
Ep. ad monach. 3 [C]

---

⁴¹ Omission due to homoioteleuton.
⁴² It is likely that the first quotation is simply an abbreviated form of the longer quotation.

Lac. (𝔓⁴⁶)

.1)   1. κυριον Ath 𝔓⁴⁶ ℵ* A B C 33 1739
        2. κυριον Ιησουν Χριστον ℵᶜ D F G L Ψ 049 104 876 2423*
        3. κυριον ημων Ιησουν Χριστον K P 223 2423ᶜ

---

1 Cor 16:23
ἡ χάρις τοῦ κυρίου ἡμῶν Ἰησοῦ Χριστοῦ μεθ᾽ ὑμῶν
Ep. ad monach. 3 [C]

Lac. 𝔓⁴⁶

.1)   1. ημων Ath A L P 33 223
        2. omit ℵ B C D F G K Ψ 049 104 876 1739 2423

.2)   1. Χριστου Ath ℵᶜ A C D F G K L P Ψ 049 104 223 876 1739 2423
        2. omit ℵ* B 33

---

2 Cor 1:10
καὶ ῥύσεται, εἰς ὃν ἠλπίκαμεν
Or. III c. Ar. 13 [C]

.1)   1. και ρυσεται Ath 𝔓⁴⁶ ℵ B C P 33
        2. omit A D* Ψ
        3. και ρυεται Dᶜ F G K L 049 104 223 876 1739 2423

ηλπικαμεν Ath 𝔓⁴⁶ ℵ A B C D F G K L P Ψ 049 33 104 223 1739 2423]
        ελπικαμεν 876

---

2 Cor 1:23
μάρτυρα τὸν Θεὸν ἐπικαλοῦμαι ἐπὶ τὴν ἐμαυτοῦ ψυχήν
Apol. ad Const. 3.2 [C]

οὐκ ἀγνοοῦντες αὐτοῦ τὰ νοήματα
Ep. ad ep. Aeg. et Lib. 3.2 [Ad]

ἐμαυτοῦ Ath] ἐμην 𝔓⁴⁶ ℵ A B C D F G 33 223 876 1739 2423

---

2 Cor 2:11

Οὐ γὰρ αὐτοῦ τὰ νοήματα ἀγνοοῦμεν
Or. I c. Ar. 51 [C]

Οὐ γὰρ αὐτοῦ τὰ νοήματα ἀγνοοῦμεν
Vita Ant. 22.4 [C]

———————

2 Cor 2:15

χριστοῦ (γὰρ) εὐωδία ἐσμὲν ἐν τοῖς σῳζομένοις
Ep. ad Amun 63 [C]

———————

Lac. P
.1)   1. εσμεν Ath K
      2. εσμεν τω θεω 𝔓⁴⁶ ℵ A B C D F G L Ψ 049 33 104 223 876 1739
         2423

Χριστου ευωδια Ath 𝔓⁴⁶ ℵ A B C D G* K L Ψ 049 33 104 223 876 1739
2423] Χριστι ευωδρια F Gᶜ

———————

2 Cor 2:17

κεκαπηλευκέναι τὸν λόγον
Apol. c. Ar. 47 [Ad]

———————

2 Cor 3:2

γινωσκομένη τε καὶ ἀναγινωσκομένη
Ep. ad Jov. 1.3 [C]

σὺ γὰρ ἐμοὶ ἐπιστολή, κατὰ τὸ γεγραμμένον, ἐπιγινωσκομένη καὶ ἀναγινωσκομένη ἐν καρδίᾳ
Ep. ad Rufin. 77 [All]

———————

2 Cor 3:16

ἐπιστρέψατε πρὸς Κύριον
Or. I c. Ar. 11 [Ad]

Περιέλοιμεν τὸ κάλυμμα
Or. II c. Ar. 77 [All]

———————

2 Cor 3:17

ὁ δὲ κύριος τὸ πνεῦμά ἐστι
Or. I c. Ar. 11 [C]

_____

2 Cor 4:6

ἀπὸ σκότους ἡ ἀλήθεια ὑμῖν λάμψει
Or. III c. Ar. 28 [All]

_____

2 Cor 4:11

ἀεὶ γὰρ ἡμεῖς οἱ ζῶντες
De decretis 20 [C]; Ep. ad Afros 5.6 [C]

.1)   1. αει Ath ℵ A B C D K L P 049 104 223 876 1739 2423
        2. ει 𝔓⁴⁶ F G
        3. omit Ψ 33⁴³

_____

2 Cor 4:18

ἀλλὰ μόνα τὰ πρόσκαιρα καὶ τὰ σωματικὰ εἶναι τὰ καλά
Or. c. gentes 8.6-7 [All]

_____

Lac. A

_____

2 Cor 5:10

τοὺς πάντας ἡμᾶς παραστῆναι δεῖ ἔμπροσθεν τοῦ βήματος τοῦ Χριστοῦ,
ἵνα κομίσηται ἕκαστος, πρὸς ἃ διὰ τοῦ σώματος ἔπραξεν, εἴτε ἀγαθόν, εἴτε
φαῦλον
Or. de Inc. Verb. 56.5 [C]

_____

Lac. A

_____

.1)   1. προς α δια Ath
        2. τα ιδια 𝔓⁴⁶
        3. τα δια ℵ B C K P Ψ 049 33 104 223 876 1739 2423
        4. α δια D F G
        5. omit L

_____

⁴³ Omission via homoioteleuton.

.2)   1. του σωματος Ath D* F G
2. του σωματος προς α 𝔓⁴⁶ ℵ B C K P 049 33 104 223 876 1739
2423
3. προς α L
4. του σωματος ο Ψ

.3)   1. φαυλον Ath ℵ C 33 1739
2. κακον 𝔓⁴⁶ B D F G K L P Ψ 049 104 223 876 2423

παραστηναι Ath] φανερωθεναι 𝔓⁴⁶ ℵ B C D F G K L P Ψ 049 33 104 223
876 1739 2423
εμπροσθεν Ath 𝔓⁴⁶ ℵ B C D K L P Ψ 049 33 104 223 876 1739 2423]
ενπροσθεν F G

---

2 Cor 5:14

ἡ γὰρ ἀγάπη τοῦ Χριστοῦ συνέχει ἡμᾶς κρίναντας τοῦτο, ὅτι εἰ εἷς ὑπὲρ
πάντων ἀπέθανεν, ἄρα οἱ πάντες ἀπέθανον +
Or. de Inc. Verb. 10.2 [C]

πάντες ἡμεῖς ἀπεθάνομεν
Or. I c. Ar. 41 [All]

Lac. (𝔓⁴⁶)[inc. τοῦτο], A

.1)   1. Χριστου Ath ℵ B C D F G K L Ψ 049 104 223 876 1739 2423
2. θεου P 33

.2)   1. οτι ει Ath ℵᶜ C 104 223 876 1739 2423
2. οτι 𝔓⁴⁶ ℵ* B D F G K L P Ψ 049 33

.3)   1. αρα οι παντες απεθανον Ath ℵᶜ B C D F G K L P Ψᶜ 33 104 223
876 1739 2423
2. αρα οι παντες απεθανεν ℵ*
3. omit[44] 𝔓⁴⁶ Ψ* 049

κριναντας Ath ℵ B C D K L P Ψ 049 104 223 876 1739 2423] κριναντες F
G; κρινοντας 33[45]
υπερ παντων Ath 𝔓⁴⁶ ℵ B C D F G K L Ψ 049 33 223 876 1739 2423] omit
104

---

[44] These three mss (𝔓⁴⁶ Ψ* 049) omit per homoioteleuton.

[45] Swanson shows ms 33 as a witness to κριναντας but Tischendorf notes the correct reading.
Reuben Joseph Swanson, ed., *New Testament Greek Manuscripts: 2 Corinthians. Variant Readings
Arranged in Horizontal Lines Against Codex Vaticanus* (Wheaton: Tyndale House, 2005).

2 Cor 5:15

+ καὶ ὑπὲρ πάντων ἀπέθανεν, ἵνα ἡμεῖς μηκέτι ἑαυτοῖς ζῶμεν, ἀλλὰ τῷ
ὑπὲρ ἡμῶν ἀποθανόντι καὶ ἀναστάντι
Or. de Inc. Verb. 10.2 [C]

Lac. A C

.1)   1. και υπερ παντων απεθανεν Ath ℵ B C D K L P Ψᶜ 33 104 223
            876 1739 2423
         2. και υπερ παντων απεθανεν χριστος F G
         3. omit⁴⁶ 𝔓⁴⁶ Ψ* 049

ημεις Ath] οι ζωντες 𝔓⁴⁶ ℵ B C D F G K L P Ψ 049 33 104 223 876 1739
   2423
ζωμεν Ath] ζωσιν 𝔓⁴⁶ ℵ B C D F G K L P Ψ 049 33 104 223 876 1739 2423
τω Ath 𝔓⁴⁶ ℵ B C D F G K L P Ψ 049 33 104 876 1739 2423] τω χριστος
   223
ημων Ath] αυτων 𝔓⁴⁶ ℵ B C D F G K L P Ψ 049 33 104 223 876 1739 2423
ανασταντι Ath] εγερθεντι 𝔓⁴⁶ ℵ B C D F G K L P Ψ 049 33 104 223 876
   1739 2423
αποθανοντι Ath 𝔓⁴⁶ ℵ B D F G K L P Ψ 049 33 104 223 876 1739 2423]
   απεθανοντι C

----

2 Cor 5:17

ὥστε εἴ τις ἐν Χριστῷ καινὴ κτίσις, τὰ ἀρχαῖα παρῆλθεν, ἰδοὺ γέγονε
καινά⁴⁷
Or. II c. Ar. 65 [C]

τὰ ἀρχαῖα παρῆλθεν, ἰδοὺ γέγονε τὰ πάντα καινά +
De decretis 19 [C]

τὰ ἀρχαῖα παρῆλθεν, ἰδοὺ γέγονε καινά +
Ep. ad Afros 5.4 [C]

ἐν Χριστῷ Ἰησοῦ καινὴ κτίσις
Or. II c. Ar. 69 [Ad]

----

⁴⁶ Omission per homoioteleuton.
⁴⁷ While Athanasius omits τα παντα in this quotation (and in the quotation from *Ep. ad Afros*)
it cannot be reasonably argued that Athanasius knew two versions; one with and one without. Note
Fee's comment concerning a similar issue in Origen's text that "One surely is not prepared, on the
basis of the shortened form of citation, to argue that Origen is using two different texts, one with
and one without the clause!". Fee, "Text of John in Origen and Cyril," 303. Therefore the collation is
made against the reconstructed version noted as TEXT.

TEXT: ὥστε εἴ τις ἐν Χριστῷ καινὴ κτίσις, τὰ ἀρχαῖα παρῆλθεν, ἰδοὺ γέγονε τὰ πάντα καινά

Lac. A

.1) 1. τα παντα καινα Ath 33 223
2. καινα 𝔓⁴⁶ ℵ B C D* F G 876 1739 2423
3. καινα τα παντα Dᶜ K L P Ψ 049 104

---

2 Cor 5:18
+ τὰ δὲ πάντα ἐκ τοῦ θεοῦ
De decretis 19 [C]

+ τὰ δὲ πάντα ἐκ τοῦ θεοῦ
Ep. ad Afros 5.4 [C]

Lac. A

.1) 1. του θεου Ath 𝔓⁴⁶ ℵ B C K L P Ψ 049 33 104 223 876 2423
2. θεου D F G
3. omit 1739

---

2 Cor 5:19
θεὸς ἦν ἐν Χριστῷ κόσμον ἑαυτῷ καταλλάσσων
Or. III c. Ar. 6 [C]

Lac. A

εαυτω καταλλασσων Ath] καταλλασσων εαυτω 𝔓⁴⁶ ℵ B C D F G K L P Ψ
33 104 223 876 1739 2423; καταλλασσων αυτω 049

---

2 Cor 5:21
τὸν μὴ γνόντα ἁμαρτίαν ὑπὲρ ἡμῶν ἁμαρτίαν ἐποίησεν
Or. II c. Ar. 47 [C]

ἁμαρτία τε ὑπὲρ ἡμῶν γέγονε
Or. II c. Ar. 55 [All]

Lac. A

.1)   1. τον Ath 𝔓⁴⁶ ℵ* B C D F G 33 1739
       2. τον γαρ ℵᶜ K L P Ψ 049 104 223 876 2423

---

2 Cor 6:14

οὐδεμία γὰρ κοινωνία φωτὶ πρὸς σκότος
Vita Ant. 69.5 [Ad]*

καὶ οὐδεμία ἐστὶ κοινωνία φωτὶ πρὸς σκότος
De decretis 35[Ad]

οὐδεμία γὰρ κοινωνία φωτὶ πρὸς σκότος
Apol. c. Ar. 47 [Ad]

Lac. A

φωτι Ath 𝔓⁴⁶ ℵ B C F G K L P Ψ 049 33 104 223 876 1739 2423] φωτος D

---

2 Cor 6:15

οὐδὲ συμφώνησις Χριστοῦ πρὸς Βελίαρ
De decretis 35 [C]

οὐδεμία γὰρ συμφωνία Χριστῷ πρὸς Βελίαρ
Apol. c. Ar. 47 [Ad]

 Lac. A

συμφωνησις Χριστου Ath 𝔓⁴⁶ ℵ B C K L P Ψ 049 223 876 1739 2423] συμ-
    φωνη εις Χριστω F G; συμφωνησις Χριστω D; συμφωνια Χριστου
    33; συμφωνια Χριστω 104
ουδε Ath] τις δε 𝔓⁴⁶ ℵ B C F G K L P Ψ 049 33 104 223 876 1739 2423

---

2 Cor 6:16

ἐνοικήσω ἐν αὐτοῖς καὶ ἐμπεριπατήσω
Tom. ad Ant. 1.2 [C]

ἡμεῖς ναοί ἐσμεν θεοῦ ζῶντος
Or. I c. Ar. 16 [Ad]

Lac. A

2 Cor 7:1

ἀπὸ παντὸς μολυσμοῦ σαρκὸς καὶ πνεύματος, ἐπιτελοῦντες ἁγιωσύνην
ἐν φόβῳ θεοῦ
Ep. Cosm. Indic. XL; 10.7 [C]

Lac. A (33)

πνευματος Ath ℵ B C D F G K L P Ψ 049 33 104 223 876 1739 2423]
        πνευματι 𝔓⁴⁶
αγιωσυνην Ath ℵ B C D F G K L P Ψ 049 33 104 223 876 1739 2423]
        αγιοσυνης 𝔓⁴⁶
φοβῳ Ath ℵ B C D F G K L P Ψ 049 33 104 223 876 1739 2423] αγαπη 𝔓⁴⁶
μολυσμου Ath 𝔓⁴⁶ ℵ B C D F G K L P Ψ 049ᶜ 33 104 223 876 1739 2423]
        μολυμου 049*

2 Cor 8:9

πλούσιος ὢν ἐπτώχευσε δι᾽ ἡμᾶς
De sent. Dion. 10 [Ad]

Lac. A

2 Cor 10:15

οὐκ ἐν ἀλλοτρίοις καμάτοις καυχήσομαι
Apol. c. Ar. 6 [All]

Lac. A C

2 Cor 11:3

ἀπὸ τῆς ἁπλότητος καὶ τῆς ἁγνότητος
Ep. xxxix 71 [C]

ἀπατήσαντα τὴν Εὔαν
Ep. ad ep. Aeg. et Lib. 2.14 [Ad]

Lac. A C (D)[48]

.1)   1. και της αγνοτητος Ath 𝔓[46] ℵ* B G 33 104
      2. omit ℵ[c] K L P Ψ 049 223 876 1739 2423
      3. και της απλοτητος D
      4. και της αγνοτητο F

2 Cor 11:13
μετασχηματιζόμενοι[49]
Vita Ant. 23.3 [C]

Lac. A C

2 Cor 11:14
μετασχηματίσηται εἰς ἄγγελον φωτὸς
Ep. ad ep. Aeg. et Lib. 2.19-20 [C]

κἂν ὡς ἄγγελοι μετασχηματίσωνται δαίμονες
Or. III c. Ar. 49 [All]

Lac. A, C

μετασχηματίσηται Ath] μετασχηματιζεται 𝔓[46] ℵ B D F K L P Ψ 049 33
      104 223 876 1739 2423; μετασχηματιζονται G
εις αγγελον Ath 𝔓[46] ℵ B D[c] F G K L P Ψ 049 33 104 223 876 1739 2423]
      εἰς αγγελους 104; ως αγγελος D*

2 Cor 11:33
ἀπὸ τοῦ τείχους ἐν σαργάνῃ κεχάλασται καὶ ἐξέφυγε τοῦ ζητοῦντος τὰς
χεῖρας
Apol. de fuga 11.5-6 [Ad]*

διὰ σαργάνης ἀπὸ τείχους χαλασθῆναι
Apol. ad Const. 34.2 [Ad][50]

[48] Tischendorf's edition of Codex Claromontanus (D 06) shows partial lacuna here for the first hand, i.e., ἀπὸ τῆς ἀ--ότητος καὶ τῆς ἁγνότητος. Constantinus Tischendorf, ed., *Epistulae Pauli Omnes: Ex Codice Parisiensi Celeberrimo Nomine Claromontani Plerumque Dicto* (Leipzig: F. A. Brockhaus, 1852).
[49] New Testament hapax in form.
[50] Though the event is also recorded in Acts 9:24-25, it is clear that Athanasius here refers to the recounting of the event by Paul himself since he refers to the basket as σαργανης and not σπυριδι which is used in the Acts account.

ἐν σαργάνῃ χαλασθεὶς
Apol. de fuga 18.19 [All]

χαλασθεὶς ἀπὸ τοῦ τείχους
Apol. de fuga 25.13 [All]

_____

Lac. A, C

εν σαργανη Ath 𝔓⁴⁶ ℵ B D K L P Ψ 049 33 104 223 876 1739 2423] omit F
    G

_____

2 Cor 12:2
οἶδα ἄνθρωπον ἐν χριστῷ πρὸ ἐτῶν δεκατεσσάρων εἴτε ἐν σώματι,
οὐκ οἶδα, εἴτε ἐκτὸς τοῦ σώματος, οὐκ οἶδα· ὁ θεὸς οἶδε
Or. III c. Ar. 47 [C]**

οἶδα ἄνθρωπον ἐν χριστῷ
Or. III c. Ar. 47 [C]

οὐκ οἶδα
Or. III c. Ar. 47 [C] x5

ἕως τρίτου οὐρανοῦ
Apol. de fuga 20.36 [C]

εἴτε ἐν σώματι, οὐκ οἶδα, εἴτε ἐκτὸς τοῦ σώματος, οὐκ οἶδα· ὁ θεὸς οἶδεν
Vita Ant. 65.8 [C]

τρίτου οὐρανοῦ
Vita Ant. 65.9 [C]

_____

Lac. A, C (P) inc. εἴτε ἐκτὸς

εν σωματι Ath 𝔓⁴⁶ ℵ B Dᶜ F G K L Ψ 049 33 104 223 876 1739 2423] εν τω
    σωματι D*
του Ath 𝔓⁴⁶ ℵ D F G K L P Ψ 049 33 104 223 876 1739 2423] omit B
ο θεος Ath 𝔓⁴⁶ ℵ B D F G K L P Ψ 049 33 104 223 876 1739 2423] θεος
    1739

_____

2 Cor 12:4
καὶ ἤκουσεν ἄρρητα ῥήματα ἃ μὴ ἐξὸν ἀνθρώπῳ λαλῆσαι
Apol. de fuga 20.37-38 [C]

ἁρπαγέντος εἰς τὸν παράδεισον
De decretis 6 [Ad]

ἡρπάσθη καὶ εἰς τὸν παράδεισον
Apol. de fuga 20.36 [Ad]*

ἀκούσας ἄρρητα ῥήματα
Vita Ant. 65.9 [Ad]

_____

Lac. A, C

αρρητα Ath 𝔓⁴⁶ ℵ B D G K L P Ψ 049 33 104 223 876 1739 2423] αρπητα
        F
μη Ath] ουκ 𝔓⁴⁶ ℵ B D F G K L P Ψ 049 33 104 223 876 1739 2423
λαλησαι Ath 𝔓⁴⁶ ℵ B D G K L P Ψ 049 33 104 223 876 1739 2423] αλλησαι
        F
παραδεισον Ath 𝔓⁴⁶ ℵ B D G K L P Ψ 049 33 104 223 876 1739 2423]
        παραλισον F

_____

2 Cor 12:6
        ὑπὲρ ὃν βλέπει
        Or. III c. Ar. 47 [Ad]
        _____

        Lac. A, C
        _____

2 Cor 12:7
        τὴν ὑπερβολὴν τῶν ἀποκαλύψεων
        Or. III c. Ar. 47 [Ad]*
        _____

        Lac. C
        _____

αποκαλυψεων Ath 𝔓⁴⁶ ℵ A B D K L P Ψ 049 33 104 223 876 1739 2423]
        αποκαλυψ F⁵¹ G

        _____

2 Cor 12:10
        Ὅταν ἀσθενῶ, τότε δυνατός εἰμι
        Vita Ant. 7.8 [C]
        _____

οταν Ath 𝔓⁴⁶ ℵ A B C D K L P Ψ 049 33 104 223 876 1739 2423] οτε F G

_____
⁵¹ αποκλυψ.

δυνατος ειμι Ath 𝔓⁴⁶ ℵ A B C D K L P Ψ 049 33 104 223 876 1739 2423]
δυνατω εγεγωνα F G

2 Cor 13:5

Ἑαυτοὺς ἀνακρίνετε, καὶ ἑαυτοὺς δοκιμάζετε
Vita Ant. 55.6 [Ad]*

Lac. 𝔓⁴⁶ C

εαυτους δοκιμαζετε Ath ℵ B D F G K L P Ψ 049 33 104 223 876 1739
2423] omit A

Gal 1:5

ᾧ ἡ δόξα εἰς τοὺς αἰῶνας τῶν αἰώνων. Ἀμήν
Vita Ant. 94.2 [C]

Lac. C

Gal 1:8

ἄγγελος ἐξ οὐρανοῦ εὐαγγελίσηται ἡμᾶς
Ep. ad ep. Aeg. et Lib. 2.21 [C]

ἀλλὰ καὶ ἐὰν ἡμεῖς ἢ ἄγγελος ἐξ οὐρανοῦ εὐαγγελίσηται ὑμᾶς παρ' ὃ
παρελάβετε, ἀνάθεμα ἔστω
De decretis 5 [C]**

Lac. 𝔓⁴⁶ C

.1)   1. ευαγγελισηται υμᾶς Ath
       2. ευαγγελιζηται F G Ψ
       3. ευαγγελίσηται ℵ*
       4. ευαγγελίσηται ὑμιν ℵᶜ A 104
       5. υμιν ευαγγελιζηται B 1739
       6. ευαγγελιζητε υμας D
       7. ευαγγελιζεται υμιν K P⁵² 049 33 223
       8. ευαγγελιζηται υμιν L 876 2123

---

[52] Swanson's collation is incorrect for P here. He shows the reading as ευαγγελισηται. See also
Constantinus Tischendorf, *Epistulae Pauli et Catholicae*, 5:200.

.2)   1. παρελαβετε⁵³ Ath
2. ευηγγελισαμεθα υμιν ℵ A B Fᶜ K L P Ψ 049 33 104 223 876 2423
3. ευαγγελισαμεθα υμιν D G
4. ευηγγελισαμεν υμιν 1739
5. ευηγγελισαμετα ημιν F*

Gal 1:9
εἴ τις ὑμᾶς εὐαγγελίζεται παρ' ὃ παρελάβετε, ἀνάθεμα ἔστω
De decretis 5 [C]; Apol. c. Ar . 47 [C]

παρ' ὃ παρελάβομεν ἀνάθεμα
Ep. ad ep. Aeg. et Lib. 2.21-22 [Ad]

καθὼς προείρηκα, καὶ πάλιν λέγω
De decretis 5 [Ad]

Lac. 𝔓⁴⁶ C

υμας Ath ℵ A B D F G K L P 049 33 104 223 876 1739 2423] omit Ψ
παρελαβετε Ath ℵ A B D F G K L P 049 33 104 223 876 1739 2423]
        ευηγγελισαμεθα υμιν Ψ

Gal 1:16
μὴ προσαναθέμενον σαρκὶ καὶ αἵματι
Ep. ad Drac. 4.4 [Ad]

Lac. C

Gal 2:6
τῶν δοκούντων εἶναί τι
De Syn. 1 [C]

τοὺς δοκοῦντας εἶναί τι
Ep. ad Jov. 1.4 [Ad]

---

⁵³ Clark notes this reading also in ms 2401. Clark, *Eight American Praxapostoloi*. Also found in 999 and 2464 (-βεται). See Reuben Joseph Swanson, ed., *New Testament Greek Manuscripts: Galatians. Variant Readings Arranged in Horizontal Lines Against Codex Vaticanus* (Wheaton: Tyndale House, 1999).

Gal 3:5

ἐχορήγει τοῖς ἁγίοις ὡς ἴδιον τὸ πνεῦμα
Or. II c. Ar. 48 [All]

———————

Gal 3:11

ἐν νόμῳ οὐδεὶς δικαιοῦται
De Syn. 45 [C]

———————

Lac. P

———————

Gal 3:13

ἐξηγοράσας ἡμᾶς ἐκ τῆς κατάρας
Or. II c. Ar. 47 [C]

τῇ κατάρᾳ τοῦ νόμου
Or. II c. Ar. 14 [Ad]

Χριστὸς γέγονεν ὑπὲρ ἡμῶν κατάρα
Or. II c. Ar. 47 [Ad]

ὑπὲρ ἡμῶν γενόμενον κατάραν
Or. III c. Ar. 33 [Ad]

Χριστὸς ὑπὲρ ἡμῶν γέγονε κατάρα
Ep. ad Epic. 8.7-8 [Ad]

ἐγένετο κατάρα
Or. de Inc. Verb. 25.2 [All]

———————

Lac. P 2423

εξηγορασας ημας Ath] ημας εξηγορασεν 𝔓⁴⁶ ℵ A B C D F G K L P Ψ 049
    33 104 223 876 1739

———————

Gal 3:28

οὔτε ἄρσεν, οὔτε θῆλυ
Or. II c. Ar. 69 [All]

———————

Lac. 2423

Gal 4:1

ὅσῳ διαφέρει δούλων υἱὸς
Or. I c. Ar. 62 [All]

Lac. 2423

Gal 4:4

γενόμενον ἐκ γυναικὸς, γενόμενον ὑπὸ νόμον
Or. III c. Ar. 31 [C]

Lac. (P) 2423

Gal 4:6

τὸ πνεῦμα τοῦ υἱοῦ
Or. II c. Ar. 51 [C]

ἀββᾶ, ὁ πατήρ
Or. II c. Ar. 59 [C]

τὸ πνεῦμα τοῦ υἱοῦ
Or. II c. Ar. 61 [C]

ἐξαπέστειλεν ὁ θεὸς τὸ πνεῦμα τοῦ υἱοῦ αὐτοῦ εἰς τὰς καρδίας ἡμῶν
κρᾶζον· ἀββᾶ ὁ πατήρ
De decretis 31 [C]

εἰς τὰς καρδίας ἑαυτῶν τὸ πνεῦμα τοῦ υἱοῦ αὐτοῦ κρᾶζον, ἀββᾶ, ὁ πατήρ
Or. II c. Ar. 59 [Ad]

Lac. (P) expl. κραζον, 2423

.1)   1. ο θεος Ath 𝔓⁴⁶ ℵ A C D F G K L P Ψ 049 33 104 223 876
       2. omit B 1739

κραζον Ath 𝔓⁴⁶ ℵ A B C D K L P Ψ 049 33 104 223 876 1739] εν ω
       κραξομεν F G
του υιου Ath ℵ A B C D K L P Ψ 049 33 104 223 876 1739] omit 𝔓⁴⁶; του
       υιοι F G

Gal 4:8
> τοῖς φύσει μὴ οὖσι θεοῖς
> Or. II c. Ar. 14 [C]

Lac. 2423

.1)   1. φυσει μη Ath 𝔓⁴⁶ ℵ A B C D* P⁵⁴ 33 104 1739
       2. μη φυσει Dᶜ F G L Ψ 049 223 876
       3. μη K

Gal 4:12
> γίνεσθε ὡς ἐγώ
> Vita Ant. 72.4 [C]

> Γίνεσθε ὡς ἡμεῖς
> Vita Ant. 80.6 [All]

Lac. (P) 2423

Gal 4:18
> ἐζήλωσεν ἐν καλῷ
> Vita Ant. 3.3 [Ad]

Lac. 2423

Gal 4:26
> ἄνω Ἰερουσαλήμ
> Ep. Cosm. Indic. *Τοῦ αὐτοῦ ἐκ τῆς αὐτῆς* 10.13 [C]

Lac. (P)

Gal 5:6
> ἀλλὰ πίστις δι' ἀγάπης (τῆς εἰς τὸν Χριστὸν) ἐνεργουμένη
> Vita Ant. 80.6 [Ad]

---

[54] Swanson shows P as lacunose in this verse but this is incorrect. See Swanson, *New Testament Greek Manuscripts: Galatians*; also Tischendorf, *Apocalypsis et Actus Apostolorum*.

Gal 5:13

    ἐπ᾽ ἐλευθερίᾳ
    Ep. ad ep. Aeg. et Lib. 20.18 [C]

    ελευθερια Ath 𝔓⁴⁶ ℵ A B C D F G K L P Ψ 049 104 223 876 1739 2423]
        ελευθερίας 33

Gal 5:15

    ἵνα μὴ ἀλλήλους δάκνοντες ὑπὸ ἀλλήλων ἀναλωθῶσι
    Or. I c. Ar. 32 [All]*

    Lac. P

    υπ(ο) Ath 𝔓⁴⁶ ℵ A B C D F G K L P Ψ 049 33 104 876 1739 2423] απο 223

Gal 6:2

    ἀλλήλων (μὲν) τὰ βάρη βαστάζωμεν
    Vita Ant. 55.8 [Ad]

Eph 1:3

    εὐλογητὸς ὁ θεὸς καὶ πατὴρ τοῦ κυρίου ἡμῶν Ἰησοῦ Χριστοῦ[55], ὁ εὐλογήσας
    ἡμᾶς ἐν πάσῃ εὐλογίᾳ πνευματικῇ ἐν τοῖς ἐπουρανίοις ἐν Χριστῷ Ἰησοῦ
    +
    Or. II c. Ar. 75 [C]

    Lac. C 049

    .1)   1. εν Χριστω Ιησου Ath Dᶜ K
           2. εν Χριστω 𝔓⁴⁶ ℵ A B D* F G L P Ψ 33 104 1739
           3. Χριστω 223 876 2423

    και πατηρ Ath 𝔓⁴⁶ ℵ A D F G K L P Ψ 33 104 223 876 1739 2423] omit B
    του κυριου Ath 𝔓⁴⁶ ℵᶜ A B D F G K L P Ψ 33 104 223 876 1739 2423] του
        κυριου και σωτηρος ℵ*
    ημας Ath 𝔓⁴⁶ ℵᶜ A B D F G K L P Ψ 33 104 223 876 1739 2423] omit ℵ*

---

[55] εὐλογητὸς ὁ θεὸς καὶ πατὴρ τοῦ κυρίου ἡμῶν Ἰησοῦ Χριστοῦ ommitted in 𝔓⁴⁶ per homoioteleuton as noted by Kenyon. Kenyon, *Pauline Epistles, Text*, 119. Colwell and Tune classify homoioteleuton as an example of a "Dislocated Reading" and claim that such errors cannot be utilised as significant genetic variants. Colwell and Tune, "Method in Classifying," 102.

Eph 1:4

+ καθὼς ἐξελέξατο ἡμᾶς ἐν αὐτῷ πρὸ καταβολῆς κόσμου εἶναι
ἡμᾶς ἁγίους καὶ ἀμώμους κατ᾽ ἐνώπιον αὐτοῦ ἐν ἀγάπῃ +
Or. II c. Ar. 75 [C]

———————

Lac. C 049

εν αυτω Ath 𝔓⁴⁶ ℵ A B D K L P Ψ 33 104 223 876 1739 2423] εαυτω F G
προ Ath 𝔓⁴⁶ ℵ A B D K L P Ψ 33 104 223 876 1739 2423] προς F G

———————

Eph 1:5

+ προορίσας ἡμᾶς εἰς υἱοθεσίαν διὰ Ἰησοῦ Χριστοῦ εἰς ἑαυτόν
Or. II c. Ar. 75 [C]

κατὰ τὴν εὐδοκίαν τοῦ θελήματος αὐτοῦ
Or. III c. Ar. 61 [C]

ἡμᾶς προώρισεν εἰς υἱοθεσίαν
Or. II c. Ar. 76 [Ad]

εὐδοκίᾳ καὶ θελήματι
Or. III c. Ar. 64 [All]

———————

Lac. C 049

δια Ath ℵ A B D F G K L P Ψ 33 104 223 876 1739 2423] omit 𝔓⁴⁶
Ιησου Χριστου Ath 𝔓⁴⁶ ℵ A D F G K L P Ψ 33 104 223 876 1739 2423]
        Χριστου Ιησου B
εαυτον Ath] αυτον 𝔓⁴⁶ ℵ A B D F G K L P Ψ 33 104 223 876 1739 2423

———————

Eph 1:11

ἐκληρώθημεν προορισθέντες
Or. II c. Ar. 76 [C]

———————

Lac. (𝔓⁴⁶) εκληρωθ[ημεν...], C 049 2423

.1)   1. εκληρωθημεν Ath 𝔓⁴⁶ ℵ B K L P Ψ 33 104 223 876 1739
         2. εκληθημεν A D Fᶜ G
         3. εκληθησαμεν F*

———————

Eph 1:13

καὶ ὑμεῖς ἐσφραγίσθητε τῷ πνεύματι τῆς ἐπαγγελίας τῷ ἁγίῳ
Or. I c. Ar. 47 [C]

Lac. C 049 2423

υμεις Ath] υμεις ακουσαντες τον λογον της αληθειας το ευαγγελιον της
    σωτηριας υμων εν ω και πιστευσαντες 𝔓⁴⁶ ℵ A B D K L P Ψ 33
    104 223 876 1739; υμεις ακουσαντες τον λογον της αληθειας το
    ευαγγελιον σωτηριας υμων εν ω πιστευσαντες F G
εσφραγισθητε Ath 𝔓⁴⁶ ℵ A D F G K L P Ψ 33 104 223 876 1739] εσφραγι-
    σθη B

Eph 1:18

τοῖς ὀφθαλμοῖς τῆς καρδίας
Or. I c. Ar. 1 [Ad]

Lac. C 049 2423

Eph 2:2

κατὰ τὸν ἄρχοντα τῆς ἐξουσίας τοῦ ἀέρος, τοῦ νῦν ἐνεργοῦντος ἐν τοῖς
υἱοῖς τῆς ἀπειθείας
Or. de Inc. Verb. 25.5 [C]

κατὰ τὸν ἄρχοντα τῆς ἐξουσίας τοῦ ἀέρος
Vita Ant. 65.7 [C]

Lac. C 049 2423

αερος Ath] αερος του πνευματος 𝔓⁴⁶ ℵ A B D K L P Ψ 33 104 223 876
    1739; αερος τουτου πνευματος F G
τηςˢᵉᶜ Ath 𝔓⁴⁶ ℵ A B D F G K L P Ψ 33 104 876 1739] τοις 223

Eph 2:10

αὐτοῦ γάρ ἐσμεν[56] ποίημα[57], κτισθέντες ἐν Χριστῷ Ἰησοῦ
Or. II c. Ar. 56 [C]

---

[56] These first three words are lacunose in 𝔓⁴⁶.
[57] Mullen's text of Cyril incorrectly reads ποίησα though his note for lacuna in 𝔓⁴⁶ correctly
reads ποίημα. Mullen, *Text of Cyril*, 242.

αὐτοῦ γάρ ἐσμεν ποίημα κτισθέντες
Or. II c. Ar. 66 [C]

ἐπ ἔργοις ἀγαθοῖς
Or. II c. Ar. 66 [Ad]

Lac. (𝔓⁴⁶) [inc. ποίημα] C 2423

αυτου Ath 𝔓⁴⁶ ℵᶜ A B D F G K L P Ψ 049 33 104 223 876 1739] θεου ℵ*
Χριστω Ιησου Ath 𝔓⁴⁶ ℵ A B D K L P Ψ 049 33 104 223 876 1739] κυριω
    F G

Eph 2:14
ὁ μεσότοιχον τοῦ φραγμοῦ
Or. de Inc. Verb. 25.3 [C]

τὸ μεσότοιχον τοῦ φραγμοῦ λύσας, τὴν ἔχθραν ἐν τῇ σαρκὶ αὐτοῦ +
Or. II c. Ar. 55 [C]**

Lac. C 2423

εχθραν Ath 𝔓⁴⁶ ℵ A B D K L P 049 33 104 223 876 1739] εκθραν F G;
    εχραν Ψ

Eph 2:15
+ τὸν νόμον τῶν ἐντολῶν ἐν δόγμασι καταργήσας, ἵνα τοὺς δύο κτίσῃ ἐν
ἑαυτῷ εἰς ἕνα καινὸν ἄνθρωπον, ποιῶν εἰρήνην
Or. II c. Ar. 55 [C]

τὸν νόμον τῶν ἐντολῶν ἐν δόγμασι καταργήσας, ἵνα τοὺς δύο κτίσῃ ἐν
ἑαυτῷ εἰς ἕνα καινὸν ἄνθρωπον
Or. II c. Ar. ⁴⁶ [C]

Lac. C 2423

.1)   1. εαυτω Ath ℵᶜ D G K L Ψ 049 223 876
        2. αυτω 𝔓⁴⁶ ℵ* A B F P 33 104 1739

.2)   1. καινον Ath ℵ A B D L P Ψ 049 33 104 223 876 1739
        2. κοινον 𝔓⁴⁶ F G
        3. και μονον K

εν δογμασι Ath ℵ A B D F G K L P Ψ 049 33 104 223 876 1739] omit 𝔓⁴⁶
καταργησας Ath 𝔓⁴⁶ ℵ A B F G K L P Ψ 049 33 104 223 876 1739]
    καταρτισας D
εἰς ενα Ath 𝔓⁴⁶ ℵ A B D G K L P Ψ 049 33 104 223 876 1739] εινα F

Eph 2:19

καὶ ἀλλοτρίους ποτὲ ὄντας γενέσθαι συμπολίτας τῶν ἁγίων
Ep. Cosm. Indic. *Τοῦ αὐτοῦ ἐκ τῆς αὐτῆς*; 10.13 [All]

Lac. 2423

Eph 2:20

τὸν θεμέλιον τῶν ἀποστόλων
De Syn. 54 [Ad]

Lac. 2423

Eph 3:6

σύσσωμοι[58]
Or. II c. Ar. 61 [Ad]

Eph 3:7

οὗ (καὶ) γέγονε διάκονος
Or. II c. Ar. 54 [Ad]

Eph 3:15

πᾶσα πατριὰ ἐν οὐρανοῖς καὶ ἐπὶ γῆς ὀνομάζεται
Or. I c. Ar. 23 [C]

  .1)   1. ουρανοις Ath 𝔓⁴⁶ ℵ A B C D F G K L Ψ 049 33 223 876 1739
            2423
            2. ουρανω P 104

Eph 3:17

ἐν ἀγάπῃ ἐρριζωμένοι καὶ τεθεμελιωμένοι +
Or. de Inc. Verb. 16.2 [C]

---

[58] Biblical hapax in form and root.

Eph 3:18

+ ἵνα ἐξισχύσητε καταλαβέσθαι σὺν πᾶσι τοῖς ἁγίοις τί τὸ πλάτος καὶ μῆκος καὶ ὕψος καὶ βάθος +
Or. de Inc. Verb. 16.2 [C]

.1)   1. υψος και βαθος Ath 𝔓⁴⁶ B C D F G P 33
       2. βαθος και υψος ℵ A K L Ψ 049 104 223 876 1739 2423

εξισχυσητε Ath 𝔓⁴⁶ ℵ A B C Dᶜ F G K L Ψ 049 33 223 876 1739 2423]
ισχυσητε D*; αισχυσητε P⁵⁹
καταλαβεσθαι Ath ℵ A B C D F G K L P Ψ 33 223 876 1739 2423] κατα-
λαμβανεσθαι 𝔓⁴⁶; καταβαλεσθαι 049

Eph 3:19

+ γνῶναί τε τὴν ὑπερβάλλουσαν τῆς γνώσεως ἀγάπην του Χριστοῦ· ἵνα πληρωθῆτε εἰς πᾶν τὸ πλήρωμα τοῦ θεοῦ
Or. de Inc. Verb. 16.2 [C]

.1)   1. τε⁶⁰ Ath 𝔓⁴⁶ ℵ A B C Dᶜ K L P Ψ 049 33 104 223 876 1739 2423
       2. omit D* F G

.2)   1. πληρωθητε εις Ath ℵ A C D F G K L P Ψ 049 104 223 876 1739
         2423
       2. πληρωθη 𝔓⁴⁶ B 33

της γνωσεως αγαπην Ath 𝔓⁴⁶ ℵ B C D F G K L P Ψ 049 33 104 223 876
    1739 2423] αγαπην της γνωσεως A
του θεου 𝔓⁴⁶ ℵ B C D F G K L P Ψ 049 104 223 876 1739 2423] εις υμας 33

Eph 4:3

τὸν σύνδεσμον τῆς εἰρήνης
Ep. ad Afros 10.1 [Ad]

---

[59] The scribe of P has an unusual abbreviation for the final epsilon at the end of the word here. Instead of forming the uncial epsilon (E) a short line with a final trailing dot is appended onto the base of the preceding tau (T). This abbreviated form for τε is not unusual in P being found in numerous other locations (e.g. 2 Cor 12:20, 13:11; Gal 1:4, 5:15 et al.) but it is unclear why it is used since τε is often found in longhand, including just above the abbreviation noted in Eph 3:18. Tischendorf, *Epistulae Pauli et Catholicae*, 226.

[60] Normally the presence or absence of particles or conjunctions at the beginning of a phrase is not considered, except where the verse is part of a longer quotation, the control witnesses indicate the presence of a variant and Athanasius clearly aligns with a particular reading as in this case.

τηρεῖν τὸν σύνδεσμον τῆς ὁμονοίας καὶ εἰρήνης
De decretis 35 [All]

_____

Lac. 2423

_____

Eph 4:4

ἓν σῶμα καὶ ἓν πνεῦμα
Or. III c. Ar. 22 [C]

_____

Lac. 2423

_____

Eph 4:5

εἷς κύριος, μία πίστις, ἓν βάπτισμα
De Syn. 54 [C]

εἷς κύριος, μία πίστις
Tom. ad Ant. 1.1 [C]

_____

Lac. 2423

_____

Eph 4:6

πάντα δὲ διὰ πάντων
Or. de Inc. Verb. 8.1 [All]

_____

Lac. 2423

_____

Eph 4:9

κατωτέρων μερῶν τῆς γῆς,
Or. I c. Ar. 45 [Ad]*

_____

Lac. 2423

.1)   1. μερη (Ath) ℵ A B C Dᶜ K L P Ψ 049 33 104 223 876 1739
       2. omit 𝔓⁴⁶ D* F G

_____

Eph 4:10
ὁ (γαρ) καταβὰς, αὐτός ἐστι καὶ ὁ ἀναβάς
Or. I c. Ar. 44 [C]

πεπλήρωκεν αὐτὸς συνὼν τῷ ἑαυτοῦ Πατρί
Or. de Inc. Verb. 8.1 [All]

Lac. 2423

Eph 4:13
εἰς ἄνδρα τέλειον
Or. II c. Ar. 74 [All]; Or. III c. Ar. 22 [All]

Lac. 2423

Eph 4:14
ἀνέμῳ παντὶ καὶ κλύδωνι περιφέρεσθαι
Hist. Arian. 78 [All]

Lac. 2423

Eph 4:24
ἐνδύσασθε τὸν καινὸν ἄνθρωπον, τὸν κατὰ θεὸν κτισθέντα ἐν ὁσιότητι
καὶ δικαιοσύνη τῆς ἀληθείας
Or. II c. Ar. 46 [C]

Lac. C

.1)   1. οσιοτητι και δικαιοσυνη Ath ℵ*
        2. δικαιοσυνη και οσιοτητι 𝔓⁴⁶ ℵᶜ A B D F G K L P Ψ 049 33 104
           223 876 1739 2423

.2)   1. της αληθειας Ath 𝔓⁴⁶ ℵ A B K L P Ψ 049 33 104 223 876 1739
           2423
        2. και αληθεια D F G

Eph 4:26

ὁ ἥλιος μὴ ἐπιδυέτω ἐπὶ τῷ παροργισμῷ ὑμῶν
Vita Ant. 55.4 [C]

ἐπιδῦναι τὸν ἥλιον ἐπὶ τῇ λύπῃ
Apol. c. Ar. 21 [All]

———————

Lac. 𝔓⁴⁶ C

.1)   1. τω Ath ℵᶜ D F G K L P Ψ 049 33 104 223 876 1739ᶜ 2423
        2. omit ℵ* A B 1739*

επι Ath ℵ A B F G K L P Ψ 049 33 104 223 876 2423] εν D

———————

Eph 4:30

λυπεῖν ἐν τούτῳ τὸ πνεῦμα
Apol. c. Ar. 34 [All]

———————

Lac. C

———————

Eph 5:1

γίνεσθε οὖν μιμηταὶ τοῦ Θεοῦ, ὡς τέκνα ἀγαπητά+
Or. III c. Ar. 10 [C]

———————

Lac. C

———————

Eph 5:2

+καὶ περιπατεῖτε ἐν ἀγάπῃ, καθὼς καὶ ὁ Χριστὸς ἠγάπησεν ἡμᾶς
Or. III c. Ar. 10 [C]

———————

Lac. C

———————

Eph 5:6

μηδεὶς ὑμῶν ἀπατάσθω
Ep. ad ep. Aeg. et Lib. 8.3 [Ad]

———————

Lac. (𝔓⁴⁶)[expl. μηδεὶς] C

Eph 5:14

ἔγειραι, ὁ καθεύδων, καὶ ἀνάστα ἐκ τῶν νεκρῶν, καὶ ἐπιφαύσει σοι ὁ Χριστός
Or. III c. Ar. 46 [C]

Lac. C

των Ath ℵ A B D F G K L P Ψ 049 33 104 223 876 1739 2423] omit 𝔓⁴⁶
επιφαυσει σοι ο Χριστος Ath 𝔓⁴⁶ ℵ A B F G K L P Ψ 049 33 104 223 876
      1739 2423] επιψαυσεις του Χριστου D

Eph 5:19

ψαλμῶν καὶ ᾠδῶν πνευματικῶν
Ep. Cosm. Indic. *Τοῦ αὐτοῦ ἐκ τῆς αὐτῆς;* 10.13 [Ad]*

Lac. C

.1)   1. πνευματικαις (Ath) ℵ A D F G K L P Ψ 049 33 104 223 876 1739
          2423
       2. omit 𝔓⁴⁶ B

Eph 5:27

μὴ ἔχουσαν σπῖλον ἢ ῥυτίδα, ἤ τι τῶν τοιούτων, ἀλλ᾽ ἵνα ᾖ ἁγία καὶ ἄμωμος
Or. II c. Ar. 67 [C]

Lac. C

η τι Ath 𝔓⁴⁶ ℵᶜ A B D F G K L P Ψ 049 33 104 223 876 1739 2423] omit ℵ*

Eph 6:11

τὰς μεθοδείας τοῦ ἐχθροῦ
Vita Ant. 7.3 [Ad]

τὰς τοῦ ἐχθροῦ μεθοδείας
Vita Ant. 55.13 [Ad]

Lac. C

Eph 6:12

ἐστὶν ἡμῖν ἡ πάλη, (ὡς εἶπεν ὁ Ἀπόστολος), οὐ[61] πρὸς αἷμα καὶ σάρκα, ἀλλὰ πρὸς τὰς ἀρχὰς, καὶ πρὸς τὰς ἐξουσίας, πρὸς τοὺς κοσμοκράτορας τοῦ σκότους τούτου, πρὸς τὰ πνευματικὰ τῆς πονηρίας, ἐν τοῖς ἐπουρανίοις
Vita Ant. 21.3 [C]

οὐ πρὸς αἷμα καὶ σάρκα, ἀλλὰ πρὸς τοὺς ἀντικειμένους δαίμονας
Vita Ant. 51.2 [Ad]

πρὸς ἐκεῖνον γάρ ἐστιν ἡμῖν διὰ τούτων ἡ πάλη
Or. I c. Ar. 10 [All]

τὸν μὲν ἐν τῷ ἀέρι ἐνεργοῦντα διάβολον καθελών
Ep. Cosm. Indic. XXII; 10.4 [All]

Lac. C

.1)   1. σκοτους Ath 𝔓[46] ℵ* A B D* F G 33 1739*
        2. σκοτους του αιωνος ℵ[c] D[c] K L P Ψ 049 104 223 876 1739[c] 2423

αρχας, και προς τας εξουσιας Ath] αρχας, προς τας εξουσιας ℵ A B K L P
        Ψ 049 33 104 223 876 1739 2423; μεθοδιας 𝔓[46]; αρχας, και εξου-
        σιας D; αρχας εξουσιας F G
εν τοις επουρανιοις Ath ℵ A B D F G K L P Ψ 049 33 104 223 876 1739
        2423] omit 𝔓[46]

Eph 6:13

ἀναλάβετε τὴν πανοπλίαν τοῦ θεοῦ, ἵνα δυνηθῆτε ἀντιστῆναι ἐν τῇ ἡμέρᾳ τῇ πονηρᾷ
Vita Ant. 65.8 [C]

Lac. C

αναλαβετε Ath 𝔓[46] ℵ A B D F G K L P Ψ 049 33 104 223 876 1739 2423]
        αναβαλετε D
δυνηθητε Ath ℵ A B D F G K L P Ψ 049 33 104 223 876 1739 2423]
        δυνητε 𝔓[46]

---

[61] Though classified as a Citation, the position of ου constitutes the one clear adaptation of the quote and is therefore not noted as a variant.

ἀντιστῆναι Ath 𝔓⁴⁶ ℵ A B D F G K L P Ψ 049 33 104 223 1739 2423]
        στῆναι 876

Phil 1:17

κἀγὼ τὸν Χριστὸν καταγγέλλω
Ep. ad ep. Aeg. et Lib. 9.5 [Ad]*

Lac. 𝔓⁴⁶ C L⁶² 104

.1)   1. τον χριστον (Ath) ℵᶜ A D K P 049 33 223 876 2423
         2. χριστον ℵ* B F G Ψ 1739

Phil 1:23

ἀναλύσαντές εἰσι σὺν Χριστῷ
Apol. c. Ar. 23 [All]

Phil 1:29

τεθάρρηκα γαρ ὅτι ὑπέρ χριστοῦ πάσχων
Narr. Ath. [All]

Phil 2:5

τοῦτο φρονείσθω ἐν ὑμῖν, ὃ καὶ ἐν Χριστῷ Ἰησοῦ+
Or. I c. Ar. 40 [C]

.1)   1. τουτο Ath ℵ* A B C Ψ 33
         2. τουτο γαρ 𝔓⁴⁶ ℵᶜ D F G K L P 049 104 223 876 1739 2423

.2)   1. φρονεισθω Ath Cᶜ K L P Ψ 049 104 223 876 2423
         2. φρονειτε 𝔓⁴⁶ ℵ A B C* D F G 33 1739

Phil 2:6

+ ὃς ἐν μορφῇ θεοῦ ὑπάρχων, οὐχ ἁρπαγμὸν ἡγήσατο τὸ εἶναι ἴσα θεῷ +
Or. I c. Ar. 40 [C]

Ὅς, ἐν μορφῇ θεοῦ ὑπάρχων, οὐχ ἁρπαγμὸν ἡγήσατο τὸ εἶναι ἴσα
θεῷ +
Or. III c. Ar. 29 [C]

------

⁶² Lacuna via homoioteleuton.

Ὅς ἐν μορφῇ θεοῦ ὑπάρχων, οὐχ ἁρπαγμὸν ἡγήσατο, τὸ εἶναι ἴσα θεῷ +
Or. I c. Ar. 47 [C]

Ὅς ἐν μορφῇ θεοῦ ὑπάρχων
Or. II c. Ar. 53 [C]; Or. III c. Ar. 59 [C]

ἐν μορφῇ θεοῦ ὑπάρχων
Tom. ad Ant. 7.1 [C]

ἐν μορφῇ θεοῦ ὑπάρχων
Or. I c. Ar. 42 [C]; Or. I c. Ar. 50 [C]

ἐν μορφῇ θεοῦ
Or. I c. Ar. 44 [C]

ὃς ἐν μορφῇ θεοῦ ὑπάρχων οὐχ ἁρπαγμὸν ἡγήσατο τὸ εἶναι ἴσα θεῷ
De sent. Dion. 8 [C]

οὐχ ἁρπαγμὸν ἡγήσατο τὸ εἶναι ἴσα θεῷ
De Syn. 49 [C]

ἐν μορφῇ θεοῦ ὄντα
Or. I c. Ar. 43 [Ad]

ὁ ἐν μορφῇ θεοῦ ὑπάρχων
Or. II c. Ar. 14 [Ad]; Or. III c. Ar. 6 [Ad]

ἴσα Θεῷ ὑπάρχων
Or. III c. Ar. 51 [Ad]

ἐν μορφῇ θεοῦ ὢν οὐχ ἁρπαγμὸν ἡγήσατο τὸ εἶναι ἴσα θεῷ +
De sent. Dion. 10 [Ad]

ἴσα θεω
Or. I c. Ar. 41 [All]; Or. I c. Ar. 35 [All]

ἴσά τῷ θεῷ
Or. III c. Ar. 27 [All]

.1)   1. το Ath ℵ A B C D K L P Ψ 049 33 104 223 876 1739 2423
        2. omit 𝔓⁴⁶ F G

αρπαγμον Ath 𝔓⁴⁶ ℵ A B C Dᶜ F G K L P Ψ 049 33104 223 876 1739 2423]
αρπακμον D*

Phil 2:7

+ ἀλλ’ ἑαυτὸν ἐκένωσε μορφὴν δούλου λαβών, ἐν ὁμοιώματι ἀνθρώπων
γενόμενος, καὶ σχήματι εὑρεθεὶς ὡς ἄνθρωπος +
Or. I c. Ar. 40 [C]

+ ἀλλ’ ἑαυτὸν ἐκένωσε, μορφὴν δούλου λαβών, ἐν ὁμοιώματι ἀνθρώπων
γενόμενος, καὶ σχήματι εὑρεθεὶς ὡς ἄνθρωπος +
Or. III c. Ar. 29 [C]

+ ἀλλ’ ἑαυτὸν ἐκένωσε, μορφὴν δούλου λαβών
Or. I c. Ar. 47 [C]

Ἑαυτὸν ἐκένωσε, μορφὴν δούλου λαβών
Or. II c. Ar. 1 [C]

ἀλλ’ ἑαυτὸν ἐκένωσε μορφὴν δούλου λαβών
De sent. Dion. 10 [C]

λαβὼν τὴν τοῦ δούλου μορφὴν
Ep. ad ep. Aeg. et Lib. 17.6 [Ad]

Τὴν μορφὴν ἔλαβε τοῦ δούλου
Or. II c. Ar. 53 [Ad]

λαβὼν δούλου μορφήν
Or. III c. Ar. 30 [Ad]

ἔλαβε δούλου μορφήν
Tom. ad Ant. 7.1 [Ad]

ἔλαβε δούλου μορφὴν
Or. I c. Ar. 50 [Ad]

τὴν τοῦ δούλου μορφὴν ἀνέλαβε
Or. I c. Ar. 38 [All]

εἰλήφει δούλου μορφὴν +
Or. I c. Ar. 42 [All]

καὶ δοῦλον ἀνθ’ ἡμῶν καὶ ὑπὲρ, ἡμῶν γενέσθαι
Or. I c. Ar. 43 [All]

ἔλαβε τὴν τοῦ δούλου μορφὴν
Or. I c. Ar. 41 [All]

δούλου τε μορφὴν ἔλαβεν
Or. I c. Ar. 43 [All]

ἐν τῇ μορφῇ τοῦ δούλου ἦν
Or. II c. Ar. 10 [All]

δούλου μορφὴν ἔλαβεν
Or. II c. Ar. 14 [All]

σχήματι ἄνθρωπον
Or. II c. Ar. 16 [All]

τὴν τοῦ δούλου μορφὴν ἀνέλαβεν
Or. II c. Ar. 50 [All]

τοῦ δούλου μορφὴν λαμβάνων
Or. II c. Ar. 51 [All]

σχήματι εὑρεθεὶς ὡς ἄνθρωπος
Or. II c. Ar. 52 [All]

τῆς δουλείας ἔλαβε μορφήν
Or. III c. Ar. 34 [All]

ἐνεδύσατο δούλου μορφὴν
De Syn. 45 [All]

ανθρωπων Ath ℵ A B C D G K L P Ψ 049 33 104 223 876 1739 2423]
      ανθρωπου 𝔓⁴⁶; ανδρωπων F

Phil 2:8

+ ἐταπείνωσεν ἑαυτὸν, γενόμενος ὑπήκοος μέχρι θανάτου, θανάτου δὲ
σταυροῦ +
Or. I c. Ar. 40 [C]

+ ἐταπείνωσεν ἑαυτὸν, γενόμενος ὑπήκοος μέχρι θανάτου, θανάτου δὲ
σταυροῦ
Or. III c. Ar. 29 [C]

ἐταπείνωσεν ἑαυτὸν
Or. III c. Ar. 30 [C]; Or III c. Ar. 52 [C]

γενόμενος ὑπήκοος μέχρι θανάτου
Or. I c. Ar. 38 [C]

ἐταπείνωσε[63]
Or. I c. Ar. 41 [C]

ἐταπείνωσεν ἑαυτὸν μέχρι θανάτου, θανάτου δὲ σταυροῦ
Or. II c. Ar. 53 [Ad]

ἐταπείνωσεν ἑαυτὸν μέχρι θανάτου +
Or. I c. Ar. 44 [Ad]

ἐταπείνωσεν ἑαυτὸν μέχρι θανάτου
Or. I c. Ar. 44 [Ad]

ταπεινῶσαι ἑαυτὸν
Or. I c. Ar. 43 [All]

ἐταπείνωσεν ἑαυτὸν συγχωρήσας μέχρι θανάτου
Or. I c. Ar. 44 [All]

+ καὶ ταπεινώσας ἦν ἑαυτὸν μέχρι θανάτου
Or. I c. Ar. 42 [All]

.1)   1. μεχρι Ath 𝔓⁴⁶ ℵ A B C K L P Ψ 049 33 104 223 876 1739 2423
           2. αχρι D F G

υπηκοος Ath 𝔓⁴⁶ ℵ A B C D K L P Ψ 049 33 104 223 876 1739 2423]
           υπηκος F G
θανατου δὲ Ath 𝔓⁴⁶ A B C D F G K L P Ψ 049 33 104 223 876 1739 2423]
           θανατου δε του ℵ

Phil 2:9
    ὑπὲρ πᾶν ὄνομα
    Ep. ad ep. Aeg. et Lib, 3.23-24 [C]

    + διὸ καὶ ὁ θεὸς αὐτὸν ὑπερύψωσε, καὶ ἐχαρίσατο αὐτῷ ὄνομα τὸ ὑπὲρ
    πᾶν ὄνομα +
    Or. I c. Ar. 40 [C]

---

[63] Though only one word, the context shows the quotation is clearly from Phil 2:8.

διὸ καὶ ὁ θεὸς αὐτὸν ὑπερύψωσε, καὶ ἐχαρίσατο αὐτῷ ὄνομα τὸ ὑπὲρ πᾶν
ὄνομα +
Or. I c. Ar. 37 [C]

διὸ καὶ ὁ θεὸς αὐτὸν ὑπερύψωσεν
Or. I c. Ar. 43 [C]

Διὸ καὶ ὁ Θεὸς αὐτὸν ὑπερύψωσε
Or. I c. Ar. 44 [C]

ὑπερύψωσε[64]
Or. I c. Ar. 41 [C]; Or. I c. Ar. 43 [C]

ἐχαρίσατο αὐτῷ
Or. I c. Ar. 42 [C]

διὰ τοῦτο ὑπερύψωσε
Or. I c. Ar. 44 [Ad]

+ διὸ καὶ ὁ Θεὸς ὑπερύψωσεν αὐτόν
Or. I c. Ar. 44 [All]

Ὁ Θεὸς αὐτὸν ὑπερύψωσε,
Or. I c. Ar. 45 [All]

ὁ Θεὸς αὐτῷ ἐχαρίσατο·
Or. I c. Ar. 45 [All]

.1)   1. αυτω Ath D F G K L P Ψ 049 104 223 876 2423
       2. αυτω το 𝔓[46] ℵ A B C 33 1739

ονομα Ath 𝔓[46] ℵ A B C D K L P Ψ 049 33 104 223 876 1739 2423] ονομα
εις F G

Phil 2:10
+ ἵνα ἐν τῷ ὀνόματι Ἰησοῦ πᾶν γόνυ κάμψῃ ἐπουρανίων, καὶ ἐπιγείων, καὶ
καταχθονίων +
Or. I c. Ar. 40 [C]

+ ἵνα ἐν τῷ ὀνόματι Ἰησοῦ πᾶν γόνυ κάμψῃ ἐπουρανίων καὶ ἐπιγείων, καὶ
καταχθονίων
Or. I c. Ar. 37 [C]

[64] This is a biblical hapax in form.

ἵνα ἐν τῷ ὀνόματι Ἰησοῦ κάμψῃ πᾶν γόνυ
Or. I c. Ar. 38 [Ad]

πᾶν γόνυ κάμπτει
Or. II c. Ar. 16 [Ad]

ἐν τῷ ὀνόματι τούτῳ τὰ γόνατα κάμπτουσαν αὐτῷ
Or. I c. Ar. 42 [All]

.1)　　1. Ιησου Ath 𝔓⁴⁶ ℵ𝄓 A B C D F G K L P Ψ 049 33 104 223 1739 2423
　　　2. Ιησου Χριστου ℵ* 876

Phil 2:11
+ καὶ πᾶσα γλῶσσα ἐξομολογήσηται, ὅτι κύριος Ἰησοῦς Χριστὸς εἰς δόξαν
θεοῦ πατρός
Or. I c. Ar. 40 [C]

εἰς δόξαν Θεοῦ Πατρός
Or. I c. Ar. 42 [C]

.1)　　1. εξομολογησηται Ath 𝔓⁴⁶ ℵ B Fᶜ 223 1739 2423
　　　2. εξομολογησεται A C D F* G K L P Ψ 049 33 104⁶⁵ 876

κυριος Ιησους Χριστος Ath 𝔓⁴⁶ ℵ A B C D L P Ψ 049 33 104 223 876
2423] κυριος Ιησους F G; εις κυριος Ιησους Χριστος 1739; Χριστος
κυριος Κ

Phil 3:13
τῶν ὄπισθεν ἐπιλανθανόμενος, τοῖς δὲ ἔμπροσθεν ἐπεκτεινόμενος
Vita Ant. 7.11 [C]

ἐπεκτείνεσθαι
Or. III c. Ar. 52 [Ad]

τοῖς ἔμπροσθεν ἐπεκτεινόμενοι, τῶν δὲ ὄπισθεν ἐπιλανθανόμενοι
Or. III c. Ar. 49 [All]

Lac. C 049

.1)　　1. τοις δε Ath 𝔓⁴⁶ ℵ A B K L P Ψ 33 104 223 876 1739 2423
　　　2. εις δε τα D F G

---

⁶⁵ NA²⁷ incorrectly lists 104 as reading εξομολογησηται.

τῶν ὀπισθεν Ath] τα μεν οπισω 𝔓⁴⁶ ℵ A B D F G L P Ψ 33 104 223 876
 1739 2423;τα μεν ουν οπισω K
επεκτεινομενος Ath 𝔓⁴⁶ ℵ A B D K L P Ψ 33 104 223 876 1739 2423]
 απεκτεινομενος F G

Phil 3:14
 κατὰ σκοπὸν διώκω, εἰς τὸ βραβεῖον τῆς ἄνω κλήσεως Ἰησοῦ Χριστοῦ
 Or. c. gentes 5.24-25 [C]

 εἰς τὸ βραβεῖον τῆς ἄνω κλήσεως
 Ep. Cosm. Indic. XXVIII; 10.5 [C]

 κατὰ σκοπὸν διώκων εἰς τὸ βραβεῖον τῆς ἄνω κλήσεως
 Ep. Cosm. Indic. XLIII; 10.11 [C]

 κατὰ σκοπὸν ἐδίωκον εἰς τὸ βραβεῖον τῆς ἄνω κλήσεως
 Ep. ad Drac. 8.1 [C]

 ἡ κλῆσις ἄνωθέν ἐστι
 Ep. Cosm. Indic. XLIII; 10.9 [All]

Lac. C 049

 .1) 1. εις Ath 𝔓⁴⁶ ℵ A B Ψ 33 1739
   2. επι D F G K L P 104 223 876 2423

Ιησου Χριστου Ath] του θεου εν Χριστου Ιησου ℵ A B Dᶜ K L P Ψ 33 104
 223 876 1739 2423; θεου 𝔓⁴⁶; του θεου εν κυριω Ιησου Χριστου D*;
 εν κυριω Ιησου Χριστου F G

Phil 3:20
 τὸ πολίτευμα ἡμῶν ἐν οὐρανοῖς
 Ep. Cosm. Indic. XLIII; 10.9 [Ad]

Lac. C

Phil 3:21
 τὸ ταπεινὸν ἡμῶν σῶμα
 Or. I c. Ar 43 [All]

Lac. C

———————

Phil 4:1

χαρὰν καὶ στέφανον
Ep. ad Drac. 4.4 [Ad]

———————

Lac. C

———————

Phil 4:8

ταῦτα λογίζεσθε
Vita Ant. 91.5 [C]

———————

Lac. C

———————

Phil 4:22

Καίσαρος οἰκίας
Hist. Arian. 52 [C]

———————

Lac. C

———————

Col 1:5

ἐλπὶς ἐν οὐρανοῖς ἀπόκειται
Vita Ant. 2.2 [All]

———————

Col 1:12

εὐχαριστοῦντες τῷ θεῷ καὶ πατρὶ τῷ ἱκανώσαντι ἡμᾶς εἰς τὴν μερίδα τοῦ
κλήρου τῶν ἁγίων ἐν τῷ φωτί +
De decretis 17 [C]

———————

Lac. (𝔓⁴⁶)

.1)   1. τω θεω και πατρι Ath Cᶜ 104 223 1739ᶜ
        2. αμα τω πατρι 𝔓⁴⁶ B
        3. τω θεω πατρι ℵ
        4. τω πατρι A C* D K L P Ψ 049 33 876 1739* 2423
        5. θεω τω πατρι F G

.2)   1. ικανωσαντι Ath 𝔓⁴⁶ ℵ A C Dᶜ K L P Ψ 049 104 223 876 1739
          2423
        2. καλεσαντι D* F G 33
        3. καλεσαντι και ικανωσαντι B

εν Ath ℵ A B D F G K L P Ψ 049 33 104 223 876 1739 2423] omit C

_____

Col 1:13

+ ὃς ἐρρύσατο ἡμᾶς ἐκ τῆς ἐξουσίας τοῦ σκότους καὶ μετέστησεν εἰς τὴν
βασιλείαν τοῦ υἱοῦ τῆς ἀγάπης αὐτοῦ +
De decretis 17 [C]

_____

Lac. (𝔓⁴⁶)

ερρυσατο Ath ℵ A B C D F K L P Ψ 049 33 104 223 876 1739 2423]
        ευρυσατο G

_____

Col 1:14

+ ἐν ᾧ ἔχομεν τὴν ἀπολύτρωσιν, τὴν ἄφεσιν τῶν ἁμαρτιῶν +
De decretis 17 [C]

λύτρωσις ἀπὸ τῶν ἁμαρτιῶν
Or. I c. Ar. 49 [All]

_____

Lac. 𝔓⁴⁶

.1)   1. την αφεσιν Ath ℵ A B C F G K L P Ψ 049 33 104 1739
        2. omit D
        3. δια του αιματος αυτου την αφεσιν 223 876 2423

εχομεν Ath ℵ A C D F G K L P Ψ 049 33 104 223 876 2423] εσχομεν B

_____

Col 1:15

ὅς ἐστι (γὰρ) εἰκὼν τοῦ θεοῦ τοῦ ἀοράτου, πρωτότοκος πάσης κτίσεως +
Or. c. gentes 41.27-30 [C]

ὅς ἐστιν εἰκὼν τοῦ θεοῦ τοῦ ἀοράτου, πρωτότοκος πάσης κτίσεως +
Or. II c. Ar. 45 [C]**

ὅς ἐστιν εἰκὼν τοῦ θεοῦ τοῦ ἀοράτου
Or. III c. Ar. 59 [C]

+ ὅς ἐστιν εἰκὼν τοῦ θεοῦ τοῦ ἀοράτου, πρωτότοκος πάσης κτίσεως +
De decretis 17 [C]

ὅς ἐστιν εἰκὼν τοῦ θεοῦ τοῦ ἀοράτου
De Syn. 29 [C]

πρωτότοκος πάσης τῆς κτίσεως
Or. I c. Ar. 39 [Ad]

πρωτότοκός πάσης τῆς κτίσεως
Or. II c. Ar. 63 [Ad]

πρωτότοκός ἐστι πάσης τῆς κτίσεως
Or. II c. Ar. 63 [Ad]

πρωτότοκος δὲ πάσης κτίσεως
Or. II c. Aι. 63 [Ad]

πρωτότοκος τῆς κτίσεως
Or. II c. Ar. 62 [All]; Or. II c. Ar. 75 [All]

πάσης τῆς κτίσεως
Or. II c. Ar. 64 [All]

_____

Lac. 𝔓⁴⁶

ος Ath ℵ A B C D K L P Ψ 049 33 104 223 876 1739 2423] ο F G
πρωτοτοκος Ath ℵ A B C D G K L P Ψ 049 33 104 223 876 1739 2423]
        πρωτοκος F

_____

Col 1:16
+ ὅτι ἐν αὐτῷ ἐκτίσθη τὰ πάντα τά τε ἐν τοῖς οὐρανοῖς καὶ ἐπὶ τῆς γῆς,
τὰ ὁρατὰ καὶ τὰ ἀόρατα, εἴτε θρόνοι, εἴτε κυριότητες, εἴτε ἀρχαὶ, εἴτε
ἐξουσίαι· τὰ πάντα δι' αὐτοῦ καὶ εἰς αὐτὸν ἔκτισται +
Or. II c. Ar. 45 [C]**

ὅτι ἐν αὐτῷ ἐκτίσθη τὰ πάντα
Or. II c. Ar. 62 [C]

πάντα δι' αὐτοῦ⁶⁶
Or. I c. Ar. 39 [C]

_____

⁶⁶ Though this phrase is also found in John 1:3 it is clear from the context that Athanasius has in mind Col 1:16. Brogan does not include this quotation as being derived from the Johannine reference. See Brogan, "Text of the Gospels," 132–134.

δι' αὐτοῦ
Or. II c. Ar. 41 [C]

+ ὅτι ἐν αὐτῷ ἐκτίσθη τὰ πάντα τά τε ἐν τοῖς οὐρανοῖς καὶ τὰ ἐπὶ τῆς
γῆς τὰ ὁρατὰ καὶ τὰ ἀόρατα, εἴτε θρόνοι εἴτε κυριότητες εἴτε ἀρχαὶ εἴτε
ἐξουσίαι, τὰ πάντα δι' αὐτοῦ καὶ εἰς αὐτὸν ἔκτισται +
De decretis 17 [C]

ὅτι ἐν αὐτῷ ἐκτίσθη τὰ πάντα
De sent. Dion. 2 [C]

+ ὅτι δι' αὐτοῦ καὶ ἐν αὐτῷ συνέστηκε τὰ πάντα τά τε ὁρατὰ καὶ τὰ
ἀόρατα
Or. c. gentes 41.27-30 [Ad]

τά τε ὁρατὰ καὶ τὰ ἀόρατα
Or. II c. Ar. 39 [Ad]

ἀρχάς τε καὶ ἐξουσίας, καὶ θρόνους καὶ κυριότητας
Or. III c. Ar 10 [Ad]

θρόνοι καὶ ἐξουσίαι, καὶ κυριότητες
Or. II c. Ar. 27 [Ad]

ἐν αὐτῷ ἐκτίσθη τὰ πάντα
Or. II c. Ar. 31 [Ad]

πάντα γὰρ δι' αὐτοῦ
De Syn. 52 [Ad]

εἴτε ἄγγελος, εἴτε θρόνος, εἴτε κυριότης, καὶ ἐξουσία
Or. II c. Ar. 49 [All]

εἴτε ἄγγελοι, εἴτε ἀρχάγγελοι, εἴτε ἀρχα
Or. II c. Ar. 49 [All]

πάντα δι' αὐτοῦ γέγονε
Or. II c. Ar. 51 [All]

ἐν αὐτῷ τὰ πάντα ἐκτίσθη
Or. II c. Ar. 51 [All]

ἐν αὐτῷ τὰ πάντα ἐκτίσθη
Ep. ad Afros 4.5 [All]

.1) 1. τα παντα τα τε Ath C
     2. τα παντα τα ℵᶜ A Dᶜ L P 049 104 223 876 2423
     3. τα παντα 𝔓⁴⁶ ℵ* B D* F G Ψ 33 1739
     4. παντα τα K

.2) 1. ουρανοις και τα Ath⁶⁷ ℵᶜ A C D F G K L P 049 104 223 876 2423
     2. ουρανοις και 𝔓⁴⁶ ℵ* B Ψ 33 1739

εκτισται Ath 𝔓⁴⁶ ℵ A B C D K L P Ψ 049 33 104 223 876 1739 2423]
    κεκτεισται F G
και τα αορατα Ath 𝔓⁴⁶ ℵ A B C D F G K L P Ψ 049 33 104 223 876 2423]
    και αορατα 1739
εξουσιαι τα Ath ℵ A B C D F G K L P Ψ 049 33 104 223 876 1739 2423]
    εξουσιαι οτι 𝔓⁴⁶

Col 1:17
    + καὶ αὐτός ἐστι πρὸ πάντων
    Or. II c. Ar. 45 [C]

    αὐτός ἐστι πρὸ πάντων
    Or. I c. Ar. 39 [C]

    πρὸ πάντων
    Or. II c. Ar. 49 [C]; Or. II c. Ar. 50 [C]

    ἐν αὐτῷ συνέστηκε
    Or. II c. Ar. 63 [C]

    + καὶ αὐτός ἐστι πρὸ πάντων καὶ τὰ πάντα ἐν αὐτῷ συνέστηκεν
    De decretis 17 [C]

    ἐν αὐτῷ τὰ πάντα συνέστηκεν
    Or. II c. Ar. 71 [Ad]

    ἐν ᾧ συνέστηκε
    Or. III c. Ar. 44 [Ad]

    καὶ ἐν αὐτῷ συνέστηκε
    De Syn. 52 [Ad]

---

[67] Athanasius witnesses to both readings. However since he clearly knew the longer reading it is likely this was contained in his *Vorlage* and the collation is made against that reading.

πάντα δι' αὐτοῦ ἐγένετο, (καὶ) ἐν αὐτῷ συνέστηκεν
Or. II c. Ar. 50 [All]

καὶ ἐν αὐτῷ τὰ πάντα συνέστηκεν
Or. I c. Ar. 12 [All]

τὰ ἄλλα πάντα συνέστηκέ
Or. I c. Ar. 15 [All]

ἐν ᾧ τὰ πάντα
Or. III c. Ar. 1 [All]

.1)   1. τα παντα εν Ath ℵ A B C K L P Ψ 049 33ᶜ 104 223 876 1739 2423
          2. τα παντα 𝔓⁴⁶
          3. παντα F G
          4. παντα εν D 33*

Col 1:18

καὶ αὐτός ἐστιν ἡ κεφαλὴ τῆς ἐκκλησίας
Or. c. gentes 41.30 [C]

αὐτός ἐστιν ἡ κεφαλὴ τοῦ σώματος τῆς ἐκκλησίας, ὅς ἐστιν ἀρχὴ πρωτότοκος ἐκ τῶν νεκρῶν, ἵνα γένηται ἐν πᾶσιν αὐτὸς πρωτεύων
Or. II c. Ar. 65 [C]**

ὅς ἐστιν ἀρχὴ πρωτότοκος ἐκ τῶν νεκρῶν, ἵνα γένηται ἐν πᾶσιν αὐτὸς
πρωτεύων
Or. II c. Ar. 60 [C]

ἐκ τῶν νεκρῶν
Or. II c. Ar. 61 [C]

πρωτότοκος δὲ ἐκ τῶν νεκρῶν
Or. II c. Ar. 63 [Ad]

τὸν ἐκ νεκρῶν δι' ἡμᾶς πρωτότοκον γενόμενον κύριον
Or. I c. Ar. 8 [All]

ἐν πᾶσιν αὐτὸν πρωτεύειν
Or. II c. Ar. 64 [All]

.1)   1. ος Ath ℵ A B C D K L P Ψ 049 33 104 223 876 1739 2423
       2. ο 𝔓⁴⁶ F G

.2)   1. αρχη Ath ℵ A C D F G K L P Ψ 049 223 876 2423
       2. η αρχη 𝔓⁴⁶ B 104 1739
       3. απαρχη 33

.3)   1.πρωτοτοκος εκ Ath ℵᶜ A B C D F G K L P Ψ 049 33 104 223
              876 1739 2423
       2.πρωτοτοκος 𝔓⁴⁶ ℵ*

.4)   1. η κεφαλη Ath 𝔓⁴⁶ ℵ B C D F G K L P Ψ 049 104 223 876 1739
              2423
       2. κεφαλη A 33

Col 2:3

ἐν ᾧ καὶ οἱ θησαυροὶ τῆς γνώσεως πάσης εἰσὶν ἀπόκρυφοι
Ep. ad ep. Aeg. et Lib. 16.15-16 [C]

Lac. F, G

.1)   1. της γνωσεως Ath
       2. της σοφιας και γνωσεως 𝔓⁴⁶ ℵ* B C D* Ψ 33 223 1739 2423
       3. της σοφιας και της γνωσεως ℵᶜ A Dᶜ K L P 049 104 876

και Ath] εισιν παντες 𝔓⁴⁶ ℵ A B C D K L P Ψ 049 33 104 223 876 1739
       2423
πασης εισιν Ath] omit 𝔓⁴⁶ ℵ A B C D K L P Ψ 049 33 104 223 876 1739
       2423

Col 2:4

πιθανολογίας⁶⁸
Or III c. Ar. 1 [All]

Lac. F, G

Col 2:9

τὸ πλήρωμα τῆς θεότητος
Ep. ad ep. Aeg. et Lib. 16.15 [C]

---

⁶⁸ This is a New Testament hapax and so it is most likely this is the verse reference Athanasius is alluding to.

σωματικῶς[69]
Or. III c. Ar. 31 [C]

ἐν αὐτῷ κατοικεῖ πᾶν τὸ πλήρωμα τῆς θεότητος σωματικῶς
De Syn. 38 [C]

πλήρωμα θεότητός
Or III c. Ar. 1 [Ad]

πλήρωμα τῆς τοῦ πρώτου καὶ μόνου θεότητος
Or. III c. Ar. 6 [All]

τὸ πλήρωμα τῆς τοῦ Πατρὸς θεότητός
Or. III c. Ar. 6 [All]

Col 2:15

ἀπεκδυσάμενος τὰς ἀρχὰς καὶ τὰς ἐξουσίας[70]
Or. de Inc. Verb. 45.5 [C]

ἐθριάμβευσεν ἐν τῷ σταυρῷ[71]
Or. de Inc. Verb. 45.5 [Ad]

ἐν αὐτῷ τούτους ἀποδυσάμενος, παρεδειγμάτισεν (ὁ σωτήρ)
Vita Ant. 35.3 [All]

Col 3:1

καθημένου ἐν δεξιᾷ τοῦ πατρός
Or. I c. Ar. 61 [All]

Col 3:11

πάντα καὶ ἐν πᾶσιν ἔσται ὁ Χριστός
Or. II c. Ar. 69 [C]

Lac. 𝔓[46]

---

[69] Although only one word, it is listed here since Athanasius' discussion clearly indicates that it is a citation and it is a New Testament hapax in this form.

[70] Though this quotation and the next one are both taken from one longer quotation in *Or. de Inc. Verb.* 45.5, they are separated here as the first part is clearly a Citation and the second half is more properly an Adaptation.

[71] τω σταυρω is an Adaptation from verse 14.

εσται ο Χριστος Ath] Χριστος 𝔓⁴⁶ ℵ A B C D K L P Ψ 049 33 104 223 876
1739 2423

Col 3:21

μὴ ἀθυμεῖτε, τέκνα
Vita Ant. 34.1 [All]

Lac. P

Col 4:6

τὸν δὲ λόγον εἶχεν ἠρτυμένον τῷ θείῳ ἅλατι
Vita Ant. 73.4 [All]

Lac. P

---

1 Thess 3:11

αὐτὸς δὲ ὁ θεὸς καὶ πατὴρ ἡμῶν, καὶ ὁ κύριος Ἰησοῦς χριστὸς κατευθύναι
τὴν ὁδὸν ἡμῶν πρὸς ὑμᾶς
Or. III c. Ar. 11 [C]

Lac. 𝔓⁴⁶ C P

.1)   1. κυριος Ιησους Χριστος Ath
        2. κυριος ημων Ιησους ℵ A B Ψ 33 1739
        3. κυριος ημων D*
        4. κυριος ημων Ιησους Χριστος Dᶜ F G K L 049 104 223 876 2423

---

1 Thess 4:1

ἀλλ᾽ ἵνα θεῷ καλῶς ἀρέσωμεν
Vita Ant. 34.1 [All]

Lac. 𝔓⁴⁶ C P

---

1 Thess 4:9

θεοδίδακτος γενόμενος ὁ μακάριος
Vita Ant. 66.2 [All]

Lac. 𝔓⁴⁶ C P 049

---

1 Thess 5:17

προσεύχεσθαι ἀδιαλείπτως
Vita Ant. 3.6 [Ad]

Lac. 𝔓⁴⁶ C 049

---

1 Thess 5:18

τοῦτο γὰρ θέλημα θεοῦ ἐν Χριστῷ Ἰησοῦ εἰς ὑμᾶς
Or. III c. Ar. 61 [C]

τὸ θέλημα τοῦ θεοῦ ἐν Χριστῷ Ἰησοῦ ἐστιν
Or. III c. Ar. 65 [Ad]

Lac. 𝔓⁴⁶ C 049

.1)   1. θελημα Ath ℵ B Dᶜ K L P Ψ 33 104 223 876 1739 2423
       2. εστιν θελημα A D* F G

.2)   1. θεου Ath ℵᶜ B D F G K L P Ψ 33 104 223 876 1739 2423
       2. του θεου ℵ* A

εν Χριστω Ιησου εις υμας Ath ℵ B D F G K L P 33 104 223 1739 2423]
    εις υμας εν Χριστω Ιησου A; εν Χριστω Ιησου προς ημας 876; εν
    Χριστω εις υμας Ψ

---

1 Thess 5:24

πιστὸς ὁ καλῶν ὑμᾶς, ὃς καὶ ποιήσει
Or. II c. Ar. 10 [C]

Lac. C 049

ποιησει Ath 𝔓⁴⁶ ℵ A B D G K L P Ψ 33 104 223 876 1739 2423] ποιησαι F

---

2 Thess 2:3

ὁ υἱὸς τῆς ἀνομίας
Hist. Arian. 77 [Ad]

Lac. 𝔓⁴⁶ C 049

---

2 Thess 3:10
Ὁ δὲ ἀργὸς μηδὲ ἐσθιέτω
Vita Ant. 3.6 [Ad]

Lac. 𝔓⁴⁶ C 049

---

2 Thess 3:18
ἡ χάρις τοῦ κυρίου ἡμῶν Ἰησοῦ Χριστοῦ μετὰ πάντων ὑμῶν
Or. III c. Ar. 51 [C]

Lac. 𝔓⁴⁶ C 049

υμων (Ath)⁷² ℵ* B 33 1739] υμων αμην ℵᶜ A D F G K L P Ψ 104 223 876
    2423
ημων Ath ℵ A B D K L P Ψ 33 104 223 876 1739 2423] omit F G

---

1 Tim 1:4
ἐν μύθοις καὶ γενεαλογίαις ἀπεράντοις
Hist. Arian. 66 [C]

Lac. 𝔓⁴⁶ B C 049 2423

εν Ath] omit ℵ A D F G K L P Ψ 33 104 223 876 1739

---

1 Tim 1:7
μὴ γινωσκοντες μήτε ἃ λέγουσι μήτε περὶ τίνων διαβεβαιοῦνται
Or. I c. Ar. 30 [C]

νοοῦσιν ἃ λέγουσιν
Apol. de fuga 2.26 [Ad]

νοοῦντες μήτε πῶς πιστεύουσι μήτε περὶ τίνων διαβεβαιοῦνται
De Syn. 1 [Ad]

---

72 Since it cannot be concluded that Athanasius witnesses to the omission of αμην (the quotation as it is being an argument from silence) this cannot be taken as a significant variant.

μὴ νοῶν αὐτὸς ἃ λέγει, μήτε περὶ τίνων διαβεβαιοῦται
Or. III c. Ar. 2 [All]

μήτε εἰδότα περὶ ὧν λέγει μήτε περὶ ὧν διαβεβαιοῦται
De Syn. 37 [All]

Lac. 𝔓⁴⁶ B C 049, 2423 [inc. τίνων]

γινωσκοντες Ath] νοουντες⁷³ ℵ A D F G K L P Ψ 33 104 223 876
τινων Ath ℵ A D F G K L Ψ 33 104 223 876] τινος P

---

1 Tim 1:8
καλὸς ὁ νόμος, ἐάν τις αὐτῷ νομίμως χρῆται
De Syn. 45 [C]

Lac. 𝔓⁴⁶ B C 049

.1)   1. χρηται Ath ℵ D F G K L Ψ 33 104 223 876 1739 2423
         2. χρησηται A P

αυτω Ath ℵ D F G K L Ψ 33 104 223 876 1739 2423] αυτον P

---

1 Tim 1:17
τῷ δὲ βασιλεῖ τῶν αἰώνων
De Syn. 49 [C]

Lac. 𝔓⁴⁶ B C 049

---

1 Tim 1:19
περὶ τὴν πίστιν ἐναυάγησαν
Ep. ad ep. Aeg. et Lib. 21.10 [C]

ἐναυάγησαν περὶ τὴν πίστιν
Or. III c. Ar. 58 [Ad]

καὶ περὶ τὴν πίστιν ναυαγήσαντες
Or. c. gentes 6.13 [All]

---

⁷³ It appears Athanasius did know νοουντες since he uses it in some of the quotations classified as Adapatations.

Lac. 𝔓⁴⁶ B C 049

εναυαγησαν Ath ℵ D G K L P Ψ 33 104 223 876 1739 2423] εναυγαγησαν
   A; αναγισαν F

1 Tim 1:20
   Ὑμέναιος (δὲ) καὶ Ἀλέξανδρος
   Ep. ad ep. Aeg. et Lib. 21.9 [C]

   Ὑμέναιον (δὲ) καὶ Ἀλεχανδρον
   Or. I c. Ar. 2 [Ad]

   Ὑμέναιον καὶ Ἀλέχανδρον
   Or. I c. Ar. 54 [Ad]

   Lac. 𝔓⁴⁶ B C 049

1 Tim 2:7
   διδάσκαλός (ἐστιν) ἐθνῶν ἐν πίστει καὶ ἀληθείᾳ
   De Syn. 39 [C]

   Lac. 𝔓⁴⁶ B C 049, 2423 [expl. εθνῶν]

   πιστει Ath D F G K L P Ψ 33 104 223 876 1739] γνωσει ℵ; πνευματι A

1 Tim 3:2
   δεῖ τὸν ἐπίσκοπον ἀνεπίληπτον εἶναι
   Hist. Arian. 3 [C]

   εἴ τίς ἐστιν ἀνεπίληπτος
   Apol. ad Const. 28.3 [All]

   Lac. 𝔓⁴⁶ B C 049 2423

   .1)   1. ανεπίληπτον Ath K L P Ψ 104 223 876 1739
           2. ανεπίλημπτον ℵ A D F G 33

1 Tim 3:8

διακόνους ἠθέλησεν εἶναι διλόγους
De decretis 5 [All]

Lac. 𝔓⁴⁶ B C 049 2423

1 Tim 4:1

ἐν ἐσχάτοις καιροῖς ἀποστήσονταί τινες τῆς ὑγιαινούσης πίστεως,
προσέχοντες πνεύμασι πλάνης καὶ διδασκαλίαις δαιμόνων
Ep. ad ep. Aeg. et Lib. 20.11-12 [C]

ἐν ὑστέροις καιροῖς ἀποστήσονταί τινες τῆς ὑγιαινούσης πίστεως,
προσέχοντες πνεύμασι πλάνης καὶ διδασκαλίαις δαιμονων +
Or. I c. Ar. 8 [C]**

ὅτι ἐν ὑστέροις καιροῖς ἀποστήσονταί τινες τῆς ὑγιαινούσης πίστεως
προσέχοντες πνεύμασι πλάνοις καὶ διδασκαλίαις δαιμονίων
De decretis 35 [C]

προσέχειν πνεύμασι πλάνης
Ep. ad ep. Aeg. et Lib. 21.24 [Ad]

οὐκ ἔστι γὰρ τῶν ἀποστόλων αὕτη ἡ διδασκαλία, ἀλλὰ τῶν δαιμόνων
Vita Ant. 82.13 [All]

Lac. 𝔓⁴⁶ B 049 2423

υστεροις Ath ℵ A C D F G K L P Ψ 104 223 876 1739] εσχατοις Ath⁷⁴ 33
υγιαινουσης Ath] omit ℵ A C D F G K L P Ψ 33 104 223 876 1739
 προσεχοντες Ath ℵ A C D F G L P Ψ 33 104 223 876 1739] και
        προσεχοντες Κ
και διδασκαλίαις Ath ℵᶜ A C F G K L Ψ 33 104 223 876 1739] και διδα-
        σκαλιας ℵ* P; διδασκαλιαις D
δαιμονων Ath] δαιμονιων Ath⁷⁵ ℵ A C D F G K L P Ψ 33 104 223 876
        1739

1 Tim 4:4

πᾶν κτίσμα θεοῦ καλὸν, καὶ οὐδὲν ἀπόβλητον μετ᾽ εὐχαριστίας
λαμβανόμενον
Or. II c. Ar. 45 [C]

---

[74] Athanasius knew both forms of this variant and it cannot therefore stand as significant.
[75] Clearly, Athanasius knew both forms here also.

Lac. 𝔓⁴⁶ B 049 2423

θεου Ath ℵ A C D F G K L Ψ 33 104 223 876 1739] omit P

1 Tim 4:8
ἡ δὲ ἐπαγγελία τῆς αἰωνίου ζωῆς
Vita Ant. 16.5 [All]

Lac. 𝔓⁴⁶ B 049 2423

1Tim 4:13
προσέχωμεν, (ὡς εἶπεν ὁ Ἀπόστολος), τῇ ἀναγνώσει
Or. III c Ar. 28 [Ad]

προσέχειν τῇ ἀναγνώσει
De decretis 10 [Ad]

καὶ τοῖς ἀναγνώσμασι προσέχων
Vita Ant. 1.3 [All]

καὶ γὰρ προσεῖχεν οὕτω τῇ ἀναγνώσει
Vita Ant. 3.7 [All]

Lac. 𝔓⁴⁶ B 049 2423

1 Tim 4:14
μὴ ἀμέλει τοῦ ἐν σοὶ χαρίσματος, ὃ ἐδόθη σοι μετὰ ἐπιθέσεως τῶν χειρῶν
τοῦ πρεσβυτερίου
Apol. ad Const. 26.5 [C]

μὴ ἀμέλει τοῦ ἐν σοὶ χαρίσματος
Ep. ad Drac. 4.2 [C]

Lac. 𝔓⁴⁶ B 049 2423

χαρισματος Ath ℵ A C D F G K L Ψ 33 104 223 876 1739] χρισματος P
σοι μετα Ath] σοι δια προφητειας μετα ℵ A C D F G K L P Ψ 33 104 223
    876 1739

πρεσβυτεριου Ath ℵᶜ A C D F G K L P Ψ 33 104 223 876 1739] πρεσβυτε-
ρου ℵ*

---

1 Tim 5:16

Εἴ τίς ἐστι πιστὴ χήρας ἔχουσα
Or. II c. Ar. 6 [All]

Lac. 𝔓⁴⁶ B 049 2423

---

1 Tim 6:4

λογομαχίαις[76]
Ep. ad Jov. 4.1 [Ad]

Lac. 𝔓⁴⁶ B C 049 2423

---

1 Tim 6:5

πορισμὸν ἡγησαμένου τὴν εὐσέβειαν
De Syn. 37 [Ad]

Lac. 𝔓⁴⁶ B C 049 2423

---

1 Tim 6:12

καὶ ἀγωνιζόμενος τοῖς τῆς πίστεως ἄθλοις
Vita Ant. 47.1 [All]

Lac. 𝔓⁴⁶ B C 049 2423

---

1 Tim 6:13

(μᾶλλον) ζωογονεῖ τὰ πάντα
Or. III c. Ar. 1 [Ad]*

Lac. 𝔓⁴⁶ B C 049 2423

.1)   1. ζωογονουντος (Ath) A D F G P Ψ 33 104 1739
        2. ζωοποιουντος ℵ K L 223 876

---

[76] Biblical hapax.

1 Tim 6:15
  ἦν καιροῖς ἰδίοις δείξει[77]
  Or. de Inc. Verb. 10.5 [C]

  Lac. 𝔓[46] B C 049 2423

  δείξει Ath ℵ A F G K L P Ψ 33 104 223 876 1739] δειξαι D

2 Tim 1:8
  συγκακοπάθησον τῷ εὐαγγελίῳ, κατὰ δύναμιν θεοῦ +
  Or. II c. Ar. 75 [C]

  Lac. 𝔓[46] B 049 2423

  .1) 1. συγκακοπάθησον Ath C K Ψ 104 223 876 1739
       2. συνκακοπάθησον ℵ A[78] D F G L P 33

2 Tim 1:9
  + τοῦ σώσαντος ἡμᾶς καὶ καλέσαντος κλήσει ἁγίᾳ· οὐ κατὰ τὰ ἔργα ἡμῶν,
  ἀλλὰ κατὰ οἰκείαν πρόθεσιν καὶ χάριν, τὴν δοθεῖσαν ἡμῖν ἐν Χριστῷ Ἰησοῦ
  πρὸ χρόνων αἰωνίων +
  Or. II c. Ar. 75 [C]

  Lac. 𝔓[46] B 049 2423

  κατα οικειαν Ath] κατα ιδιαν ℵ A C D K L P Ψ 33 104 223 876 1739; καθ
       ιδιαν F G
  αγια Ath ℵ A C D F G K P Ψ 33 104 223 876 1739] τη αγια L
  εν Χριστω Ιησου προ χρονων αιωνιων Ath ℵ[c] A C D F G K L Ψ 33 104
       223 876 1739] προ χρονων αιωνιων εν Χριστω Ιησου P; εν Χριστω
       Ιησου προ χρονων αιωνιαν ℵ*

2 Tim 1:10
  + φανερωθεῖσαν δὲ νῦν διὰ τῆς ἐπιφανείας τοῦ σωτῆρος ἡμῶν Ἰησοῦ
  Χριστοῦ, καταργήσαντος μὲν τὸν θάνατον, φωτίσαντος δὲ τὴν ζωήν
  Or. II c. Ar. 75 [C]

[77] Note also 1 Tim 2:6 and Titus 1:3 where καιροις ιδιοις is also found.
[78] Hansell cites the reading incorrectly for A and D. Hansell, *Novum Testamentum Graece*.

κατήργησε τὸν θάνατον
Or. I c. Ar. 59 [Ad]

καταργῆσαι τὸν θάνατον
Or. II c. Ar. 81 [Ad]

κατηργήσας τὸν θάνατον
Apol. ad Const. 33.1 [Ad]

———————

Lac. 𝔓⁴⁶ B 049 2423

.1)   1. Ιησου Χριστου Ath ℵᶜ C Dᶜ F G K L P Ψ 33 104 223 876 1739
       2. Χριστου Ιησου ℵ* A D*

.2)   1. την ζωην Ath D
       2. ζωην ℵ A C F G K L P Ψ 33 104 223 876 1739

φανερωθεισαν Ath ℵ A C D F G L P Ψ 33 104 223 876 1739] φανερωθε-
   ντος K
σωτηρος Ath ℵ A C D F G K L P 33 104 223 876 1739] κυριος Ψ
καταργησαντος Ath ℵ A C F G K L P Ψ 33 104 223 876 1739] του
   καταργησαντος D

———————

2 Tim 2:13
εἰ ἀπιστήσομεν, ἐκεῖνος πιστὸς μένει· ἀρνήσασθαι γὰρ ἑαυτὸν οὐ
δύναται.
Or. II c. Ar. 10 [C]

———————

Lac. 𝔓⁴⁶ B, (F G)[inc. εκεινος], 049 2423

.1)   1. αρνησασθαι γαρ Ath ℵ* A* C D F G L P 33 104 1739
       2. αρνησασθαι ℵᶜ Aᶜ K Ψ 223 876

απιστησομεν Ath] απιστουμεν ℵ A C D K L P Ψ 33 104 223 876 1739
εκεινος Ath ℵ A C D F G K L P Ψ 33 104 876 1739] κακεινος 223

———————

2 Tim 2:14
λογομαχεῖν ἐπ᾽ οὐδὲν χρήσιμον
Tom. ad Ant. 8.2 [C]

μὴ προσέχειν τοῖς λογομαχοῦσι
Ep. ad Ioan. et Ant. 2 [All]

Lac. 𝔓⁴⁶ B 049 2423

.1)   1. επ ουδεν Ath ℵ* A C P 33
         2. εις ουδεν ℵᶜ D K L Ψ 104 223 876 1739
         3. επ ουδενει γαρ F G⁷⁹

.2)   1. λογομαχειν Ath ℵ* Cᶜ D F G K L P Ψ 33 104 223 876 1739
         2. λογομαχει A C*
         3. λογομαχεις ℵᶜ

2 Tim 2:17
ὡς γάγγραιναν, (ἔχουσαν) νομὴν
Ep. ad ep. Aeg. et Lib. 5.30 [C]

Ὑμέναιος καὶ Φίλητος
De decretis 35 [C]

Lac. 𝔓⁴⁶ B 049 2423

.1)   1. γαγγραινα(ν) Ath ℵ A C K L P Ψ 33 104 223 876 1739
         2. γανγραινα D F G

2 Tim 2:18
λέγοντες τὴν ἀνάστασιν ἤδη γεγονέναι
Or. I c. Ar. 54 [C]

Lac. 𝔓⁴⁶ B 049 2423

.1)   1. την Ath A C D K L P Ψ 104 223 876 1739
         2. omit ℵ F G 33

2 Tim 2:26
τῆς τοῦ διαβόλου παγίδος
Or. III c. Ar. 67 [C]

Lac. 𝔓⁴⁶ B 049 2423

⁷⁹ NA²⁷ incorrectly shows the reading for F & G as επ ουδεν

2 Tim 3:9

καὶ γὰρ καὶ ἡ τούτων ἀσέβεια πᾶσιν ἔκδηλός ἐστιν
Vita Ant. 89.4 [All]

———————

Lac. 𝔓⁴⁶ B 049 2423

———————

2 Tim 3:11

ἐκ πάντων με ἐρρύσατο ὁ κύριος
Or. III c. Ar. 13 [C]

οἵους διωγμοὺς ὑπήνεγκα, καὶ ἐκ πάντων με ἐρρύσατο ὁ κύριος καὶ ῥύσεται
Apol. de fuga 20.32-33 [C]

———————

Lac. 𝔓⁴⁶ B 049 2423

παντων Ath ℵ A C D G K L P Ψ 33 104 223 876 1739] πατων F
κυριος Ath ℵ A C F G K L P Ψ 33 104 223 876 1739] θεος D
και ρυσεται Ath] omit ℵ A C D F G K L P Ψ 33 104 223 876 1739

———————

2 Tim 3:12

ὅσοι μὲν θέλουσιν εὐσεβῶς ζῆν ἐν Χριστῷ, διωχθήσονται +
Ep. ad ep. Aeg. et Lib. 20.13 [Ad]*

ὅσοι θέλουσιν εὐσεβῶς ζῆν ἐν Χριστῷ, διωχθήσονται
Apol. de fuga 21.16 [Ad]

———————

Lac. 𝔓⁴⁶ B 049 2423

.1)   1. ευσεβως ζην Ath C D F G K L Ψ 223 876
        2. ζην ευσεβως ℵ A P 33 104 1739

———————

2 Tim 3:13

+ πονηροὶ δὲ ἄνθρωποι καὶ γόητες προκόψουσιν ἐπὶ τὸ χεῖρον, πλανῶντες καὶ πλανώμενοι
Ep. ad ep. Aeg. et Lib. 20.13-14 [C]

———————

Lac. 𝔓⁴⁶ B 049 2423

γοητες Ath ℵ A C G K L P Ψ 33 104 223 876 1739] γοηται D; γονταις F
προκοψουσιν Ath ℵ A C D K L P Ψ 33 104 223 876 1739] προοιψουσειν
    F G
το χειρον Ath ℵ A C F G K L P Ψ 33 104 223 876] πλειον 1739

2 Tim 3:16
τῆς θεοπνεύστου γραφῆς
Or. III c. Ar. 28 [Ad]; 29 [Ad]

Lac. 𝔓⁴⁶ B 049 2423

2 Tim 4:6
ἐγὼ γὰρ ἤδη σπένδομαι, καὶ ὁ καιρὸς τῆς ἀναλύσεώς μου ἐφέστηκε
Apol. de fuga 18.24-25 [C]

καιρός ἐστι κἀμὲ λοιπὸν ἀναλῦσαι
Vita Ant. 89.3]All]

Lac. 𝔓⁴⁶ B (P) 049 2423

.1)   1. αναλυσεως μου Ath ℵ A C F G P 33 104 1739
       2. εμης αναλυσεως D K L Ψ 223 876

2 Tim 4:7
τὴν πίστιν τετηρήκαμεν
Ep. ad ep. Aeg. et Lib. 23.21 [Ad]

εἰ τὴν πίστιν τετήρηκε
Vita Ant. 33.6 [Ad]

τὸν καλὸν ἀγῶνα ἀγωνισάμενος
Ep. ad Drac. 4.5 [Ad]

Lac. 𝔓⁴⁶ B (P) 049 2423

2 Tim 4:8
ἀλλὰ καὶ πᾶσι τοῖς ἠγαπηκόσι τὴν ἐπιφάνειαν
Ep. ad ep. Aeg. et Lib. 23.24 [C]

Lac. 𝔓⁴⁶ B (P) 049 2423

.1)   1. πασι Ath ℵ A C Dᶜ F G K L P Ψ 33 104 223 876
       2. omit D* 1739

τοις ηγαπηκοσι Ath ℵᶜ A C D F G K L P Ψ 33 104 223 876 1739] omit ℵ*

Titus 1:11
ἐπιστομισθῶσι[80]
Or. I c. Ar. 7 [Ad]

Lac. 𝔓⁴⁶ B 049 2423

Titus 1:12
κρῆτες ἀεὶ ψεῦσται
De Syn. 39 [C]

Lac. 𝔓⁴⁶ B 049 2423

Titus 1:13
ὑγιαίνουσαν[81] τὴν τῆς πίστεως διάνοιαν
Or. I c. Ar. 54 [All]

Lac. 𝔓⁴⁶ B 049 2423

Titus 1:14
ἀποστρεφομένων τὴν ἀλήθειαν
Ep. ad ep. Aeg. et Lib. 20.12 [C]; Or. I c. Ar. 8 [C]; De decretis 35 [C]

Lac. 𝔓⁴⁶ B 049 2423

Titus 1:15
πάντα μὲν γὰρ καθαρὰ τοῖς καθαροῖς, τῶν δὲ ἀκαθάρτων καὶ ἡ συνείδησις
καὶ τὰ πάντα μεμόλυνται
Ep. ad Amun 64 [All]

---

[80] New Testament hapax.
[81] New Testament hapax in form.

Lac. 𝔓⁴⁶ B 049 2423

Titus 2:8

μηδὲν ἔχων λέγειν περὶ ἡμῶν φαῦλον
Vita Ant. 65.8 [C]

Lac. 𝔓⁴⁶ B 049 2423

.1)   1. λεγειν περι ημων Ath ℵ A C D F G P 33 104 876 1739
         2. περι ημων λεγειν K L Ψ 223

Titus 2:14

λυτρώσηται[82]
Or. I c. Ar. 60 [C]

Lac. 𝔓⁴⁶ B 049 2423

λυτρωσηται Ath ℵ A C D F G K L Ψ 33 104 223 876 1739] λυτρωσεται P

Titus 3:4

Ἀγαθὸς γὰρ ὢν καὶ φιλάνθρωπος ὁ Θεός
Or. c. gentes 35.1 [All][83]

Lac. 𝔓⁴⁶ B 049 2423

Titus 3:11

αὐτοκατάκριτός[84]
Or. III c. Ar. 47 [C]

Lac. 𝔓⁴⁶ (A) B 049 2423

---

[82] New Testament hapax.

[83] φιλάνθρωπος is found only twice in the New Testament. Here in Titus 3:4 and also in Acts 28:2. The context makes it clear that Athanasius is alluding to the reference in Titus rather than Acts.

[84] Though only one word, this is a New Testament hapax and so it is likely that Athanasius is referring to this verse.

Heb 1:1

πολυμερῶς καὶ πολυτρόπως πάλαι ὁ θεὸς λαλήσας τοῖς πατράσιν ἐν τοῖς
προφήταις +
Or. I c. Ar. 55 [C]

πολυμερῶς καὶ πολυτρόπως
De decretis 1 [C]

πολυμερῶς καὶ πολυτρόπως πάλαι ὁ θεὸς λαλήσας τοῖς πατράσιν ἐν τοῖς
προφήταις +
De decretis 17 [C]

———————

Lac. C F G 049 223

πατρασιν Ath 𝔓⁴⁶* ℵ A B D K L P Ψ 33 104 876 1739 2423] add ημων 𝔓⁴⁶ᶜ

———————

Heb 1:2

+ ἐπ’ ἐσχάτου τῶν ἡμερῶν τούτων ἐλάλησεν ἡμῖν ἐν υἱῷ
Or. I c. Ar. 55 [C]

ἐπ’ ἐσχάτου τῶν ἡμερῶν
Or. I c. Ar. 55 [C]

+ ἐπ’ ἐσχάτου τῶν ἡμερῶν τούτων ἐλάλησεν ἡμῖν ἐν υἱῷ, ὃν ἔθηκεν
ληρονόμον πάντων· δι’ οὗ καὶ ἐποίησε τοὺς αἰῶνας
De decretis 17 [C]

δι’ οὗ καὶ τοὺς αἰῶνας καὶ τὰ ὅλα πεποίηκε
De Syn. 16 [Ad]

δι’ οὗ ἐποίησε τοὺς αἰῶνας
Or. I c. Ar. 12 [All]

δι’ οὗ καὶ οἱ αἰῶνες
Or. I c. Ar. 13 [All]; Or. II c. Ar. 77 [All]

πάντων ὧν κληρονόμος
Or. III c. Ar. 36 [All]

καὶ διὰ τοῦ ἰδίου υἱοῦ λελάληκεν ἡμῖν
Vita Ant. 81.3 [All]

———————

Lac. C F G 049 223

.1)   1. εποιησε τους αιωνας Ath 𝔓⁴⁶ ℵ A B D* 33 104 1739ᶜ
         2. τους αιωνας εποιησε Dᶜ K L P Ψ 876 1739* 2423

και Ath ℵ A B D K L P Ψ 33 104 1739 2423] omit 𝔓⁴⁶
εσχατου Ath 𝔓⁴⁶ ℵ A B D K L P 33 104 1739 2423] εσχατων Ψ

Heb 1:3

ὃς ὢν ἀπαύγασμα⁸⁵ τῆς δόξης, καὶ χαρακτὴρ τῆς ὑποστάσεως αὐτοῦ
Ep. ad ep. Aeg. et Lib. 13.22-23 [C]

ὃς ὢν ἀπαύγασμα τῆς δόξης καὶ χαρακτὴρ τῆς ὑποστάσεως αὐτοῦ
Or. I c. Ar. 12 [C]; Or. III c. Ar. 65 [C]

δι' ἑαυτοῦ καθαρισμὸν τῶν ἁμαρτιῶν ἡμῶν ποιησάμενος, ἐκάθισεν
ἐν δεξιᾷ τῆς μεγαλωσύνης +
Or. I c. Ar. 55 [C]

ὃς ὢν ἀπαύγασμα
Or. I c. Ar. 24 [C]

ὃς ὢν ἀπαύγασμα τῆς δόξης καὶ χαρακτὴρ τῆς ὑποστάσεως
Or. II c. Ar. 32 [C];

ὃς ὢν ἀπαύγασμα τῆς δόξης
Or. III c. Ar. 59 [C]

ὃς ὢν ἀπαύγασμα τῆς δόξης, καὶ χαρακτὴρ τῆς ὑποστάσεως αὐτοῦ
Ep. ad Afros 4.3 [C]

ἀπαύγασμα⁸⁶
Ep. ad Afros 6.1 [C]

χαρακτὴρ
Or. I c. Ar. 9⁸⁷ [C]; Or. I c. Ar. 20 [C]

---

⁸⁵ A nonsense variant in P reads απαυασμα. See Tischendorf, *Epistulae Pauli et Catholicae*, 281.

⁸⁶ Though only one word it is a biblical hapax

⁸⁷ Though only one word it is a New Testament hapax and while also appearing in the LXX (at Lev. 13:28), the use of ὑποστάσεως, following in context, indicates the reference is from the Hebrews passage.

ὃς ὢν ἀπαύγασμα τῆς δόξης καὶ χαρακτὴρ τῆς ὑποστάσεως αὐτοῦ
De decretis 12 [C]; De sent. Dion. 8 [C]

τὸν δὲ χαρακτῆρα τῆς ὑποστάσεως
Or. II c. Ar. 33 [Ad]

ἀπαύγασμα αὐτοῦ
Or. III c. Ar. 1 [Ad]

ἀπαύγασμα τῆς δόξης, καὶ χαρακτὴρ τῆς τοῦ Πατρὸς ὑποστάσεως
Ep. ad Afros 5.4 [Ad]

εἰκὼν αὐτοῦ τὸ ἀπαύγασμα· καὶ οὔσης ὑποστάσεως, ἔστι ταύτης ὁ χαρακτὴρ
Or. I c. Ar. 20 [All]

ἀπαύγασμα τοῦ Πατρὸς
Or. I c. Ar. 20 [All]

ἀπαύγασμα καὶ χαρακτὴρ
Or. I c. Ar. 49 [All]

καὶ τῶν ἁμαρτιῶν καθαρισμὸς
Or. I c. Ar. 55 [All]

χαρακτῆρα πρὸς τὴν ὑπόστασιν
Ep. ad Afros 6.1 [All]

Lac. C F G 049 223

.1)   1. δι εαυτου Ath 876 1739ᶜ
    2. δι αυτου 𝔓⁴⁶
    3. αυτου ℵ A B P Ψ 33 104
    4. αυτου δι εαυτου Dᶜ K L 1739* 2423
    5. αυτου δι αυτου D*⁸⁸

.2)   1. των αμαρτιων ημων ποιησαμενος Ath ℵᶜ Dᶜ 33
    2. των αμαρτιων ποιησαμενος 𝔓⁴⁶ ℵ* A B D* P 1739
    3. ποιησαμενος των αμαρτιων ημων K L 104 876 2423
    4. ποιησαμενος των αμαρτιων Ψ

---

⁸⁸ NA²⁷ shows an intermediate correction for D as being αυτου alone. I.e. reading #3 with ℵ A B P Ψ 33 81.

.3)   1. δεξια Ath 𝔓⁴⁶ ℵ A B D K L P Ψ 33 104 1739
       2. δεξια του θρονου 876 2423

μεγαλωσυνης Ath] μεγαλωσυνης εν υψηλοις 𝔓⁴⁶ ℵ* A B D K L P Ψ 33
104 1739; μεγαλωσυνης εν τοις υψηλοις 876

Heb 1:4
+ τοσούτῳ κρείττων γενόμενος[89] τῶν ἀγγέλων
Or. I c. Ar. 55 [C]

τοσούτῳ κρείττων γενόμενος τῶν ἀγγέλων, ὅσῳ διαφορώτερον παρ'
αὐτοὺς κεκληρονόμηκεν ὄνομα
Or. I c. Ar. 53 [C]

τοσούτῳ κρείττων γενόμενος τῶν ἀγγέλων
Or. I c. Ar. 54 [C]; Or. I c. Ar. 55 [C] x2; Or. I c. Ar. 59 [C]; Or. II c. Ar. 1 [C];
Or. II c. Ar. 18 [C]; De sent. Dion. 10 [C]; De sent. Dion. 11 [C]

κρείττων γενόμενος τῶν ἀγγέλων
Or. III c. Ar. 1 [C]

γενόμενος κρείττων
Or. I c. Ar. 61 [Ad]

γέγονε τοσούτῳ κρείττων
Or. I c. Ar. 62 [Ad]

γενόμενος κρείττων τῶν ἀγγέλων
Or. I c. Ar. 64 [Ad]

κρείττων γέγονε τῶν ἀγγέλων
Or. I c. Ar. 64 [All]

Lac. C F G 049 223

.1)   1. των Ath ℵ A D K L P Ψ 33 104 876 1739 2423
       2. omit 𝔓⁴⁶ B

οσω Ath 𝔓⁴⁶ ℵ A B D L P Ψ 33 104 876 1739 2423] οσω και K

---

[89] Ψ reads γεναμενος here but this is clearly a scribal error.

Heb 1:5

τίνι γὰρ εἶπέ ποτε τῶν ἀγγέλων· υἱός μου εἶ σύ;
Or. I c. Ar. 57 [C]; Or. I c. Ar. 62 [C]

———

Lac. C F G 049 223

ποτε των αγγελων Ath 𝔓⁴⁶ ℵ A B Dᶜ K L P Ψ 33 104 876 1739 2423] των
αγγελων ποτε D*

———

Heb 1:6

καὶ προσκυνησάτωσαν αὐτῷ πάντες ἄγγελοι θεοῦ
Or. I c. Ar. 40 [C]; Or. I c. Ar. 61 [C]; Or. II c. Ar. 23 [C]

ὅταν εἰσαγάγῃ τὸν πρωτότοκον εἰς τὴν οἰκουμένην, λέγει· καὶ προσκυνησάτωσαν αὐτῷ πάντες ἄγγελοι θεοῦ
Or. II c. Ar. 64 [C]

καὶ προσκυνησάτωσαν (γὰρ) αὐτῷ πάντες ἄγγελοι θεοῦ
De Syn. 49 [C]

ἦν γὰρ πάλιν, καὶ πρὶν γένηται ἄνθρωπος προσκυνούμενος, ὥσπερ εἴπο-
μεν, ὑπό τε τῶν ἀγγέλων
Or. I c. Ar. 42 [All]

———

Lac. (𝔓⁴⁶) C F G 049, (223)[inc. αγγελοι]

οταν Ath] οταν δε παλιν 𝔓⁴⁶ ℵ A B D K L P Ψ 33 104 876 1739 2423
εισαγαγη Ath ℵ A B D K L P Ψ 33 104 876 1739 2423] αγαγη⁹⁰ 𝔓⁴⁶

———

Heb 1:7

καὶ πρὸς μὲν τοὺς ἀγγέλους λέγει· ὁ ποιῶν τοὺς ἀγγέλους αὐτοῦ πνεύματα
καὶ τοὺς λειτουργοὺς αὐτοῦ πυρ φλέγον
Or. I c. Ar. 57 [C]

———

Lac. (𝔓⁴⁶) [expl. μεν... inc. πυρος]⁹¹, C F G 049

---

⁹⁰ This word is almost totally lacunose in 𝔓⁴⁶. Kenyon has conjecturally reconstructed as αγαγ]
η. However a reconstruction on a copy of the photographic plate (fol. 21r.) indicates that there is
enough line length to allow for εισαγαγη. Therefore it is unclear as to why Kenyon would conjecture
αγαγη only. It also means that this variant cannot be considered as genetically significant. See
Kenyon, *Pauline Epistles, Text*, f. 21r.
⁹¹ The text between μεν and πυρος is lacunose in 𝔓⁴⁶, consisting of the last two missing lines

αγγελους Ath ℵ A B K L P Ψ 33 104 223 876 1739 2423] αγγελους αυτου
 D
πνευματα Ath ℵ A B K L P Ψ 33 104 223 876 1739 2423] πνευμα D
πυρ φλεγον Ath] πυρος φλογα ℵ 𝔓⁴⁶ A B D K L P Ψ 33 104 223 876 1739
 2423

Heb 1:8

ὁ θρόνος σου, ὁ Θεὸς, εἰς τὸν αἰῶνα τοῦ αἰῶνος
Or. I c. Ar. 58 [C]

Lac. C F G 049

του αιωνος Ath 𝔓⁴⁶ ℵ A D K L P Ψ 104 223 1739 2423] omit B 33; και εις
 τον αιωνα του αιωνος 876

Heb 1:9

διὰ τοῦτο ἔχρισέ σε ὁ θεὸς, ὁ θεός σου ἔλαιον ἀγαλλιάσεως παρὰ τοὺς
μετόχους σου
Or. I c. Ar. 37 [C]

παρὰ πάντας τοὺς μετόχους αὐτοῦ, ἐλαίῳ ἀγαλλιάσεως
Or. I c. Ar. 47 [All]

Lac. C F G 049

ελαιον Ath 𝔓⁴⁶ ℵ A B Dᶜ K L P Ψ 33 104 223 876 1739 2423] ελεος D*

Heb 1:10

καὶ σὺ κατ' ἀρχὰς, κύριε, τὴν γῆν ἐθεμελίωσας, καὶ ἔργα τῶν χειρῶν σου
εἰσὶν οἱ οὐρανοί +
Or. I c. Ar. 36 [C]

καὶ σὺ κατ' ἀρχὰς, κύριε, τὴν γῆν ἐθεμελίωσας, καὶ ἔργα τῶν χειρῶν σου
εἰσὶν οἱ οὐρανοί +
Or. I c. Ar. 58 [C]

καὶ σὺ κατ' ἀρχὰς, κύριε, τὴν γῆν ἐθεμελίωσας
Or. II c. Ar. 57 [C]

---

of folio 21ʳ.

καὶ σὺ κατ' ἀρχὰς, κύριε, τὴν γῆν ἐθεμελίωσας, καὶ ἔργα τῶν χειρῶν σου εἰσὶν οἱ οὐρανοί
Or. II c. Ar. 71 [C]

θεμελιώσαντα
Or. I c. Ar. 57 [All]

Lac. C F G 049

Heb 1:11

+ αὐτοὶ ἀπολοῦνται, σὺ δὲ διαμένεις· καὶ πάντες ὡς ἱμάτιον παλαιωθήσονται
+
Or. I c. Ar. 36 [C]

+ αὐτοὶ ἀπολοῦνται, σὺ δὲ διαμένεις
Or. I c. Ar. 58 [C]

Lac. C F G 049

Heb 1:12

+ καὶ ὡσεὶ περιβόλαιον ἑλίξεις αὐτούς, καὶ ἀλλαγήσονται· σὺ δὲ ὁ αὐτὸς εἶ, καὶ τὰ ἔτη σου οὐκ ἐκλείψουσιν
Or. I c. Ar. 36 [C]

Lac. C F G 049

.1)   1. ελιξεις Ath 𝔓⁴⁶ A B Dᶜ K L P Ψ 33 104 223 876 1739 2423
        2. αλλαξεις ℵ* D*
        3. ειλιξεις ℵ ᶜ

.2)   1. αυτους και Ath Dᶜ K L P Ψ 33 104 223 876 2423
        2. αυτους ως ιματιον και 𝔓⁴⁶ ℵ A B 1739
        3. αυτους ως ιματιον D*

.3)   1. ο αυτος Ath 𝔓⁴⁶ ℵ A B D K L P Ψ 223 876 1739 2423
        2. αυτος 33 104

συ δε Ath 𝔓⁴⁶ ℵᶜ A B D K L P Ψ 33 104 223 876 1739 2423] συ δε και ℵ*

Heb 1:13
> ἐν δεξιᾷ κάθηται
> Or. I c. Ar. 55 [All]

Lac. C F G 049

Heb 1:14
> λειτουργικὰ πνεύματά εἰσιν εἰς διακονίαν ἀποστελλόμενοι
> Or. III c. Ar. 14 [C]

> λειτουργικὸν πνεῦμα εἰς διακονίαν ἀποστελλόμενος
> Or. I c. Ar. 62 [Ad]

Lac. C F G 049

.1)   1. αποστελλομενοι Ath 104
       2. αποστελλομενα $\mathfrak{P}^{46}$ ℵ A B D K L P Ψ 33 223 876 1739 2423

λειτουργικα πνευματα εισιν Ath] εισιν λειτουργικα πνευματα $\mathfrak{P}^{46}$ ℵ A B
       D K L P^{92} Ψ 33 104 223 876 1739 2423
διακονιαν Ath $\mathfrak{P}^{46}$ ℵ A D K L P Ψ 33 104 223 876 1739 2423] διακονιας B

Heb 2:1
> διὰ τοῦτο δεῖ περισσοτέρως προσέχειν ἡμᾶς τοῖς ἀκουσθεῖσι, μήποτε
> παραρρυῶμεν +
> Or. I c. Ar. 59 [C]

Lac. C F G 049

.1)   1. δει περισσοτερως προσεχειν ημας Ath $\mathfrak{P}^{46}$ A B D
       2. περισσοτερως δει προσεχειν ημας ℵ
       3. δει περισσοτερως ημας προσεχειν K L P 104 223 2423
       4. δει προσεχειν ημας περισσοτερως 33
       5. δει περισσοτερως προσεχειν 876
       6. δει ημας περισσοτερως προσεχειν Ψ
       7. omit 1739

---

[92] The facsimile of Tischendorf for P shows a typographical error. The printed reading indicates ΠΝΑ (written as nomina sacra) followed by ΓΑ when ΠΝΑΤΑ (written as nomina sacra) is clearly intended. Tischendorf, *Epistulae Pauli et Catholicae*, 283.

δια τουτο Ath 𝔓⁴⁶ ℵ A B D K L P Ψ 33 104 223 876 2423] omit 1739
τοις ακουσθεισι μηποτε παραρρυωμεν Ath 𝔓⁴⁶ ℵ A B D K L P Ψ 33 104
     223 876 2423] omit 1739

———————

Heb 2:2

+ εἰ γὰρ ὁ δι' ἀγγέλων λαληθεὶς λόγος ἐγένετο βέβαιος, καὶ πᾶσα παράβα-
σις καὶ παρακοὴ ἔλαβεν ἔνδικον μισθαποδοσίαν +
Or. I c. Ar. 59 [C]

δι' ἀγγέλων ἐλαλήθη
Or. I c. Ar. 59 [Ad]

———————

Lac. C F G 049

.1)   1. ελαβεν ενδικον Ath 𝔓⁴⁶ ℵ A B D K L P 104 223 876 1739 2423
          2. ενδικον ελαβεν Ψ 33

δι αγγελων Ath 𝔓⁴⁶ ℵ A B D K P 33 104 223⁹³ 876 1739 2423] δι αγγελου
     L; omit Ψ

———————

Heb 2:3

+ πῶς ἡμεῖς ἐκφευξόμεθα, τηλικαύτης ἀμελήσαντες σωτηρίας; ἥτις,
ἀρχὴν λαβοῦσα λαλεῖσθαι διὰ τοῦ κυρίου ὑπὸ τῶν ἀκουσάντων, εἰς ἡμᾶς
ἐβεβαιώθη
Or. I c. Ar. 59 [C]

———————

Lac. (𝔓⁴⁶) C F G 049

———————

Heb 2:9

τὸν δὲ βραχύ τι παρ' ἀγγέλους ἠλαττωμένον βλέπομεν Ἰησοῦν, διὰ τὸ
πάθημα τοῦ θανάτου δόξῃ καὶ τιμῇ ἐστεφανωμένον, ὅπως χάριτι θεοῦ
ὑπὲρ παντὸς γεύσηται θανάτου
Or. de Inc. Verb. 10.2 [C]

———————

Lac. F G 049

———————

οπως χαριτι Ath 𝔓⁴⁶ ℵ A B C D K L P Ψ 33 104 223 876 2423] οπως χωρις
     1739*; οπας χαριτι 1739ᶜ

———————

⁹³ The text in Clark's edition is as follows: δι' αΑγελων. Clark, *Eight American Praxapostoloi.*
Most likely this is a typesetting/printing error.

γεύσηται Ath 𝔓⁴⁶ ℵ A B C Dᶜ K L P Ψᵛⁱᵈ 33 104 223 876 1739 2423]
γεύσεται D*

Heb 2:10
ἔπρεπε γὰρ αὐτῷ δι' ὃν τὰ πάντα, καὶ δι' οὗ τὰ πάντα, πολλοὺς υἱοὺς εἰς δόξαν
ἀγαγόντα τὸν ἀρχηγὸν τῆς σωτηρίας αὐτῶν διὰ παθημάτων τελειῶσαι
Or. de Inc. Verb. 10.3 [C]

δι' ὃν τὰ πάντα καὶ δι' οὗ τὰ πάντα
Ep. ad ep. Aeg. et Lib. 15.5-6 [C]

δι' ὃν τὰ πάντα, καὶ δι' οὗ τὰ πάντα
De decretis 35 [C]

Lac. F G 049

αυτων Ath 𝔓⁴⁶ ℵ A B C D K L P Ψ 33 104 223 1739 2423] ημων 876

Heb 2:14
ἐπεὶ οὖν τὰ παιδία κεκοινώνηκεν αἵματος καὶ σαρκός, καὶ αὐτὸς παραπλησίως μετέσχε τῶν αὐτῶν, ἵνα διὰ τοῦ θανάτου καταργήσῃ τὸν τὸ κράτος
ἔχοντα τοῦ θανάτου, τουτέστι τὸν διάβολον +
Or. de Inc. Verb. 10.4 [C]**

καταργήσῃ τὸν τὸ κράτος ἔχοντα τοῦ θανάτου, τουτέστιν τὸν διάβολον
+
Or. de Inc. Verb. 20.6 [C]

ἐπεὶ οὖν τὰ παιδία κεκοινώνηκεν αἵματος καὶ σαρκός, καὶ αὐτὸς παραπλησίως μετέσχε τῶν αὐτῶν, ἵνα διὰ τοῦ θανάτου καταργήσῃ τὸν τὸ
κράτος ἔχοντα τοῦ θανάτου, τουτέστι τὸν διάβολον +
Or. II c. Ar. 8 [C]

ἐπεὶ τὰ παιδία κεκοινώνηκεν αἵματος καὶ σαρκός, καὶ αὐτὸς παραπλησίως
μετέσχε τῶν αὐτῶν, ἵνα διὰ τοῦ θανάτου καταργήσῃ τὸν τὸ κράτος ἔχοντα
τοῦ θανάτου⁹⁴, τὸν διάβολον +
Or. II c. Ar. 55 [C]

παραπλησίως ἡμῖν μετέσχε καὶ αὐτὸς αἵματος καὶ σαρκός
Or. II c. Ar. 9 [All]

---

⁹⁴ Athanasius here omits τουτεστιν – See above. However it is clear he knows the word is
usually present. Here is a case which advises caution concerning how instances of word omissions in
quotations are handled. Such instances provide clues which other cases do not always provide.

θανάτῳ τὸν θάνατον κατήργησε
Or. III c. Ar. 57 [All]

ὅτι τὸν ἡμῶν θάνατον καταργῆσαι θέλων
De decretis 14 [All]

Lac. F G 049

.1)   1. αιματος και σαρκος Ath 𝔓⁴⁶ ℵ A B C D P 33 1739
        2. σαρκος και αιματος K L Ψ 104 223 876 2423

των αυτων Ath 𝔓⁴⁶ ℵ A B C K L P Ψ 33 104 223 876 1739 2423] των
    αυτων παθηματων D
θανατουᵖʳⁱ Ath 𝔓⁴⁶ ℵ A B C K L P Ψ 33104 223 876 1739 2423] θανατου
    θανατον D
μετεσχε Ath 𝔓⁴⁶ ℵ A B C D K L P 33 104 223 876 1739 2423] μετεσχηκεν
    Ψ

Heb 2:15
    + καὶ ἀπαλλάξῃ τούτους, ὅσοι φόβῳ θανάτου διὰ παντὸς τοῦ ζῆν ἔνοχοι
    ἦσαν δουλείας
    Or. de Inc. Verb. 10.4 [C]

    + καὶ ἀπαλλάξῃ τούτους, ὅσοι φόβῳ θανάτου διὰ παντὸς τοῦ ζῆν ἔνοχοι
    ἦσαν δουλείας
    Or. de Inc. Verb. 20.6 [C]

    + καὶ ἀπαλλάξῃ τούτους, ὅσοι φόβῳ θανάτου διαπαντὸς τοῦ ζῆν ἔνοχοι
    ἦσαν δουλείας +
    Or. II c. Ar. 8 [C]

    + καὶ ἀπαλλάξῃ τούτους, ὅσοι φόβῳ θανάτου διὰ παντὸς τοῦ ζῆν ἔνοχοι
    ἦσαν δουλείας
    Or. II c. Ar. 55 [C]

    ἀπαλλάξῃ πάντας ἡμᾶς, ὅσοι φόβῳ θανάτου διὰ παντὸς τοῦ ζῆν ἔνοχοι
    ἦμεν δουλείας
    De decretis 14 [Ad]

Lac. F G 049

απαλλαξη Ath 𝔓⁴⁶ ℵ B C D K L P Ψ 33 104 223 876 1739 2423] αποκα-
ταλλαξη A

_____

Heb 2:16

+ οὐ γὰρ δήπου ἀγγέλων ἐπιλαμβάνεται, ἀλλὰ σπέρματος Ἀβραὰμ ἐπιλαμβάνεται +
Or. II c. Ar. 8 [C]

σπέρματος (γὰρ) Ἀβραὰμ ἐπιλαμβάνεται
Ep. ad Epic. 5.1-2 [C]

_____

Lac. F G 049

αλλα σπερματος Αβρααμ επιλαμβανεται Ath 𝔓⁴⁶ ℵ A B C D K L P Ψ 33
104ᶜ 223 876 1739 2423] omit 104*[95]

_____

Heb 2:17

+ ὅθεν ὤφειλε κατὰ πάντα τοῖς ἀδελφοῖς ὁμοιωθῆναι, ἵνα ἐλεήμων γένηται καὶ πιστὸς ἀρχιερεὺς τὰ πρὸς τὸν θεὸν, εἰς τὸ ἱλάσκεσθαι τὰς ἁμαρτίας
τοῦ λαοῦ +
Or. II c. Ar. 8 [C]

γέγονεν ἐλεήμων καὶ πιστὸς ἀρχιερεὺς
Or. II c. Ar. 8 [All]

ἀρχιερεὺς ὠνομάσθη, καὶ γέγονεν ἐλεήμων καὶ πιστός
Or. II c. Ar. 8 [All]

_____

Lac. F G 049

.1)   1. τας αμαρτιας Ath 𝔓⁴⁶ ℵ B C D K L P 104 223 876 1739 2423
        2. ταις αμαρτιαις A Ψ 33

_____

Heb 2:18

+ ἐν ᾧ γὰρ πέπονθεν αὐτὸς πειρασθείς, δύναται τοῖς πειραζομένοις
βοηθῆσαι +
Or. II c. Ar.8 [C]

_____

Lac. F G 049

_____
[95] Ommission via homoioteleuton. The corrector has inserted the words in the margin.

πεπονθεν αυτος Ath ℵ A B C K L P Ψ 33 104 223 876 1739 2423]
   πεποθεν⁹⁶ αυτος 𝔓⁴⁶; αυτος πεπονθεν D
πειρασθεις Ath 𝔓⁴⁶ ℵᶜ A B C D K L P Ψ 33 104 223 876 1739 2423] omit
   ℵ*

Heb 3:1

+ ὅθεν, ἀδελφοὶ ἅγιοι, κλήσεως ἐπουρανίου μέτοχοι, κατανοήσατε τὸν
ἀπόστολον καὶ ἀρχιερέα τῆς ὁμολογίας ἡμῶν Ἰησοῦν +
Or. II c. Ar. 8 [C]

ὅθεν, ἀδελφοὶ ἅγιοι, κλήσεως ἐπουρανίου μέτοχοι, κατανοήσατε τὸν
ἀπόστολον καὶ ἀρχιερέα τῆς ὁμολογίας ἡμῶν Ἰησοῦν +
Or. II c. Ar. 1 [C]

ὅθεν, ἀδελφοὶ ἅγιοι, κλήσεως ἐπουρανίου μέτοχοι, κατανοήσατε τὸν
ἀπόστολον καὶ ἀρχιερέα τῆς ὁμολογίας ἡμῶν Ἰησοῦν +
Or. II c. Ar. 7 [C]

ὅθεν, ἀδελφοὶ ἅγιοι, κλήσεως ἐπουρανίου μέτοχοι, κατανοήσατε τὸν
ἀπόστολον καὶ ἀρχιερέα τῆς ὁμολογίας ἡμῶν, Ἰησοῦν +
Or. I c. Ar. 53 [C]

ἀπόστολον καὶ +
Or. II c. Ar. 10 [C]

Lac. F G 049

.1)   1. Ιησουν Ath 𝔓⁴⁶ ℵ A B C* D* P 33 1739
      2. Ιησουν χριστον Cᶜ Dᶜ K L Ψ 104 223 876 2423

κατανοησατε Ath 𝔓⁴⁶ ℵ A B C K L P Ψ 33 104 223 876 1739 2423]
   κατανοησετε D

Heb 3:2

+ πιστὸν ὄντα τῷ ποιήσαντι αὐτόν
Or. I c. Ar. 53 [C]

+ πιστὸν ὄντα τῷ ποιήσαντι αὐτόν
Or. II c. Ar. 1 [C]

---

⁹⁶ Kenyon notes this as an error from πενονθεν. However it appears that πενονθεν is itself an error pro πεπονθεν since the perfect reduplicates the stem resulting in πεπ- and not πεν-. Kenyon, *Pauline Epistles, Text*, 24.

+ πιστὸν ὄντα τῷ ποιήσαντι αὐτόν
Or. II c. Ar. 7 [C]

+ πιστὸν ὄντα τῷ ποιήσαντι αὐτόν
Or. II c. Ar. 8 [C]

+ πιστὸν ὄντα τῷ ποιήσαντι αὐτὸν
Or. II c. Ar. 10 [C]

πιστὸν ὄντα τῷ ποιήσαντι αὐτόν
Or. II c. Ar. 1 [C] x2; Or. II c. Ar. 6 [C]; Or. II c. Ar. 7 [C]; Or. II c. Ar. 8 [C];
Or. II c. Ar. 9 [C]; Or. II c. Ar. 11 [C]; Or. III c. Ar. 1 [C]; De sent. Dion. 10
[C]; De sent. Dion. 11 [C]

πιστὸν ὄντα
Or. II c. Ar. 6 [C]

τῷ ποιήσαντι αὐτὸν
Or. II c. Ar. 5 [C]

Lac. F G 049

Heb 3:3
ἐπεὶ ὥρα ὑμᾶς καὶ τοῦ ἀρχιτέκτονος τὴν τιμὴν εἰς τὴν ὑπ᾽ αὐτοῦ γενομένην
οἰκίαν
Vita Ant. 76.4 [All]

Lac. F G 049

Heb 3:5
ὁ μὲν Μωσῆς θεράπων
Or. II c. Ar. 10 [All]

Lac. F G 049

Heb 3:6

ὁ δὲ Χριστὸς Υἱός κἀκεῖνος μὲν πιστὸς εἰς τὸν οἶκον, οὗτος δὲ ἐπὶ τὸν
οἶκον
Or. II c. Ar. 10 [All]

_____

Lac. F G 049

_____

Heb 4:12

ζῶν γὰρ ὁ λόγος τοῦ θεοῦ, καὶ ἐνεργής, καὶ τομώτερος ὑπὲρ πᾶσαν
μάχαιραν δίστομον, καὶ διικνούμενος μέχρι μερισμοῦ ψυχῆς καὶ πνεύματος, ἁρμῶν τε καὶ μυελῶν, καὶ κριτικὸς ἐνθυμήσεων +
Or. II c. Ar. 72 [C]

ζῶν ἐστιν ὁ Λόγος τοῦ Θεοῦ καὶ ἐνεργής, καὶ τομώτερος ὑπὲρ πᾶσαν
μάχαιραν δίστομον, καὶ διικνούμενος ἄχρι μερισμοῦ ψυχῆς καὶ πνεύματος, ἁρμῶν τε καὶ μυελῶν, καὶ κριτικὸς ἐνθυμήσεων καὶ ἐννοιῶν καρδίας
+
Or. II c. Ar. 35 [Ad]

Ὁ μὲν γὰρ τοῦ Θεοῦ Υἱὸς ζῶν καὶ ἐνεργής
Or. de Inc. Verb. 31.3 [All]

_____

Lac. F G 049

.1)   1. ενθυμησεων Ath 𝔓⁴⁶ ℵ A B K L P Ψ 33 104 223 876 1739 2423
         2. ενθυμησεως C D

.2)   1. ψυχης Ath 𝔓⁴⁶ ℵᶜ A B C L P Ψ 33 104 1739
         2. omit ℵ*⁹⁷
         3. ψυχης τε D K 223 876 2423

ενεργης Ath 𝔓⁴⁶ ℵ A C D K L P Ψ 33 104 223 876 1739 2423] εναργης B
διικνουμενος Ath 𝔓⁴⁶ ℵ A B C Dᶜ K L P Ψ 33 104 223 876 1739 2423]
        δεικνυμενος D*
μεχρι Ath] αχρι 𝔓⁴⁶ ℵ A B C K L P Ψ 33 104 223 876 1739 2423; αχρις D
και εννοιων καρδιας Ath 𝔓⁴⁶ ℵ A B C K L P Ψ 33 104 223 876 1739 2423]
        εννοιων τε καρδιας D

_____

⁹⁷ Osburn does not note that ψυχης has been added supralinearly as a correction. See Osburn,
Text of the Apostolos in Epiphanius, 160.

Heb 4:13

+ καὶ οὐκ ἔστι κτίσις ἀφανὴς ἐνώπιον αὐτοῦ, πάντα δὲ γυμνὰ καὶ τετραχηλισμένα τοῖς ὀφθαλμοῖς αὐτοῦ, πρὸς ὃν ἡμῖν ὁ λόγος
Or. II c. Ar. 72 [C]

Πάντα δὲ γυμνὰ καὶ τετραχηλισμένα τοῖς ὀφθαλμοῖς αὐτοῦ, πρὸς ὃν ἡμῖν
ὁ λόγος
Or. II c. Ar. 72 [C]

+ καὶ οὐκ ἔστι κτίσις ἀφανὴς ἐνώπιον αὐτοῦ, πάντα δὲ γυμνὰ καὶ τετραχηλισμένα τοῖς ὀφθαλμοῖς αὐτοῦ, πρὸς ὃν ἡμῖν ὁ λόγος
Or. II c. Ar. 35 [Ad]

Lac. ($\mathfrak{P}^{46}$)[expl. προς ον] F G 049

κτισις Ath ℵ A B C Dᶜ K L P Ψ 33 104 223 876 1739 2423] κρισις D*

Heb 6:12

τὰς ἐπαγγελίας κληρονομῆσαι
Ep. ad ep. Aeg. et Lib. 23.23 [Ad]

Lac. F G 049

Heb 6:18

ἀδύνατόν ἐστιν, αὐτὸν ψεύσασθαι
Or. II c. Ar. 6 [All]

Lac. F G 049

Heb 6:19

ἄγκυραν τῆς πίστεως
Or. III c. Ar. 58 [All]

Lac. F G 049

Heb 6:20

(ἔνθα) πρόδρομος ὑπὲρ ἡμῶν εἰσῆλθεν Ἰησοῦς
Or. I c. Ar. 41 [C]

πρόδρομος ὑπὲρ ἡμῶν εἰσῆλθεν Ἰησοῦς
Ep. Cosm. Indic. XLV; 10.12 [C]

(ὁ αὐτὸς) πρόδρομος ὑπὲρ ἡμῶν εἰσελθὼν
Ep. Cosm. Indic. XLIII; 10.10 [Ad]

_____

Lac. F G 049

_____

Heb 7:10

(Λευὶς) ἔτι ἦν ἐν τῇ ὀσφύι
Or. I c. Ar. 26 [Ad]

_____

Lac. F G 049

_____

Heb 7:19

οὐδὲν γὰρ ἐτελείωσεν ὁ νόμος, ἐπεισαγωγὴ δὲ κρείττονος
ἐλπίδος
Or. I c. Ar. 59 [C]

οὐδένα τετελείωκε
Or. I c. Ar. 59 [All]

ὁ νόμος οὐδένα τετελείωκε
De Syn. 45 [All]

_____

Lac. F G 049

.1)   1. επεισαγωγη Ath 𝔓⁴⁶ ℵ A B C Dᶜ K L P Ψᵛⁱᵈ 33 104 223 876
            1739ᶜ 2423
        2. επεισαγωγης D* 1739*

ουδεν Ath ℵ A B C D K L P Ψ 33 104 223 876 1739 2423] ου 𝔓⁴⁶

_____

Heb 7:22

κατὰ τοσοῦτον κρείττονος διαθήκης γέγονεν ἔγγυος
Or. I c. Ar. 59 [C]

γέγονεν ἔγγυος
Or. I c. Ar. 60 [C]

τοσούτῳ κρείττων γέγονεν ἔγγυος ὁ Ἰησοῦς
Or. I c. Ar. 64 [Ad]

Lac. F G 049

.1)   1. τοσουτον Ath ℵ^c D^c K L Ψ 104 223 876 1739 2423
        2. τοσουτο 𝔓⁴⁶ ℵ* A B C D* P 33

.2)   1. κρειττονος Ath 𝔓⁴⁶ ℵ^c A C^c D K L P Ψ 104 223 876 1739 2423
        2. και κρειττονος ℵ* B C* 33

.3)   1. ο Ιησους Ath L P
        2. Ιησους 𝔓⁴⁶ ℵ A B C D K Ψ 33 104 223 876 1739 2423

Heb 7:24
        ἀπαράβατον[98]
        Or. II c. Ar. 9 [C]

Lac. F G 049

Heb 8:6
        νυνι διαφορωτέρας τετύχηκε λειτουργίας, ὅσῳ καὶ κρείττονός ἐστι
        διαθήκης μεσίτης, ἥτις ἐπὶ κρείττοσιν ἐπαγγελίαις νενομοθέτηται
        Or. I c. Ar. 59 [C]

Lac. C F G 049

.1)   1. νυνι Ath 𝔓⁴⁶ᶜ ℵ A D^c K L P Ψ 33 104 104 223 876 1739 2423
        2. νυν 𝔓⁴⁶* [99] B D*

.2)   1. τετυχηκε Ath P Ψ 33 104 223 876 1739
        2. τετυχεν 𝔓⁴⁶ ℵ* A D* K L
        3. τετευχεν ℵ^c B D^c 2423

.3)   1. εστι διαθηκης Ath ℵ* A B D L Ψ 33 104 223 876 1739 2423
        2. διαθηκης εστιν 𝔓⁴⁶ ℵ^c K P

---

[98] Biblical hapax in form and root.
[99] The first hand of 𝔓⁴⁶ wrote νυν with a (corrected) ι added superlinearly.

.4)   1. και Ath 𝔓⁴⁶ ℵ A B Dᶜ L P Ψ 33 104 223 876 1739 2423
           2. omit D* K

διαφορωτερας Ath 𝔓⁴⁶ ℵ A B D K L P Ψ 33 104 223 876 1739 2423] σοι
διαφορωτερας D
κρειττονος Ath 𝔓⁴⁶ A B D K L P Ψ 33 104 223 876 1739 2423] κρειττονο-
σιν ℵ*; κρειττονο ℵᶜ ¹⁰⁰

Heb 9:12[101]

αἰωνίαν λύτρωσιν εὑράμενος
Ep. Cosm. Indic. XLV; 10.12 [C]

Lac. C F G Ψ 049

ευραμενος Ath 𝔓⁴⁶ ℵ A B Dᶜ K L P 33 104 223 876 1739 2423*] ευρομενος
D* 2423ᶜ

Heb 9:23

ἀνάγκη οὖν τὰ μὲν ὑποδείγματα τῶν ἐν τοῖς οὐρανοῖς τούτοις καθαρίζε-
σθαι· αὐτὰ δὲ τὰ ἐπουράνια κρείττοσι θυσίαις παρὰ ταύτας
Or. I c. Ar. 59 [C]

Lac. B F G 049

.1)   1. καθαριζεσθαι Ath 𝔓⁴⁶ ℵ A C K L P Ψ 33 104 223 876 2423
           2. καθαριζεται D 1739

δε Ath 𝔓⁴⁶ ℵ A C D K L P Ψ 104 223 876 1739 2423] τε 33
ταυτας Ath ℵ A C Dᶜ K L P Ψ 33 104 223 876 1739 2423] ταυταις 𝔓⁴⁶;
           ταυτης D*

Heb 9:24

(εἰς) ἀντίτυπα τῶν ἀληθινῶν, ἀλλ’ εἰς αὐτὸν τὸν οὐρανὸν νῦν ἐμφα-
νισθῆναι τῷ προσώπῳ τοῦ θεοῦ ὑπὲρ ἡμῶν
Or. I c. Ar. 41 [C]

---

[100] A clear case of homoioteleuton here in ℵ with the correction inserted in the margin below
the text column.
[101] Winstedt incorrectly specifies the reference as Heb viii.12. Winstedt, *The Christian
Topography of Cosmas Indicopleustes*, 298.

Lac. B F G 049

.1)   1. εμφανισθηναι Ath 𝔓⁴⁶ ℵ C Dᶜ K L P Ψ 33 104 223 876 1739 2423
            2. ενφανισθηναι A¹⁰² D*

πϱοσωπω Ath 𝔓⁴⁶ᶜ ℵ A C D K L P Ψ 33 104 223 876 1739 2423] πϱοσωπου
𝔓⁴⁶* ¹⁰³

Heb 9:26

ἐπὶ συντελείᾳ τῶν αἰώνων
Or. I c. Ar. 25 [C]; Or. I c. Ar. 29 [C]; Or. II c. Ar. 68 [C]

ἅπαξ ἐπὶ συντελείᾳ τῶν αἰώνων
Or. III c. Ar. 30 [C]

ἐπὶ συντελείᾳ τῶν αἰώνων
Tom. ad Ant. 7.1 [C]

ἐπὶ δὲ συντελείᾳ τῶν αἰώνων
Or. III c. Ar. 29 [Ad]

ἐπὶ δὲ συντελείᾳ τῶν αἰώνων
Apol. de fuga 11.15 [Ad]

Lac. (𝔓⁴⁶)[inc. αἰώνων], B F G 049

Heb 9:27

ἀπόκειται τοῖς ἀνθρώποις ἅπαξ ἀποθανεῖν
Ep. ad Ser. 4 [C]

Lac. B F G 049

Heb 10:1

τῶν μελλόντων ἀγαθῶν
Vita Ant. 14.7 [C]

(πεϱὶ) τῶν μελλόντων ἀγαθῶν
Vita Ant. 42.7 [C]

---

¹⁰² Hansell incorrectly transcribes A as here reading εμφανισθηναι. However the facsimile of the ms clearly shows otherwise with no correction. Tischendorf notes the reading correctly. See Hansell, *Novum Testamentum Graece*; also Tischendorf, *Novum Testamentum Graece*.
¹⁰³ In 𝔓⁴⁶ the first hand wrote πϱοσωπου with a (second hand) corrector adding ω superlinearly over ου.

Lac. B F G 049

Heb 10:5

σῶμά μοι κατηρτίσατο
Or. II c. Ar 47 [All]

καταρτίσας (, ὡς γέγραπται,) σῶμα
Or. II c. Ar 47 [All]

Lac. B F G 049

Heb 10:14

τετελείωκε[104]
Or. II c. Ar 9 [C]

Lac. B F G 049

Heb 10:20

διὰ τοῦ καταπετάσματος, τοῦτ᾽ ἔστιν τῆς σαρκὸς αὐτοῦ
Or. de Inc. Verb. 25.5 [C]

ἡμῖν ὁδὸν πρόσφατον καὶ ζῶσαν
Or. II c. Ar. 65 [C]

διὰ τοῦ καταπετάσματος, τουτέστι διὰ τῆς σαρκὸς αὐτοῦ
Or. II c. Ar. 65 [C]**

ἡμῖν τὴν[105] ὁδὸν πρόσφατον
Ep. Cosm. Indic. Τοῦ αὐτοῦ ἐκ τῆς αὐτῆς; 10.13 [C]

Lac. (𝔓[46]) B F G 049 876[106]

---

[104] Biblical hapax in form.

[105] Since Athanasius witnesses to both the presence and absence of the article, this variant shall not be considered.

[106] Clark notes that 876 has 10:16-11:7 "on two 16th century (?) supplied leaves." See Clark, *Eight American Praxapostoloi*, 199. Therefore these verses are considered as lacunose for the collation.

διαˢᶜᶜ Ath D] omit Ath¹⁰⁷ 𝔓⁴⁶ ¹⁰⁸ ℵ A C K L P Ψ 33 104 223 1739 2423
και Ath 𝔓⁴⁶ ℵ A C K L P Ψ 33 104 223 1739 2423] omit D

Heb 11:3
πίστει νοοῦμεν κατηρτίσθαι τοὺς αἰῶνας ῥήματι θεοῦ, εἰς τὸ μὴ ἐκ φαινο-
μένων τὸ βλεπόμενον γεγονέναι
De decretis 18 [C]

Lac. B C F G 049 876

.1)   1. το βλεπομενον Ath 𝔓⁴⁶ ℵ A D* P 33 1739
       2. τα βλεπομενα Dᶜ K L Ψ 104 223 876 2423

κατηρτισθαι Ath ℵ A D K L P Ψ 33 223 2423] κατηρτισται 𝔓⁴⁶
θεου Ath 𝔓⁴⁶ ℵ A D K L P Ψ 33 223 2423] του θεου 876; omit 104

Heb 11:5
Ἐνὼχ γοῦν οὕτω μετετέθη
Or. III c. Ar. 52 [All]

Lac. B C F G 049 876

Heb 11:6
ὁ δὲ κύριος μισθαποδότης αὐτῶν ἐστιν
Ep. I ad Orsis. [All]

Lac. B C F G 049 876

Heb 11:32
Γεδεὼν, Βαρὰκ, Σαμψὼν, Ἰεφθαὲ, Δαβίδ τε καὶ Σαμουὴλ
Ep. ad ep. Aeg. et Lib. 21.12 [C]

Lac. B C F G 049

---

[107] Athanasius appears to know the phrase both with and without δια. Therefore it cannot be cited as a significant variant.

[108] In 𝔓⁴⁶ δια is omitted from a conjectural reconstruction of lacuna of the last two lines.

.1)   1. Βαρακ Ath 𝔓⁴⁶ ℵ A 33 1739
        2. Βαρακ τε K L P Ψ 104 223 876 2423
        3. και Βαρακ D*
        4. και Βαρακ τε Dᶜ

.2)   1. Σαμψων Ath 𝔓⁴⁶ ℵ A 33 1739
        2. και Σαμψων D K L P Ψ 104 223 876 2423

.3)   1. Ιεφθαε Ath 𝔓⁴⁶ ℵ A 33 104
        2. και Ιεφθαε D K L P Ψ 223 876 1739 2423

Δαβιδ τε Ath ℵ A D K L P Ψ 33 104 223 876 1739 2423] omit τε 𝔓⁴⁶

Heb 11:35
    κρείττονος ἀναστάσεως
    Or. de Inc. Verb. 21.1 [C]

Lac. B C F G 049

αναστάσεως Ath 𝔓⁴⁶ ℵ A D K L P Ψ 33 104 223 876 2423] επαγγελιας
    1739

Heb 11:37
    περιερχόμενοι ἐν μηλωταῖς, ἐν αἰγείοις δέρμασιν, ὑστερούμενοι,
    κακουχούμενοι
    Apol. de fuga 16.12-15 [C]

Lac. B C F G 049

περιερχομενοι Ath] περιηλθον 𝔓⁴⁶ ℵ A D K L P Ψ 33 104 223 876 1739
    2423
υστερουμενοι Ath] υστερουμενοι θλειβομενοι 𝔓⁴⁶ ℵ A D K L P Ψ 33 104
    223 876 1739 2423

Heb 11:38
    ἐπὶ ἐρημίαις πλανώμενοι, καὶ ἐν σπηλαίοις καὶ ταῖς ὀπαῖς τῆς γῆς
    Apol. de fuga 16.12-15 [C]

Lac. B C F G 049

.1)   1. επι Ath 𝔓⁴⁶ ℵ A P 33 1739
         2. εν D K L Ψ 104 223 876 2423

πλανωμενοι Ath] πλανωμενοι και ορεσιν 𝔓⁴⁶ ℵ A D K L P Ψ 33 104 223
         876 1739 2423
εν Ath] omit 𝔓⁴⁶ ℵ A D K L P Ψ 33 104 223 876 1739 2423

Heb 12:1
δι᾽ ὑπομονῆς τρέχομεν τὸν προκείμενον ἡμῖν ἀγῶνα
Apol. de fuga 21.17-18 [C]

ἡμῖν ἀγῶνος, καὶ προκειμένου
Ep. ad ep. Aeg. et Lib. 21.20-21 [All]

Lac. (𝔓⁴⁶)[expl. προκειμενον], B C F G 049

υπομονης Ath 𝔓⁴⁶ ℵ A D K L P Ψ 33 104 876 1739 2423] υπονης 223

Heb 12:18
οὐ γὰρ προσεληλύθατε, (λέγων) ψηλαφωμένῳ ὄρει καὶ κεκαυμένῳ πυρὶ
καὶ γνόφῳ καὶ ζόφῳ καὶ θυέλλῃ +
Ep. Cosm. Indic. XLIII; 10.11 [C]

Lac. B F G 049

.1)   1. ορει Ath D K L P Ψ 104 223 876 1739 2423
         2. omit 𝔓⁴⁶ ℵ A C 33

.2)   1. και ζοφω Ath ℵ* A C D* P 33 104
         2. και σκοτει 𝔓⁴⁶ Ψ
         3. και σκοτω ℵᶜ Dᶜ L 223 876 1739 2423
         4. omit K

ψηλαφωμενω Ath 𝔓⁴⁶ ℵ A D K L P Ψ 33 223 876 1739 2423]
         ψηλαφουμενω 104

Heb 12:19
+ καὶ σάλπιγγος ἤχῳ καὶ φωνῇ ῥημάτων
Ep. Cosm. Indic. XLIII; 10.11 [C]

Lac. B F G 049

Heb 12:22

ἀλλὰ προσεληλύθατε Σιὼν ὄρει καὶ πόλει θεοῦ ζῶντος, Ἰερουσαλὴμ ἐπου-
ρανίῳ καὶ μυριάσιν ἀγγέλων, πανηγύρει +
Ep. Cosm. Indic. XLIII; 10.11 [C]

Lac. B F G 049

αλλα Ath 𝔓⁴⁶ ℵ C D K L P Ψ 33 104 223 876 1739 2423] ου γαρ A
και πολει Ath 𝔓⁴⁶ ℵ A C K L P Ψ 33 104 223 876 1739 2423] πολει D
Ιερουσαλημ επουρανιω Ath 𝔓⁴⁶ ℵ A C K L P Ψ 33 104 223 876 1739 2423]
      επουρανίω Ιερουσαλημ D
μυριασιν Ath 𝔓⁴⁶ ℵ A C K L P Ψ 33 104 223 876 1739 2423] μυριων αγιων
      D*; μυριασιν αγιων Dᶜ
πανηγυρει Ath 𝔓⁴⁶ ℵ A C D K L P Ψ 33 104 876 1739 2423] πανηγυριζει
      223

Heb 12:23

+ καὶ ἐκκλησίᾳ πρωτοτόκων ἀπογεγραμμένων ἐν οὐρανοῖς
Ep. Cosm. Indic. XLIII; 10.11 [C]

τῇ τῶν πρωτοτόκων ἐν οὐρανοῖς ἐκκλησίᾳ
Ep. ad ep. Aeg. et Lib. 19.14-15 [Ad]

Lac. B F G 049

.1)   1. απογεγραμμενων εν ουρανοις Ath 𝔓⁴⁶ ℵ A C D L P Ψ 33 104
           1739
        2. εν ουρανοις απογεγραμμενων K 223 876 2423

Heb 13:3

καὶ ὡς συνδεδεμένος αὐτοῖς
Vita Ant. 46.7 [All]

Lac. B F G 049

Heb 13:4

Τίμιος ὁ γάμος καὶ ἡ κοίτη ἀμίαντος
Ep. ad Amun 67 [C]

πόρνους καὶ μοιχοὺς
Ep. ad Amun 68 [C]

Lac. B F G 049

γαμος Ath] γαμος εν πασιν 𝔓⁴⁶ ℵ A C D K L P Ψ 33 104 223 876 1739
    2423

Heb 13:6
κύριος (γὰρ, φησὶν), ἐμοὶ βοηθός· οὐ φοβηθήσομαι τί ποιήσει μοι
ἄνθρωπος
Or. III c. Ar. 54 [C]

Lac. B F G 049

.1)   1. βοηθος Ath ℵ* C* P 33 1739
        2. βοηθος και 𝔓⁴⁶ ℵᶜ A Cᶜ D K L Ψ 104 223 876 2423

Heb 13:8
Ἰησοῦς Χριστὸς χθὲς καὶ σήμερον ὁ αὐτὸς, καὶ εἰς τοὺς αἰῶνας
Or. II c. Ar. 10 [C]; Ep. ad Epic. 5.23 [C]; De decretis 35 [C]

Ἰησοῦς (γὰρ) Χριστὸς, χθὲς καὶ σήμερον ὁ αὐτὸς καὶ εἰς τοὺς αἰῶνας
Or. I c. Ar. 36 [C]

Ἰησοῦς Χριστὸς χθὲς καὶ¹⁰⁹ σήμερον (καὶ) ὁ αὐτός ἐστιν εἰς τοὺς αἰῶνας
Or. I c. Ar. 48 [Ad]

Lac. B F G 049

.1)   1. χθες Ath K L P Ψ 104 223 876 2423
        2. εχθες¹¹⁰ 𝔓⁴⁶ ℵ A C* D* 33 1739

ο αυτος Ath ℵ A C D K L P Ψ 33 104 223 876 1739 2423] αυτος 𝔓⁴⁶

Heb 13:14
οὐ γὰρ ἔχομεν ὧδε μένουσαν πόλιν, ἀλλὰ τὴν μέλλουσαν ἐπιζητοῦμεν
Ep. Cosm. Indic. XLIII; 10.9 [C]

---

¹⁰⁹ In 𝔓⁴⁶ the first hand has omitted και but this has been added superlinearly as a correction.
¹¹⁰ Attic form in Athanasius (Kenyon notes the form also in ℵ A C* D*). Cf Walter Bauer, *A Greek-English Lexicon of the New Testament and Other Early Christian Literature* (2d ed.; Chicago: University of Chicago Press, 1979), 881; Kenyon, *Pauline Epistles, Text*, 50.

Lac. B F G L 049

CATHOLIC EPISTLES

James 1:8
διψύχους καὶ ἀκαταστάτους ὄντας ἐν πάσαις ταῖς ὁδοῖς αὐτῶν
De decretis 4 [Ad]

Lac. 325

James 1:12
ἀπολήψεσθε (δὲ) τὸν στέφανον τῆς ζωῆς, ὃν ἐπηγγείλατο ὁ θεὸς τοῖς
ἀγαπῶσιν αὐτόν
Ep. ad ep. Aeg. et Lib. 23.21-22 [C]

Lac. 325

.1)   1. αποληψεσθε Ath
         2. λημψεται ℵ A B
         3. ληψεται C L Ψ 049 33 105 201 323 1022 1424 1739 2423

.2)   1. ο θεος Ath 33vid [111] 323 1739
         2. omit ℵ A B Ψ
         3. κυριος C
         4. ο κυριος L 049 105 201 1022 1424 2423

στεφανον Ath ℵ A B C L Ψ 049 33 201 323 1022 1739 2423] αμαραντι-
νον[112] στεφανον 1424

James 1:15
ἡ (δὲ) ἐπιθυμία, συλλαβοῦσα, τίκτει ἁμαρτίαν· ἡ δὲ ἁμαρτία, ἀποτελε-
σθεῖσα ἀποκύει θάνατον
Vita Ant. 21.1 [C]

---

[111] The ABMC copy of the microfilm for MS 33 shows water damage of the MS at this point and hence it is difficult to verify the reading here. NA[27] indicates MS 33 omits ὁ θεός.

[112] The scribe of 1424 has clearly interpolated ἀμαραντινον here (due to its association in his mind with στέφανον) but which is otherwise a New Testament hapax found only in 1 Pet 5:4.

Lac. (33)[113] 325

η[pr] Ath ℵ A B L Ψ 049 33[vid] 105 201 323 1022 1424 1739 2423] omit C

James 1:17
παραλλαγή (τις) ἢ τροπῆς ἀποσκίασμα
Ep. ad Afros 8.3 [C]

Lac. (33) 325

.1)   1. αποσκιασμα Ath ℵ[c] A C L Ψ 049 33 105 201 323 1022 1424
            1739 2423
         2. αποσκιασματος ℵ* B

ἢ Ath ℵ A B C 049 33 105 201 323 1022 1424 1739 2423] οὐδε Ψ

James 1:18
βουληθεὶς ἀπεκύησεν ἡμᾶς λόγῳ ἀληθείας
Or. III c. Ar. 61 [C]

Lac. (33) 325

James 1:20
ὀργὴ ἀνδρὸς δικαιοσύνην θεοῦ οὐ κατεργάζεται
Vita Ant. 21.1 [C]

Lac. (33) 325

.1)   1. ου κατεργαζεται Ath C* L 049 105 201 323 1022 1424 1739
            2423
         2. ουκ εργαζεται ℵ A B Cc Ψ

James 1:22
μη μονον ακροαται, αλλα και ποιηται
Ep. Cosm. Indic. 11; 10.3 [All]

---

[113] This verse in the MS is not strictly lacunose but the microfilm shows the codex with extreme water damage in this area rendering it difficult to verify the reading.

Lac. 325

---

1 Peter 1:25

τὸ δὲ ῥῆμα τοῦ κυρίου
Ep. ad Afros 2.3 [C]

του Ath] omit 𝔓⁷² ℵ A B C L Ψ 049 33 105 201 323 325 1022 1424 1739
    2423

---

1 Peter 2:22

ὃς ἁμαρτίαν (γάρ, φησίν), οὐκ ἐποίησεν, οὐδὲ εὑρέθη δόλος ἐν τῷ στόματι
αὐτοῦ
Or. de Inc. Verb. 17.7 [C]

ευρεθη Ath 𝔓⁷² A B C L Ψ 049 33 105 201 323 325 1022 1424 1739 2423] ο
    ευρεθη ℵ
στοματι Ath 𝔓⁷²ᶜ ℵ A B C L Ψ 049 33 105 201 325 1022 1424 1739 2423]
    στοματ 323; σοματι 𝔓⁷²*

---

1 Peter 2:24

ἀνήνεγκεν αὐτὰς τῷ σώματι ἐπὶ τὸ ξύλον
Or. II c. Ar. 47 [C]

τῷ σώματι ἑαυτοῦ τὰς ἁμαρτίας ἡμῶν ἀνήνεγκεν ἐπὶ τοῦ ξύλου
Or. I c. Ar. 62 [Ad]

ἀναφέρων τὰς ἁμαρτίας ἡμῶν ἐπὶ τὸ ξύλον τῷ σώματι αὐτοῦ
Or. III c. Ar. 31 [Ad]

αυτας Ath] εν 𝔓⁷² ℵ A B C L Ψ 049 33 105 201 323 325 1022 1424 1739
    2423
σωματι Ath] σωματι αυτου 𝔓⁷² ℵ A B C L Ψ 049 33 105 201 323 325 1022
    1424 1739 2423

---

1 Peter 2:25

ἐπίσκοπον ψυχῶν
De sent. Dion. 8 [All]

---

1 Peter 3:6
τὸν Ἀβραὰμ κύριον ἐκάλει
Or. II c. Ar. 3 [All]

_____

1 Peter 3:18
θανατωθεὶς σαρκὶ
Or. I c. Ar. 44 [C]

_____

.1)   1. σαρκι Ath 𝔓⁷² A*vid Ψ
       2. μεν σαρκι ℵ Aᶜ B C L 049 33 105 201 323 325 1022 1424 1739
          2423

_____

1 Peter 3:19
ὅτε αὐτὸς ἐπορεύθη κηρύξαι καὶ τοῖς ἐν φυλακῇ πνεύμασιν
Ep. ad Epic. 5.26 27 [Ad]*

_____

φυλακη Ath 𝔓⁷² ℵ A B L Ψ 049 33 105 201 323 325 1022 1424 1739 2423]
φυλακη κατακεκλεισμενοις C

_____

1 Peter 3:22
ὑποταγέντων αὐτῷ ἀγγέλων
Or. III c. Ar. 40 [C]

καὶ ἀγγέλων καὶ δυνάμεων
De sent. Dion. 8 [All]

_____

Lac. (33)

_____

1 Peter 4:1
Χριστοῦ οὖν παθόντος ὑπὲρ ἡμῶν σαρκί
Or. III c. Ar. 31 [C]; 34 [C]

Χριστοῦ οὖν παθόντος (θεότητι, ἀλλ᾽) ὑπὲρ ἡμῶν σαρκὶ
Or. III c. Ar. 34 [C]

σαρκὶ πέπονθε
Or. III c. Ar. 53 [All]

σαρκὶ μὲν πάσχων
Tom. ad Ant. 7.3 [All]

.1)   1. παθοντος υπερ ημων σαρκι Ath ℵᶜ A L 33 105 201 325 1022
           1424 2423
        2. αποθανοντος υπερ υμων σαρκι ℵ*
        3. παθοντος σαρκι 𝔓⁷² B C Ψ 323 1739
        4. παθοντος εν σαρκι 049*
        5. παθοντος εν σαρκι υπερ ημῶν 049ᶜ

1 Peter 4:4

τῶν μὴ συντρεχόντων[114] αὐτοῖς
Apol. de fuga 2.31 [Ad]

1 Peter 4:19

ὥστε καὶ οἱ πάσχοντες κατὰ τὸ θέλημα τοῦ θεοῦ, πιστῷ κτίστῃ παρατιθέ-
σθωσαν τὰς ἑαυτῶν ψυχάς
Or. II c. Ar. 9 [C]

Lac. C

.1)   1. πιστω Ath 𝔓⁷² ℵ A B Ψ 1739
        2. ως πιστω L 049 105 201 323 325 1022 1424 2423
        3. πιστως τω 33

.2)   1. εαυτων ψυχας Ath 1739
        2. ψυχας αυτων 𝔓⁷² ℵ A L Ψ 049 33 105 201 323 325 1022 1424
           2423
        3. ψυχας B

1 Peter 5:3

τύπος γενόμενοι
Ep. ad ep. Aeg. et Lib. 23.19-20 [Ad]

Lac. C

1 Peter 5:8

ὁ ἀντίδικος ἡμῶν διάβολος
Ep. ad ep. Aeg. et Lib. 1.13-14 [C]

---

[114] This form is a New Testament hapax.

περιήρχετο γὰρ πάλιν ὡς λέων
Vita Ant. 7.2 [Ad]

περιέρχεται ὡς λέων ζητῶν τίνα καταπίῃ
Hist. Arian. [Ad]

ὡς λέων ζητῶν τινα ἁρπάσῃ καὶ καταπιη
Ep. ad ep. Aeg. et Lib. 1.23 [All]

ὡς λέοντες ζητοῦντες
Hist Arian. 11 [All]

Lac. C

.1)   1. διαβολος Ath ℵ A B C L Ψ 049 105 201 323 325 1022 1424 1739
        2423
        2. ο διαβολος 𝔓⁷² 33

---

2 Peter 1:4

(ἵνα) γένησθε θείας κοινωνοὶ φύσεως
Or. I c. Ar. 16 [C]

κοινωνοὶ γενόμενοι θείας φύσεως
Or. III c. Ar. 40 [Ad]

ποιήσῃ τοὺς ἀνθρώπους κοινωνῆσαι θείας καὶ νοερᾶς φύσεως
Vita Ant. 74.4 [All]

κοινωνοι φυσεως Ath 𝔓⁷² A B C L Ψ 049 33 105 201 323 325 1022 1424
1739 2423] φυσεως κοινωνοι ℵ

---

2 Peter 1:11

ὁ κύριος καὶ σωτὴρ ἡμῶν Ἰησοῦς χριστὸς
Ep. ad ep. Aeg. et Lib. 1.1 [All]

---

2 Peter 1:17

λαβὼν παρὰ θεοῦ τιμὴν καὶ δόξαν
Or. III c. Ar. 40 [C]

.1) 1. θεου Ath
  2. του θεου πατρος ℵ C Ψ
  3. θεου πατρος 𝔓⁷² A B L 049 33 105 201 323 325 1022 1424 1739
   2423

---

2 Pet 2:22
 τὰ ἴδια ἐξεράματα
 Or. II c. Ar. 1 [All]

 ὡς κύνες εἰς τὸ ἴδιον ἐξέραμα τῆς ἀσεβείας ἐπέστρεψαν
 De decretis 4 [All]

 κυλιόμενοι ὡς ἐν βορβόρῳ
 De decretis 9 [All]

---

1 John 2:7
 οὐκ ἐντολὴν καινὴν δίδωμι ὑμῖν, ἀλλ᾽ ἐντολὴν παλαιάν, ἣν ἠκούσατε ἀπ᾽
 ἀρχῆς
 De decretis 5 [C]

 ουκ εντολην καινην Ath ℵ A B C L Ψ 049 105 201 323 325 1022 1424 1739
  2423] ου καινην 33
 διδωμι Ath] γραφω ℵ A B C L Ψ 049 33 105 201 323 325 1022 1424 1739
  2423
 ηκουσατε Ath] ειχετε ℵ A B C L Ψ 049 33 105 201 325 1022 1424 1739
  2423; εχετε 323

---

1 John 2:19
 μεθ᾽ ἡμῶν
 Or. I c. Ar. 1 [C]

---

1 John 2:20
 καὶ ἡμεῖς χρίσμα ἔχομεν ἀπὸ τοῦ ἁγίου
 Or. I c. Ar. 47 [C]

 εχομεν Ath] εχετε ℵ A B C L Ψ 049 33 105 201 323 325 1022 1424 1739
 2423

---

1 John 2:23

ἀρνούμενος τὸν υἱὸν
Or. I c. Ar. 4 [C]

---

1 John 3:2

φανερωθῇ, ὅμοιοι αὐτῷ ἐσόμεθα
De Syn. 53 [C]

ομοιοι Ath ℵ A B C L Ψ 049ᶜ 33 105 201 323 325 1022 1424 1739 2423]
        ομοι 049*

---

1 John 3:5

καὶ οἴδατε, ὅτι ἐκεῖνος ἐφανερώθη, ἵνα τὰς ἁμαρτίας ἡμῶν ἄρῃ· καὶ ἁμαρτία ἐν αὐτῷ οὐκ ἔστι
Or. III c. Ar. 34 [C]

.1)   1. ημων Ath ℵ C L Ψ 049 105 201 325 1022 1424 2423
           2. omit A B 33 323 1739

οιδατε Ath A B C L Ψ 049 33 105 201 323 325 1022 1424 1739 2423]
        οιδαμεν ℵ
εν αυτω ουκ εστι Ath A B C L Ψ 049 33 105 201 323 325 1022 1424 1739
        2423]   ουκ εστι εν αυτω ℵ

---

1 John 3:8

εἰς τοῦτο (γὰρ) ἐφανερώθη
Or. II c. Ar. 69 [C]

Lac. (C)

---

1 John 4:1

μὴ παντὶ πνεύματι πιστεύετε
Ep. ad ep. Aeg. et Lib. 3.19 [C]

μὴ παντὶ πνεύματι πιστεύωμεν
Vita Ant. 38.5 [Ad]

Lac. (C)

---

1 John 4:9

ἀπέστειλεν ὁ θεὸς τὸν υἱὸν αὐτοῦ τὸν μονογενῆ
Or. II c. Ar. 62 [Ad]

_____

Lac. C

_____

1 John 5:20

καί ἐσμεν ἐν τῷ ἀληθινῷ, ἐν τῷ υἱῷ αὐτοῦ Ἰησοῦ Χριστῷ. οὗτός ἐστιν ὁ
ἀληθινὸς θεὸς καὶ ἡ ζωὴ ἡ αἰώνιος
Ep. ad ep. Aeg. et Lib. 13.13-14 [C]

θεὸς ἀληθινὸς
Ep. ad Afros 5.4 [Ad]

θεὸν ἀληθινὸν
Ep. ad Afros 5.6 [Ad]

_____

Lac. C

.1)   1. η ζωη η αιωνιος Ath L 105 201
       2. ζωη αιωνιος ℵ A B 33 323 325 1022 1424 1739 2423
       3. ζωην αιωνιον παρεχων Ψ
       4. η ζωη αιωνιος 049

εσμεν Ath ℵ A B L Ψ 049 33 105 201 325 1022 1424 1739 2423] ωμεν 323
Ιησου Χριστω Ath ℵᶜ (ℵ* -του) B L 049 33 105 201 323 325 1022 1424
       1739 2423] omit A

_____

3 John 11

δεῖ γὰρ τὰ καλὰ μιμεῖσθαι
Vita Ant. 72.4]All]

_____

Jude 6

τοῦ διαβόλου, τοῦ μὴ τηρήσαντος τὴν ἰδίαν τάξιν
Vita Ant. 26.4 [All]

_____

REVELATION

Rev 1:8

τάδε λέγει ὁ ὢν καὶ ὁ ἦν καὶ ὁ ἐρχόμενος ὁ παντοκράτωρ
De Syn. 49 [Ad]

———————

Rev 8.9

καὶ ἀπέθανε τὸ τρίτον μέρος τῶν κτισμάτων τῶν ἐν τῇ θαλάσσῃ, τὰ
ἔχοντα ψυχάς
Or. II c. Ar. 45 [C]

———————

Lac. (A) [expl ψ....], C

μερος Ath ℵ] omit A P 046 Andreas Oecumenius
κτισματων τῶν Ath ℵ A[115] P Andreas Oecumenius] κτισματων 046
ψυχας Ath P 046 Andreas Oecumenius] ψυχην ℵ

———————

Rev 22:2

ξύλον ζωῆς
Or. II c. Ar. 37 [C]

———————

Lac. C (P)

ξυλον ζωης Ath A P 046 Andreas Oecumenius] omit ℵ

———————

Rev 22:9

ὅρα μή· σύνδουλός σου εἰμὶ καὶ τῶν ἀδελφῶν σου τῶν προφητῶν καὶ τῶν
τηρούντων τοὺς λόγους τοῦ βιβλίου τούτου· τῷ θεῷ προσκύνησον
Or. II c. Ar. 23 [C]

———————

Lac. C P

προφητων καὶ Ath ℵ A 046 Oecumenius] προφητων Andreas

———————

———————
[115] των is lacunose in A (the upper corner of the page is missing) but it is clear allowance
has been made for the presence of the word at the end of the first line, in the second column of the
folio.

4
THE METHODOLOGY OF TEXTUAL ANALYSIS

In order to accurately analyse Athanasius' text of the Apostolos it is necessary to utilise a carefully defined methodology. The methodology that has been used in previous studies of the Greek Fathers is a combination of a quantitative analysis and the Comprehensive Profile Method. This chapter will also discuss the use of an alternative method known as multivariate analysis and specifically the technique of producing multidimensional scaling maps in both two dimensions (2D) and three dimensions (3D) as well as related output consisting of Dendrograms and Optimal Cluster maps. Each of these methodologies will be discussed in turn.

QUANTITATIVE ANALYSIS

Quantitative analysis is used to clarify the relationship of Athanasius' text of the Apostolos to the text found in a selected range of New Testament manuscript witnesses on both an individual manuscript and aggregate text-type basis. This is done by calculating the percentage of agreement of the text of Athanasius with these other witnesses over a range of carefully selected significant units of textual variation.[1] The method as used in contemporary textual studies was initially developed by Colwell and Tune in response to a recognition of the "insurmountable deficiencies" of the earlier traditional methodology that had been used for over two hundred years of classifying New Testament manuscripts by tabulating their agreements whenever they varied from an arbitrary 'standard' text—most often the *Textus Receptus*.[2] Colwell and Tune's method on the other hand required

---

[1] See the previous discussion in Chapter 2 for details of the manuscripts selected as representatives of the various text-types.

[2] Ehrman notes that while the earlier method may have proved to be a "rough and ready" measure of textual consanguinity, "overlooking documentary agreements in readings *shared* with the *TR*—readings that often prove to be very ancient, if not genuine—can seriously skew the picture of textual alignments." Ehrman, *Didymus*, 187–188; See also Ernest C. Colwell and Ernest W. Tune, "The Quantitative Relationships Between Ms Text-Types" in *Biblical and Patristic Studies in Memory of Robert Pierce Casey* (ed. J. Neville Birdsall and Robert W. Thompson; Frieberg im Breisgau: Herder, 1963), 25–32. For further discussion concerning the flaws inherent in the earlier traditional methodology see Fee, "Codex Sinaiticus in John."; also Ehrman, "Methodological Developments.";

that in any area of text which is sampled the total amount of variation be taken into account—not just the variants from some text used as a "norm".[3] To fulfil this requirement selected representative witnesses of the various commonly accepted text-types are collated fully against each other in all places where the witness of interest—in this case Athanasius' text of the Apostolos—is extant. Then all instances of significant variation units amongst all the selected witnesses are recorded and percentages of agreement calculated for the relationship of all witnesses over the units of variation.[4]

An influential aspect of Colwell and Tune's methodology was to define a text-type relationship for a group of manuscript witnesses as being an agreement of more than 70% with a gap of about 10% from the next text-type.[5] Several subsequent studies were able to demonstrate that this 'rule-of-thumb' held generally for the Alexandrian witnesses at least though refinements of the method were also suggested.[6] In particular W. L. Richards demonstrated that no set level of agreement among manuscripts of a group can be anticipated at the outset, but rather the various textual groups must be allowed to set their own level of agreements since these will vary.[7] The results of Ehrman's quantitative analysis of the Gospels text of Didymus the Blind did not achieve the expected levels of text-type percentage agreement or separation.[8] Therefore he suggested that "the Colwell-Tune rule of thumb... should be lowered somewhat in view of the special character of patristic quotations and allusions that occur frequently but sporadically, lowered perhaps to a >65% agreement of a witness with group members with a 6–8% disparity between groups."[9] Brogan subsequently adopted Ehrman's suggested modified percentage agreement figures as a guide in his study of Athanasius' text of the Gospels.[10] This highlights the somewhat arbitrary nature of the Colwell-

---

Larry W. Hurtado, *Text-Critical Methodology and the pre-Caesarean Text: Codex W in the Gospel of Mark* (SD 43; Grand Rapids: Eerdmans, 1981), 5.

[3] Colwell and Tune, "Quantitative Relationships", 25.

[4] For discussion on the term 'significant variation unit' see Eldon Jay Epp, "Toward the Clarification of the Term 'Textual Variant'," in *Studies in the Theory and Method of New Testament Textual Criticism* (ed. Eldon J. Epp and Gordon D. Fee; SD 45; Grand Rapids: Eerdmans, 1993); Epp, "It's All about Variants," 275ff.

[5] Colwell and Tune suggest that "the quantitative definition of a text-type is a group of manuscripts that agree more than 70 per cent of the time and is separated by a gap of about 10 per cent from its neighbours. Both these elements seem to us to be significant." Colwell and Tune, "Quantitative Relationships, " 28.

[6] See Fee, "Text of John in Origen and Cyril." Fee showed that the agreement of the Primary Alexandrians was greater than 80% while a 70% agreement level held true for the Secondary Alexandrians. His later study on the text of $\mathfrak{P}^{75}$, $\mathfrak{P}^{66}$ and Origen confirmed these results. Fee, "The Myth of Early Textual Recension in Alexandria."; See also Richards, *Classification of the Greek Manuscripts.*

[7] For example, in his study on the text of the Johannine Epistles, Richards demonstrated that the level of agreement for members of the Byzantine subgroups was around 90%. Richards, *Classification of the Greek Manuscripts.*

[8] Ehrman, *Didymus*, 194–195.

[9] Ibid., 202. Ehrman prefaces the 65% figure with the ± symbol but this is clearly incorrect since this is a 'lower limit' (> 'greater than') percentage figure and not a 'range' percentage amount.

[10] See Brogan, "Text of the Gospels," 187. On the basis of the low level of Clement's proportional

Tune rule and the ease with which it has been susceptible to modification on the basis of unfavorable results argues against the inherent robustness and adequacy of the associated definition of text-type identification. This is a matter that will be taken up again in discussion on the alternative methodology of multivariate analysis.

As noted earlier, in order to determine the relationship of Athanasius' text of the Apostolos with a range of selected New Testament manuscript witnesses it is necessary to calculate the percentage agreement between witnesses. While the related calculations may be processed by hand this can be extremely laborious and prone to error and therefore as an alternative this study utilizes a custom Python script in order to automate the process.[11] The first step required is to tabulate in a multistate data matrix the raw data that is available in the critical apparatus concerning all significant variation units.[12] A partial sample of the first few columns from the data of Athanasius' text for Romans is shown below and on the next page

	Rom. 1.19.1	Rom. 1.19.2	Rom. 1.21.1	Rom. 1.24.1	Rom. 1.26.1	Rom. 1.27.1
Ath	1	1	1	1	1	1
P46	NA	NA	NA	NA	NA	NA
U1	1	1	1	2	1	2
U1C	1	1	1	2	1	2
A	1	1	1	2	1	1
B	1	1	1	2	1	2
C	1	1	1	2	1	3
D	2	1	2	1	2	1
F	NA	NA	NA	NA	NA	NA
G	2	1	2	1	2	1

agreements Cosaert asks the question as to whether a further revision of Colwell and Tune's group classification level is required, "even beyond Ehrman's suggested adjustment to 65%? In the case of Clement's citations, at least in Matthew, the answer appears to be a cautious yes." Cosaert, *Text of the Gospels in Clement*, 233.

[11] Python is an open-source dynamic object-oriented programming language that runs on all major (and many minor) computing platforms including those of Windows™, Apple™ and Linux™ and utilises simple text scripts to instruct the program 'interpreter' to perform the required steps. Being 'open-source', the Python program is freely available and can be easily accessed and downloaded from the official Python website: http://www.python.org/. For further details on Python see Mark Lutz and David Ascher, *Learning Python* (Sebastopol, Calif.: O'Reilly, 1999).

[12] The designation 'multistate' refers to the presentation of the data for the significant variation unit readings by the use of a unique numeral for each reading (1,2,3,4,etc). Refer also to the earlier description (in Chapter 2) for the data presentation of the significant variation units in the Critical Apparatus in Chapter 3. The use of multistate data is distinguished from the alternative presentation format using binary data which will be discussed in the following section on multivariate analysis.

K	1	2	1	1	1	2
L	1	2	1	1	1	2
P	1	2	1	1	1	1
U44	1	1	1	1	1	1
U49	1	2	1	1	1	3
M33	1	1	1	2	1	1
M104	1	2	1	2	1	1
M223	1	1	1	1	1	3
M876	1	2	1	1	1	3
M1739	1	1	1	2	1	1
M2423	1	1	1	1	1	2

A number of aspects concerning the nomenclature in this table should be noted. The sigla for the manuscripts are listed in the first column and then the data for each significant variation unit is listed in the subsequent columns.[13] The symbol 'U' is prefixed to the sigla of all uncial manuscripts rather than the customary '0' used in the Gregory-Aland designation.[14] This nomenclature has been adopted following the example set by Finney in his unpublished dissertation on the text of the Epistle to the Hebrews.[15] Finney notes that the main advantage of using 'U' to designate the Greek uncials is that it allows the application of "a simple system that can be applied across the various manuscript categories, allowing the use of a plain 'P' for papyri, 'U' for uncials, 'M' for minuscules... This scheme has positive advantages when it comes to mapping exercises where the initial '0' might be confused with a Gregory-Aland number, and in situations in which special fonts cannot be used [in the output maps]."[16] Therefore the designation 'U1' refers to the uncial (majuscule) manuscript 01 ℵ Codex Sinaiticus.

The second aspect to note is that the final 'C' used as a suffix in the identification for Codex Sinaiticus refers to the correctors of this manuscript.[17] A separate listing is provided only for this particular manuscript in order to allow for a direct comparison with the data analysis presented in Brogan's study on

---

[13] Refer to the sub-folder *SourceData* (available in the *Athanasius.zip* file located on the SBL website) for the relevant files containing details of the tabulated data sources used in the analysis of Athanasius' text of the Apostolos.

[14] See Aland et al., eds., *NA²⁷*, Appendix I, Codices Graeci et Latini.

[15] Finney, "Epistle to the Hebrews".

[16] See ibid., 2. The Gregory–Aland nomenclature is however utilised in the output data charts in Chapters 5 and 6.

[17] In this study no distinction is made between the various correctors. For details of the correctors of Codex Sinaiticus refer to H. J. M. Milne, T. C. Skeat and Douglas Cockerell, *Scribes and Correctors of the Codex Sinaiticus* (London: British Museum, 1938); also Dirk Jongkind, *Scribal Habits of Codex Sinaiticus* (TS 3/5; Piscataway, N.J.: Gorgias, 2007).

the Gospels text of Athanasius.[18] The designation NA (not available) is used to indicate missing or ambiguous data in the manuscript evidence which is most often due to lacunose passages but may also sometimes be due to the difficulty of determining a particular reading, for example, in a water damaged portion of a manuscript.

In the columns below the references to the significant variation units are the numerals identifying the various readings which the manuscripts witness. These data matrices must then be transposed, the column containing the significant variation unit references removed and saved as comma delimited files (.csv) in order to present the matrices in the appropriate format and file-type required by the Python script.[19] From the source data matrix composed of n rows and p columns the Python script calculates a symmetrical p x p data matrix of percentage agreement between all manuscripts.[20] These percentage agreement data matrices are presented in Appendix A and in the document: *Addenda to the Book. Donker–Apostolos of Athanasius.pdf* which is available on the SBL website associated with this book.

In his study on the text of Matthew in the writings of Basil of Caesarea, Racine discussed the need to calculate the (previously ignored) margin of error associated with the calculation of proportional agreement between manuscript witnesses.[21] He noted this was necessary since the source data used to calculate the proportional agreements is essentially a fragmentary text and as such must be considered a 'sample' that represents the 'population' which is equated to the otherwise inaccessible complete text of the Father's New Testament exemplar.[22] The task then is to determine the extent to which the sample accurately represents the complete population since as a general rule, the larger the sample size, the more likely it is to represent the population with a conversely smaller margin of error.[23] Therefore along with calculating the proportional agreements it is necessary to

---

[18] See Brogan, "Text of the Gospels," 190ff.

[19] It is relatively easy to transpose data matrices in common spreadsheet programs such as Microsoft Excel™. The transpose process essentially reverses the arrangement of the columns and rows. Refer to the sub-folder *SourceData* (located in the *Athanasius.zip* file on the SBL website) for the relevant files containing details of the tabulated data sources used in the analysis of Athanasius' text of the Apostolos. The filename for the Python script that is used to process the source data files is: *MssCompare.py*. Refer to the document *Addenda to the Book. Donker-Apostolos in Athanasius. pdf* (located in the *Athanasius.zip* file on the SBL website), for details of this Python script and how it is used.

[20] In these matrices which are rectangular and symmetrical it is only necessary to show the lower left diagonal portion of the table. Also the centre line figures of the diagonal are ignored since the agreement of a witness with itself is of no interest.

[21] Racine noted that in previous studies on the texts of the Fathers scholars had "neglected calculating this error correction. This oversight does not make their results void, but leads to a false impression of accuracy." Racine, *Text of Matthew in Basil*, 241.

[22] Ibid., 241; See also Cosaert, *Text of the Gospels in Clement*, 223; For further discussion on the relationship of samples and populations see Peter Sprent, *Quick Statistics: An Introduction to non-parametric methods* (Harmondsworth: Penguin Books, 1981), 49ff.

[23] For discussion on the relationship of sample size and variation see David S. Moore and George P. McCabe, *Introduction to the Practice of Statistics* (New York: Freeman, 2003), 265ff.

calculate the margin of error. This is done by multiplying the standard deviation of the proportional agreement by the t-score associated with a particular confidence level. The formula used to calculate the standard deviation is:[24]

$$\sigma p = \sqrt{\frac{p(100 - p)}{n}}$$

The notation for the formula is as follows: σp is the standard deviation of the proportional distribution where p is the percentage agreement for each manuscript pair calculated (previously) and n is the sample size which equates to the number of significant variation units used in the comparison between each pair of manuscripts.[25] Once the standard deviation is calculated it is then multiplied by the standardized score associated with a specific confidence level which is found in a 'distribution of t' chart.[26] While various confidence levels can be used (typically 90%, 95%, 99%) this study uses 95%.[27] For a confidence level of 95% the value of t in a t-chart is found to be (1.96). The standard deviation is multiplied by 1.96 to calculate the error margin (ie σp x t = ± error margin). A typical example will suffice to demonstrate this process. In the text of the

---

[24] It should be noted here that one minor modification has been made to the formula used by Racine and subsequently Cosaert which is that 'n–1' in the denominator of the fraction within the square root has been replaced by 'n' alone. This is because for cases where the sample is small (<10%) compared to the population size—which is almost certainly the case with Athanasius' text of the Apostolos (and for texts of the Fathers generally)—the standard deviation for a sample can be approximated by using 'n' rather than 'n–1'. This modification has the advantage of simplifying the formula. See ibid., 374; also Derek Rowntree, *Statistics Without Tears: A Primer for Non-mathematicians* (London: Penguin Books, 1981), 100. Cosaert also applied a minor modification to the formula used by Racine. He opted to use t-scores exclusively (rather than also using z-scores as per Racine) whereas Racine indicated that it was only necessary to use t-scores for samples less than 30. See Racine, *Text of Matthew in Basil*, 242, n. 7. However, as Cosaert points out, even for sample sizes greater than 30, "there is so little difference between the two tables [of z and t scores] ... that it makes little sense to switch back and forth between the two." Cosaert, *Text of the Gospels in Clement*, 224.

[25] The Python script *MssCompare.py* is also used to tabulate the number of comparisons used as the basis for the percentage agreement calculations. See the document *Addenda to the Book. Donker-Apostolos in Athanasius.pdf* and the sub-folder: *Agreement and Comparison Counts Docs* (both located in the *Athanasius.zip* file on the SBL website) for the relevant output data matrices. The *Addenda* also provides details of this Python script and how it is used.

[26] A distribution of t-table can be found in most statistical handbooks. This study uses the t-table found in Chris Spatz and James O. Johnstone, *Basic Statistics: Tables of Distributions* (Belmont, California: Wadsworth, 1981), 349. See also Rowntree, *Statistics Without Tears*, 77; Moore and McCabe, *Introduction*, T-11, Table D.

[27] The choice of confidence level is related to significance testing in which there are two opposite risks. The first is that one may accept a statistical result as significant when it is not. This is known as a TYPE I error and is guarded against by using a high level of confidence (typically 99%). This would be used in cases where a wrong decision would have severe consequences, for example in medical trials or personal safety contexts. However as the confidence level is increased there is also the increasing risk of *rejecting* a statistical result as being significant even when it is. This is known as a TYPE II error and is guarded against by using a lower confidence level. For these reasons, in cases which are not considered 'critical' a confidence level of 95% is commonly used. See Rowntree, *Statistics Without Tears*, 119. also Moore and McCabe, *Introduction*, 475ff.

Pauline Epistles, Athanasius has a 59.5% (=*p*) agreement with Codex Sinaiticus (ℵ) over 168 (=*n*) units of variation.[28] Therefore:

$$\sigma_p = \sqrt{\frac{59.5\,(100-59.5)}{168}} = 3.78$$

Then the standard deviation (3.78) is multiplied by the t-score (1.96) and the result is 7.4%. Therefore the error margin for the 59.5% agreement of Athanasius with Codex Sinaiticus (ℵ) in the Pauline Epistles with a 95% confidence level is ±7.4%. In this study the error margins will be presented in a separate matrix following the related data matrix of percentage agreements. Once these agreements have been calculated it is possible to tabulate manuscript relationships with Athanasius ranked ordinally from highest percentage agreement to lowest. The ordinal charts for Athanasius' agreements with the range of selected New Testament manuscripts are also presented in Chapter 5.

In order to determine Athanasius' textual affinity with the various text-types the manuscript witnesses are arranged into groups and the aggregate relationships of known group members are calculated. While these ordinal tables provide an initial indication of text type affinity they cannot be regarded as statistically significant.[29] It is, however, possible to determine this using the ordinal data by applying a non-parametric statistical significance test known as the Mann-Whitney *U* (Wilcoxon) test.[30] This test determines the probability that two samples—one of which is Athanasius' alignment with a specific text-type, and the other, the remaining manuscripts—come from the same distribution. A low probability, generally less than 0.05 (=5% or 1 in 20) indicates a statistically significant relationship of Athanasius with that specific group.

While there are various statistical computer software packages that provide the required functionality to perform a Mann-Whitney text, this study utilizes the open-source statistical programming environment known as 'The R Project

[28] Refer to the Percentage Agreement chart in Chapter 5. The number of units of variations is also calculated by the Python script *MssCompare.py* and the respective output charts can be found in the sub-folder: *Agreement and Comparison Counts Docs* (located in the *Athanasius.zip* file on the SBL website).

[29] This appears to be a weakness of previous studies inasmuch as numerous claims for 'significance' (properly understood as a statistical term) are made for small differences of proportional agreement between manuscripts or text-type alignments within the Quantitative or Group Profile analysis but without any statistical verification provided to support the claims. For example, Osburn notes that in the quantitative analysis of Epiphanius' text in 2 Corinthians, his agreement with the Old Egyptian (Primary Alexandrian) is at 64.0% with the Byzantine text being "significantly higher" at 68.1%. There is however no verification that this constitutes a 'significant' difference in proportional agreement. See Osburn, *Text of the Apostolos in Epiphanius*, 225. Osburn is not alone. Ehrman claims Didymus' agreement with the Early Alexandrian text group at 73% in John 1:1–6:46 is "significantly greater" than his agreement with the Late Alexandrian at 70% (3% less), though again without statistical verification to support the claim. See Ehrman, *Didymus*, 213–214.

[30] Non-parametric tests are utilised when the normality of the respective distribution cannot be assumed or, as in the present case, when the data consists of ranks. See Rowntree, *Statistics Without Tears*, 125; also Myles Hollander and Douglas A. Wolfe, *Nonparametric Statistical Methods* (New York: John Wiley & Sons, 1973).

for Statistical Computing', more commonly identified simply as 'R'.[31] To perform the Mann-Whitney test within the R console it is necessary to specify the two samples used in the test. This may be done by entering two values at the command prompt in the R console, x and y where x represents the first sample which is the concatenation of the percentage agreements for the specific text-type under consideration. Then y represents the second sample which is the concatenation of all the remaining manuscripts. Again an example may suffice. For the Pauline Epistles, where the affinity of Athanasius with all the Alexandrian manuscripts is being tested the following is entered at the R console command prompt;[32]

x<-c(59.5,58.3,50.4,51.6,61.3,62.2,58.1,61.3,67.8)[33]

where x represents a concatenation of all the Alexandrian manuscripts. Then y is specified which in this case represents the concatenation of all the remaining manuscripts;

y<-c(55.7,55.2,51.2,51.4,50.0,51.5, 44.6,41.9,39.5)

Then the Mann-Whitney (Wilcoxon) test function is entered at the command prompt as;

wilcox.exact (x,y, alternative="g", paired=FALSE, conf.level=0.95)[34]

---

[31] This is an open-source statistics package, available for Windows™, Apple™ and Linux™ systems. Instructions on how to install the software (which is freely available) are provided on the R project website. For further information on downloading, installation and use of R see the website: http://www.r-project.org/ ; also R Development Core Team, "R: A language and environment for statistical computing," (2007) No pages. Online: http://www.r-project.org/. One of the advantages of R is that apart from the extensive core functionality provided within the base package, extra packages, of which there are many (all freely available), may be easily installed to add extra functionality. Specifically the package, *exactRankTests* provides the *wilcox.exact* function which is equivalent to the Mann-Whitney test. Packages may be installed and loaded into the R environment from within R by the use of the drop down 'Packages' command located along the top row of the R window. For purposes of comparison and verification the Mann-Whitney test was also conducted using the commercially available MINTAB™ statistical software program. The output from both packages was found to be equivalent.

[32] The command prompt within the R console is identified as >. Therefore all commands are entered after this prompt. In the example cited above the complete text as indicated is entered exactly as shown beginning with the x or y.

[33] In this case x represents a concatenation of the percentage agreements of all the Alexandrian manuscripts. The percentage agreements used in this example are taken from the quantitative data results presented in Chapter 5.

[34] When both x and y are given and paired is FALSE, a Wilcoxon rank sum test (equivalent to the Mann-Whitney test) is carried out. In this case, the null hypothesis is that the location of the distributions of x and y differ by the mean (μ). The argument *alternative="g"* designates that the alternative hypothesis is that x is 'greater than' (shifted to the right of) y which would be the case if Athanasius is significantly associated with a particular text-type. The *wilcox.exact* function produces exact p-values in the presence of ties of which there are numerous examples in the Athanasian data. For further information concerning the Man-Whitney test see David F. Bauer, "Constructing

The result is calculated as 'p-value = 0.000905'. This equates to a percentage probability of 0.09% which is much less than the upper limit of 5% necessary to determine statistical significance. As such it can be concluded that Athanasius is indeed significantly related to the (All) Alexandrian text-type. However, before specific conclusions can be drawn on the basis of this result, it will first need to be compared to the results obtained for the Alexandrian sub-groups as well as the other remaining text-type groups.[35] A "major drawback" of the use of a quantitative analysis alone and one which Ehrman claims is frequently over-looked is that while the method is able to determine a witness's agreements with individual representatives of the known textual groups, "it cannot at all measure what is equally important: a witness's attestation of readings shared by the members of these groups."[36] For that reason a complementary method known as the Comprehensive Group Profile method is also used.

COMPREHENSIVE PROFILE METHOD

While the quantitative analysis focuses on the external evidence of Athanasius' affinity with a range of selected manuscripts (albeit on the basis of textual variations), the Comprehensive Profile Method focuses on Athanasius' text-type affinity on the basis of readings. That is to say that in order to determine to what extent Athanasius may be classed as a good Alexandrian witness, it is necessary to analyse the degree to which he preserves characteristic Alexandrian group readings. While other methods have been proposed to achieve this aim, such as the Claremont profile method, the Comprehensive Profile Method developed by Ehrman for his study on the Gospels text of Didymus has generally been adopted in subsequent studies of the Greek Fathers.[37] It does not replace the quantitative

---

Confidence Sets Using Rank Statistics," *Journal of the American Statistical Association* 67 (1972); also Hollander and Wolfe, *Nonparametric Statistical Methods*, 27–33; Reinhard Bergmann, John Ludbrook and Will P. J. M. Spooren, "Different Outcomes of the Wilcoxon-Mann-Whitney Test from Different Statistics Packages," *The American Statistician* 54, no. 1 (2000).

[35] Refer to Chapter 5 for the complete results of the Mann-Whitney test performed to determine Athanasius' affinity with the various text-types.

[36] Ehrman, "Use of Group Profiles," 466. The problem as noted by Fee in his study on the text of John 4 in Origen and Cyril is that the occasional—sometimes frequent—occurrence of accidental agreements in error among otherwise unrelated manuscripts can artificially raise the level of their proportional relationship making them appear to be more closely related than they actually are. See Fee, "Text of John in Origen and Cyril," 367–369.

[37] See Ehrman, *Didymus*, 223ff; See also Mullen, *Text of Cyril*, 305ff; Racine, *Text of Matthew in Basil*, 255ff; Osburn, *Text of the Apostolos in Epiphanius*, 181ff; Cosaert, *Text of the Gospels in Clement*, 251ff. For information concerning the Claremont Profile Method see Frederik Wisse, *The Profile Method for the Classification and Evaluation of Manuscript Evidence, as Applied to the Continuous Text of the Gospel of Luke* (SD 44; Grand Rapids: Eerdmans, 1982); also Epp, "Claremont Profile Method." The Institut für Neutestamentliche Textforschung (INTF) in Münster, Germany under the direction of Gerd Mink has developed an alternative classification system referred to as the Coherence Based Genealogical Method (CBGM) which produces stemmata of manuscripts based on the initial creation of individual local stemma at all points of variation. See Gerd Mink, "Eine umfassende Genealogie der neutestamentlichen Überlieferung," *NTS* 39 (1993), 481–499;

analysis but is designed to function complimentarily only after the proportional relationship of the Father's text to individual representatives of the known textual groups has been established.[38] As such the group profile analysis is intended to clarify the findings of a quantitative analysis and where necessary to modify the conclusions derived from it by means of a comprehensive evaluation of group readings which are preserved extensively among members of a group as well as of those readings unique to each group.

This evaluation is performed through the use of three specific profiles: 1) An inter-group profile compiles readings uniquely or primarily preserved by witnesses belonging to one of the known textual groups. 2) An intra-group profile compiles readings found extensively among members of one group regardless of the reading's attestation in members of other groups. 3) A combination of the inter and intra-group profiles such that readings in this profile "are those supported by all or most representatives of a group (as determined by the intra-group profile) but by few or no other witnesses (as determined by the inter-group profile)."[39] The definitions used to establish a reading's status within the three profiles are provided below.

Inter-Group Profile.

Distinctive Readings: Defined as readings shared by most members of a group but not found in any other witnesses. Alexandrian: More than half of the group members and no others.[40] Western: More than one group manuscript and no others.[41] Byzantine: More than half of the group members and no others.[42]

---

also Gerd Mink,, "Editing and Geneological Studies: The New Testament," *Literary and Linguistic Computing* 15 (2000). While this method has only been applied to the Catholic Epistles with the rest of the New Testament to follow, it holds promise, especially since the data for witness relationships is based on the full text where the number of significant variation units used for comparison numbers in the thousands.

[38] Ehrman, "Methodological Developments," 44.

[39] Refer to Ehrman, *Didymus*, 226–227 for definitions.

[40] This also applies to both the Primary and Secondary Alexandrian sub-groups. This definition represents a modification from that initially used by Ehrman. He defined a reading as Distinctive Alexandrian when it was "found in at least two Early Alexandrian witnesses, half of the Late Alexandrian, and no others." The modified definition was also used by Brogan who notes that it will be subsequently used by Ehrman, Fee and Homes in their forthcoming analysis of Origen's text of John. See Brogan, "Text of the Gospels," 228, n. 9. See the main text for discussion on the necessity of modifications to Ehrman's original definition specifically for the category of 'Primary Readings' in the inter-group profile.

[41] This definition also represents a departure from Ehrman's original definition which was: "Readings found in at least one Greek manuscript and two Old Latin manuscripts (when their witness can be adduced) and no others. When the Old Latin cannot be used, readings found in two Greek witnesses." As has been noted earlier, no Old Latin manuscript witnesses have been used in the present study and therefore the definition has been modified to reflect the revised context.

[42] Ehrman's original definition was: "Readings found in all but one of the Byzantine witnesses and no others." The revised definition was also used by Brogan.

Exclusive Readings: Readings shared by at least two members of the same group and no others, and excluding Distinctive readings which have already been determined.

Primary Readings: Readings that have more than 50% group support and twice as much group support (expressed as a percentage) as non-group support (expressed as a percentage).

This definition of 'Primary' readings follows Osburn's suggested modifications based on his review of problems inherent in Ehrman's original definition.[43] Osburn notes two difficulties in Ehrman's procedure that "skew data." First Osburn asks "why exclusive inter-group readings are included to profile a Father's total agreements with a particular group, when by definition an exclusive reading is a secondary or minority reading for that group[?]"[44] The problem is that the inclusion of such readings does not represent accurately a Father's agreements with a group and while the combined inter and intra-group profile eliminates these minority readings the independent value of the inter-group profile is correspondingly weakened.[45]

The second problem is how primary readings are reckoned since Ehrman's profile allowed mixed readings to be counted as primary for a group that supports readings uniformly (= all group mss support) even when the reading is supported predominantly (= up to ⅔ group support) by another group. Osburn observes that such readings appear to be mixed rather than primary for either group. He claims that "this problem is more significant than the previous one in that the combined profile does not filter out these readings as it did the exclusive ones. Clearly, a revision to the method is necessary to provide accurate data."[46]

---

[43] Ehrman's original definition for the Primary readings was: At least two group members and greater group than non-group support, either Uniform (100% and no other Uniform support and only one other ⅔ group support), Predominant (⅔ group support and no other group Uniform or Predominant), or less than ⅔ (more group than non-group support). See Osburn, Text of the Apostolos in Epiphanius, 181ff. Mullen also encountered difficulty in his attempt to analyse the text of the Pauline corpus in Cyril of Jerusalem. In the inter-group profile Cyril's text had its highest level of Distinctive support from the Alexandrian group (39.1%) as against the Byzantine (23.8%). However in the Primary Readings the support is reversed with Byzantine (65.9%) higher than the Alexandrian (54.8%). Mullen's conclusion is that "primary readings are generally less indicative of text-type than are the distinctive readings because primary readings are shared with one or more witnesses of other textual groups." Mullen, Text of Cyril, 378. Osburn encountered the same problem in his initial attempt to analyse the text of Romans in Epiphanius using Ehrman's original definition for Primary readings.

[44] Osburn, Text of the Apostolos in Epiphanius, 182.

[45] Ibid., 182. Mullen found that Cyril's support for Exclusive Alexandrian (24%) and Byzantine readings (33.3%) was reversed in comparison to the Distinctive Alexandrian (39.1%) and Byzantine (23.8%) readings and helps to explain why he chose to focus on the Distinctive readings rather than the Exclusive or Primary readings in the inter-group profile. Mullen, Text of Cyril, 378. Also 336–337 on the text of John.

[46] Osburn, The Text of the Apostolos in Epiphanius of Salamis, 183.

Intra-Group Profile.

Uniform Readings: Defined as readings shared by all group manuscripts (except lacuna) regardless of attestation in other groups.

Predominant Readings: Defined as readings shared by more than 60% of all group witnesses (except lacuna) regardless of attestation in other groups.[47]

Combination inter and intra-group Profile: Defined as readings that are Uniform or Predominant that are also Distinctive, Exclusive or Primary.

While a full presentation of the Group Profile results can be found in Chapter 6, it will be instructive to provide here a representative sample of the results for Athanasius' text of Acts 1–12.

1. Athanasius' Attestation of **Inter-Group** Readings in Acts 1–12

	Distinctive Rdgs[48]		Exclusive Rdgs		Primary Rdgs		Agree Total	Total Rdgs	% Agree	±% Error
Alex	3[49]	5[50]	0	1	2	2	5	8	63	34
Byz	0	0	0	0	0	1	0	1	0	0
West	0	0	0	0	0	0	0	0	0	0

2. Athanasius' Attestation of **Intra-Group** Readings in Acts 1–12

	Uniform Rdgs		Predominant Rdgs		Agree Total	Total Rdgs	% Agree	±% Error
Alex	2	2	10	13	12	15	80	20
- Primary	9	12	5	7	14	19	74	20
- Secondary	3	4	9	12	12	16	75	21
Byz	6	12	4	7	10	19	53	22
West	2	7	7	10	9	17	53	24

---

[47] This also represents a slight modification from Ehrman's original definition for Predominant which was: Readings shared by at least two-thirds of all group witnesses with text. The revised definition is in line with that used by Brogan and its adoption allows a more direct comparison with his results for the Gospels text of Athanasius. Brogan, "Text of the Gospels," 231.

[48] The specific identification of the readings is provided in footnotes referenced in the profile tables for the respective genre and section in Chapter 6.

[49] The first figure is the number of (Distinctive Alexandrian) readings supported by Athanasius. The identification of the readings is provided in footnotes for each category in the respective profile table.

[50] The second figure is the number of (Distinctive Alexandrian) readings compared. This arrangement is typical in all the Group Profile Tables. For example here Athanasius supports 3 out of 5 total (Distinctive Alexandrian) readings.

3. Athanasius' Attestation of **Uniform or Predominant** Readings in Acts 1–12 that are also Distinctive, Exclusive or Primary.

	Uniform Rdgs		Predominant Rdgs		Agree Total	Total Rdgs	% Agree	±% Error
Alex	0	0	4	5	4	5	80	35
Byz	0	1	0	0	0	1	0	0
West	0	0	0	0	0	0	0	0

Discussion of the specific results for Acts 1–12 will be suspended until Chapter 6. However a number of general aspects evident in these results should be noted here. The first aspect to note is the relatively low total number of readings that qualify under the various definitions within each of the three profiles. The results for Athanasius' text of Acts 1–12 is not unusual since Osburn's results for the same section of Acts in Epiphanius of Salamis were comparable. For example, the number of total readings for the Alexandrian text in the inter-group profile (i.e. an aggregate of Distinctive, Exclusive and Primary readings) is 8 for Athanasius compared to a total of 10 readings for Epiphanius.[51]

In the intra-group profile (which generally includes more readings than for the inter-group profile) the total readings for Athanasius in the Alexandrian group is 15 compared to 11 for Epiphanius. In the third profile which is a combination of inter and intra group profiles, the total number of Alexandrian readings for Athanasius is 5 compared to 8 for Epiphanius. The percentage agreements are then calculated on a relatively few readings compared to the generally much greater numbers used in the quantitative analysis. The problem here is that the numbers are so low as to produce potentially wild fluctuations and contradictory results. For example, in the combination inter and intra-group profile for the text of Acts 1–12, Epiphanius agrees with 5 Alexandrian group readings out of 8 total readings for a 62.5% agreement. He agrees with 4 Byzantine group readings out of a total of 10 for 40% agreement. But he happens to agree with the single Western Uniform reading to show a percentage agreement for that text group of 100% even though the overall group profile analysis in Acts shows that Epiphanius' agreement with the Western group is otherwise "negligible".[52] This problem can be overcome by only analyzing larger blocks of text to increase the number of qualifying readings, but such an approach defeats the aim of analyzing smaller sections of text in order to detect the presence of block-mixture and text-type shifts.[53]

---

[51] See Osburn, *Text of the Apostolos in Epiphanius*, 203.

[52] The 100% agreement of Epiphanius with the Western group in the third profile on the basis of one sample reading also carried through to the *whole* of the text of Acts since there were no Western Readings for Acts 13–28 to dilute this figure. See ibid., 202–203.

[53] For example Ehrman discovered that Didymus' text shifts decidedly away from the Alexandrian at John 6:47 and was able to verify this in the Group Profile analysis of John 6:47–21:25. See Ehrman, *Didymus*, 235.

A corollary to the use of low (sample) numbers of readings for percentage agreement calculations is the correspondingly much larger error margins than those associated with the results of the quantitative analysis. This aspect has not been noted in previous studies on the Fathers. While Racine and Cosaert calculate and display error margins for the results of the quantitative analysis they are silent on the equivalent need to calculate and display error margins for the results of the group profile analysis. The greater error margins associated with the group profile analysis suggests that their inclusion is even more urgent than for the quantitative analysis. Note for example the ±34% error margin for the Alexandrian text in the inter-group profile for Athanasius. In the intra-group profile, no error margin is less than 20%. Recognition of the extent of these error margins challenges the confidence which has been placed in the results of a Group Profile analysis in previous studies of the Fathers.

The previous discussions concerning the Quantitative and Comprehensive Group Profile analysis have highlighted the usefulness but also the problems and shortcomings associated with the current methodologies.[54] The question then arises as to whether there exists an alternative methodology that is not encumbered with such limitations and which is able to utilise advances made in areas such as computer technology and statistical analysis and which can be readily adapted to a textual analysis of the Fathers. Specifically a methodology known as multivariate analysis holds great potential and is particularly suitable for analysis of textual and manuscript relationships since it can be used to produce useful graphical output as a way of more clearly displaying manuscript relationships and text-type alignments.

MULTIVARIATE ANALYSIS

Cosaert claims that the presentation of percentage agreement matrices (tables) containing the full quantitative analysis of all the witnesses to one another are of "little use" due to the limited number of citations recovered in the texts of the Fathers.[55] For example he refers to Brogan's presentation of agreement chart(s) for the text of Athanasius in each of the four Gospels but notes that the chart "serves no real purpose to his study. In each case the chart is merely identified with no further discussion or reference to its findings."[56] Certainly this criticism is correct insofar as previous studies have utilised only one 'dimension' (column) of the full data available in these matrices in their analysis when they only make use of the data pertaining to the proportional agreements for the range of manuscripts

---

[54] Broman suggests that the current methodologies of Quantitative and Group Profile analysis can be regarded as two heuristic attempts to measure something that could be more clearly modelled by using a theoretical ideal text by means of a probability distribution against which a Father's text could be compared. This is similar to Finney's concept of a 'synthetic text' produced using computer simulation. See Broman. n.p; also Timothy J. Finney, "Analysis of Textual Variation," n.p. [cited 17 April 2009]. Online: http://purl.org/tfinney/ATV/book/.

[55] See Cosaert, *Text of the Gospels in Clement*, 227.

[56] Ibid., 227–28.

against the Father's text in a quantitative analysis while essentially ignoring the remaining majority of the data of proportional agreements of all the manuscripts (apart from the Father's text) with one another.

Cosaert however is incorrect when he concludes that this data is of "little use" since properly utilised and analyzed the full data from such matrices can reveal important information about the relationships between a Father's text and that of the range of selected manuscripts.[57] The problem is that the analytical method typically adopted in previous studies of the Fathers, does not include any component which is able to utilise and analyse the full dimensionality of the data available in the proportional agreements matrices. This is a deficiency in the current methodology but one which can be satisfactorily overcome by the use of multivariate analysis.[58] Multivariate analysis, as the name suggests, involves the analysis of more than one variable or dimension of data.[59]

Consider the sample data from Athanasius' text of Romans presented earlier:

	Rom. 1.19.1	Rom. 1.19.2	Rom. 1.21.1	Rom. 1.24.1	Rom. 1.26.1	Rom. 1.27.1
Ath	1	1	1	1	1	1
P46	NA	NA	NA	NA	NA	NA
U1	1	1	1	2	1	2
U1C	1	1	1	2	1	2
A	1	1	1	2	1	1
B	1	1	1	2	1	2
C	1	1	1	2	1	3

---

[57] One might ask, for example, why the proportional agreements between a Father's text and the range of manuscripts is useful in a Quantitative analysis but the remaining proportional agreements results for the relationships of the manuscripts among themselves, which is based upon the same source data, is of "little or no value." See Ehrman, *Didymus*, 201.

[58] I am indebted to Tim Finney whose work on the text of the Epistle to the Hebrews introduced me to the potential of multivariate analysis as a particularly useful methodology for text-critical study of the Apostolos of Athanasius and whose influence will be recognised throughout the section on multivariate analysis. See Finney, "Epistle to the Hebrews"; also Finney, "Analysis of Textual Variation." Other computer based methods for analysing manuscript relationships have been investigated; for example cladistics. See Stephen C. Carlson, "The Origin(s) of the 'Caesarean' Text" (paper presented at the Annual Conference of the SBL, San Antonio, Tex., 20 November 2004).

[59] For general introductions to the use of multivariate analysis see Christopher Chatfield and Alexander J. Collins, *Introduction to Multivariate Analysis* (London: Chapman and Hall, 1980); also Bryan F. J. Manly, *Multivariate Statistical Methods: A Primer* (London: Chapman & Hall, 1994). Afifi, Clarke and May note that the expression *multivariate analysis* "is used to describe analyses of data that are multivariate in the sense that numerous observations or variables are obtained for each individual or unit studied." See Abdelmonem Afifi, Virginnia A. Clark and Susanne May, *Computer-Aided Multivariate Analysis* (4th ed.; Boca Raton, Fla.: Chapman & Hall, 2004), 3.

Using text-critical nomenclature various aspects of this data can be identified. There are the witnesses, variation units and unique readings. Multivariate
analysis, however, utilizes different terminology. Venables and Ripley note that
"Multivariate analysis is concerned with datasets that have more than one response
variable for each observational or experimental unit. The datasets can be sum-
marized by data matrices X with n rows and p columns, the rows representing
the observations or cases, and the columns the variables."[60] The data presented in
the matrix above represents the 'dataset', the manuscript witnesses correspond
to 'cases', the variation units correspond to 'variables' and the different readings
correspond to unique states of each variable.[61] While variables can be encoded as
nominal, ordinal, interval or ratio data, the unique states of each reading are here
encoded as nominal data by a one-to-one mapping of states to numerical labels
(1, 2, 3, 4, etc).[62] The data in the table is classified as multistate data rather than
the alternative binary data which has only two states.[63] As noted earlier, missing
data is identified by NA.

The methodology as presented here involves a number of elements. 1)
Constructing a dissimilarity data matrix (essentially the complement of a percentage agreements matrix) from the multistate form of the significant variation
units data; 2) Calculating critical values of dissimilarity and determining statistically significant relationships between manuscripts; 3) Plotting two dimension
(2D) and three dimension (3D) multidimensional scaling (MDS) maps which can
display the relative distance relationship between mss as well as visually identifying text type affinity; 4) Plotting dendrograms and optimal cluster maps.

1. Dissimilarity data matrix: The reason that a dissimilarity matrix is calculated rather than a percentage agreement (=similarity) matrix is that it can be
used to identify witnesses that share a statistically significant level of agreement.[64]
To do that we must convince a 'sceptic' that the observed level of agreement of
any two manuscript witnesses is not merely coincidental.[65] One way to do this

---

[60] W. N. Venables and B. D. Ripley, *Modern Applied Statistics with S* (New York: Springer,
2002), 301. The designation *S* in the title refers to the *S* statistical language which is the precursor to
R. *R* has been developed as open-source software whereas *S* continues to be available as a supported
commercial product.

[61] See Finney, *Analysis of Textual Variation*, sec. 2.1.

[62] For discussion on the different data types see Roderick Floud, *An Introduction to
Quantitative Methods for Historians* (London: Methuen, 1973), 8. The numerals used are not
inherently significant but serve merely as labels to distinguish the different states.

[63] It is only necessary to encode the data as binary if the intention is to utilise Primary
Components Analysis (PCA) which is a specific technique within multivariate analysis. However
since the more general multivariate analysis as presented here can adequately process multistate
data, this method of encoding the data will be retained. It is possible to convert multistate data into
binary data if necessary.

[64] Dissimilarity is used in preference rather than a measure of similarity (which is the
complement) since there is a direct correspondence between an increase in the measure of
dissimilarity and an increase in the distance between witnesses.

[65] Finney, *Analysis of Textual Variation*, sec. 3.5.1.

is to consider a 'normal distribution' of dissimilarity which includes the range of agreements between witnesses that can be expected to occur by chance. Then lower and upper critical values of dissimilarity are calculated. The observed level of dissimilarity between any two witnesses is then compared with these critical values. From a statistical perspective any dissimilarity that falls *outside* that range of critical values can be considered significant. That is, any extremely low or high values of *dissimilarity* imply *statistically significant relationship*. Refer to the normal distribution curve diagram below (Figure 1). The lower and upper critical values are (commonly) taken to be –2 x Standard Deviation (= Error; –2SE) and +2 x Standard Deviation (=Error; +2SE) respectively.[66]

Figure 1: Normal Distribution Curve

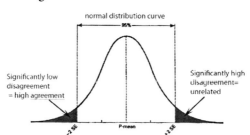

Any level of dissimilarity *less* than –2SE indicates that there is a statistically significant agreement (=significant similarity) between the respective witnesses and any level of dissimilarity *more* than +2SE indicates the respective witnesses are significantly dissimilar. In order to calculate the dissimilarity for each pair of witnesses it is necessary to apply an appropriate dissimilarity coefficient. In the present study the *simple matching distance* is used since it is applicable to multistate data.[67] It is defined as:

$$SMD = \frac{Nd}{Nc}$$

where *Nd* is the number of variation units where the pair of witnesses disagree and *Nc* is the total number of variation units compared.[68] Any variation

---

[66] ±2 x SE is commonly used since it represents 95% of the area under the normal distribution curve which equates to a 95% confidence level. See Rowntree, *Statistics Without Tears*, 75.

[67] Other dissimilarity coefficients are the Jaccard distance and the Euclidean distance. They are only applicable to binary data and therefore not suitable for use here. Since the simple matching distance coefficient satisfies the three conditions;

1) $d_{rs} \geq 0$ *for every* r,s
2) $d_{rs} = 0$ *if* r *is identical to* ,s
3) $d_{rs} = d_{sr}$ *for every* r,s

and a fourth condition known as the metric inequality; $d_{rt} + d_{ts} \geq d_{rs}$ *for every* r,s,t then the coefficient is a 'metric' or distance. Therefore the dissimilarity matrix also functions as a distance matrix. See Chatfield and Collins, *Introduction to Multivariate Analysis*, 191–192.

[68] Thus the value of SMD will always be 0 > SMD > 1. It should also be observed that the

units where at least one of the witnesses contains missing data (NA) are excluded. The Python script (*MssCompare.py*) used earlier to calculate percentage agreement matrices can also be used to calculate dissimilarity matrices.[69] These matrices are presented in Chapter 7.

2. Calculating critical values of dissimilarity and determining statistically significant relationships between manuscripts: In order to calculate the lower and upper critical values of dissimilarity it is necessary to construct a normal distribution of probabilities of random agreement (i.e. agreements expected to occur by chance) between two artificial 'pseudo-witnesses'.[70] The critical values

---

measure of dissimilarity is precisely the complement of the measure of similarity. (ie $d = 1-s$).

[69] Refer to the document *Addenda to the Book. Donker-Apostolos in Athanasius.pdf* (located in the *Athanasius.zip* file on the SBL website) for details of the appropriate command switch used to calculate dissimilarity matrices using *MssCompare.py*. Finney has written an *R* script to produce dissimilarity matrices (called *diss.r*). However at the time of producing the dissimilarity matrices in the present study Finney's script was unsuitable as it used what he refers to as an 'exclusive' strategy. That is, in a first pass it eliminates from a source data matrix all columns of variation units which are undefined (NA), for a specified witness of interest (e.g., Athanasius), then in a second pass it eliminates complete rows of witnesses that still contain *any* missing data. The reason for this strategy is to derive a matrix that contains no missing data such that critical values of dissimilarity calculated from it would apply equally to all witnesses included in the matrix. However an important issue is that all witnesses that still contain missing data (NA) after the first pass are eliminated. This is the case with many of the selected witnesses in the present study and their elimination from the data output and subsequent analysis is unacceptable. Therefore Finney's *R* script could not be used and the alternative Python script was developed. Subsequently, following ongoing private discussion on this issue, Finney revised his methodology to incorporate an alternative 'inclusive' strategy which allows for the presence of NA in the data of any witness by only eliminating missing data related to a pair of witnesses prior to calculating dissimilarity on the remaining variation units and which, as a result, closely reflects the procedure applied in the Python script. See Finney, *Analysis of Textual Variation*, sec. 2.5. It is also possible to calculate dissimilarity matrices from percentage agreement matrices since dissimilarity is simply the complement of proportional agreement. To convert from percentage agreement to dissimilarity the following equation is applied: *Dissimilarity* = 1– (*percentage agreement* ÷ 100). The resultant dissimilarity coefficient calculated using this formula only equates to the Simple Matching distance and the Jaccard distance but not the Euclidean distance.

[70] Finney indicates that "An artificial pseudo-witness can be generated by randomly choosing a reading at each variation unit such that a reading's probability of selection is the same as its relative frequency of occurrence among a sample set of witnesses. By definition any two of these pseudo-witnesses are unrelated: their readings are the result of random selection, not common ancestry. Lack of relationship does not imply lack of agreement, however. In fact, the probability of agreement between two randomly generated texts at a particular variation unit may be quite high." Ibid., sec. 3.5.2. The probability at a variation unit is calculated by summing the probabilities of combinations of the relevant variation unit's readings that produce agreement. Using simple matching distance the equation is $p\ (random\ agreement) = \sum p(x)^2$. For example, of the nineteen witnesses that cover the first variation unit at Rom 1:27, nine (including Athanasius) support the first reading, six support the second and four support the third. The relative frequencies of occurrence are therefore 9/19, 6/19 and 4/19 respectively. The probability of random agreement is $(9/19)^2 + (6/19)^2 + (4/19)^2 = 0.368$. Once the probability of random agreement for each variation unit is calculated, it is possible to calculate the probability of any number of agreements between two pseudo-witnesses and a distribution of probabilities of random agreement can be constructed by plotting the probability of each number of agreements from zero up to the total number of variation units included in the source data.

are the lower and upper bounds that bracket the values of the number of agreements between these witnesses that can be expected to occur in 95% of cases. Conversely in only 5% of cases can values be expected to fall outside this range and therefore it is reasonably safe to assume that a value outside the range defined by the critical values is not due to chance and is therefore statistically significant. The technique used to calculate the lower and upper critical values based on the distribution of probabilities of random agreements employs a so-called 'Monte Carlo' calculation since it can cope with large numbers of variations but also return reasonably definitive results.[71] The 'Monte Carlo' calculation, which has similarities to a game of chance, operates as follows:

"At its heart lies a random number generator that acts like a roulette wheel [hence the name for the technique], producing one of a range of possible outcomes. In the present case, each trial produces a set of n numerals, where n is the number of variation units. The random number generator is constrained such that the probability of producing a particular number is equal to the relative frequency of the corresponding reading or trait among a set of witnesses. The dissimilarity between this 'text' and another one produced in the same way is then calculated using a selected distance measure and stored in an array. Once a preset number of trials has [sic] been performed, the array of dissimilarities is sorted into ascending order and the critical values are obtained by referencing particular values. For example, given an alpha value of 0.05 [=95% range, = ±2SE] and 10,000 trials, the upper (or lower) critical value of dissimilarity is found in the 9,750[th] (or 250th) cell of the sorted array."[72]

An R script, montecarlo.r, functions as outlined here and calculates lower and upper critical values.[73] Since the script requires the specification of a witness of interest, it is necessary to run it for each witness in the dissimilarity matrix. This is because the calculations of dissimilarity for each witness in comparison

---

[71] The name 'Monte Carlo' was popularized by two physicists, Stanislaw Ulam and Nicholas Metropolis who worked at Los Alamos in the 1940's. See Nicholas Metropolis, "The Beginning of the Monte Carlo Method," Los Alamos Science Special Issue (1987); also Nicholas Metropolis and Stanislaw Ulam, "The Monte Carlo Method," Journal of the American Statistical Association 44, no. 247 (1949). Two other possible techniques are: 1) A technique based on a binomial distribution but which makes a number of assumptions about probabilities of readings in order to do so. These assumptions are: a) every variation unit has only two readings; b) the probability of agreement is the same for all variation units; c) the reading of one variation unit has not effect on the reading of another variant. Finney notes the first two conditions are not satisfied by the New Testament textual evidence. 2) A technique that makes exact calculations based on the actual probabilities of readings. However the computations involved are so demanding that it is only feasible for use with small numbers of variation units. For example exact calculations involving more than 40 variation units would take months to complete. See Finney, Analysis of Textual Variation, sec. 3.5.3.1.

[72] See Finney, Analysis of Textual Variation, sec 3.5.3.3. The Monte Carlo technique is essentially a contemporary application of statistical sampling which uses the raw procesing power available in modern desktop computers.

[73] Refer to the document Addenda to the Book. Donker-Apostolos in Athanasius.pdf and the sub-folder: Agreement and Comparison Counts Docs (both located within the Athanasius.zip file, available on the SBL website) for details of the montecarlo.r script and the arguments required.

to other witnesses in the matrix are based on varying numbers of total variation units and hence the calculations of lower and upper critical values for each respective witness are also based on the same number of total variation units.[74]

Once critical values have been obtained they can be presented in a table with the respective witnesses arranged ordinally from lowest to highest dissimilarity relative to Athanasius. The tables are presented in Chapter 7. Then the values of dissimilarity are inspected to determine which of the following categories the witness falls into: a) Witnesses with dissimilarities less than the lower critical value (LCV). Witnesses in this category may be considered to have a statistically significant relationship with the text of Athanasius. b) Witnesses with dissimilarities within the range defined by the lower and upper critical values. Witnesses in this category cannot be considered to show any significant relationship with the text of Athanasius. c) Witnesses with dissimilarities greater than the upper critical value (UCV). Witnesses in this category may be considered to evidence a statistically significant difference from the text of Athanasius. The value in calculating critical values of dissimilarity is that they provide a statistically cognizant method for determining relationships between the text of Athanasius and the range of witnesses included in the dissimilarity matrix and therefore provide an appropriate level of confidence when making claims of 'significance' for those relationships.

3. Plotting two dimension (2D) and three dimension (3D) multidimensional scaling (MDS) maps: While these tests (above) have value in providing statistically verifiable results, the relationships between witnesses can also be observed using multidimensional scaling (MDS) which is able to produce graphical 'maps' from the data in the dissimilarity matrices.[75] Cleveland notes that:

---

[74] As a result the procedure outlined in the present study varies from that advocated by Finney. His procedure utilises an 'exclusive' strategy whereby the dissimilarity matrix is calculated on the basis of a source data matrix from which all witnesses (rows) are removed that still contain missing values (NA) after the first pass. See Finney, *Analysis of Textual Variation*, sec. 3.5.4. The primary motivation for such a procedure is that the lower and upper critical values calculated on the basis of such source data apply to all the witnesses in the dissimilarity matrix. However, as noted earlier, another result is that many manuscript witnesses originally included in the source data are removed. Since a requirement in this study is to retain *all* of the selected witnesses in the dissimilarity matrix an alternative procedure is required. The solution is to calculate lower and upper critical values for each witness in turn since these values will apply to a comparison between the witness itself and Athanasius (who is never eliminated since his text contains no missing data). In practice it will be observed from the critical values tables that a number of witnesses may share the same critical values since these values are calculated on the basis of similar comparison counts of total variation units.

[75] For a general introductions to the use of multidimensional scaling see Trevor F. Cox and Michael A. A. Cox, *Multidimensional Scaling* (Monographs on Statistics and Applied Probability 88; Boca Raton, Fla.: Chapman & Hall, 2001); also John Maindonald and John Braun, *Data Analysis and Graphics using R–An Example Based Approach* (Cambridge: Cambridge University Press, 2007); Edward R. Tufte, *The Visual Display of Quantitative Information* (Cheshire, Conn.: Graphics Press, 1983); Patrick J.F. Groenen and Michael van de Velden, "Multidimensional scaling," in *Econometric Institute Report EI 2004-15* (Erasmus Universiteit Rotterdam, 2004). The technique

Data display is critical to data analysis. Graphs allow us to explore data to see overall patterns and to see detailed behavior; no other approach can compete in revealing the structure of data so thoroughly. Graphs allow us to view complex mathematical models fitted to the data, and they allow us to assess the validity of such models.[76]

Multivariate analysis such as that represented by principal component analysis (PCA) and multidimensional scaling (MDS) are, as Finney notes, "an optimal means of characterizing a witness" since they have "greater classificatory power" than *ad-hoc* indices such as 'percentage of Byzantine readings' or 'percentage of Alexandrian readings.'[77]

One of the primary advantages in using MDS maps to represent the relationships between witnesses is that they both utilise and display a far greater proportion of the available information contained in a dissimilarity matrix than can be portrayed in an ordinal percentage agreement list. This may be seen from the analogy of a list of data for various geographical locations; certain 'dimensions' of information may be listed such as distance between cities, direction from one city to another, population size, etc. Then consider the ease with which this information can be clearly observed on a printed map which is only two dimensions though more 'dimensions' may be represented by, for example, size of a circle to represent relative population size of a city. The analogy can be applied to the relationships between witnesses. With the current methodology, the proportional agreement tables are essentially uni-dimensional even though the full number of 'dimensions' of the source data equates to as many manuscript witnesses as are used in the comparative analysis. Just as a map is generally deemed an efficient means of displaying the relationship between locations, so also multidimensional scaling 'maps' have characteristics which allow them to be ideal tools for displaying the textual relationship between witnesses.[78] The use of MDS maps to display the textual relationships of New Testament manuscript witnesses is not new, though none have as yet focussed on utilizing MDS on the text of the Fathers.[79] Previous exploratory studies have produced maps using

---

used here is the more common 'classical' or metric multidimensional scaling as opposed to non-metric or 'ordinal' multidimensional scaling. See J. C. Thorpe, "Multivariate Statistical Analysis for Manuscript Classification," n.p. [cited 1 December 2008]. Online: http://rosetta.reltech.org/TC/vol07/Thorpe2002.html, sec. 48, 49. For details of the mathematical formulae used in classical multidimensional scaling see Brian Everitt, *An R and S-Plus Companion to Multivariate Analysis* (London: Springer, 2005), 94–96.

[76] See William S. Cleveland, *The Elements of Graphing Data* (New Jersey: Hobart Press, 1994), 5.

[77] See Finney, *Analysis of Textual Variation*, sec. 4.2, 4.6.1.

[78] The advantage of MDS is that it is a statistical technique for data 'reduction' whereby the first dimension of a map 'explains' the greatest proportion of the original data and then each successive dimension accounts for correspondingly less. The aim is that in a relatively few dimensions the map can adequately 'explain' a large proportion of the original data. How well it is able to do this depends on the inherent dimensionality of the original data.

[79] Thorpe has written a helpful introductory article on the use of multivariate analysis for manuscript classification and Finney's important contribution has already been acknowledged. Thorpe notes, "There is no reason why multidimensional scaling should not be successfully applied

only two dimensions (2D), primarily due to the limitations of earlier computer technology.

This study, however, utilizes the graphics display capabilities of contemporary computer systems to simulate the relationship of witnesses in what may be termed a three-dimensional 'textual space'. Two dimensions are convenient since 2D maps can be presented easily in print form. However, the addition of a third dimension has the potential to enhance our perspective on the relationships between witnesses. A simple analogy is that of stars in space. Looking into the night sky (the equivalent of a two-dimensional perspective) one might be tempted to conclude that many of the stars observed are in close proximity to one another. Only by travelling about the cosmos though, could one gain a true perspective of the relationships of the various constellations. This textual 'space' can be readily simulated using contemporary, basic computing facilities.

The R software package includes a dedicated graphics library (rgl) which is used to produce three-dimensional (3D) plots that can be interactively manipulated, for example dynamically rotated, so that relationships between witnesses can be more easily observed. This study provides both two-dimensional plots of maps depicting the relationships between witnesses used in the analysis of Athanasius' text of the Apostolos and then also plots of three-dimensional maps shown from various viewpoints due to the limitation of representing them in print form.[80] A further advantage in using three dimensions rather than just two is that a greater proportion of information from the source data can be represented. For example, the 2D map for Athanasius' text of the Pauline corpus represents 64% of the full variability of the source data (a reasonably high figure for this type of plot) whereas the 3D map incorporates 71% of the source data. These maps are found in Chapter 7.

---

to manuscript classification as it requires nothing more than a dissimilarity matrix to proceed."See Thorpe, "Multivariate Statistical Analysis," sec. 52; also Wieland Willker, "Principal Component Analysis of Manuscripts of the Gospel of John," n.p. [cited 1 December 2998] Online: http://www-user.uni-bremen.de/~wie/pub/Analysis-PCA.html. While not having a specific focus on text-critical issues, James Libby's research on the grammatical structure of the New Testament Greek using multivariate data reduction (MDR) has direct relevance since his output is likewise presented by means of three dimensional (3D) maps. James A. Libby, "An Introduction to the Use of Advanced Data Reduction Approaches to Address Longstanding Issues in Biblical Studies" (paper presented at the Annual Conference of the SBL, San Diego, 19 November 2007). One of the distinct advantages in mapping the text of the Fathers using MDS is that since they can be 'located' both chronologically and geographically, their texts may serve as fixed points of reference against which other manuscript witnesses may be evaluated.

[80] In order to demonstrate the advantage of presenting MDS maps in three dimensions, sample .gif files for all the 3D maps plotted in Chapter 7 are available for download from the SBL website associated with this book which, when opened, display the maps in dynamic rotation. Preferably the R program should be installed, along with all scripts used in the present study as well as all source data files which the scripts process. Using these resources it is possible to reproduce the 3D maps within the R environment allowing for dynamic interaction and further observation. The appropriate R installation source files (for whichever computing platform is being used) can be freely accessed from the R website: www.r-project.org/. The R scripts used to produce the 2D and 3D MDS maps are: cmds-ath-2d.r and cmds-ath-3d.r and are available on the SBL website

4. Plotting dendrograms and optimal cluster maps: Other graphical output that holds potential for analyzing relationship of witnesses are those produced using cluster analysis. Thorpe notes that the purpose of cluster analysis "is to classify objects into a relatively small number of clusters, the intention being that members of the same cluster should be more similar to one another than they are to objects outside the cluster." Two methods that will be utilised here produce dendrograms and optimal cluster maps. Dendrograms are the result of a hierarchical clustering technique which uses a tree diagram to indicate the distinction between clusters and sub-clusters.[81] It is important to note that dendrograms are not to be equated with diagrams displaying genealogy of manuscript witnesses. In dendrograms individual witnesses only appear at the tips of the branches of the tree. Those most similar join to form clusters which are combined at successively higher levels until one complete cluster is formed. Therefore while dendrograms cannot be taken to represent chronological descent they may still reveal useful information concerning the inherent classification of the witnesses involved. This highlights one of the advantages in using multivariate analysis for witness classification in that the various text-type affinities that may exist among the witnesses is resolved from the data and not imposed externally as a pre-defined set of categories.[82]

The dendrograms presented here use an agglomerative technique. Various criteria can be applied for combining clusters such as; a) single-link: the minimum distance between an object in group A and one in group B; b) complete-link: the maximum distance between an object in group A and one in group B; group-average: the average of distances between all possible object pairs, where one object is in group A and the other is in group B; d) Ward's criterion: Uses a method besides proximity by combining at each step those two items which produce the least increase of within-group sums of squared distances.[83] The dendrograms presented in Chapter 7 are calculated using the R script, cluster.r and are based on single-link, group-average and Ward's method.

---

[81] Murrell discusses the use of the graphics capabilities in R to produce dendrograms. See Paul Murrell, R Graphics (Boca Raton, Fla.: Chapman & Hall, 2006), 40–42. Such is the rapid development of graphics capabilities of modern computer statistical packages that though Murrell's book was published as recently as 2006, he makes no reference to the rgl graphics library (for R) used in this study. See also Afifi, Clark and May, Computer-Aided Multivariate Analysis, 432ff.

[82] Chatfield and Collins note that "the basic aim of cluster analysis is to find the 'natural groupings', if any, of a set of individuals... This set of individuals may form a complete population or be a sample from some larger population. More formally, cluster analysis aims to allocate a set of individuals to a set of mutually exclusive, exhaustive, groups such that individuals within a group are similar to one another while individuals in different groups are dissimilar." Chatfield and Collins, Introduction to Multivariate Analysis, 212.

[83] See Finney, Analysis of Textual Variation, sec. 4.5.1. Thorpe designates four criteria as: a) Nearest Neighbour; b) Furthest Neighbour; c) Mean Distance; d) Centroid: "This method requires a full set of coordinates to be present for all of the objects to be classified. It calculates the centroid coordinates of each cluster, then the Euclidean distances between each pair of centroids. The pair with the least distance is merged before proceeding to the next iteration." Thorpe, "Multivariate Statistical Analysis," sec. 59.

Optimal partitioning cluster maps are a further means of observing classification of witnesses. The method used to produce this type of map partitions the data into a predetermined number of groups by clustering witnesses around representative objects called *medoids*.[84] The *R* script *cluster.r* is also used to construct clusters by adding witnesses to the nearest medoids in such a way as to minimise the sum of dissimilarities of group members.[85] Since the three major text-types of Alexandrian, Byzantine and Western are represented in the quantitative and group profile analysis for Acts and the Pauline Epistles, maps for three groups are constructed in order to observe whether the *a priori* classification of witnesses is reflected in the clustering evident in the maps. The Alexandrian witnesses are also divided into Primary and Secondary sub-groups and therefore maps for four clusters are presented. For the Catholic Epistles two groups, Byzantine and Alexandrian are considered and therefore maps with two and three clusters are produced.

---

[84] Medoids are distinct from cluster means or centroids in that they are representative members of the data set whose average dissimilarity to all the (other) objects in their respective cluster is minimal. See Leonard Kaufman and Peter J. Rousseeuw, *Finding Groups in Data: An Introduction to Cluster analysis* (New York: Wiley, 1989); also Mark J. van der Laan, Katherine S. Pollard and Jennifer Bryan, "A New Partitioning Around Medoids Algorithm," n.p. [cited 18 October 2008]. Online: http://www.bepress.com/ucbbiostat/paper105.

[85] See Finney, *Analysis of Textual Variation*, sec. 4.5.3.

5
QUANTITATIVE ANALYSIS

The results of a quantitative analysis for the Apostolos of Athanasius are presented here with the genres of Acts, the Pauline Epistles and the Catholic Epistles analyzed separately.[1]

ACTS

A review of the data for Acts in Table 4 shows that the alignment of witnesses by textual groups is even more clearly distinguished than will be observed in the Pauline Epistles (following).[2]

Table 4: Agreement of Manuscripts with Athanasius in Acts: Ordinal List

Witness	No. Agreements	No. Occurrences	% Agreement	±% Error
81	32	41	78	13
B	34	45	76	13
1891	34	45	76	13
A	33	45	73	13
Ψ	33	45	73	13
ℵ	32	45	71	13
630	32	45	71	13
1175	32	45	71	13
1704	32	45	71	13
945	31	45	69	14
1739	31	45	69	14
$\mathfrak{P}^{74}$	29	43	67	14

---

[1] The data from Revelation is not analyzed as there are insufficient significant variation units to enable any meaningful results to be produced. Finney claims that a minimum acceptable sample size of twelve significant variation units are required to enable any statistically significant results to be obtained. On this basis Mullen's claim that "as few as six points of variation" can give good results is questionable, though it should be noted that Mullen's comments are not made with reference to quantitative analysis but profile methods. See Finney, *Analysis of Textual Variation*, sec. 3.4.4; Mullen, *Text of Cyril*, 305, 360.

[2] Refer Table 68 (Appendix A) for the full Percentage Agreement Matrix for Acts (Complete Corpus).

Witness	No. Agreements	No. Occurrences	% Agreement	±% Error
P	29	44	66	14
C	26	41	63	15
H	27	45	60	14
1073	27	45	60	14
L	19	32	59	17
049	26	45	58	14
1352	26	45	58	14
383	11	21	52	21
E	23	45	51	15
614	22	45	49	15
D	14	36	39	16

Of the top eleven witnesses, nine are Secondary Alexandrian, though MS C which had the highest agreement with Athanasius in the Paulines, is not amongst them but is found further down the list at 63%.[3] In general the proportional agreements are higher for all groups than those found in the Paulines.

As a result of Geer's observation concerning the changing textual character of MS 33 in Acts, Osburn analyzed Acts both in its entirety and in two divisions, chapters 1–12 and 13–28.[4] This division is also adopted here.

Table 5: Agreements with Athanasius in Acts 1–12 and 13–28

(Order of columns: Witness; No. Agreements; No. Comparisons; **% Agreement with Athanasius**; ±% Error)

Acts 1–12					Acts 13–28				
1891	16	19	**84**	16	1175	21	26	**81**	15
B	15	19	**79**	18	81	17	22	**77**	18
81	15	19	**79**	18	A	20	26	**77**	16
ℵ	13	19	**68**	21	Ψ	20	26	**77**	16
A	13	19	**68**	21	630	20	26	**77**	16
Ψ	13	19	**68**	21	𝔓74	19	26	**73**	17
1704	13	19	**68**	21	ℵ	19	26	**73**	17
1739	13	19	**68**	21	B	19	26	**73**	17
630	12	19	**63**	22	P	19	26	**73**	17
945	12	19	**63**	22	945	19	26	**73**	17
𝔓74	10	17	**59**	23	1704	19	26	**73**	17
C	11	19	**58**	22	1739	18	26	**69**	18
H	11	19	**58**	22	1891	18	26	**69**	18

[3] This is not surprising in view of the complex history of this manuscript. See Metzger and Ehrman, *Text of the New Testament*, 69–70.

[4] Geer, "The Two Faces."; also Osburn, *Text of the Apostolos in Epiphanius*, 200.

Acts 1–12					Acts 13–28			
1175	11	19	**58**	22	C	15	22	**68**	19
P	10	18	**56**	23	1073	17	26	**65**	18
049	10	19	**53**	22	E	16	26	**62**	19
1073	10	19	**53**	22	H	16	26	**62**	19
1352	10	19	**53**	22	L	16	26	**62**	19
L	3	6	**50**	40	049	16	26	**62**	19
614	8	19	**42**	22	1352	16	26	**62**	19
D	6	15	**40**	25	614	14	26	**54**	19
E	7	19	**37**	22	383	11	21	**52**	21
383	-	-	**Lac.**	-	D	8	21	**38**	21

The proportional agreements for text-type groups in Table 6 show that there is very little distinction (0.1%) between the Primary and Secondary Alexandrian groups in the Acts corpus.

Table 6: Percentage Agreement of Witnesses with Athanasius in Acts: By Text Type

a) Primary Alexandrian

Witness	Agreements	Comparisons
B	34	45
ℵ	32	45
$\mathfrak{P}^{74}$	29	43
Total	95	133
Agreement=	**71.4% (±7.7%)**	

b) Secondary Alexandrian

Witness	Agreements	Comparisons
81	32	41
1891	34	45
A	33	45
Ψ	33	45
630	32	45
1175	32	45
1704	32	45
1739	31	45
945	31	45
C	26	41
Total	316	442
Agreement=	**71.5% (±4.2%)**	
Total	411	575
All Alexandrian Agreement=	**71.5% (±3.7%)**	

c) Byzantine

Witness	Agreements	Comparisons
P	29	44
H	27	45
1073	27	45
L	19	32
1352	26	45
049	26	45
Total	154	256
	Agreement=	**60.2% (±6.0%)**

d) Western

Witness	Agreements	Comparisons
383	11	21
E	23	45
614	22	45
D	14	36
Total	70	147
	Agreement=	**47.6% (±8.1%)**

Taken together however, the Alexandrian group demonstrates a substantial disparity to the Byzantine which is the next closest group (71.5% compared to 60.2%) and as a result satisfies Ehrman's definition of at least a 65% group affinity with a 6–8% disparity to the next group. Of further interest is the fact that all groups have weaker proportional agreement in the first section (1–12) of Acts than the second (13–28) (See Table 7).

Table 7: Percentage Agreement of Athanasius with Text-Type Groups in Acts Corpus and in Two Sections; Chapters 1–12 and 13–28

Groups	Acts: Corpus	Acts: 1–12[5]	Acts: 13–28
All Alexandrian	71.5	68.2	73.9
Primary Alexandrian	71.4	69.1	73.1
Secondary Alexandrian	71.5	67.9	74.2
Byzantine	60.2	54.0	64.1
Western	47.6	40.0	52.0

In particular the Byzantine and Western have more than 10% greater affinity in chapters 13–28. As noted in Chapter 4, a test to determine the statistical significance of Athanasius' alignment with the various textual groupings in

---

[5] Refer to Appendix A for the relevant tables of percentage agreement by text-type group in Acts 1–12 and 13–28.

sections of the Apostolos can be made using a Mann-Whitney (Wilcoxon) test. The strong support for the Alexandrian group throughout Acts is also reflected in the results of such a test (Table 8).

Table 8: Mann–Whitney (Wilcoxon) Test: Acts

Text Type	P value (to 3 significant digits)	% Probability (<5% = significant)
Acts: Corpus		
All Alexandrian	1.75e-06	0.000175
Primary Alexandrian	0.106	10.6
Secondary Alexandrian	0.0005	0.05
Byzantine	0.968	96.8
Western	1	100
Acts: 1–12		
All Alexandrian	6.03e-06	0.000603
Primary Alexandrian	0.0786	7.86
Secondary Alexandrian	0.0016	0.16
Byzantine	0.987	98.7
Western	1	100
Acts: 13–28		
All Alexandrian	1.92e-05	0.00192
Primary Alexandrian	0.187	18.7
Secondary Alexandrian	0.0006	0.06
Byzantine	0.952	95.2
Western	1	100

Of note is the clear result not only for the significance of the All Alexandrian group but also of the Secondary Alexandrian group in both sections and the corpus. This even applies in Acts 1–12 where the proportional agreements in Table 7 show that the Primary Alexandrian group is higher than the Secondary Alexandrian group (69.1% compared to 67.9%).

This result is surprising but can be attributed to the importance of the *distribution* of proportional agreements of witnesses within a group and not just the percentage values when conducting a Mann-Whitney test.[6] The results here demonstrate that applying a Mann-Whitney (Wilcoxon) test to proportional agreements data provides a viable, statistically cognizant alternative to Ehrman's suggested modification of the Colwell-Tune rule, especially since significant agreement is determined from the data itself and not from the application of an *ad hoc* measure.

---

[6] For example the standard deviation for the Primary Alexandrian group is 10.0 but only 8.3 for the Secondary Alexandrian group in Acts 1–12.

PAULINE EPISTLES

The Pauline Epistles are analyzed as an entire corpus and by epistle; Romans, 1 Corinthians, 2 Corinthians to Titus (inclusive) and Hebrews so as to enable detection of possible shifts in textual alignments.

Table 9 presents an ordinal chart of the percentage agreements for all the witnesses with Athanasius arranged from highest percentage agreement to lowest.[7]

Table 9: Agreement of Manuscripts with Athanasius in the Pauline Epistles: Ordinal List

Witness	No. Agreements	No. Comparisons	% Agreement	±% Error
C	80	118	67.8	8.4
P	102	164	62.2	7.4
33	103	168	61.3	7.4
A	95	155	61.3	7.7
$\aleph^c$	101	168	60.1	7.4
$\aleph$	100	168	59.5	7.4
1739	98	168	58.3	7.5
104	97	167	58.1	7.5
L	93	167	55.7	7.5
223	90	163	55.2	7.6
Ψ	92	168	54.8	7.5
$\mathfrak{P}^{46}$	65	126	51.6	8.7
049	51	99	51.5	9.8
K	75	146	51.4	8.1
876	86	168	51.2	7.6
B	71	141	50.4	8.3
2423	74	148	50.0	8.1
D	75	168	44.6	7.5
G	54	129	41.9	8.5
F	47	119	39.5	8.8

There are 168 significant variation units in the Pauline Epistles corpus and for each epistle respectively: Romans=21, 1 Corinthians=40, 2 Corinthians–Titus=71[8],

---

[7] Table 76 to Table 85 (See Appendix A) present the percentage agreement matrices for the entire Pauline corpus and each epistle, along with their related error margin matrices.

[8] Since there were too few variation units in each of the individual epistles, 2 Corinthians (14), Galatians (4), Ephesians (14), Philippians (10), Colossians (11), 1 Thessalonians (3), 1 Timothy (3), 2 Timothy (11) and Titus (1) were combined as one epistolary section. Osburn preserved 2 Corinthians as a separate epistle but combined Galatians–Hebrews. Mullen combined 1 Thessalonians–Titus though his analysis of other epistles individually was on the basis of very few samples. For example his data for Galatians included only seven points of variation, and Philippians only one!

Hebrews=36.[9] As noted earlier, the text-type groups considered in the Pauline Epistles are; Primary Alexandrian, Secondary Alexandrian, Byzantine and Western.[10]

Secondary Alexandrian witnesses occupy the first five top level positions followed by a number of Primary Alexandrians. Codex Ephraemi Syri Rescriptus (C 04) has the highest agreement with Athanasius even though it is based on the second lowest number of comparisons (118). The associated error margin is 8.4%. This level of error margin is similar to Cosaert's results for Clement of Alexandria though the highest error margin for Athanasius of 9.8% for MS 049 (based on the lowest number of comparisons = 99) is far lower than some of the aberrant figures obtained by Cosaert.[11] The 67.8% agreement of C with Athanasius is higher than the 62.4% agreement obtained by Brogan in the Gospels text of Athanasius.

A review of Table 10 shows the proportional agreement of C with Athanasius for each epistle of the Pauline Epistles is respectively; Romans = 63%,1 Corinthians = 58%, 2 Corinthians–Titus = 78%, and Hebrews = 63%.

---

[9] In comparison, Osburn used a total of 129 variation units in the Pauline Epistles while Mullen used 175. See Osburn, *Text of the Apostolos in Epiphanius*, 216; Mullen, *Text of Cyril*, 351ff.

[10] Osburn used the terminology of 'Old Egyptian' and Late Egyptian' to refer to the Primary and Later Alexandrian text-type groups respectively. He also delineates 'family 1739' as a sub-group within the 'Egyptian' group though this will not be treated separately here since the main focus will be a comparison with Brogan's results for Athanasius' text of the Gospels. See Osburn, *Text of the Apostolos in Epiphanius*, 38–39.

[11] For example Cosaert includes Athanasius in the list of proportional agreements of manuscripts with Clement in Matthew (though he does not include Athanasius in the subsequent data analysis). Athanasius' agreement with Clement is 77.8% but with a ±30.9% error margin since the comparison is based on only nine variation units. As noted earlier, this is too few to determine reliable results. Cosaert, *Text of the Gospels in Clement*, 226.

Table 10: Agreements with Athanasius in Romans, 1 Corinthians, 2 Corinthians–Titus and Hebrews

(Order of columns: Witness; No. Agreements; No. Comparisons;
% Agreement with Athanasius; ±% Error)

Romans					1 Corinthians					2 Corinthians–Titus					Hebrews				
A	14	21	**67**	20	A	24	38	**63**	15	C	39	50	**78**	11	P	26	36	**72**	15
C	12	19	**63**	22	33	25	40	**63**	15	104	45	70	**64**	11	33	25	36	**69**	15
א	13	21	**62**	21	C	19	33	**58**	17	P	44	69	**64**	11	אᶜ	24	36	**67**	15
אᶜ	13	21	**62**	21	א	23	40	**58**	15	223	45	71	**63**	11	A	24	36	**67**	15
Ψ	13	21	**62**	21	𝔓⁴⁶	20	35	**57**	16	אᶜ	43	71	**61**	11	104	24	36	**67**	15
L	12	21	**57**	21	P	20	38	**53**	16	K	43	71	**61**	11	1739	24	36	**67**	15
P	12	21	**57**	21	אᶜ	21	40	**53**	15	33	42	71	**59**	11	א	23	36	**64**	16
049	12	21	**57**	21	1739	21	40	**53**	15	876	42	71	**59**	11	C	10	16	**63**	24
223	12	21	**57**	21	Ψ	20	40	**50**	15	1739	42	71	**59**	11	𝔓⁴⁶	22	36	**61**	16
33	11	21	**52**	21	L	19	40	**48**	15	2423	30	51	**59**	14	B	14	24	**58**	20
876	11	21	**52**	21	B	18	40	**45**	15	L	41	70	**59**	12	L	21	36	**58**	16
1739	11	21	**52**	21	104	18	40	**45**	15	א	41	71	**58**	11	223	17	31	**55**	18
2423	11	21	**52**	21	049	12	28	**43**	18	Ψ	40	71	**56**	12	Ψ	19	36	**53**	16
𝔓⁴⁶	4	8	**50**	34	D	17	40	**43**	15	B	31	56	**55**	13	876	19	36	**53**	16
104	10	21	**48**	21	223	16	40	**40**	15	A	33	60	**55**	13	2423	17	36	**47**	16
K	8	17	**47**	24	2423	16	40	**40**	15	049	27	50	**54**	14	K	16	36	**44**	16
D	9	21	**43**	21	F	15	38	**39**	16	D	34	71	**48**	12	D	15	36	**42**	16
G	9	21	**43**	21	G	15	38	**39**	16	G	30	70	**43**	12	F	Lac.			
B	8	21	**38**	21	K	8	22	**36**	20	𝔓⁴⁶	19	47	**40**	14	G	Lac.			
F	4	11	**36**	28	876	14	40	**35**	15	F	28	70	**40**	11	049	Lac.			

It is clear that in Romans and Hebrews the agreement of MS C with Athanasius is similar to the average result from the Gospels, but the higher agreement in 2 Corinthians–Titus is responsible for raising the average agreement in the Pauline Epistles. Table 10 also demonstrates the movement of witnesses relative to each other in the various epistles. For example, though C agrees with Athanasius at 63% in both Romans and Hebrews it is second highest in Romans (after A) but only eighth highest in Hebrews. This is due to the higher average agreements in the latter epistle.[12] The generally higher error margins associated with the results for the individual epistles due to the lower number of sample variation units should also be noted and urges caution in the use of these results. Nevertheless, Table 10, along with Table 9, demonstrates the highest general agreement of Athanasius with Secondary Alexandrian witnesses followed by the Primary Alexandrians and the Byzantines while having least agreement with the Western witnesses.

---

[12] This may be partly due to the fact that MSS F, G and 049 are lacunose in Hebrews.

Since P was not used in Brogan's study of the Gospels text of Athanasius no further comment on this manuscript will be made here. The agreement of 33 at 61.3% in the Pauline Epistles (see Table 9) is also generally lower than the 67.4% result in the Gospels.[13] The comparison of A must be applied with caution since it is associated with a Secondary Alexandrian text-type in the Pauline Epistles but a Byzantine text-type in the Gospels. Therefore one might expect a higher proportional agreement of Athanasius with A in the Paulines than in the Gospels. This however is not the case with 61.3% agreement in the Paulines but a higher 67.9% agreement in the Gospels. Why this might be the case will be discussed shortly when reviewing the proportional relationships arranged according to textual groupings (Table 11 and the summary data in Table 12). The correction of Codex Sinaiticus ($\aleph^c$) shows agreement of 60.1% with Athanasius in the Paulines compared to 71.1% in the Gospels while the original hand of Codex Sinaiticus ($\aleph$) shows 59.5% agreement in the Paulines and 62.1% in the Gospels. The differentiation between the original and corrected hands of Codex Sinaiticus is much lower in the Paulines (60.1–59.5 = 0.6%) than in the Gospels (71.1%–62.1% = 9.0%).

Codex Laurensis (Ψ 044) should also be noted here. In both the Gospel and the Pauline Epistles Ψ is classified as a Secondary Alexandrian though its agreement with Athanasius in the Gospels is 77% but only 54.8% in the Paulines.[14] Osburn noted a shift of text type in Ψ on the basis of the results of Morrill's analysis of manuscript classifications in 1 Corinthians in which he noted that Ψ has a mixed text much closer to the Byzantine tradition.[15] In order to test this, Ψ was included in the present analysis. Ψ has a proportional agreement of 62% with Athanasius in Romans which drops to only 50% in 1 Corinthians but rises again to 56% in 2 Corinthians–Titus and 53% in Hebrews.[16] Therefore it does appear that there is some shift in 1 Corinthians though the result for 2 Corinthians –Titus mitigates the severity of the shift. Nevertheless in the tables which present the proportional agreements by textual groupings, the results for the Secondary Alexandrian will be shown both with and without the inclusion of Ψ. A clearer picture of Athanasius' affinity with the various textual groups can be seen by looking at the data of proportional agreements by text-type groups, both for the Pauline corpus as a whole and for the individual epistles (Table 11 and Tables for individual epistles in Appendix A). Table 11 shows the data for the Pauline corpus.

[13] See Brogan, "Text of the Gospels," 220ff.

[14] See Greenlee, *New Testament Textual Criticism*, 117–118; also Metzger and Ehrman, *Text of the New Testament*, 313.

[15] See Osburn, *Text of the Apostolos in Epiphanius*, 213; Bruce Morrill, "The Classification of the Greek Manuscripts of First Corinthians" (M.A. Thesis, Harding Graduate School of Religion, 1981).

[16] Refer to Appendix A: Percentage Agreement Tables–Witnesses by text-type for individual Pauline epistles.

Table 11: Percentage Agreement of Witnesses with Athanasius in the Pauline
Epistles: By Text Type

a) Primary Alexandrian

Witness	Agreements	Comparisons
ℵ	100	168
1739	98	168
B	71	141
$\mathfrak{P}^{46}$	<u>65</u>	<u>126</u>
Total	334	603
	Agreement=	**55.4% (±4.0%)**

b) Secondary Alexandrian

Witness	Agreements	Comparisons	
33	103	168	
P	102	164	
104	97	167	
A	95	155	
C	80	118	
Total	477	772	(w/o Ψ & ℵ^c)
	Agreement=	**61.8% (±3.4%)**	
ℵ^c	101	168	
Ψ	92	168	
Total	670	1108	(w Ψ & ℵ^c)
	Agreement=	**60.5% (±2.9%)**	
Total	811	1375	
All Alexandrian Agreement=	**59.0% (±2.6%)**		(w/o Ψ & ℵ^c)

c) Byzantine Witnesses

Witness	Agreements	Comparisons
L	93	167
223	90	163
876	86	168
K	75	146
2423	74	148
049	51	99
Total	469	891
	Agreement=	**52.6% (±3.3%)**

d) Western Uncials

Witness	Agreements	Comparisons
D	75	168
G	54	129
F	47	119
Total	176	416
	Agreement=	**42.3% (±4.7%)**

Athanasius' highest agreement is with the Secondary Alexandrian group at 61.8% (68.3% in the Gospels) followed by the Primary Alexandrian at 55.4% (66.8% in the Gospels), the Byzantine at 52.6% (64.8% in the Gospels) and then the Western group at 42.3% (44.9% in the Gospels). While the order of text-type agreement is maintained when compared with the Gospels data, it is also clear that the percentages of agreement for the Pauline Epistles are generally lower with well over 10% difference in the case of the Primary Alexandrian and Byzantine groups. None of the textual groups demonstrates agreement of at least 65% with Athanasius and therefore do not to qualify under Ehrman's modification to the Colwell-Tune rule for identification of a Father with a particular text-type, though the 6.4% disparity between the Secondary and Primary Alexandrian groups do satisfy the second part of Ehrman's modified rule requiring a 6–8% gap between text-type groups. The Alexandrian witnesses considered together have a proportional agreement with Athanasius of 59% compared to 67.7% in the Gospels. A review of the data for proportional agreement by text-type groups for each epistle provides further clarification. This can be seen in the summary data of Table 12.

Table 12: Percentage Agreement of Athanasius with Text-Type Groups in the
Pauline Epistles Corpus and Individual Epistles

Groups	Corpus	Romans[16]	1 Cor	2 Cor–Titus	Hebrews
Alexandrian	59.0	54.6	54.7	59.5	65.8
Primary	55.4	50.7	52.9	54.3	62.9
Secondary	61.8	57.3	56.1	63.4	68.1
Byzantine	52.6	54.1	40.5	59.4	51.4
Western	42.3	41.5	40.5	43.6	41.7

In all epistles the Secondary Alexandrian group shows the highest agreement with Athanasius. However the next highest group varies. In Romans
the Secondary Alexandrian group (57.3%) is followed by the Byzantine group
(54.1%), then by the Primary Alexandrian (50.7%) and then the Western (41.5%).
This order also applies in 2 Corinthians–Titus where the Secondary Alexandrian
agreement (63.4%) is followed next by the Byzantine group (59.4%), then the
Primary Alexandrian (54.3%) and finally the Western group (43.6%). In comparison, 1 Corinthians and Hebrews reflect the order of the Pauline corpus;
the highest agreement is with the Secondary Alexandrian group, then Primary
Alexandrian, Byzantine and finally Western. The fluctuations from the corpus
average for the Secondary Alexandrians in each epistle are; Romans (–4.5%), 1
Corinthians (–5.7%), 2 Corinthians–Titus (+1.6%), Hebrews (+6.3%). The reason
for this pattern is unclear. At the very least the data above indicates that while the
Secondary Alexandrian text-type has the highest support in Athanasius' writings in the Pauline Epistles, the Byzantine influence is not inconsiderable and
competes with the Primary Alexandrian in some epistles.[18]

The influence of MS Ψ as a special case, (along with ℵ^c)[19] is considered in
the proportional agreement for the Secondary Alexandrian group. When these
two are included in the calculations for the Pauline corpus the percentage drops
by 1.3% (from 61.8% to 60.5%). By epistle the results are; Romans (+1.3%), 1
Corinthians (–1.5%), 2 Corinthians–Titus (–1.5%), Hebrews (–2.6%). It is clear
that Ψ is a stronger Secondary Alexandrian witness in Romans than in the
remaining epistles and tends to confirm the conclusion that there is a shift in Ψ
toward the Byzantine text-type in 1 Corinthians.

---

[17] Refer to Appendix A for the relevant tables of percentage agreement by text-type for individual epistles in the Pauline corpus.

[18] In Romans, Athanasius' agreement with Secondary Alexandrian group is 57.3% but the
Byzantine is not much less at 54.1%. In 2 Corinthians–Titus his agreement with the Secondary
Alexandrian is 63.4% while the Byzantine agreement is 59.4% which is almost equivalent to the
Alexandrian group average of 59.5% and well above the Primary Alexandrian agreement of 54.3%.
See Table 12.

[19] Brogan calculates totals for the Secondary Alexandrian group both with and without ℵ^c
for each gospel (though not in the aggregate totals). In order to allow for direct comparison this
procedure is also carried out in the present study.

The results of a Mann–Whitney (Wilcoxon) test for the Pauline Epistles are presented in Table 13.[20]

Table 13: Mann–Whitney (Wilcoxon) Test: Pauline Epistles

Text Type	P value (to 3 significant digits)	% Probability (<5% = significant)
Pauline Epistles: Complete Corpus		
All Alexandrian	0.000905	**0.09**
Primary Alexandrian	0.390	39
Secondary Alexandrian	0.000350	**0.035**
Byzantine	0.851	85
Western	1	100
Pauline Epistles: Romans		
All Alexandrian	0.129	12.9
Primary Alexandrian	0.650	65
Secondary Alexandrian	0.0541	5.41
Byzantine	0.0984	9.84
Western	0.997	99.7
Pauline Epistles: 1 Corinthians		
All Alexandrian	6.17e-05	**0.00617**
Primary Alexandrian	0.0830	8.3
Secondary Alexandrian	0.00502	**0.502**
Byzantine	0.992	99.2
Western	0.952	95.2
Pauline Epistles: 2 Corinthians–Titus		
All Alexandrian	0.197	19.7
Primary Alexandrian	0.882	88.2
Secondary Alexandrian	0.0179	**1.79**
Byzantine	0.184	18.4
Western	0.996	99.6
Pauline Epistles: Hebrews		
All Alexandrian	0.000400	**0.04**
Primary Alexandrian	0.294	29.4
Secondary Alexandrian	0.00233	**0.233**
Byzantine	0.994	99.4
Western	1	100

Athanasius has significant agreement with the Secondary Alexandrian group in both the corpus and in each epistle except for Romans where the result of 5.41% is just outside the P value statistic of <5% in order to be considered

---

[20] Table 14 contains a comparison with the data from Athanasius' text of the Gospels. See Brogan, "Text of the Gospels," 184–224.

significant. The results for the Pauline corpus and for the individual epistles are conclusive; corpus (0.035%), 1 Corinthians (0.502%), 2 Corinthians–Titus (1.79%), Hebrews (0.233%). It appears that Romans is a special case in the Pauline Epistles for Athanasius. A review of the data for Romans in Table 12 provides some clues to help explain this result. As noted earlier, in Romans the Secondary Alexandrian group shows the highest agreement with Athanasius (57.3%) followed by the Byzantine group (54.1%). These two groups are separated by 3.2% and the result is that the stronger influence of the Byzantine text-type is enough to dilute the otherwise significant affinity of Athanasius' text with the Secondary Alexandrian text-type in Romans.

This strong Byzantine influence is also reflected in the Mann–Whitney results for the corpus (All Alexandrian) in Romans which is 12.9% and therefore well outside the 5% maximum required for significance. Another interesting result relates to the epistles 2 Corinthians–Titus. While the Secondary Alexandrian group shows significant agreement (1.79%) the All Alexandrian result is not significant (19.7%) and again the influence of the Byzantine group is evident here. Table 12 shows that the difference between the Secondary Alexandrian and Byzantine groups is 4% and though this is not enough to cancel the significance of the Secondary Alexandrian group it does weaken it (compare 1.79% for 2 Corinthians–Titus against 0.035% for the corpus, 0.502% for 1 Corinthians and 0.233% for Hebrews). However, the difference of only 0.5% between the Byzantine and All Alexandrian groups in Romans (refer to Table 12) is enough to undermine the statistical significance of the latter group. This demonstrates that it is possible to successfully utilise standard statistical tests for significance using even (very) close results for proportional agreement.[21]

Table 14: Comparison Mann–Whitney (Wilcoxon) Test: Athanasius in the Gospels

Text Type	P value (to 3 significant digits)	% Probability (<5% = significant)
All Alexandrian	0.00262	**0.262**
Primary Alexandrian	0.144	14.4
Secondary Alexandrian	0.0226	**2.26**
Byzantine	0.330	33.0
Western	1	100

---

[21] It is necessary to recognise the provisional nature of these results when taking into account the higher error margins associated with the proportional agreements used in the calculations of the Mann-Whitney test, especially where the sample sizes are smaller as is the case when analyzing the epistles individually.

CATHOLIC EPISTLES

Table 15: Agreements with Athanasius in the Catholic Epistles

(Order of columns: Witness; No. Agreements; No. Comparisons; % Agreement with Athanasius; ±% Error)

Witness	No. Agreements	No. Comparisons	% Agree	±% Error
L	6	12	50	28
105	6	12	50	28
201	6	12	50	28
1739	6	12	50	28
C	4	9	44	32
A	5	12	42	28
Ψ	5	12	42	28
1022	5	12	42	28
1424	5	12	42	28
2423	5	12	42	28
325	3	8	38	27
$\mathfrak{P}^{72}$	2	6	33	38
049	4	12	33	27
323	4	12	33	27
33	3	11	27	26
ℵ	3	12	25	25
B	2	12	17	21

Since the Western text-type has no apparent support in the Catholic Epistles, the only two groups considered here are the Alexandrian and Byzantine.[22] In contrast to previous results in Acts and the Pauline Epistles, Athanasius' strongest affinity is with the Byzantine text (43%) rather than the Alexandrian (35%) in the Catholic Epistles as can be seen from Table 16.

---

[22] For comments concerning lack of a Western witness in the Catholic Epistles see Metzger and Ehrman, *Text of the New Testament*, 309, n.19. Wasserman suggested that Osburn could have included more than just the two Alexandrian and Byzantine groups in his analysis of the Catholic Epistles in Epiphanius by including, for example, the Harclensis group. This suggestion has not been adopted here in order to maintain a direct comparison with the textual groupings as used by Brogan in the Gospels as well as with Osburn's results in the Catholic Epistles. See Tommy Wasserman, review of Carroll D. Osburn, *The Text of the Apostolos in Epiphanius of Salamis*, *RBL* [http://www.bookreviews.org] (2005), 3.

Table 16: Percentage Agreement of Witnesses with Athanasius in the Catholic Epistles: By Text Type

a) Alexandrian Witnesses

Witness	Agreements	Comparisons
1739	6	12
C	4	9
A	5	12
Ψ	5	12
$\mathfrak{P}^{72}$	2	6
323	4	12
33	3	11
ℵ	3	12
B	2	12
Total	34	98
Agreement=		**35% (±9%)**

b) Byzantine Witnesses

Witness	Agreements	Comparisons
105	6	12
201	6	12
L	6	12
1022	5	12
1424	5	12
2423	5	12
325	3	8
049	4	<u>12</u>
Total	40	92
Agreement=		**43% (±10%)**

This is similar to Osburn's results for Epiphanius.[23] His agreement with the Byzantine group was far greater at 80% with the Alexandrian group agreement at

---

[23] There appears to be a number of errors in the presentation of the Quantitative and Group Profile analysis results for the Catholic Epistles in Osburn's study. Osburn states that "selected MSS from Family 1739 in Acts are included in the quantitative analysis [of the Catholic Epistles] because of the close relationship of Epiphanius' text of Acts to that group." Osburn, *The Text of the Apostolos in Epiphanius of Salamis*, 208. However the only manuscript witness from Family 1739 included in the Alexandrian [Egyptian] group is MS 1739 itself. See ibid., 210, Table 21. There the proportional agreement of MS 1739 with Epiphanius is 40%. However in the summary data in Table 22, *Family 1739* is listed as a separate group with a proportional agreement of 58.8%. Further, the reference in Table 22 to being a summary of the statistical data in Tables 18–20 appears to be incorrect since there is no Table 18 and therefore while Table 22 refers to Tables 18–20 it actually summarizes Tables 19–21. The Totals data in Table 23 for the Byzantine group is also missing. It should show seven agreements out of nine total (7/9) for a proportional agreement of 77%. Also the final comment below this table should read; "Agreeing with the one Distinctive [not *exclusive*] Byzantine

49%. Caution is necessary when considering the results for Athanasius, since the analysis is based on a total of only twelve readings. As noted earlier, this figure equates to the lower limit for statistically meaningful data.[24] The error margins are correspondingly high with such low samples (see Appendix A; Table 98) and therefore while the results provide some basic conclusions they are necessarily provisional in nature. While there is an 8% disparity between the Byzantine and Alexandrian groups, the generally low overall agreements indicate that Athanasius cannot be considered to have a strong affinity with either group.

This is confirmed by the Mann–Whitney test (see Table 17) although the 5.84% result for the Byzantine group lies just outside the 5% maximum for determining Athanasius' significant alignment with that group.

Table 17: Mann–Whitney (Wilcoxon) Test: Catholic Epistles

Text Type	P value (to 3 significant digits)	% Probability (<5% = significant)
Alexandrian	0.949	94.9
Byzantine	0.0584	5.84

Nevertheless, the conclusion on the basis of the data presented here is that Athanasius appears to have a stronger affinity with the Byzantine group than the Alexandrian in the Catholic Epistles and that this is the only place he does so in the Apostolos and indeed the whole of the New Testament. It is to be expected that a Group Profile Analysis will clarify the picture of the Catholic Epistles as well as that of Acts and the Pauline Epistles.

---

reading, Epiphanius also reads six of eight primary Byzantine texts." Wasserman also noted that Osburn indicates his analysis is based on a total of thirteen readings in the Catholic Epistles (p. 255) but the tabular data shows only a maximum of ten (Tables 20–21). Wasserman, review of Osburn, 4. Osburn does list a total of thirteen readings in (his) Table 24 (Intra-Group Profile) for the Byzantine group but this is surely an error as it is not possible to have an aggregate total of readings in any category of the Group Profiles that is greater than the highest number of comparisons used in the quantitative analysis. Unfortunately Osburn does not indicate which are the relevant readings used in each category of the group profile analysis as this would have enabled verification of his data. Therefore the results for the Group Profiles in particular should be treated with caution.

[24] See Finney, *Analysis of Textual Variation*, sec. 3.4.4. Osburn's analysis being based on a sample of only ten variation units render the decimal points, specified in his proportional agreements results, superfluous. See Osburn, *Text of the Apostolos in Epiphanius*, 211, Table 22.

6
GROUP PROFILE ANALYSIS

The group profile analysis is designed to supplement the quantitative analysis discussed in the previous chapter by focussing on Athanasius' preservation of readings characteristic of the various textual groupings. The three sections in the Apostolos of Acts, the Pauline Epistles and the Catholic Epistles will be considered in turn.

ACTS

The results of a group-profile analysis of Acts confirm the conclusions derived from the quantitative analysis of an even clearer distinction between the Alexandrian textual group and the Byzantine and Western groups than that observed in the Pauline Epistles.

The only positive result in the inter-group profile for Acts (Table 18) is the 47% agreement of Athanasius with the Alexandrian group since there are no agreements for the Byzantine and Western groups.

Table 18: Athanasius' Attestation of Inter-Group Readings in Acts

	Distinctive Rdgs		**Exclusive** Rdgs		**Primary** Rdgs		Agree Total	Total Rdgs	**%** **Agree**	**±%** **Error**
Alex	4	7	0	5	4	5	8	17	**47**	24
Byz	0	1	0	0	0	4	0	5	**0**	0
West	0	2	0	0	0	1	0	3	**0**	0

Lack of agreement for these two groups in the Acts data is not an anomaly as it is observed again in the combined group profile (Table 19)[1] for the corpus as well as in the inter and combined profiles of the two sections of Acts (1–12 and 13–28).

---

[1] As discussed in Chapter 4, this profile is a combination of the inter and intra-group profiles and provides Athanasius' attestation of Uniform and Predominant readings that are also Distinctive, Exclusive or Primary.

Table 19: Athanasius' Attestation of Uniform or Predominant Readings in Acts
That Are Also Distinctive, Exclusive or Primary

	Uniform Rdgs		Predominant Rdgs		Agree Total	Total Rdgs	% Agree	±% Error
Alex	3	3	4	7	7	10	70	28
Byz	0	3	0	2	0	5	0	0
West	0	1	0	0	0	1	0	0

The intra-group profile (Table 20) shows a very strong agreement of
Athanasius with the (All) Alexandrian group at 82% and with support in the sub-
groups being stronger for the Primary Alexandrian at 76% than the Secondary
Alexandrian at 74%.

Table 20: Athanasius' Attestation of Intra-Group Readings in Acts

	Uniform Rdgs		Predominant Rdgs		Agree Total	Total Rdgs	% Agree	±% Error
Alex	9	9	22	29	31	38	82	12
- Primary	22	27	12	18	34	45	76	13
- Secondary	16	18	15	24	31	42	74	13
Byz	18	31	8	14	26	45	58	14
West	7	14	10	16	17	30	57	18

This slightly higher support for the Primary Alexandrian than the Secondary
Alexandrian group is contrary to the general pattern established in the Pauline
Epistles and in the results for the quantitative analysis for Acts. There the
proportional agreement was only 0.1% separation in favour of the Secondary
Alexandrian group, though it was noted that this order was reversed in Acts 1–12
but restored again in Acts 13–28.

A review of the intra-group profiles for the two sections, 1–12 and 13–28
(Appendix A; Table 75, and Table 23–following) shows that the Secondary
Alexandrian group has 1% higher support in Acts 1–12 (at 75%) but the Primary
Alexandrian has 4% higher support (at 77%) in Acts 13–28.

When faced with such fluctuations, the results of a Mann-Whitney test would
appear to provide a more statistically verifiable result. Support for the Byzantine
and Western groups in the intra-group profile (Table 20) are nearly equivalent at
58% and 57% respectively. The combined profile (Table 19) also shows Athanasius
strong support for the Alexandrian group at 70% while, as noted earlier, there is
no agreement at all with the Byzantine and Western groups.

The results of the inter-group profile for Acts 1–12 (Table 21) show a much
higher proportional agreement for the Alexandrian group at 63% than in the

Acts corpus (47%); however, again there is no agreement with the Byzantine and Western groups.[2]

Table 21: Athanasius' Attestation of Inter-Group Readings in Acts 1–12

	Distinctive[3] Rdgs		Exclusive[4] Rdgs		Primary[5] Rdgs		Agree Total	Total Rdgs	% Agree	±% Error
Alex	3	5	0	1	2	2	5	8	63	34
Byz	0	0	0	0	0	1	0	1	0	0
West	0	0	0	0	0	0	0	0	0	0

This phenomenon is restricted only to Acts and not the whole of the Apostolos, and is verified by the Mann-Whitney results for Acts reviewed in the previous chapter. In both the corpus and the two sub-sections of Acts the Mann-Whitney results for the Western group is consistently 100% indicating an extremely *non*-significant relationship. The results for the Byzantine group are almost as conclusive in indicating *non*-significant relationship with results of 96% for the corpus, 98% for Acts 1–12 and 95% for Acts 13–28.[6] Therefore the results of the group profile analysis in Acts confirm that Athanasius' support for the Byzantine and Western groups in Acts is minimal and the results of the Mann-Whitney test demonstrate just how statistically *in*significant this support is.

The results from the inter-group profile in Acts 13–28 (Table 22) show that Athanasius' support for the Alexandrian group is much weaker at 33% compared to Acts 1–12.

Table 22: Athanasius' Attestation of Inter-Group Readings in Acts 13–28

	Distinctive[7] Rdgs		Exclusive[8] Rdgs		Primary[9] Rdgs		Agree Total	Total Rdgs	% Agree	±% Error
Alex	1	2	0	4	2	3	3	9	33	31
Byz	0	1	0	0	0	3	0	4	0	0
West	0	2	0	0	0	1	0	3	0	0

---

[2] For the Byzantine group there are no distinctive or exclusive readings and Athanasius does not support the single primary reading. There are no readings at all recorded for the Western group in the inter-group readings profile.

[3] Note that Athanasius *preserves* the respective readings where the final numeral is '1' (eg 2.23.1.**1**). Athanasius *does not* preserve the respective readings where the final numeral is *other* than '1' (eg 1.8.1.**2** or 2.22.2.**3**). The Distinctive Alexandrian Readings in Acts 1–12 are: 1.8.1.2, 2.22.1.2, 2.23.1.1, 2.36.2.1, 7.56.1.1.

[4] The Exclusive Alexandrian Reading in Acts 1–12 is: 8.33.1.2.

[5] Note that the Group Profile classification term 'Primary' used here is not to be confused with the text-type classification 'Primary Alexandrian' which is specified only in the Intra-Group Profile as a subset category type under Uniform or Predominant (see below n. 10). The Primary Alexandrian Readings in Acts 1–12 are: 2.22.2.1, 2.23.2.1; The Primary Byzantine Reading in Acts 1–12 is: 2.22.2.3.

[6] Refer to the results for the Mann-Whitney test for Acts in Chapter 5.

This result contradicts the quantitative analysis since there the proportional agreement was higher in Acts 13–28 at 73.9% than in Acts 1–12 at 68.2%. This may be a statistical anomaly since the profile analysis is based on only nine readings. In comparison the intra-group profile (Table 23) shows that Athanasius' support for the Alexandrian group is 83%.

Table 23: Athanasius' Attestation of Intra-Group Readings in Acts 13–28

	Uniform[10]		**Predominant**[11]		Agree	Total	**%**	**±%**
	Rdgs		Rdgs		Total	Rdgs	**Agree**	**Error**
Alex	7	7	12	16	19	23	83	15
- Primary	13	15	7	11	20	26	77	16
- Secondary	13	14	6	12	19	26	73	17
Byz	13	19	4	7	17	26	65	18
West	5	7	3	6	8	13	62	26

His support for the Byzantine and Western groups is also stronger, at 65% and 62% respectively, than the equivalent result in Acts 1–12.

In the combined profile for Acts 1–12 (Table 24) and 13–28 (Table 25), Athanasius' support for the Alexandrian group is at 80% and 60% respectively though these results are based on even fewer readings (five only) than in the

---

[7] The Distinctive Alexandrian Readings in Acts 13–28 are: 14.17.2.2, 14.17.4.1; The Distinctive Byzantine Reading in Acts 13–28 is: 17.31.1.2; The Distinctive Western Readings in Acts 13–28 are: 13.32.1.2, 17.28.1.2.

[8] The Exclusive Alexandrian Readings in Acts 13–28 are: 13.22.1.2, 14.17.5.2, 17.30.1.2, 25.16.1.2.

[9] The Primary Alexandrian Readings in Acts 13–28 are: 14.15.5.1, 14.17.6.2, 25.16.2.1; The Primary Byzantine Readings in Acts 13–28 are: 13.23.2.3, 14.15.6.2, 25.16.2.2; The Primary Western Reading in Acts 13–28 is: 25.16.4.2.

[10] The Uniform (All) Alexandrian Readings in Acts 13–28 are: 13.32.1.1, 14.15.5.1, 14.17.1.1, 14.17.4.1, 17.28.1.1, 17.31.1.1, 25.16.2.1; The Uniform Primary Alexandrian Readings in Acts 13–28 are: 13.22.1.2, 13.23.1.1, 13.32.1.1, 14.15.1.1, 14.15.2.1, 14.15.3.2, 14.15.4.1, 14.15.5.1, 14.17.1.1, 14.17.4.1, 17.28.1.1, 17.30.2.1, 17.31.1.1, 25.16.1.1, 25.16.2.1; The Uniform Secondary Alexandrian Readings in Acts 13–28 are: 13.22.2.1, 13.23.2.1, 13.32.1.1, 14.15.5.1, 14.15.6.1, 14.17.1.1, 14.17.2.2, 14.17.4.1, 17.28.1.1, 17.30.1.1, 17.31.1.1, 25.16.2.1, 25.16.3.1, 25.16.4.1; The Uniform Byzantine Readings in Acts 13–28 are: 13.22.2.1, 13.23.2.1, 13.32.1.1, 14.15.5.1, 14.15.6.1, 14.17.1.1, 14.17.2.2, 14.17.4.1, 17.28.1.1, 17.30.1.1, 17.31.1.1, 25.16.2.1, 25.16.3.1, 25.16.4.1; The Uniform Western Readings in Acts 13–28 are: 14.17.2.1, 14.17.4.2, 14.17.5.1, 17.30.1.1, 17.31.1.1, 25.16.1.1, 25.16.4.2

[11] The Predominant (All) Alexandrian Readings in Acts 13–28 are: 13.22.1.3, 13.22.2.1, 13.23.2.1, 14.15.1.1, 14.15.2.1, 14.15.3.2, 14.15.4.1, 14.15.6.1, 14.17.2.2, 14.17.3.1, 14.17.5.1, 14.17.6.2, 17.30.1.1, 25.16.3.1, 25.16.4.1, 25.16.5.1; The Predominant Primary Alexandrian Readings in Acts 13–28 are: 13.22.2.1, 13.23.2.1, 14.15.6.1, 14.17.2.2, 14.17.3.2, 14.17.5.1, 14.17.6.2, 17.30.1.2, 25.16.3.1, 25.16.4.1, 25.16.5.1; The Predominant Secondary Alexandrian Readings in Acts 13–28 are: 13.22.1.3, 14.15.1.1, 14.15.2.1, 14.15.3.2, 14.15.4.1, 14.17.2.2, 14.17.3.1, 14.17.5.1, 14.17.6.2, 17.30.2.3, 25.16.1.2, 25.16.5.1; The Predominant Byzantine Readings in Acts 13–28 are: 13.23.2.3, 14.15.1.1, 14.15.2.1, 14.17.3.1, 14.17.4.2, 17.31.1.2, 25.16.3.1; The Predominant Western Readings in Acts 13–28 are: 13.22.1.3, 13.22.2.1, 14.15.1.1, 14.15.3.2, 14.15.5.2, 14.17.6.1.

inter-group profile and are therefore associated with correspondingly larger error margins.

Table 24: Athanasius' Attestation of Uniform or Predominant Readings in Acts 1–12 That Are Also Distinctive, Exclusive or Primary

	Uniform[12] Rdgs		Predominant[13] Rdgs		Agree Total	Total Rdgs	% **Agree**	±% **Error**
Alex	0	0	4	5	4	5	**80**	35
Byz	0	1	0	0	0	1	**0**	0
West	0	0	0	0	0	0	**0**	0

Table 25: Athanasius' Attestation of Uniform or Predominant Readings in Acts 13–28 That Are Also Distinctive, Exclusive or Primary

	Uniform[14] Rdgs		Predominant[15] Rdgs		Agree Total	Total Rdgs	% **Agree**	±% **Error**
Alex	3	3	0	2	3	5	**60**	43
Byz	0	2	0	2	0	4	**0**	0
West	0	1	0	0	0	1	**0**	0

Summary: Despite potential anomalies due to the use of very small samples it is clear that the group profile in Acts confirms Athanasius' strong support for the Alexandrian group. The results for the Primary and Secondary Alexandrian sub-groups however are so close as to preclude a determination of Athanasius' clear preference for either group.

---

[12] The Uniform Byzantine Reading in Acts 1–12 that is also Distinctive, Exclusive or Primary is: 2.22.2.3.

[13] The Uniform Alexandrian Readings in Acts 1–12 that are also Distinctive, Exclusive or Primary are: 2.22.1.2, 2.22.2.1, 2.23.1.1, 2.36.2.1, 7.56.1.1.

[14] The Uniform Alexandrian Readings in Acts 13–28 that are also Distinctive, Exclusive or Primary are: 14.15.5.1, 14.17.4.1, 25.16.2.1; the Uniform Byzantine Readings in Acts 13–28 that are also Distinctive, Exclusive or Primary are: 14.15.6.2, 25.16.2.2; The Uniform Western Reading in Acts 13–28 that is also Distinctive, Exclusive or Primary is: 25.16.4.2.

[15] The Predominant Alexandrian Readings in Acts 13–28 that are also Distinctive, Exclusive or Primary are: 14.17.2.2, 14.17.6.2; The Predominant Byzantine Readings in Acts 13–28 that are also Distinctive, Exclusive or Primary are: 13.23.2.3, 17.31.1.2.

Table 26: Summary of Comprehensive Group Profile Statistical Data in Table 18–Table 25 (Percentage Agreement with Athanasius) for Acts

Inter-Group Readings	Corpus	Chs 1–12	Chs 13–28
Alexandrian	47	63	33
Byzantine	0	0	0
Western	0	0	0
Intra-Group Readings			
Alexandrian	82	80	83
-Primary	76	74	77
-Secondary	74	75	73
Byzantine	58	53	65
Western	57	53	62
Combination Inter & Intra- Group Readings			
Alexandrian	70	80	60
Byzantine	0	0	0
Western	0	0	0

PAULINE CORPUS

The inter-group profile in Table 27 indicates Athanasius' proportional agreement with distinctive, exclusive and primary readings in three textual groups, Alexandrian, Byzantine and Western.

Table 27: Athanasius' Attestation of Inter-Group Readings in the Pauline Epistles

	Distinctive Rdgs		**Exclusive** Rdgs		**Primary** Rdgs		Agree Total	Total Rdgs	**%** **Agree**	**±%** **Error**
Alex	15	28	3	31	2	3	20	62	**32**	12
Byz	0	7	0	1	5	38	5	46	**11**	9
West	1	32	0	0	4	30	5	62	**8**	7

While the percentages for this profile are, as expected, generally lower than those reached in the quantitative analysis, the results here suffice to demonstrate that Athanasius definitely used an Alexandrian text.[16] The concern here is not

---

[16] Osburn notes that since it is rare for all members of a textual group to agree on a particular reading, "one cannot expect large totals or high percentages of agreement in these categories." Osburn, *Text of the Apostolos in Epiphanius*, 230.

to obtain a certain level of agreement such as the 65% suggested in the quantitative analysis but rather, as Cosaert states, "one should look for a group witness
to share a stronger level of agreement with one textual group than another,
regardless of the percentage level."[17] The 32% agreement of Athanasius with the
Alexandrian group is less than the 41% (approximately)[18] result for the Gospels
but the disparity to the next group (Byzantine) is greater in the Pauline Epistles
(31–11=20% in the Paulines; 41–27=14% in the Gospels). In comparison the
agreements for Epiphanius in the Paulines are generally higher but the disparity
from the Alexandrian group (highest) to the Byzantine group is much smaller
(46–38=8%).[19]

As noted in Chapter 4, Mullen essentially ignored exclusive and primary
readings and focussed on distinctive readings. On that basis the results for
Cyril of Jerusalem in the Paulines show that Cyril has stronger support for
the Alexandrian group at 39% with a 15% gap to the Byzantine group which
has the next strongest support.[20] A focus on the distinctive readings alone for
Athanasius reveals that his support for the Alexandrian group is overwhelming
at 53% (=15/28) compared to the Byzantine group at 0% (=0/7) and the Western
group at 3% (=1/32). These figures are higher than the results for Athanasius in
the Gospels where his support there for distinctive readings of the Alexandrian
group is 43% (=3/7) compared to 20% (=1/5) for the Byzantine group and 0%
(=0/24) for the Western group.[21] Athanasius' support for exclusive readings in
the Pauline Epistles is not strong since he agrees with only three readings out of
thirty one (≈9%) in the Alexandrian group but he does not agree with the single
Byzantine reading and there are no exclusive Western readings. Though there are
far less primary Alexandrian readings than for the other groups, his agreement is
again much higher at 66% (=2/3) compared to the Byzantine at 13% (=5/38) and
the Western at 13% (=4/30).

The results for the intra-group profile in Table 28 further reinforce the
strength of Athanasius' support for the Alexandrian group at 72% but also demonstrate his support for the Secondary Alexandrian sub-group at 69% compared
to 63% for the Primary Alexandrian sub-group.

---

[17] Cosaert, Text of the Gospels in Clement, 257.
[18] Where total readings in the inter-group profile are less than one hundred (which is generally
the case) results showing decimal places are unjustified and therefore the figures presented here are
rounded to the nearest whole percent.
[19] See Osburn, Text of the Apostolos in Epiphanius, 226, Table 38.
[20] Both figures here are approximate. The actual figures are: for the Alexandrian group =
39.1%; for the Byzantine group = 23.8% though these results are based on number of readings
samples of only 23 and 21 respectively.
[21] See Brogan, "Text of the Gospels," 234, Table 11; Totals.

Table 28: Athanasius' Attestation of Intra-Group Readings in the Pauline Epistles

	Uniform Rdgs		**Predominant** Rdgs		Agree Total	Total Rdgs	**%** **<u>Agree</u>**	**±%** Error
Alex	19	26	83	115	102	141	72	7
–Primary	50	78	33	53	83	131	63	8
–Secondary	49	62	59	94	108	156	69	7
Byz	70	116	13	43	83	159	52	8
West	62	134	8	33	70	167	42	7

The Byzantine group follows at 52% and then the Western at 42%. Since this profile is designed to indicate the extent and strength of a witness's attestation within each group, a high level of proportional agreement, ideally 65–70%, is important here, particularly in the uniform readings.[22] While the results for the total readings show Athanasius' strong support for the Alexandrian groups, it is particularly apparent in the case of the uniform readings. Athanasius' support for the Secondary Alexandrian group is even higher at 79% (=49/62) compared to the (All) Alexandrian at 73% (=19/26) and the Primary Alexandrian at 64% (=50/78). A comparison with the results of Athanasius' text in the Gospels is as follows; Athanasius' support for the (All) Alexandrian group in the Paulines is 72% compared to 79.4% in the Gospels, 63% for the Primary Alexandrian group in the Paulines compared to 72.4% in the Gospels, 69% for the Secondary Alexandrian group in the Paulines compared to 76.5% in the Gospels and his support for the Byzantine group is 52% in the Paulines compared to 66% in the Gospels.[23] In comparison, while these groups demonstrate some differences in proportional agreement between the Paulines and the Gospels, Athanasius' support for the Western group remains much more consistent at 42% in the intra-group profile.[24]

This general pattern is maintained in the combination inter and intra-group profile as shown in Table 29.

---

[22] See Cosaert's discussion on this profile. Cosaert, *Text of the Gospels in Clement*, 259.

[23] See Brogan, "Text of the Gospels," 241, Table 12; 256, Table 17. Epiphanius has a 76% agreement with the All Alexandrian group, 62.4% for the Primary Alexandrian (Old Egyptian) and a high 81.1% for the Secondary Alexandrian (Late Egyptian) group. Cyril has a 65.3% agreement with the All Alexandrian group. Mullen does not provide a breakdown of the Alexandrian group into sub-groups. See Osburn, *Text of the Apostolos in Epiphanius*, 226; Mullen, *Text of Cyril*, 378. Brogan noted that in the Gospels Athanasius' attestation of predominant readings is generally lower than his attestation of uniform readings. This pattern is also consistently maintained in the Epistles. See Brogan, "Text of the Gospels," 240.

[24] In the inter-group profile his support for the Western group is also reasonably consistent at 8% in the Pauline corpus and 10% in the Gospels.

Table 29: Athanasius' Attestation of Uniform or Predominant Readings That Are Also Distinctive, Exclusive or Primary in the Pauline Epistles

	Uniform Rdgs		Predominant Rdgs		Agree Total	Total Rdgs	% Agree	±% Error
Alex	2	2	12	20	14	22	64	20
Byz	4	24	1	14	5	38	13	11
West	5	40	0	17	5	57	9	7

Athanasius' support for the Alexandrian group in the Paulines is 64% compared with 73% in the Gospels. His support for the Byzantine group is a very low 13% in the Paulines compared with 27% in the Gospels but his meagre proportional agreement with the Western group is hardly changed at 9% in the Paulines and 11% in the Gospels. From these results it may be concluded that Athanasius witnesses to a more mixed and independent text in the Pauline Epistles compared to that in the Gospels though that mixture is primarily influenced by the Alexandrian and Byzantine textual groupings whereas any influence from the Western text is minimal. Since the quantitative analysis revealed differences in the Romans section of the Pauline Epistles compared to the textual character of the remaining sections, it will be of value to analyse each section in more detail with a group profile analysis.

One of the first things to note when analyzing smaller sections with a group profile analysis is that the relatively low samples of total readings produce correspondingly larger error margins. For example, in the inter-group profile for Romans (Table 30), the error margin for the Alexandrian group on the basis of only five total readings is a relatively high 35%.

Table 30: Athanasius' Attestation of Inter-Group Readings in Romans

	Distinctive[25] Rdgs		Exclusive[26] Rdgs		Primary[27] Rdgs		Agree Total	Total Rdgs	% Agree	±% Error
Alex	1	4	0	1	0	0	1	5	20	35
Byz	0	0	0	0	0	3	0	3	0	0
West	0	6	0	0	2	5	2	11	18	23

In the third profile (Table 31) which is a combination of the inter and intra-group profiles and therefore tends to retain even less readings than the inter-group profile, there are only two total readings with a corresponding 69% error margin.

---

[25] The Distinctive Alexandrian Readings are: 1.24.1.2, 1.27.3.1, 1.27.4.2, 3.30.1.2; The Distinctive Western Readings are: 1.19.1.2, 1.21.1.2, 1.26.1.2, 3.29.1.2, 15.10.1.4, 15.19.1.4.

[26] The Exclusive Alexandrian Reading is: 6.18.1.3.

[27] The Primary Byzantine Readings are: 1.19.2.2, 1.27.1.3, 3.29.1.3; The Primary Western Readings are: 1.27.2.2, 8.22.1.2, 9.32.1.1, 10.20.2.2, 12.4.1.1.

Table 31: Athanasius' Attestation of Uniform or Predominant Readings That
Are Also Distinctive, Exclusive or Primary in Romans

	Uniform[28]		Predominant[29]		Agree		%	
	Rdgs		Rdgs		Total	Rdgs	**Agree**	**±% Error**
Alex	0	0	1	2	1	2	**50**	69
Byz	0	0	0	2	0	2	**0**	0
West	2	9	0	1	2	10	**20**	25

The generally very small samples involved in the group profile analysis require
that the results be treated with due caution.[30] That small samples can cause unexpected anomalies is demonstrated in the inter-group profile for Romans (Table
30). Athanasius' strongest support is maintained for the Alexandrian group at
20% though this is significantly lower than the 32% in the inter-group profile for
the Pauline corpus. However the next closest group is the Western being only
2% less at 18% since the Byzantine group registers 0%. This result is at odds with
the previous data concerning Athanasius' support for the Western group and
hence such results must be evaluated in the light of other results from both the
quantitative and group profile analysis.[31] In this case Athanasius does not agree
with any of the (only) three primary readings for the Byzantine group and there
are no distinctive or exclusive readings.

The second profile, the intra-group profile (Table 32), generally witnesses
to more readings than the inter group profile and so the error margins are correspondingly lower. Nonetheless, they are still of concern ranging from 21% to
24%.

---

[28] The Uniform Western Readings that are also Distinctive, Exclusive or Primary are: 1.19.1.2,
1.21.1.2, 1.26.1.2, 1.27.2.2, 8.22.1.2, 9.32.1.1, 10.20.2.2, 12.4.1.1, 15.19.1.4.

[29] The Predominant Alexandrian Readings that are also Distinctive, Exclusive or Primary
are: 1.24.1.2, 1.27.3.1; The Predominant Byzantine Readings that are also Distinctive, Exclusive or
Primary are: 1.19.2.2, 3.29.1.3; The Predominant Western Reading that is also Distinctive, Exclusive
or Primary is: 3.29.1.2.

[30] Racine acknowledges that, at least in terms of the first profile (inter-group profile), the value
of results are mitigated by the fact that they rest on small samples "so that the rates of agreement
could likely be accidental." Racine, *Text of Matthew in Basil*, 258–259. Displaying the respective
error margins is pertinent to this issue.

[31] The Byzantine result is clearly less than expected but results of 0% are not uncommon in the
various group profiles and will be noted as they are encountered. Mullen also recorded numerous
results of 0% in various epistles of the Pauline corpus as part of his analysis of the text of Cyril of
Jerusalem. See Mullen, *New Testament Text of Cyril*, 354ff.

Table 32: Athanasius' Attestation of Intra-Group Readings in Romans

	Uniform[30] Rdgs		Predominant[31] Rdgs		Agree Total	Total Rdgs	% Agree	±% Error
Alex	3	5	8	13	11	18	**61**	23
- Primary	5	9	4	8	9	17	**53**	24
- Secondary	6	8	7	12	13	20	**65**	21
Byz	7	13	3	7	10	20	**50**	22
West	8	19	1	2	9	21	**43**	21

The larger samples better reflect the proportional agreements encountered previously in the results for the Pauline corpus. Athanasius shows strongest agreement with the Secondary Alexandrian group at 65% followed by the All Alexandrian group at 61% and only then the Primary Alexandrian at 53%. The Byzantine and Western follow at 50% and 43% respectively in a pattern that has been typically encountered in the quantitative analysis.

The combination profile (Table 31) shows Athanasius' strongest support for the Alexandrian group at 50% followed by the Western group at 20% since there is again no Byzantine support registered, though these results are on the basis of only two readings in the case of both the Alexandrian and Byzantine groups.[34] Athanasius' support for the Western group at 20% is unusual, being the strongest Western agreement in the combined profile for any of the epistles as seen from a review of the summary data in Table 33.[35]

---

[32] The Uniform (All) Alexandrian Readings are: 1.19.1.1, 1.21.1.1, 1.26.1.1, 8.28.2.2, 15.19.1.2; The Uniform Primary Alexandrian Readings are: 1.19.1.1, 1.19.2.1, 1.21.1.1, 1.24.1.2, 1.26.1.1, 3.29.1.1, 3.30.1.2, 8.28.2.2, 15.19.1.2; The Uniform Secondary Alexandrian Readings are: 1.19.1.1, 1.21.1.1, 1.26.1.1, 1.27.2.1, 8.28.2.2, 10.20.1.1, 10.20.2.1, 15.19.1.2; The Uniform Byzantine Readings are: 1.19.1.1, 1.21.1.1, 1.24.1.1, 1.26.1.1, 1.27.3.2, 1.27.4.1, 6.18.1.2, 8.22.1.1, 8.28.1.2, 9.32.1.2, 10.20.1.1, 10.20.2.1, 12.14.1.2; The Uniform Western Readings are: 1.19.1.2, 1.19.2.1, 1.21.1.2, 1.24.1.1, 1.26.1.2, 1.27.1.1, 1.27.2.2, 1.27.3.2, 1.27.4.1, 1.27.5.1, 3.30.1.1, 6.18.1.2, 8.22.1.1, 8.28.1.2, 8.28.2.2, 9.32.1.1, 10.20.2.2, 12.4.1.1, 15.19.1.4.

[33] The Predominant (All) Alexandrian Readings are: 1.19.2.1, 1.24.1.2, 1.27.1.2, 1.27.2.1, 1.27.3.1, 1.27.5.1, 3.29.1.1, 6.18.1.2, 8.22.1.1, 8.28.1.2, 9.32.1.2, 10.20.1.1, 10.20.2.1; The Predominant Primary Alexandrian Readings are: 1.27.1.2, 1.27.2.2, 1.27.3.1, 1.27.4.2, 1.27.5.1, 6.18.1.2, 10.20.1.1, 12.4.1.1; The Predominant Secondary Alexandrian Readings are: 1.19.2.1, 1.24.1.2, 1.27.1.1, 1.27.3.1, 1.27.5.1, 3.29.1.1, 3.30.1.1, 6.18.1.2, 8.22.1.1, 8.28.1.2, 9.32.1.2, 12.4.1.2; The Predominant Byzantine Readings are: 1.19.2.2, 1.27.2.1, 1.27.5.1, 3.29.1.3, 3.30.1.1, 8.28.2.2, 15.19.1.2; The Predominant Western Readings are: 3.29.1.2, 10.20.1.1.

[34] Low samples were also noted by Cosaert in the inter group profile for Matthew in the data from Clement of Alexandria, particularly in the case of distinctive and exclusive readings such that he could conclude only that "Clements support of distinctive and exclusive readings in the first profile reveals little useful information for determining his textual affinity in Matthew." Cosaert, *Text of the Gospels in Clement*, 257.

[35] The next highest is in 2 Corinthians–Titus at 10%.

Table 33: Summary of Comprehensive Group Profile Statistical Data (Percentage Agreement with Athanasius) for the Pauline Epistles

Inter-Group Readings	Corpus	Rom	1 Cor	2 Cor–Titus	Heb
Alexandrian	32	20	38	23	47
Byzantine	11	0	8	6	21
Western	8	18	0	8	8
Intra-Group Readings					
Alexandrian	72	61	72	74	76
-Primary	63	53	59	62	79
-Secondary	69	76	61	68	79
Byzantine	52	50	35	61	50
Western	42	43	43	42	42
Combination Inter & Intra- Group Readings					
Alexandrian	64	50	100	50	63
Byzantine	13	0	9	15	17
Western	9	20	0	10	9

As noted in the quantitative analysis for Romans, this epistle appears to represent an exception to the pattern evident among the Pauline Epistles as regards Athanasius' text and this relatively strong support for the Western group may help to explain the exceptional textual character of that epistle for Athanasius.

The inter-group profile for 1 Corinthians (Table 34) shows nearly double the agreement of Athanasius with the Alexandrian group (at 38%) than for Romans (20%) and the error margin is also reduced (though still large) due to the greater number of sample readings (16 as against 5 in Romans).

Table 34: Athanasius' Attestation of Inter-Group Readings in 1 Corinthians

	Distinctive[36] Rdgs		Exclusive[37] Rdgs		Primary[38] Rdgs		Agree Total	Tot Rdgs	% **Agree**	±% **Error**
Alex	4	6	2	10	0	0	6	16	**38**	24
Byz	0	2	0	0	1	11	1	13	**8**	14
West	0	8	0	0	0	7	0	15	**0**	0

---

[36] The Distinctive Alexandrian Readings are: 4.6.3.1, 8.8.1.1, 9.22.1.2, 11.2.1.1, 15.55.1.2, 16.22.1.1; The Distinctive Byzantine Readings are: 5.13.1.3, 6.10.1.2; The Distinctive Western Readings are: 4.6.5.4, 8.8.1.3, 9.22.1.3, 10.13.1.2, 11.2.2.3, 15.53.1.3, 15.54.1.5, 15.55.1.4.

The 8% agreement of Athanasius with the Byzantine group is much weaker than that for the Alexandrian group while no support is recorded in this profile for the eight distinctive and seven primary readings of the Western group. In the intra-group profile for 1 Corinthians (Table 35) Athanasius shows stronger support for the (All) Alexandrian group at 72% ahead of the Secondary Alexandrian at 61% and the Primary Alexandrian at 59%.

Table 35: Athanasius' Attestation of Intra-Group Readings in 1 Corinthians

	Uniform[39] Rdgs		**Predominant**[40] Rdgs		Agree Total	Total Rdgs	**%** **Agree**	**±%** **Error**
Alex	4	5	19	27	23	32	**72**	16
- Primary	11	17	8	15	19	32	**59**	17
- Secondary	12	15	10	21	22	36	**61**	16
Byz	10	25	3	12	13	37	**35**	15
West	15	30	2	10	17	40	**43**	15

Although there are only five uniform readings for the (All) Alexandrian group, Athanasius agrees with four of them. In this profile the Western group shows stronger support at 43% than the Byzantine at only 35%. Since the proportional agreement for the Western group in the intra-group profiles of the epistles

---

[37] The Exclusive Alexandrian Readings are: 1.4.1.2, 2.9.1.2, 3.16.2.2, 5.4.1.2, 5.4.1.4, 5.13.1.2, 8.6.1.2, 15.53.1.1, 15.54.1.1, 16.23.2.2.

[38] The Primary Byzantine Readings are: 1.23.1.2, 4.6.4.2, 5.7.1.2, 8.8.1.2, 9.16.1.2, 9.22.1.4, 12.26.1.1, 15.33.1.2, 15.47.1.3, 15.54.1.4, 15.55.1.3; The Primary Western Readings are: 2.4.1.2, 4.6.2.2, 9.16.2.2, 14.33.1.2, 15.10.1.3, 15.48.1.2, 16.22.1.2.

[39] The Uniform (All) Alexandrian Readings are: 4.6.2.1, 4.6.3.1, 4.6.5.2, 6.10.1.1, 10.13.1.1; The Uniform Primary Alexandrian Readings are: 3.16.1.1, 3.20.1.2, 4.6.2.1, 4.6.3.1, 4.6.4.1, 4.6.5.2, 5.7.1.1, 6.10.1.1, 8.8.1.1, 9.16.1.1, 9.22.1.2, 10.13.1.1, 11.2.1.1, 11.2.2.2, 15.55.1.2, 16.22.1.1, 16.23.1.2; The Uniform Secondary Alexandrian Readings are: 1.4.1.1, 1.23.1.1, 1.24.1.2, 4.6.1.2, 4.6.2.1, 4.6.3.1, 4.6.5.2, 5.13.1.1, 6.10.1.1, 8.6.1.1, 10.13.1.1, 15.33.1.1, 15.45.1.1, 15.48.1.1; The Uniform Byzantine Readings are: 1.24.1.2, 2.9.1.1, 3.16.2.1, 4.6.3.2, 5.4.1.1, 5.7.1.2, 5.13.1.3, 8.6.1.1, 8.8.1.2, 9.16.1.2, 9.16.2.1, 9.22.1.4, 10.13.1.1, 11.2.1.2, 11.2.2.2, 11.3.1.2, 12.26.1.1, 14.33.1.3, 15.10.1.1, 15.47.1.3, 15.48.1.1, 15.53.1.2,15.54.1.4, 15.55l.3, 16.23.2.1; The Uniform Western Readings are: 1.4.1.1, 1.23.1.1, 1.24.1.2, 2.9.1.1, 3.16.1.1, 3.16.2.1, 3.20.1.2, 4.6.1.2, 4.6.3.2, 4.6.4.1, 5.13.1.1, 6.10.1.1, 8.6.1.1, 9.16.1.1, 9.16.2.2, 9.22.1.3, 10.13.1.2, 11.2.1.2, 11.2.2.3, 12.26.1.2, 15.10.1.3, 15.22.1.1, 15.33.1.1, 15.45.1.1, 15.47.1.1, 15.48.1.2, 15.55.1.4, 16.22.1.4, 16.23.1.2, 16.23.2.1.

[40] The Predominant (All) Alexandrian Readings are: 1.4.1.1, 1.23.1.1, 1.24.1.2, 2.9.1.1, 3.16.1.1, 3.16.2.1, 3.20.1.2, 4.6.1.2, 4.6.4.1, 5.7.1.1, 5.13.1.1, 8.6.1.1, 8.8.1.1, 9.16.1.1, 9.16.2.1, 11.2.1.1, 11.2.2.2, 12.26.1.2, 14.33.1.3, 15.22.1.1, 15.33.1.1, 15.45.1.1, 15.48.1.1, 15.53.1.2, 16.22.1.1, 16.23.1.2, 16.23.2.1; The Predominant Primary Alexandrian Readings are: 1.23.1.1, 1.24.1.2, 2.41.4, 2.9.1.1, 4.6.1.2, 9.16.2.1, 12.26.1.2, 14.33.1.3, 15.10.1.3, 15.22.1.1, 15.33.1.1, 15.45.1.1, 15.47.1.1, 15.48 1 1, 16.23.2.2; The Predominant Secondary Alexandrian Readings are: 2.4.1.3, 2.9.1.1, 3.16.1.1, 2.9.1.1, 3.16.1.1, 3.16.2.1, 3.20.1.2, 4.6.4.2, 8.8.1.2, 9.16.1.1, 9.16.2.1, 9.22.1.4, 11.2.1.1, 11.2.2.2, 12.26.1.2, 14.33.1.3, 15.22.1.1, 15.47.1.3, 15.53.1.2, 15.55.1.3, 16.23.2.1; The Predominant Byzantine Readings are: 1.23.1.2, 2.4.1.3, 3.16.1.1, 3.20.1.2, 4.6.1.2, 4.6.2.1, 4.6.4.2, 4.6.5.2, 6.10.1.2, 15.45.1.1, 16.22.1.2, 16.23.1.2; The Predominant Western Readings are: 2.4.1.2, 4.6.2.2, 4.6.5.4, 5.4.1.1, 5.7.1.1, 8.8.1.3, 11.3.1.2, 14.33.1.2, 15.53.1.3, 15.54.1.5.

is very consistent (43% in Romans, 43% in 1 Corinthians, 42% in 2 Corinthians–Titus, 42% in Hebrews), it appears that in 1 Corinthians Athanasius' support for the Byzantine group is unusually weak rather than his support for the Western group being particularly strong. The combined inter and intra-group profile for 1 Corinthians (Table 36) shows that Athanasius' support for the Alexandrian group is 100% although this result is based on only four readings.

Table 36: Athanasius' Attestation of Uniform or Predominant Readings That Are Also Distinctive, Exclusive or Primary in 1 Corinthians

	Uniform[41] Rdgs		**Predominant**[42] Rdgs		Agree Total	Rdgs	**%** **Agree**	**±%** **Error**
Alex	1	1	3	3	4	4	100	0
Byz	1	8	0	3	1	11	9	17
West	0	7	0	8	0	15	0	0

His support for the Byzantine group is almost inconsequential at 9% and there is no Western support recorded.

In the inter-group profile for 2 Corinthians–Titus (Table 37) Athanasius' support for the Alexandrian group at 23% is similar to the equivalent category for Romans (at 20%) while the Byzantine and Western groups are much weaker at 6% and 8% respectively.

Table 37: Athanasius' Attestation of Inter-Group Readings in 2 Corinthians–Titus

	Distinctive[43] Rdgs		**Exclusive**[44] Rdgs		**Primary**[45] Rdgs		Agree Total	Total Rdgs	% **Agree**	**±%** **Error**
Alex	5	10	0	14	1	2	6	26	23	16
Byz	0	4	0	0	1	12	1	16	6	12
West	1	15	0	0	1	9	2	24	8	11

---

[41] The Uniform Alexandrian Reading that is also Distinctive, Exclusive or Primary is: 4.6.3.1; The Uniform Byzantine Readings that are also Distinctive, Exclusive or Primary are: 5.7.1.2, 5.13.1.3, 8.8.1.2, 9.16.1.2, 9.22.1.4, 12.26.1.1, 15.54.1.4, 15.55.1.3; The Uniform Western Readings that are also Distinctive, Exclusive or Primary are: 9.16.2.2, 9.22.1.3, 10.13.1.2, 11.2.2.3, 15.10.1.3, 15.48.1.2, 15.55.1.4.

[42] The Predominant Alexandrian Readings that are also Distinctive, Exclusive or Primary are: 8.8.1.1, 11.2.1.1, 16.22.1.1; The Predominant Byzantine Readings that are also Distinctive, Exclusive or Primary are: 1.23.1.2, 4.6.4.2, 6.10.1.2; The Predominant Western Reading that are also Distinctive, Exclusive or Primary are: 2.4.1.2, 4.6.2.2, 4.6.5.4, 8.8.1.3, 8.8.1.3, 14.33.1.2, 15.53.1.3, 15.54.1.5.

[43] The Distinctive Alexandrian Readings are: 2Cor.1.10.1.1, 2Cor.5.10.3.1, Eph.4.26.1.2, Phil.2.5.1.1, Phil.2.9.1.2, Phil.3.14.1.1, Col.1.16.2.2, 1Thess.3.11.1.2, 2Tim.2.14.1.1, 2Tim.3.12.1.2; The Distinctive Byzantine Readings are: Gal.1.8.1.8, Eph.1.3.1.3, Col.1.14.1.3, Tit.2.8.1.2; The Distinctive Western Readings are: 2Cor.5.10.1.4, 2Cor.5.10.2.1, 2Cor.5.15.1.2, 2Cor.5.18.1.2, Gal.1.8.1.2,

The results for the intra-group profile for 2 Corinthians–Titus (Table 38) are similar to those for the Pauline corpus (refer to the summary data in Table 28) with only the Byzantine group showing a slight difference at 61% compared to 50% in the Pauline corpus.

Table 38: Athanasius' Attestation of Intra-Group Readings in
2 Corinthians–Titus

	Uniform[46] Rdgs		Predominant[47] Rdgs		Agree Total	Total Rdgs	% Agree	±% Error
Alex	9	13	34	45	43	58	74	11
- Primary	20	34	13	19	33	53	62	13
- Secondary	22	29	23	37	45	66	68	11
Byz	36	51	5	16	41	67	61	12
West	24	48	5	21	29	69	42	12

Gal.1.8.2.3, Eph 3 19.1.2, Eph.4.24.2.2, Phil.2.8.1.2, Phil.3.13.1.2, Col.1.12.1.5, Col.1.12.2.2, Col.1.17.1.3, 2Tim.2.17.1.2, Col.1.18.1.2.

[44] The Exclusive Alexandrian Readings are: 2Cor.5.14.1.2, Gal.1.8.1.4, Gal.4.6.1.2, Eph.3.15.1.2, Eph.3.19.2.2, Eph.5.19.1.2, Col.1.12.1.2, Col.1.12.1.3, Col.1.18.2.2, Col.1.18.3.2, Col.1.18.4.2, 1Thess.5.18.2.2, 1Tim.1.8.1.2, 2Tim.2.14.2.2.

[45] The Primary Alexandrian Readings are: Gal.4.8.1.1, Eph.2.15.1.2; The Primary Byzantine Readings are: 2Cor.5.17.1.3, 2Cor.5.21.1.2, 2Cor.11.3.1.2, Gal.1.8.1.7, Eph.3.18.1.2, Eph.6.12.1.2, Phil.2.5.2.1, Col.1.16.1.2, 1Tim.6.13.1.2, 2Tim.2.13.1.2, 2Tim.2.14.1.2, 2Tim.4.6.1.2; The Primary Western Readings are: 2Cor.4.11.1.2, Eph.1.11.1.2, Eph.2.15.2.2, Eph.3.18.1.1, Eph.4.9.1.2, Phil.2.6.1.2, Col.1.16.1.3, 1Thess.5.18.1.2, 1Tim.3.2.1.2.

[46] The Uniform (All) Alexandrian Readings are: 2Cor.2.15.1.2, 2Cor.5.10.2.2, Gal.4.8.1.1, Eph.1.3.1.2, Eph.3.19.1.1, Eph.4.24.2.1, Phil.2.8.1.1, Phil.3.13.1.1, Col.1.14.1.1, 2Tim.1.10.2.2, 2Tim.2.17.1.1, 2Tim.4.6.1.1, Tit.2.8.1.1; The Uniform Primary Alexandrian Readings are: 2Cor.2.15.1.2, 2Cor.5.10.2.2, 2Cor.5.14.1.1, 2Cor.5.17.1.2, Gal.4.8.1.1, Eph.1.3.1.2, Eph.1.11.1.1, Eph.2.15.1.2, Eph.3.15.1.1, Eph.3.19.1.1, Eph.4.24.2.1, Eph.4.26.1.2, Eph.6.12.1.1, Phil.1.17.1.2, Phil.2.5.2.2, Phil.2.8.1.1, Phil.2.9.1.2, Phil.2.11.1.1, Phil.3.13.1.1, Phil.3.14.1.1, Col.1.14.1.1, Col.1.16.1.3, Col.1.16.2.2, Col.1.18.4.1, Col.2.3.1.2, 1Thess.3.11.1.2, 1Thess.5.18.1.1, 1Tim.1.8.1.1, 2Tim.1.10.2.2, 2Tim.2.13.1.1, 2Tim.2.14.2.1, 2Tim.2.17.1.1, 2Tim.4.6.1.1, Tit.2.8.1.1; The Uniform Secondary Alexandrian Readings are: 2Cor.2.15.1.2, 2Cor.5.10.1.3, 2Cor.5.10.2.2, 2Cor.5.14.3.1, 2Cor.5.15.1.1, 2Cor.5.18.1.1, Gal.1.8.2.2, Gal.4.6.1.1, Gal.4.8.1.1, Eph.1.3.1.2, Eph.2.15.2.1, Eph.3.19.1.1, Eph.4.9.1.1, Eph.4.24.1.2, Eph.4.24.2.1, Eph.5.19.1.1, Phil.1.17.1.1, Phil.2.6.1.1, Phil.2.8.1.1, Phil.2.10.1.1, Phil.3.13.1.1, Col.1.14.1.1, Col.1.18.1.1, Col.1.18.3.1, 2Tim.1.10.2.2, 2Tim.2.17.1.1, 2Tim.4.6.1.1, 2Tim.4.8.1.1, Tit.2.8.1.1; The Uniform Byzantine Readings are: 2Cor.1.10.3, 2Cor.4.11.1.1, 2Cor.5.10.3.2, 2Cor.5.14.1.1, 2Cor.5.18.1.1, 2Cor.5.21.1.2, 2Cor.11.3.1.2, Gal.1.8.2.2, Gal.4.6.1.1, Eph.1.11.1.1, Eph.2.15.1.1, Eph.3.15.1.1, Eph.3.18.1.2, Eph.3.19.1.1, Eph.3.19.2.1, Eph.4.9.1.1, Eph.4.24.1.2, Eph.4.24.2.1, Eph.4.26.1.1, Eph.5.19.1.1, Eph.6.12.1.2, Phil.1.17.1.1, Phil.2.5.1.2, Phil.2.5.2.1, Phil.2.6.1.1, Phil.2.8.1.1, Phil.2.9.1.1, Phil.3.13.1.1, Phil.3.14.1.2, Col.1.12.2.1, Col.1.16.2.1, Col.1.17.1.1, Col.1.18.1.1, Col.1.18.2.1, Col.1.18.3.1, Col.1.18.4.1, 1Thess.3.11.1.4, 1Thess.5.18.1.1, 1Thess.5.18.2.1, 1Tim.1.8.1.1, 1Tim.3.2.1.1, 1Tim.6.13.1.2, 2Tim.1.10.1.1, 2Tim.1.10.2.2, 2Tim.2.14.1.2, 2Tim.2.14.2.1, 2Tim.2.17.1.1, 2Tim.2.18.1.1, 2Tim.3.12.1.1, 2Tim.4.6.1.2, 2Tim.4.8.1.1; The Uniform Western Readings are: 2Cor.2.15.1.2, 2Cor.5.10.1.4, 2Cor.5.10.2.1, 2Cor.5.10.3.2, 2Cor.5.14.1.1, 2Cor.5.14.2.2, 2Cor.5.14.3.1, 2Cor.5.17.1.2, 2Cor.5.18.1.2, 2Cor.5.21.1.1, Gal.4.6.1.1, Eph.1.3.1.2, Eph.3.15.1.1, Eph.3.18.1.1, Eph.3.19.1.2, Eph.3.19.2.1, Eph.4.9.1.2, Eph.4.24.1.2, Eph.4.24.2.2, Eph.4.26.1.1, Eph.5.19.1.1, Eph.6.12.1.1, Phil.2.5.1.2, Phil.2.5.2.2, Phil.2.8.1.2, Phil.2.9.1.1,

The combined profile (Table 39) shows Athanasius' support for the Alexandrian group at 50% and hence similar to the result in Romans.

Table 39: Athanasius' Attestation of Uniform or Predominant Readings That Are Also Distinctive, Exclusive or Primary in 2 Corinthians–Titus

	Uniform[48]		Predominant[49]		Agree		%	±%
	Rdgs		Rdgs		Total	Rdgs	**Agree**	**Error**
Alex	1	1	3	7	4	8	**50**	35
Byz	1	8	1	5	2	13	**15**	20
West	2	13	0	8	2	21	**10**	13

Phil.2.10.1.1, Phil.2.11.1.2, Phil.3.13.1.2, Phil.3.14.1.2, Col.1.12.2.2, Col.1.16.1.3, Col.1.16.2.1, Col.1.18.2.1, Col.1.18.3.1, Col.1.18.4.1, Col.2.3.1.2, 1Thess.5.18.1.2, 1Thess.5.18.2.1, 1Tim.1.8.1.1, 1Tim.3.2.1.2, 1Tim.6.13.1.1, 2Tim.1.8.1.2, 2Tim.2.13.1.1, 2Tim.2.14.2.1, 2Tim.2.17.1.2, 2Tim.3.12.1.1, Titus.2.8.1.1.

[47] The Predominant (All) Alexandrian Readings are: 2Cor.1.10.1.1, 2Cor.4.11.1.1, 2Cor.5.10.1.3, 2Cor.5.14.1.1, 2Cor.5.14.3.1, 2Cor.5.15.1.1, 2Cor.5.17.1.2, 2Cor.5.18.1.1, 2Cor.5.21.1.1, 2Cor.11.3.1.1, Gal.1.8.2.2, Gal.4.6.1.1, Eph.1.11.1.1, Eph.2.15.1.2, Eph.2.15.2.1, Eph.3.15.1.1, Eph.3.19.2.1, Eph.4.9.1.1, Eph.4.24.1.2, Eph.5.19.1.1, Eph.6.12.1.1, Phil.2.5.2.2, Phil.2.6.1.1, Phil.2.9.1.2, Phil.2.10.1.1, Phil.3.14.1.1, Col.1.12.2.1, Col.1.17.1.1, Col.1.18.1.1, Col.1.18.3.1, Col.1.18.4.1, Col.2.3.1.2, 1Thess.3.11.1.2, 1Thess.5.18.1.1, 1Thess.5.18.2.1, 1Tim.1.8.1.1, 1Tim.6.13.1.1, 2Tim.1.8.1.2, 2Tim.1.10.1.1, 2Tim.2.13.1.1, 2Tim.2.14.1.1, 2Tim.2.14.2.1, 2Tim.2.18.1.1, 2Tim.3.12.1.2; The Predominant Primary Alexandrian Readings are: 2Cor.1.10.1.1, 2Cor.4.11.1.1, 2Cor.5.10.1.3, 2Cor.5.14.2.2, 2Cor.5.15.1.1, 2Cor.5.18.1.1, 2Cor.11.3.1.1, Gal.1.8.1.5, Gal.1.8.2.2, Eph.2.15.2.1, Eph.4.9.1.1, Eph.4.24.1.2, Phil.2.6.1.1, Phil.2.10.1.1, Col.1.12.2.1, Col.1.17.1.1, Col.1.18.1.1, Col.1.18.2.2, 1Thess.5.18.2.1; The Predominant Secondary Alexandrian Readings are: 2Cor.1.10.1.1, 2Cor.4.11.1.1, 2Cor.5.10.3.1, 2Cor.5.14.1.1, 2Cor.5.14.2.1, 2Cor.5.21.1.2, Gal.1.8.1.4, Eph.1.11.1.1, Eph.2.15.1.2, Eph.3.15.1.1, Eph.3.19.2.1, Eph.4.26.1.1, Eph.6.12.1.2, Phil.2.5.2.2, Phil.2.9.1.2, Phil.2.11.1.2, Phil.3.14.1.1, Col.1.12.1.4, Col.1.12.2.1, Col.1.16.1.2, Col.1.16.2.1, Col.1.17.1.1, Col.1.18.2.1, Col.1.18.4.1, Col.2.3.1.3, 1Thess.3.11.1.2, 1Thess.5.18.1.1, 1Thess.5.18.2.1, 1Tim.1.8.1.1, 1Tim.3.2.1.2, 1Tim.6.13.1.1, 2Tim.1.8.1.2, 2Tim.1.10.1.1, 2Tim.2.13.1.1, 2Tim.2.14.1.1, 2Tim.2.18.1.1, 2Tim.3.12.1.2; The Predominant Byzantine Readings are: 2Cor.2.15.1.2, 2Cor.5.10.1.3, 2Cor.5.10.2.2, 2Cor.5.14.3.1, 2Cor.5.15.1.1, Gal.4.8.1.2, Eph.1.3.1.3, Eph.2.5.2.1, Phil.2.10.1.1, Phil.2.11.1.2, Col.1.12.1.4, Col.1.16.1.2, Col.2.3.1.3, 2Tim.1.8.1.1, 2Tim.2.13.1.2, Tit.2.8.1.2; The Predominant Western Readings are: 2Cor.1.10.1.3, 2Cor.4.11.1.2, 2Cor.5.15.1.2, Gal.1.8.1.2, Gal.4.8.1.2, Eph.1.11.1.2, Eph.2.15.1.1, Eph.2.15.2.2, Phil.1.17.1.2, Phil.2.6.1.2, Col.1.12.1.5, Col.1.14.1.1, Col.1.17.1.3, Col.1.18.1.2, 1Thess.3.11.1.4, 2Tim.1.10.1.1, 2Tim.1.10.2.2, 2Tim.2.14.1.3, 2Tim.2.18.1.2, 2Tim.4.6.1.1, 2Tim.4.8.1.1.

[48] The Uniform Alexandrian Reading that is also Distinctive, Exclusive or Primary is: Gal.4.8.1.1; The Uniform Byzantine Readings that are also Distinctive, Exclusive or Primary are: 2Cor.5.21.1.2, 2Cor.11.3.1.2, Eph.3.18.1.2, Eph.6.12.1.2, Phil.2.5.2.1, 1Tim.6.13.1.2, 2Tim.2.14.1.2, 2Tim.4.6.1.2; The Uniform Western Readings that are also Distinctive, Exclusive or Primary are: 2Cor.5.10.1.4, 2Cor.5.10.2.1, 2Cor.5.18.1.2, Eph.3.18.1.1, Eph.3.19.1.2, Eph.4.9.1.2, Eph.4.24.2.2, Phil.2.8.1.2, Phil.3.13.1.2, Col.1.16.1.3, 1 Thess.5.18.1.2, 1Tim.3.2.1.2, 2Tim.2.17.1.2.

[49] The Predominant Alexandrian Readings that are also Distinctive, Exclusive or Primary are: 2Cor.1.10.1.1, Eph.2.15.1.2, Phil.2.9.1.2, Phil.3.14.1.1, 1Thess.3.11.1.2, 2Tim.2.14.1.1, 2Tim.3.12.1.2; The Predominant Byzantine Readings that are also Distinctive, Exclusive or Primary are: Eph.1.3.1.3, Eph.2.5.2.1, Col.1.16.1.2, 2Tim.2.13.1.2, Tit.2.8.1.2; The Predominant Western Readings that are also Distinctive, Exclusive or Primary are: 2Cor.4.11.1.2, 2Cor.5.15.1.2, Gal.1.8.1.2, Eph.1.11.1.2, Eph.2.15.2.2, Phil.2.6.1.2, Col.1.12.1.5, Col.1.17.1.3.

The Byzantine group receives very little support at 15% and even less for the Western group at 10%. The results for Hebrews confirm some of the fluctuations evident in the other epistles. In the inter-group profile (Table 40) the Alexandrian group at 47% has the strongest support from Athanasius to be found in any of the epistles.

Table 40: Athanasius' Attestation of Inter-Group Readings in Hebrews

	Distinctive[50] Rdgs		**Exclusive**[51] Rdgs		**Primary**[52] Rdgs		Agree Total	Total Rdgs	**%** **Agree**	**±%** **Error**
Alex	5	8	1	6	1	1	7	15	47	25
Byz	0	1	0	1	3	12	3	14	21	21
West	0	3	0	0	1	9	1	12	8	16

Support for the Byzantine group is also the strongest in any epistle at 21% while the Western group shows consistent support from Athanasius at only 8%. In the intra-group profile (Table 41) the Alexandrian groups enjoy both the strongest support and the least fluctuation of any of the epistles at 76% for the (All) Alexandrian group and 79% for both the Primary and Secondary Alexandrian groups.

Table 41: Athanasius' Attestation of Intra-Group Readings in Hebrews

	Uniform[53] Rdgs		**Predominant**[54] Rdgs		Agree Total	Total Rdgs	**%** **Agree**	**±%** **Error**
Alex	3	3	22	30	25	33	76	15
- Primary	14	18	8	10	22	28	79	15
- Secondary	0	0	19	24	19	24	79	16
Byz	15	26	2	8	17	34	50	17
West	15	36	0	0	15	36	42	16

---

[50] The Distinctive Alexandrian Readings are: 1.3.1.3, 1.12.2.2, 11.32.1.1, 11.32.2.1, 11.32.3.1, 11.38.1.1, 12.18.1.2, 13.6.1.1; The Distinctive Byzantine Reading is: 12.23.1.2; The Distinctive Western Readings are: 1.3.1.5, 1.12.2.3, 11.32.1.3.

[51] The Exclusive Alexandrian Readings are: 1.3.2.1, 1.4.1.2, 1.12.3.2, 2.1.1.2, 2.17.1.2, 7.22.2.2; The Exclusive Byzantine Reading is: 1.3.3.2.

[52] The Primary Alexandrian Reading is: 4.12.2.1; The Primary Byzantine Readings are: 1.2.1.2, 1.3.1.4, 1.3.2.3, 1.12.2.1, 2.1.1.3, 2.14.1.2, 3.1.1.2, 7.22.1.1, 11.3.1.2, 11.32.1.2, 12.18.2.3, 13.8.1.1; The Primary Western Readings are: 1.12.1.2, 2.1.1.1, 4.12.1.2, 7.19.1.2, 8.6.1.2, 8.6.2.2, 8.6.4.2, 9.23.1.2, 9.24.1.2.

[53] The Uniform (All) Alexandrian Readings are: 1.3.3.1, 8.6.4.1, 12.23.1.1; The Uniform Primary Alexandrian Readings are: 1.3.2.2, 1.3.3.1, 1.12.2.2, 1.12.3.1, 1.14.1.2, 2.2.1.1, 2.14.1.1, 2.17.1.1, 3.1.1.1, 4.12.1.1, 8.6.4.1, 9.24.1.1, 11.3.1.1, 11.32.1.1, 11.32.2.1, 11.38.1.1, 12.23.1.1, 13.8.1.2; The Uniform Secondary Alexandrian Readings are: 1.3.1.3, 1.3.3.1, 1.4.1.1, 2.14.1.1, 4.12.2.1, 7.19.1.1, 8.6.1.1, 8.6.4.1, 9.23.1.1, 12.23.1.1; The Uniform Byzantine Readings are: 1.2.1.2, 1.3.2.3, 1.4.1.1, 1.12.1.1, 1.12.2.1, 1.12.3.1, 1.14.1.2, 2.2.1.1, 2.14.1.2, 2.17.1.1, 3.1.1.2, 4.12.1.1, 7.19.1.1, 7.22.1.1, 7.22.2.1,

The Byzantine group at 50% is at approximately the same level of support as in the result for the Pauline corpus (and exactly the same as in Romans). The Western group is exactly the same at 42%. In the combined profile (Table 42) the proportional agreements for the three groups again reflect very closely the results for the Pauline corpus.

Table 42: Athanasius' Attestation of Uniform or Predominant Readings that are also Distinctive, Exclusive or Primary in Hebrews

	Uniform[55]		**Predominant**[56]		Agree		**%**	**±%**
	Rdgs		Rdgs		Total	Rdgs	**Agree**	**Error**
Alex	0	0	5	8	5	8	**63**	34
Byz	2	8	0	4	2	12	**17**	21
West	1	11	0	0	1	11	**9**	17

Athanasius' support for the Alexandrian group is 63% (compared to 64% for the corpus), 17% for the Byzantine group (13% for the corpus), and 9% for the Western group (also 9% for the corpus).

Summary: The group profile analysis of the Pauline Epistles confirms the basic conclusions of the quantitative analysis of Athanasius' strong support for the Alexandrian and more specifically the Secondary Alexandrian group followed by some support for the Byzantine group but minimal support for the Western group. However, fluctuations were noted in the epistles as regards the strength of Athanasius' support for the Alexandrian group and in Romans especially an

---

8.6.1.1, 9.23.1.1, 9.24.1.1, 11.3.1.2, 11.32.1.2, 11.32.2.2, 11.32.3.2, 11.38.1.2, 12.18.1.1, 13.6.1.2, 13.8.1.1; The Uniform Western Readings are: 1.2.1.1, 1.3.1.5, 1.3.2.2, 1.3.3.1, 1.4.1.1, 1.12.1.2, 1.12.2.3, 1.12.3.1, 1.14.1.2, 2.1.1.1, 2.2.1.1, 2.14.1.1, 2.17.1.1, 3.1.1.1, 4.12.1.2, 4.12.2.3, 7.19.1.2, 7.22.1.2, 7.22.2.1, 7.22.3.2, 8.6.1.2, 8.6.2.2, 8.6.3.1, 8.6.4.2, 9.23.1.2, 9.24.1.2, 11.3.1.1, 11.32.1.3, 11.32.2.2, 11.32.3.2, 11.38.1.2, 12.18.1.1, 12.18.2.1, 12.23.1.1, 13.6.1.2, 13.8.1.2.

[54] The Predominant (All) Alexandrian Readings are: 1.2.1.1, 1.3.1.3, 1.3.2.2, 1.4.1.1, 1.12.1.1, 1.12.2.2, 1.12.3.1, 1.14.1.2, 2.2.1.1, 2.14.1.1, 2.17.1.1, 3.1.1.1, 4.12.1.2, 4.12.2.1, 7.19.1.1, 7.22.1.2, 7.22.2.1, 7.22.3.2, 8.6.1.1, 8.6.3.1, 9.23.1.1, 9.24.1.1, 11.3.1.1, 11.32.1.1, 11.32.2.1, 11.32.3.1, 11.38.1.1, 12.18.1.2, 12.18.2.1, 13.8.1.2; The Predominant Primary Alexandrian Readings are: 1.2.1.1, 1.12.1.1, 4.12.2.1, 7.19.1.1, 7.22.1.2, 8.6.3.1, 9.23.1.1, 11.32.3.1, 12.18.1.2, 13.6.1.1; The Predominant Secondary Alexandrian Readings are: 1.2.1.1, 1.12.1.1, 1.12.2.1, 1.12.3.1, 1.14.1.2, 2.2.1.1, 2.14.1.1, 2.17.1.1, 3.1.1.1, 4.12.1.1, 7.22.1.2, 7.22.2.1, 7.22.3.2, 8.6.2.1, 8.6.3.1, 9.24.1.1, 11.3.1.1, 11.32.1.1, 11.32.2.1, 11.32.3.1, 11.38.1.1, 12.18.1.2, 12.18.2.1, 13.8.1.2; The Predominant Byzantine Readings are: 1.3.1.4, 2.1.1.3, 4.12.2.3, 7.22.3.2, 8.6.3.1, 8.6.4.1, 12.18.2.3, 12.23.1.2.

[55] The Uniform Byzantine Readings that are also Distinctive, Exclusive or Primary are: 1.2.1.2, 1.3.2.3, 1.12.2.1, 2.14.1.2, 3.1.1.2, 7.22.1.1, 11.3.1.2, 11.32.1.2; The Uniform Western Readings are: 1.3.1.5, 1.12.1.2, 1.12.2.3, 2.1.1.1, 4.12.1.2, 7.19.1.2, 8.6.1.2, 8.6.2.2, 9.23.1.2, 9.24.1.2, 11.32.1.3.

[56] The Predominant Alexandrian Readings that are also Distinctive, Exclusive or Primary are: 1.3.1.3, 1.12.2.2, 4.12.2.1, 11.32.1.1, 11.32.2.1, 11.32.3.1, 11.38.1.1, 12.18.1.2; The Predominant Byzantine Readings that are also Distinctive, Exclusive or Primary are: 1.3.1.4, 2.1.1.3, 12.18.2.3, 12.23.1.2.

overall weak Byzantine support and a correspondingly stronger Western support are evident.

CATHOLIC EPISTLES

The results of the quantitative analysis indicate that Athanasius' strongest support is for the Byzantine group rather than the Alexandrian group in the Catholic Epistles. The group profile analysis produces a similar outcome. The inter-group profile results (Table 43) show that Athanasius' strongest support is for the Byzantine group at 60% which is much greater than the 27% agreement with the Alexandrian group.

Table 43: Athanasius' Attestation of Inter-Group Readings in the Catholic Epistles

	Distinctive[57] Rdgs		**Exclusive**[58] Rdgs		**Primary**[59] Rdgs		Agree Total	Total Rdgs	**% Agree**	**±% Error**
Alex	1	3	2	8	0	0	3	11	27%	26
Byz	0	1	1	1	2	3	3	5	**60%**	43

It should be noted however, that the result for the Byzantine group has an extremely large error margin associated with it of ±43% since it is based on only five readings, consisting of one distinctive reading with which Athanasius does not agree, one exclusive reading with which he does agree and three primary readings of which Athanasius agrees with two.

The intra-group profile (Table 44) does not show such a strong differentiation between the two groups with Athanasius support for the Byzantine group at 45% and the Alexandrian group at 30%.

Table 44: Athanasius' Attestation of Intra-Group Readings in the Catholic Epistles

	Uniform[60] Rdgs		**Predominant**[61] Rdgs		Agree Total	Total Rdgs	**% Agree**	**±% Error**
Alex	0	0	3	10	3	10	30%	28
Byz	4	10	1	1	5	11	**45%**	29

---

[57] The Distinctive Alexandrian Readings in the Catholic Epistles are: 1Pet.4.1.1 3, 1Pet.4.19.1.1, 1Jn.3.5.1.2; The Distinctive Byzantine Reading in the Catholic Epistles is: Jam.1.12.1.2.

[58] The Exclusive Alexandrian Readings in the Catholic Epistles are: Jam.1.12.1.2, Jam.1.12.2.1, Jam1.12.2.2, Jam.1.17.1.2, Jam.1.20.1.2, 1Pet.3.18.1.1, 1Pet.5.8.1.2, 2Pet.1.17.1.2; The Exclusive Byzantine Reading in the Catholic Epistles is: 1Jn.5.20.1.1.

[59] The Primary Byzantine Readings in the Catholic Epistles are: 1Pet.4.1.1.1, 1Pet.4.19.1.2, 1Jn.3.5.1.1.

These results are based on eleven and ten readings respectively and so the error margins are also approximately the same at 29% and 28%. The combined profile results (Table 45) show an increased disparity with Athanasius' support for the Byzantine at 50% and for the Alexandrian group at 33%, though again the very small sample sizes (four and three only) produce correspondingly larger error margins and as a result these conclusions can only be considered tentative.

Table 45: Athanasius' Attestation of Uniform or Predominant Readings in the Catholic Epistles That Are Also Distinctive, Exclusive or Primary

	Uniform[62] Rdgs		**Predominant**[63] Rdgs		Agree Total	Total Rdgs	**%** **Agree**	**%** **Error**
Alex	0	0	1	3	1	3	33%	53
Byz	1	3	1	1	2	4	50%	49

---

[60] The Uniform Byzantine Readings in the Catholic Epistles are: Jam.1.12.1.3, Jam.1.12.2.4, Jam.1.17.1.1, Jam.1.20.1.1, 1Pet.3.18.1.2, 1Pet.4.19.1.2, 1Pet.4.19.2.2, 1Pet.5.8.1.1, 1Pet.1.17.1.3, 1Jn.3.5.1.1.

[61] The Predominant Alexandrian Readings in the Catholic Epistles are: Jam.1.12.1.3, Jam.1.17.1.1, 1Pet.3.18.1.2, 1Pet.4.1.1.3, 1Pet.4.19.1.1, 1Pet.4.19.2.2, 1Pet.5.8.1.1, 2Pet.1.17.1.3, 1Jn.3.5.1.2, 1Jn.5.20.1.2; The Predominant Byzantine Reading in the Catholic Epistles is: 1Pet.4.1.1.1.

[62] The Uniform Byzantine Readings that are also Distinctive, Exclusive or Primary in the Catholic Epistles are: Jam.1.12.2.4, 1Pet.4.19.1.2, 1Jn.3.5.1.1.

[63] The Predominant Alexandrian Readings that are also Distinctive, Exclusive or Primary in the Catholic Epistles are: 1Pet.4.1.1.3, 1Pet.4.19.1.1, 1Jn.3.5.1.2; The Predominant Byzantine Reading that is also Distinctive, Exclusive or Primary in the Catholic Epistles is: 1Pet.4.1.1.1.

7

STATISTICAL AND MULTIVARIATE ANALYSIS

A difficulty with the analysis in the previous two chapters is that of integrating the data results in a satisfactory way so as to enable a coherent picture to be drawn of Athanasius' textual affinities in the Apostolos. Multivariate analysis is an ideal method by which this can be achieved since multidimensional scaling maps provide a convenient graphical representation of the spatial relationships of the representative textual witnesses relative to the text of Athanasius and each other. This chapter presents the results of a multivariate analysis of Athanasius' text the Apostolos relative to the range of selected witnesses, utilizing the graphical output techniques discussed in Chapter 4. As in the previous chapters, the Apostolos will be analyzed by considering each genre separately. However the presentation order in this chapter will be; Pauline Epistles, Acts, Catholic Epistles. The Pauline Epistles are presented first since they contain the greatest amount of data with which to conveniently and comprehensively demonstrate the various aspects of multivariate analysis utilized here

PAULINE EPISTLES

As noted in Chapter 4, multivariate analysis, as applied in this study, is based on dissimilarity matrices rather than proportional agreement matrices. This type of matrix is used in order to enable comparison with critical values of dissimilarity so as to determine statistically significant relationships between Athanasius' text and the selected witnesses. These matrices are also used as the source data for constructing multidimensional scaling maps, dendrograms and optimal cluster maps. The five dissimilarity matrices (Table 91–Table 95; Appendix A) present the data for the corpus of the Pauline Epistles as well as for the epistles: Romans, 1 Corinthians, 2 Corinthians–Titus and Hebrews. Significant relationship between a witness of interest (in this case Athanasius) and other selected witnesses is determined by comparing the values of dissimilarity (between respective pairs of witnesses) with upper and lower critical values of dissimilarity calculated using the R script, *montecarlo.r*. Table 46 and Table 47 present the critical values of dissimilarity for the Pauline corpus.

Table 46: Critical Values of Dissimilarity Using Simple Matching Distance with Each Respective Manuscript as the Witness of Interest Relative to Athanasius: Pauline Epistles–Complete Corpus

Witness	Diss	LCV	UCV	Diss<LCV	LCV≤ Diss≤UCV	Diss>UCV
C	0.322	0.297	0.466		✓	
P	0.378	0.323	0.463		✓	
33	0.387	0.321	0.464		✓	
A	0.387	0.316	0.465		✓	
ℵᶜ	0.399	0.321	0.464		✓	
ℵ	0.405	0.321	0.464		✓	
1739	0.417	0.321	0.464		✓	
104	0.419	0.323	0.467		✓	
L	0.443	0.323	0.461		✓	
223	0.448	0.319	0.460		✓	
Ψ	0.452	0.321	0.464		✓	
𝔓⁴⁶	0.484	0.310	0.476			✓
049	0.485	0.293	0.485		✓	
K	0.486	0.322	0.473			✓
876	0.488	0.321	0.464			✓
B	0.497	0.312	0.468			✓
2423	0.500	0.318	0.473			✓
D	0.554	0.327	0.464			✓
G	0.581	0.310	0.473			✓
F	0.605	0.311	0.479			✓

Table 47: Critical Values of Dissimilarity: Pauline Epistles (Complete)

Diss < LCV	LCV ≤ Diss ≤ UCV	Diss > UCV
	C P 33 A ℵᶜ ℵ 1739 104 L 223 Ψ 049	𝔓⁴⁶ K 876 B 2423 D G F

The witnesses are arranged from lowest dissimilarity relative to Athanasius (i.e. highest agreement) to highest dissimilarity (i.e. lowest agreement) where the values of dissimilarity are obtained from the dissimilarity matrix for the Pauline corpus (Table 91, first column, Appendix A). In Table 46 two columns for the lower critical value (LCV) and upper critical value (UCV) are included. Finally, the relationship between the text of Athanasius and the respective witness is specified in one of three categories.

The categories are: a) Dissimilarity is lower than the lower critical value (LCV). Witnesses in this category may be considered to have a statistically significant relationship with the text of Athanasius[1]; b) Dissimilarity is greater than the lower critical value (LCV) but lower than the upper critical value (UCV). Witnesses in this category cannot be considered to show any significant relationship with the text of Athanasius; c) Dissimilarity is greater than the upper critical value (UCV). Witnesses in this category may be considered to indicate a statistically significant difference from the text of Athanasius.

To see clearly the relationship of Athanasius' text with the selected witnesses in the Pauline Epistles, a summary table is provided (Table 47). The first thing to note is that no witnesses occupy the first category (i.e. Diss<LCV) which means that there are no individual witnesses that share a significantly similar relationship with the text of Athanasius. This may appear surprising but it should be recalled that one conclusion from the group profile analysis was that while Athanasius should be classified as a Secondary Alexandrian, he is not a 'good' Secondary Alexandrian. What this chart makes clear is that not only does Athanasius' text have no significantly similar relationship with any of the Secondary Alexandrian witnesses but his text has no significantly similar relationship with *any* of the selected representative witnesses.[2]

In order to test the result a comparative list was compiled using Codex Sinaiticus (01 ℵ) as the witness of interest (Table 48, Table 49).

Table 48: Critical Values of Dissimilarity Using Simple Matching Distance with Each Respective Manuscript as the Witness of Interest Relative to Sinaiticus (01 ℵ): Pauline Epistles–Complete Corpus

(This is provided for purposes of comparing the results for Codex Sinaiticus with those for Athanasius)

Witness	Diss	LCV	UCV	Diss<LCV	LCV≤ Diss≤UCV	Diss>UCV
C	0.246	0.297	0.466	✓		
B	0.262	0.312	0.468	✓		
A	0.265	0.316	0.465	✓		
ℵᶜ	0.286	0.321	0.464	✓		
33	0.304	0.321	0.464	✓		
1739	0.321	0.321	0.464		✓	
𝔓⁴⁶	0.341	0.310	0.476		✓	
Ath	0.405	0.321	0.464		✓	
P	0.445	0.323	0.463		✓	
Ψ	0.488	0.321	0.464			✓
104	0.491	0.323	0.467			✓
049	0.505	0.293	0.485			✓

---

[1] The descriptions for the three categories are taken from Chapter 4.

[2] This does not mean that Athanasius shares *no* relationship with any of these witnesses; indeed he does, but they cannot be claimed as statistically significant.

Witness	Diss	LCV	UCV	Diss<LCV	LCV≤ Diss≤UCV	Diss>UCV
L	0.533	0.323	0.461			✓
D	0.542	0.327	0.464			✓
2423	0.547	0.318	0.473			✓
223	0.552	0.319	0.460			✓
876	0.566	0.321	0.464			✓
K	0.575	0.322	0.473			✓
F	0.588	0.311	0.479			✓
G	0.605	0.310	0.473			✓

Table 49: Critical Values of Dissimilarity: Pauline Epistles (Complete)–Relative to Sinaiticus (01 ℵ)

Diss < LCV	LCV ≤ Diss ≤ UCV	Diss > UCV
C B A ℵᶜ 33	1739 𝔓⁴⁶ Ath P	Ψ 104 049 L D 2423 223 876 K F G

From these tables it can be seen that ℵ shares a significantly similar relationship with C B A ℵᶜ and 33. ℵ shares no significant relationship with 1739 𝔓⁴⁶ Athanasius (Ath) and P. ℵ can be considered as significantly dissimilar to 044 104 049 L D 2423 223 876 K F and G. Table 49 demonstrates that it is possible to find witnesses sharing significantly similar (as well as dissimilar) relationships. This table also provides some surprises. Since ℵ is classified as a Primary Alexandrian, it might have been expected that this witness would be significantly related to the other well known Primary Alexandrian witnesses 𝔓⁴⁶ B and 1739. However, Table 49 shows that of these other Primary Alexandrian witnesses only B demonstrates a significantly similar relationship.

The remaining witnesses in this category come from the Secondary Alexandrian group (C A ℵᶜ 33). Further, in order of lowest dissimilarity, C precedes B (0.246 compared to 0.262). Then the second category (LCV≤Diss≤ UCV) contains 1739 and 𝔓⁴⁶ that are classified as Primary Alexandrian along with ℵ. What is going on here? First it should be noted that the testing for critical values of dissimilarity provides a reasonably rigorous assessment of significant relationship between individual witnesses, especially close relationships. This can be seen from the results for the text of Athanasius where none of the selected witnesses fulfil the criteria for close relationship when it might have been expected that possibly some of the Secondary Alexandrian witnesses would show significantly similar relationship. Second, these results constitute a challenge to the commonly accepted group classification of some of these manuscripts, especially the Primary and Secondary Alexandrian witnesses.[3] One of the primary advantages

---

[3] Wasserman has also critiqued the traditional classifications used in textual studies of the Fathers in his review of Osburn's study of the Text of Epiphanius. There he noted, using the data in the percentage agreement matrices (contra Cosaert's claim that these matrices are of no value), various incongruities whereby certain witnesses showed higher proportional agreement with

of using multivariate analysis is that it allows the sample data-set itself to determine and display manuscript relationships, rather than classification of textual groups being imposed *a priori*. With this in mind the data for Athanasius, as the witness of interest, can be more fully analyzed.

Table 47 demonstrates that witnesses having no significantly similar relationship to Athanasius belong to the Primary and Secondary Alexandrian groups as well as the Byzantine group. While no Secondary Alexandrian witnesses demonstrate a significantly similar relationship with Athanasius, the first five witnesses with lowest dissimilarity are indeed Secondary Alexandrian (C P 33 A ℵᶜ). Then follow the Primary Alexandrians, ℵ and 1739. More surprising, however, is that 𝔓⁴⁶, which is also classified as a Primary Alexandrian, appears in the category of significant dissimilarity along with some of the Byzantine witnesses and not surprisingly, all of the Western witnesses.

When analyzing the data for each of the epistles, certain similarities with, but also differences from the corpus are evident. The tables for Romans (Table 50, Table 51) indicate that here also there are no witnesses that show significant similarity with the text of Athanasius.

Table 50: Critical Values of Dissimilarity using Simple Matching Distance with Each Respective Manuscript as the Witness of Interest Relative to Athanasius: Romans

Witness	Diss	LCV	UCV	Diss<LCV	LCV≤ Diss≤UCV	Diss>UCV
A	0.333	0.190	0.571		✓	
C	0.368	0.158	0.579		✓	
ℵ	0.381	0.190	0.571		✓	
ℵᶜ	0.381	0.190	0.571		✓	
Ψ	0.381	0.190	0.571		✓	
L	0.429	0.190	0.571		✓	
P	0.429	0.190	0.571		✓	
049	0.429	0.190	0.571		✓	
223	0.429	0.190	0.571		✓	
33	0.476	0.190	0.571		✓	
876	0.476	0.190	0.571		✓	
1739	0.476	0.190	0.571		✓	
2423	0.476	0.190	0.571		✓	
𝔓⁴⁶	0.500	0.125	0.750		✓	
104	0.524	0.190	0.571		✓	
K	0.529	0.176	0.588		✓	
D	0.571	0.190	0.571		✓	
G	0.571	0.190	0.571		✓	
B	0.619	0.190	0.571			✓
F	0.636	0.091	0.636		✓	

members of other groups than with members of their own group. His conclusion was that "some of Osburn's predefined groups are problematic". See Wasserman, review of Osburn, 3.

Table 51: Critical Values of Dissimilarity: Romans

Diss < LCV	LCV ≤ Diss ≤ UCV	Diss > UCV
	A C ℵ ℵᶜ Ψ L P 049 223 33 876 1739 2423 𝔓⁴⁶ 104 K D G F	B

There is only one witness that shows significant dissimilarity with his text, the Primary Alexandrian classified manuscript, Codex Vaticanus (B). Further, of the first five witnesses with lowest dissimilarity, four (A C ℵᶜ Ψ) are classified as Secondary Alexandrian. Ψ is here particularly notable since it shows its lowest dissimilarity in Romans compared to any of the other sections. It was earlier noted that there was a change of textual character in 1 Corinthians in this witness and the results, at least in terms of the distance from the text of Athanasius, would appear to confirm this is the case.[4] Ms 104, though classified as a Secondary Alexandrian, is located well away from the other witnesses of that group just before the Byzantine witness K and the three Western witnesses D G and F with a dissimilarity to Athanasius' text of 0.524. This dissimilarity is reduced in each subsequent section but the overall result in the corpus (a dissimilarity of 0.419) still locates 104 away from the other Secondary Alexandrian witnesses with only Ψ further away. The results for Romans suggest that the character of Athanasius' text is more mixed here than in any other epistle, since all but one witness falls into the central category of no significant relationship.[5]

The tables for 1 Corinthians (Table 52, Table 53) show a slightly more defined arrangement with some of the Byzantine and all the Western witnesses located in the category of significant dissimilarity to Athanasius' text.

---

[4] The dissimilarity for Ψ increases to 0.500 in 1 Corinthians. See Table 52.

[5] The results of the Mann-Whitney test in chapter 5 also indicated the unique character of Athanasius' text in Romans compared to other sections in the Pauline Epistles. Only one witness is located in the third category of Hebrews but the other Western manuscript witnesses F and G are lacunose there.

Table 52: Critical Values of Dissimilarity Using Simple Matching Distance with Each Respective Manuscript as the Witness of Interest Relative to Athanasius: 1 Corinthians

Witness	Diss	LCV	UCV	Diss<LCV	LCV≤ Diss≤UCV	Diss>UCV
A	0.368	0.263	0.579		✓	
33	0.375	0.275	0.550		✓	
C	0.424	0.242	0.576		✓	
ℵ	0.425	0.275	0.550		✓	
𝔓⁴⁶	0.429	0.257	0.571		✓	
P	0.474	0.263	0.579		✓	
ℵᶜ	0.475	0.275	0.550		✓	
1739	0.475	0.275	0.550		✓	
Ψ	0.500	0.275	0.550		✓	
L	0.525	0.275	0.550		✓	
B	0.550	0.275	0.550		✓	
104	0.550	0.275	0.550		✓	
049	0.571	0.214	0.571		✓	
D	0.575	0.275	0.550			✓
223	0.600	0.275	0.550			✓
2423	0.600	0.275	0.550			✓
F	0.605	0.263	0.579			✓
G	0.605	0.263	0.579			✓
K	0.636	0.227	0.636		✓	
876	0.650	0.275	0.550			✓

Table 53: Critical Values of Dissimilarity: 1 Corinthians

Diss < LCV	LCV ≤ Diss ≤ UCV	Diss > UCV
	A 33 C ℵ 𝔓⁴⁶ P ℵᶜ 1739 Ψ L B 104 049 K	D 223 2423 F G 876

Again the first three witnesses with lowest dissimilarity are classified as Secondary Alexandrian while Ψ has moved further away.

The tables for 2 Corinthians–Titus (Table 54, Table 55) show that these are the only epistles where any witness is significantly similar to Athanasius' text, being C at 0.220 which has the lowest dissimilarity recorded in any of the epistles.

Table 54: Critical Values of Dissimilarity Using Simple Matching Distance with Each Respective Manuscript as the Witness of Interest Relative to Athanasius: 2 Corinthians–Titus

Witness	Diss	LCV	UCV	Diss<LCV	LCV≤ Diss≤UCV	Diss>UCV
C	0.220	0.260	0.500	✓		
104	0.357	0.271	0.486		✓	
P	0.362	0.275	0.493		✓	
223	0.366	0.282	0.493		✓	
ℵᶜ	0.394	0.282	0.493		✓	
K	0.394	0.282	0.493		✓	
33	0.409	0.282	0.493		✓	
876	0.409	0.282	0.493		✓	
1739	0.409	0.282	0.493		✓	
2423	0.412	0.255	0.510		✓	
L	0.414	0.286	0.486		✓	
ℵ	0.423	0.282	0.493		✓	
Ψ	0.437	0.282	0.493		✓	
B	0.446	0.268	0.518		✓	
A	0.450	0.267	0.500		✓	
049	0.460	0.260	0.500		✓	
D	0.521	0.282	0.493			✓
G	0.571	0.286	0.486			✓
𝔓⁴⁶	0.596	0.255	0.511			✓
F	0.600	0.286	0.486			✓

Table 55: Critical Values of Dissimilarity: 2 Corinthians–Titus

Diss < LCV	LCV ≤ Diss ≤ UCV	Diss > UCV
C	104 P 223 ℵᶜ K 33 876 1739 2423 L ℵ Ψ B A 049	D G 𝔓⁴⁶ F

It should be observed that 𝔓⁴⁶ is again found to be significantly dissimilar to Athanasius' text here in conjunction with the three Western witnesses, D F G. This does not so much reflect on the character of Athanasius' text as raise questions about the classification of 𝔓⁴⁶ as a Primary Alexandrian witness, at least in this epistolary grouping.

The results for Hebrews (Table 56, Table 57) show only D with significant dissimilarity, though F and G are lacunose in this epistle, otherwise they might have been expected to align with D.

Table 56: Critical Values of Dissimilarity Using Simple Matching Distance with Each Respective Manuscript as the Witness of Interest Relative to Athanasius: Hebrews

Witness	Diss	LCV	UCV	Diss<LCV	LCV≤ Diss≤UCV	Diss>UCV
P	0.278	0.250	0.556		✓	
33	0.306	0.250	0.556		✓	
ℵᶜ	0.333	0.250	0.556		✓	
A	0.333	0.250	0.556		✓	
104	0.333	0.250	0.556		✓	
1739	0.333	0.250	0.556		✓	
ℵ	0.361	0.250	0.556		✓	
C	0.375	0.188	0.625		✓	
𝔓⁴⁶	0.389	0.250	0.556		✓	
B	0.417	0.208	0.583		✓	
L	0.417	0.250	0.556		✓	
223	0.452	0.226	0.548		✓	
Ψ	0.472	0.250	0.556		✓	
876	0.472	0.250	0.556		✓	
2423	0.528	0.250	0.556		✓	
K	0.556	0.250	0.556		✓	
D	0.583	0.250	0.556			✓

Table 57: Critical Values of Dissimilarity: Hebrews

Diss < LCV	LCV ≤ Diss ≤ UCV	Diss > UCV
	P 33 ℵᶜ A 104 1739 ℵ C 𝔓⁴⁶ B L 223 Ψ 876 2423 K	D

In this epistle Secondary Alexandrian witnesses occupy the first five positions of lowest dissimilarity (P 33 ℵᶜ A 104) followed by two witnesses from the Primary Alexandrian group, (1739 ℵ) before C which, compared to its significantly low dissimilarity in the previous epistles (2 Corinthians–Titus), is now located approximately in the middle of the range of witnesses. Clearly there is movement of witnesses occurring between these epistles. This brings to the fore what has been previously observed in these tables; the lack of clear and consistent distinctions between textual groupings, specifically in the case of the Primary and Secondary Alexandrian witnesses. An important characteristic of the data in these tables is that it is essentially uni-dimensional being based on only one (first) column of the dissimilarity matrices. While these tables provide valuable information concerning Athanasius' textual relationship with the individual witnesses, a clearer picture of the inter-relationship of all the witnesses relative to Athanasius' text and each other can be observed in multidimensional scaling (MDS) maps.

An important difference with the methods presented in the previous chapters is that these maps are projections based on the full dimensionality of the source data contained in the dissimilarity matrices. As Finney notes

> "Given enough dimensions it is possible to obtain a set of coordinates for each witness such that every inter-witness distance is perfectly represented. However our faculty for simultaneous comprehension of multiple dimensions is limited, with three-dimensional spatial representations being the best we can be expected to understand with ease."[6]

While two-dimensional (2D) maps are presented, since their advantage is that they may be conveniently plotted, three-dimensional (3D) maps are preferable as they incorporate a greater proportion of the variability of the source data. For example, the 2D map (Figure 2) for the Pauline Epistles corpus conveys 64% of the variability of the source data whereas the 3D map (shown in Figure 3 and Figure 4) is able to convey 71%.[7]

Figure 2: Athanasius–Pauline Epistles (Complete): 2D

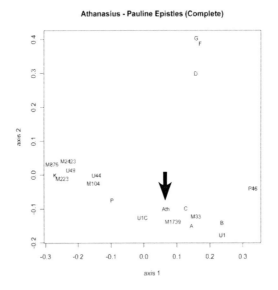

to Athanasius' text and each other can be observed in multidimensional scaling

---

[6] Finney, *Analysis of Textual Variation*, sec. 5.5. Chatfield and Collins also discuss the use of such tools as Andrews curves, Chernoff faces and weathervane plots that attempt to convey more information in a lower dimensionality. Chatfield and Collins, *Introduction to Multivariate Analysis*, 49–50.

[7] The data output of the R scripts used to produce the 2D and 3D MDS maps includes a figure that indicates the proportion of the variability of the source data represented in the respective map. For example note the proportional figures indicated below the optimal cluster maps.

Figure 3: Athanasius–Pauline Epistles (Complete): 3D View 1

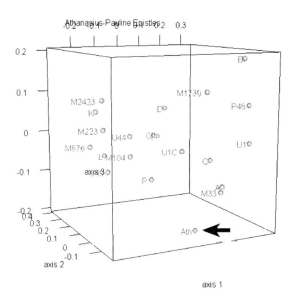

Figure 4: Athanasius–Pauline Epistles (Complete): 3D View 2

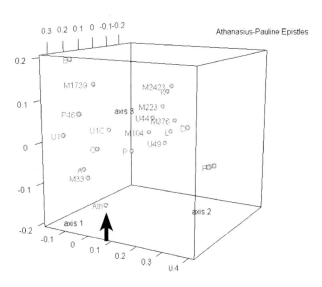

While it is possible to represent three-dimensional maps by plotting two-dimensional projections from various viewpoints, they are best observed on a computer system (in the present study using the *R* statistical program) so that they can be dynamically manipulated, thereby enabling observation from any desired viewpoint.[8]

A number of two dimensional projections of the three-dimensional map are presented as plots (Figure 3, Figure 4). Since they are based on the same source data, it is possible to recognise the relationship between the two and three-dimensional maps by observing that the vertical plane in the 2D map represents the horizontal plane in the 3D map. If the 3D map is aligned with axis 1 on the horizontal and axis 2 on the vertical (by looking at the 3D map from above) direct correspondence with the 2D map can be observed (see Figure 5).

Figure 5: Athanasius–Pauline Epistles (Complete): 3D View from x–y plane (as per 2D map)

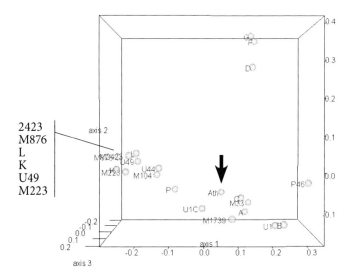

Therefore the 2D maps must be utilized with care, since witnesses that appear close together may in fact be separated by a greater distance which is more clearly observed in the 3D map. This situation is analogous to observation of stars in the night sky referred to earlier in Chapter 4. The final authority for

---

[8] Instructions to enable the generation of 'real-time' 3D MDS maps within the *R* program environment using the *rgl* graphics library are provided in the document *Addenda to the Book. Donker-Apostolos in Athanasius.pdf* available on the SBL website. An intermediate option has been provided whereby animated .gif files for each 3D map are also located on the SBL website in the subfolder: *3D gif files*. These .gif files can be downloaded and observed in any web browser and simulate dynamic rotation of the respective map about a vertical axis.

actual distances between witnesses remains the dissimilarity matrix since it is calculated directly from the source data. With this in mind the results of the two and three dimensional maps (Figure 2, Figure 3 and Figure 4) for the Pauline Epistles can be observed.

Groups of witnesses are located in a number of what are best referred to as 'clusters'.[9] The three Western witnesses, D F G, are located together well away from all other witnesses, though F and G are closer to each other than they are to D. This is expected considering the unique textual relationship between F and G. Clearly, these three witnesses form a distinct cluster which corresponds to the Western text-type group. The remaining witnesses are not so clearly distinguished especially when they are observed in the 3D map. It is, however, possible to discern two general groups that correspond approximately to the Byzantine and Alexandrian groups. Toward the left of the 2D map (Figure 2) one cluster contains M876 (=miniscule manuscript 876) K 223 2423 U49 (=uncial manuscript 049). Though not easily seen, L is also located on the 2D map in almost exactly the same position as 2423. Its presence can be verified by reference to the table of axis co-ordinates for the location of witnesses in the 2D map (Table 96).[10]

Ms 2423 is located at x= −0.231, y= 0.04 and L is located at x= −0.223, y= 0.04. It is also clearly distinguished in the 3D map (Figure 3, Figure 4). These witnesses are all classified as Byzantine. The 3D map in particular shows that they are not isolated as a distinct cluster since two manuscripts that are classified as Secondary Alexandrian witnesses, Ψ and 104 are located quite close by. This is not surprising in the case of Ψ since the mixed character of its text toward the Byzantine from 1 Corinthians onward was noted earlier. 104, however, is located closer to some of the witnesses in the Byzantine cluster than any of the Alexandrian witnesses (Primary or Secondary). The 2D map and especially the 3D map (Figure 3) show that the witnesses associated with the Alexandrian text-type are quite dispersed.

The Alexandrian witnesses commonly designated as Primary ($\mathfrak{P}^{46}$ ℵ B 1739) are located in one half of this larger Alexandrian cluster, however a number of them (ℵ 1739), are no closer to each other than they are to Secondary Alexandrian witnesses. The remaining witnesses designated as Secondary Alexandrian are generally located between the Primary Alexandrian and Byzantine witnesses. Ms P in particular lies just as close to the Byzantine cluster as it does to any other Secondary Alexandrian witness apart from Ψ and 104 whose locations have already been noted. This raises the issue of adequate identification of clusters or to use the traditional terminology, text-type groupings since P, though classified as a Secondary Alexandrian, is here almost an 'outlier' and could just as easily be

---

[9] This term is commonly used in multivariate analysis but may also be particularly suitable for discussing the relationships of witnesses in a textual 'space'. See Chatfield and Collins, *Introduction to Multivariate Analysis*, 212ff.

[10] These tables of witness coordinates are also produced by the *R* scripts that produce the 2D and 3D maps and can aid in identifying witnesses in cases where sigla are superimposed.

incorporated within the Byzantine cluster than a widely dispersed Alexandrian cluster.[11] This is an issue that will be addressed again when discussing the optimal cluster maps.

The spatial location of Athanasius' text relative to other witnesses is now easily observed, especially in the 3D map which shows his text even further away from the Secondary Alexandrian witnesses ($\aleph^c$ A C 33) than is P, though in a different direction. Athanasius' text does not appear to have been influenced by the Byzantine text-type to the extent that P is, as it has not been pulled in that direction. Neither does his text appear to be drawn toward the direction of the Western witnesses. The location of Athanasius' text relative to all other witnesses in the map indicates that it has an 'independent' element that does not come via Western or Byzantine influences.[12]

Since the 2D and 3D maps are derived from the dissimilarity matrices, and these matrices are calculated from the same source data as was used in the quantitative and group profile analyses, then as Finney notes "it follows that the co-ordinates of every plotted point in the maps are subject to sampling error as well. In general, the larger the number of variation units upon which an MDS map is based, the smaller the relative size of this error." Methods available to graphically display the associated error bounds in 2D and 3D maps are still essentially undeveloped.[13] However, the R script *cmds-incl-3d.r*, incorporates a function to estimate and display the error margin for every plotted point as a semi-transparent sphere thereby defining a region with a high probability of containing the actual location of the relevant witness.

As in previous calculations of error margins earlier in this study, a confidence level of 95% is used. The 3D MDS map (Figure 6) displays the error margins as spheres for each plotted witness in the Pauline corpus.[14]

---

[11] The term 'outlier' refers to extreme outer values that are nonetheless part of a sample set. See Rowntree, *Statistics Without Tears*, 50–51.

[12] This conclusion reflects Brogan's findings concerning the Gospels text of Athanasius when he states that "On numerous occasions, Athanasius' references to the Gospels reveal that he is using forms of the text that are not found among witnesses of the major textual traditions." Brogan, "Text of the Gospels," 261. A review of the data in Chapter 3 confirms that this is also the case for Athanasius' text of the Apostolos.

[13] Cox and Cox discuss a procedure for obtaining confidence regions for coordinates plotted in 2D MDS maps but since it is based on the method of 'maximum likelihood' is not applicable to the maps constructed here. See Cox and Cox, *Multidimensional Scaling*, 110–116.

[14] This method assume that the axis scales are equivalent otherwise the error margins would be expected to appear as ellipsoids. Finney notes that the result "is a mere approximation... but is still a useful indication of the uncertainty associated with a plotted location in an MDS map." See Finney, *Analysis of Textual Variation*, sec. 4.3.3.

Figure 6: Pauline Epistles (Complete); 3D MDS map showing error bounds (95% confidence level).

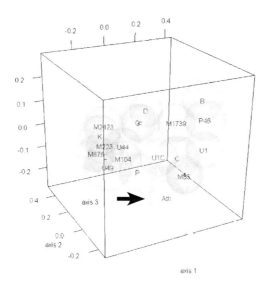

Racine's comment concerning the 'neglect' of earlier studies in the texts of the Fathers in calculating and disclosing error margins in their quantitative analyses also has a corollary here.[15] The overlapping of regions observed in Figure 6 does not invalidate the analysis based on the relative location of witnesses in the maps used in this study but rather, as Racine inferred, it should mitigate against developing a false impression of a level of accuracy that the textual data from the Fathers does not sustain.[16]

It should not be unexpected that the maps for the epistles show some movement or shifting of witness location relative to the 2D and 3D maps of the Pauline corpus. This is so because the maps for each section are based on a subset of the data used for the corpus. The tables of critical values of dissimilarity discussed earlier anticipated this movement by demonstrating the re-ordering of witnesses relative to Athanasius in the various epistles. In the 2D and 3D maps for each epistle, witness locations are based on the dissimilarity of all witnesses relative to each other and are therefore more comprehensive. Nevertheless a cause for concern in calculating maps for individual epistles is that the number of variation units in the sample data can become so low that in some cases, it drops below the minimum acceptable sample size of twelve units. This is the case in

---

[15] See Racine, *Text of Matthew in Basil*, 241.

[16] Since peripheral to the main focus of the analysis here, 3D MDS showing error bounds will not be displayed for other sections of the Apostolos in this chapter but are provided for all sections as animated .gif files available for download from the SBL website associated with this book. The 3D maps presented here display the witness locations as small spheres of fixed arbitrary size rather than points for observational clarity only.

Romans for 𝔓⁴⁶ and F. A review of Table 10 (see Chapter 5), shows that only eight variation units are specified for 𝔓⁴⁶ and only eleven variation units are specified for F.[17] Therefore these two witnesses will be excluded.[18] This can be done by re-calculating the dissimilarity matrix for Romans after excluding 𝔓⁴⁶ and F from the source data and then constructing the 2D and 3D maps based on the updated matrix using the *cmds-ath-2d.r* and *cmds-ath-3d.r* scripts or, alternately, bypassing the intermediate step of rebuilding the dissimilarity matrix by using the *cmds-incl-2d.r* and *cmds-incl-3d.r* scripts which calculate the 2D and 3D maps directly from the variation units source data.[19]

The first thing to note about the 2D map for Romans (Figure 7) is the different orientation when compared with the 2D map for the Pauline corpus.

Figure 7: Athanasius–Romans: 2D View

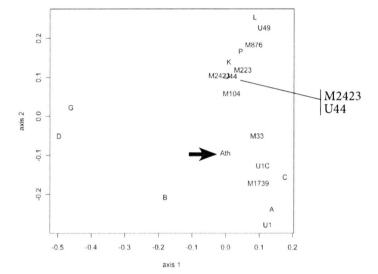

[17] The number of variation units used for comparison between some witnesses and 𝔓⁴⁶ and F are even lower. For example there are only four shared variation units between 𝔓⁴⁶ and K, while F and K share only seven variation units (Refer to Table 86; Appendix A).

[18] This approach is implemented while cognizant of the earlier stated intention to retain all witnesses for analysis. Removing 𝔓⁴⁶ and F from the dissimilarity matrix for Romans has no affect on the critical values of dissimilarity tables since these values are calculated independently for each respective witness of interest relative to Athanasius.

[19] The advantage of these latter *R* scripts is that a minimum number of sample units can be specified and the analysis will then remove any witnesses that fail to fulfil the condition of minimum units. The original dissimilarity matrices can still be consulted since the removal of specific witnesses does not affect the relative distances of all remaining witnesses. Therefore the dissimilarity matrices presented here retain all witnesses for inclusion in the critical values of dissimilarity tables even if certain witnesses are removed when constructing the multidimensional scaling maps. This occurs only in Romans, Acts 1–12 and in the Catholic Epistles where removal of witnesses will be clearly noted.

This is because the classical multidimensional scaling algorithm used to produce these maps places no constraint on the orientation of axis and inversions or rotations (both of which are the case here) are common.[20] The Western cluster is still clearly isolated, though only two witnesses (D and G) remain once F has been removed. Two clusters associated with the Byzantine and Alexandrian witnesses can again be discerned in both the 2D (Figure 7) and 3D maps (Figure 8).

Figure 8: Athanasius–Romans: 3D View

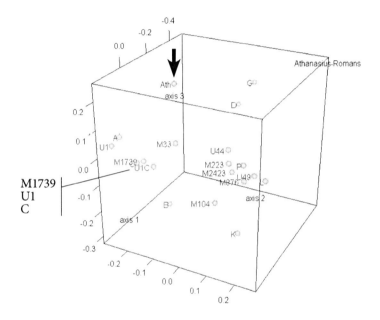

Here also some witnesses that have been classified as Secondary Alexandrian are aligned instead with the Byzantine cluster. Ms P is at the core of the Byzantine cluster whereas in the maps for the Pauline corpus it was located almost midway between both the Alexandrian and Byzantine clusters. Morrill concluded that it was a "borderline" Alexandrian and this seems to be backed up in the Aland's data for this witness.[21] They note that in Paul it has 82 Byzantine, 36 shared, 87 original and 31 singular readings (35%; 15%; 37%; 13%) and assign it to category III.[22] However, its location here indicates a strong Byzantine text in Romans. 104 is again also aligned with the Byzantine cluster, separated off by a slight distance though K is even further away as can be seen in the 3D map. Ψ is also again

---

[20] To compare this map with the map of the Pauline corpus it is necessary to first rotate the 2D map for Romans by ninety degrees clockwise and then invert about the vertical axis.

[21] See Morrill, "Classification of the Greek Manuscripts"; also Osburn, *Text of the Apostolos in Epiphanius*, 40.

[22] See Aland and Aland, *Text of the New Testament*, 113.

located with the Byzantine cluster. At almost the two opposite extremities of the Alexandrian cluster lie Athanasius and B (again best observed in the 3D map). The remaining Alexandrian witnesses are mingled and show no clear distinction between the sub-groups.

In the maps for 1 Corinthians (Figure 9 and Figure 10), F and G lie in exactly the same location.

Figure 9: Athanasius–1 Corinthians: 2D View

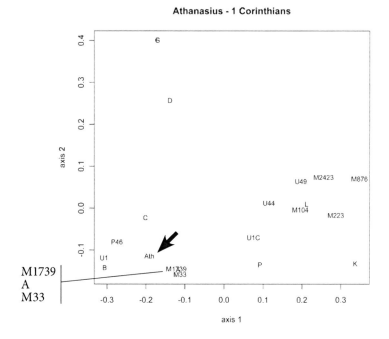

Figure 10: Athanasius–1 Corinthians: 3D View

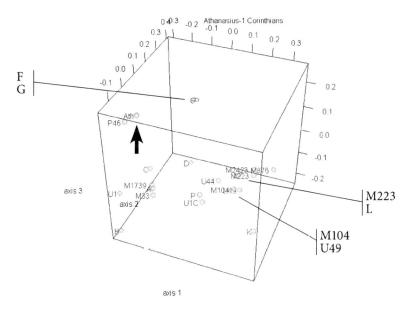

This can be verified by reference to the dissimilarity matrix which shows their dissimilarity at 0.0. The 3D map also shows that Athanasius' text and $\mathfrak{P}^{46}$ are located in the same area. This does not necessarily mean that they share the lowest dissimilarity since a review of the dissimilarity matrix shows that Athanasius' text has the lowest dissimilarity in 1 Corinthians with A at 0.368 whereas $\mathfrak{P}^{46}$ is only fifth closest at 0.429. However, once the dissimilarities of all witnesses are resolved in the 2D and 3D maps, the text of Athanasius and $\mathfrak{P}^{46}$ are located in approximately the same area in the textual space. This serves to demonstrate the improvement in explanatory power between depictions of witness relationships to Athanasius' text along a single axis (i.e., using only one dimension) that is typical in conventional analysis compared to 2D maps which can potentially incorporate another 15–20% of the source data variability, while a 3D map provides further improvement in explanatory power. This can be seen by reference to a Scree plot (Figure 11) which graphically displays the proportion of explanatory power (i.e., proportion of variability) of each dimension.[23]

---

[23] The actual values for each dimension equate to eigenvalues in Primary Components Analysis (PCA). See Afifi, Clark and May, *Computer-Aided Multivariate Analysis*, 374.

Figure 11: Scree plot showing proportion of variance for each dimension-Pauline Epistles (Complete).

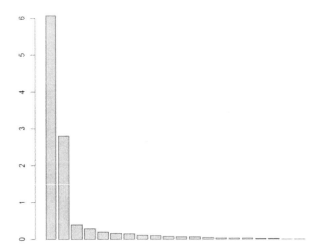

The first dimension accounts for more variation than the second, the second for more than the third, etc.[24] The Scree plot for the Pauline Epistles corpus (Figure 11) shows that, from the third dimension, the increase in cumulative proportion of variability begins to level out.

The 2D map for 2 Corinthians–Titus (Figure 12) shows greater dispersal of the Alexandrian cluster.

---

[24] See Finney, *Analysis of Textual Variation*, sec. 4.3.2.

Figure 12: Athanasius–2 Corinthians–Titus: 2D View

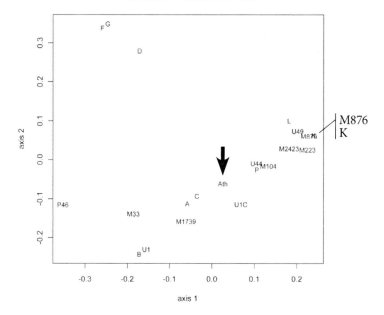

Athanasius - 2 Corinthians-Titus

Athanasius' text is now closer to the Byzantine cluster which suggests that the influence of this text-type on Athanasius' text is greatest in this section of the Pauline Epistles. P 044 and 104 are again at the periphery of the Byzantine cluster but Athanasius' text is located not so far from P. The correction of Sinaiticus (א^c) is also close to the text of Athanasius, though this has also been the case in Romans and the Pauline corpus but not so much in 1 Corinthians and Hebrews.[25]

In Hebrews (Figure 13), the Alexandrian and Byzantine clusters have separated even further compared to their general locations in 2 Corinthians–Titus.

---

[25] Brogan notes the close agreement of א^c with Athanasius' text in the Gospels. See Brogan, "Text of the Gospels," 192–193, 205, 214, 289ff; also John Jay Brogan, "Another Look at Codex Sinaiticus," in *The Bible as Book: The Transmission of the Greek Text* (eds. McKendrick and O'Sullivan; London: The British Library, 2003), 20ff.

Figure 13: Athanasius–Hebrews: 2D View

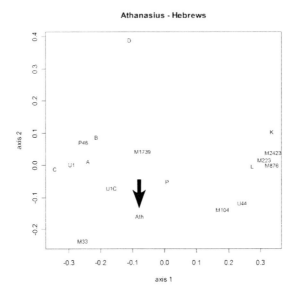

P, 044 and 104 have moved further away from the core witnesses of the Byzantine cluster. The Alexandrian cluster remains dispersed. The witnesses ℵ A and B suggest a central core but Athanasius' text is no further removed from this core than other Alexandrian witnesses such as C, 33 and 1739. Again, however, there is no clear distinction between the two Alexandrian sub-groups.

The general impression of the relationship of Athanasius' text with all the selected witnesses initially indicated by their location in a textual space can be further investigated by the use of additional graphical output. Two specific types are demonstrated here; dendrograms based on an agglomerative technique and optimal cluster maps. Figure 14–Figure 16 present dendrograms based on three different agglomerative techniques; single-linkage, group average and Ward's criterion.[26] While all three provide essentially the same result, Ward's method has been adopted as the preferred method since it tends to accentuate the vertical stem (i.e. indicating distinctiveness) which differentiates the main clusters more clearly. As noted earlier, these dendrograms cannot be equated with the results of a phylogenetic analysis, since they do not depict family-tree genealogical relationships between witnesses.[27] What is being depicted here is a similarity of textual witnesses with distinctiveness being indicated by the height of the vertical stems prior to joins with the next stem.

---

[26] These types were explained earlier in Chapter Four.
[27] Finney, *Analysis of Textual Variation*, sec. 4.5.1.

Figure 14: Dendrogram: Athanasius (Pauline Epistles), 'single' method

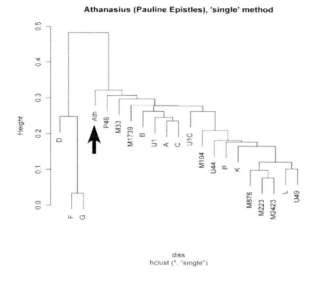

Figure 15: Dendrogram: Athanasius (Pauline Epistles), 'average' method

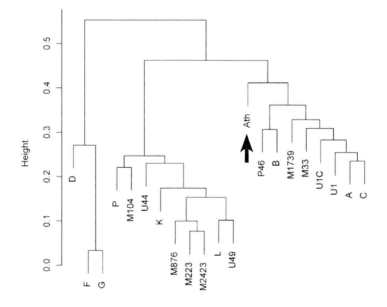

Figure 16: Dendrogram: Athanasius (Pauline Epistles), 'Ward' method

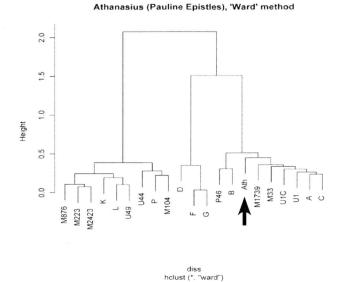

The following comments relate to Figure 16–Figure 20. Three clusters are evident in these dendrograms.

Figure 17: Dendrogram: Athanasius (Romans), 'Ward' method

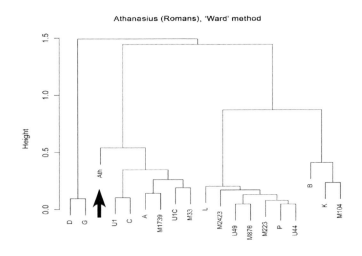

Figure 18: Dendrogram: Athanasius (1 Corinthians), 'Ward' method

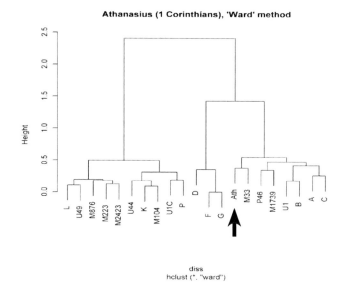

Figure 19: Dendrogram: Athanasius (2 Corinthians–Titus), 'Ward' method

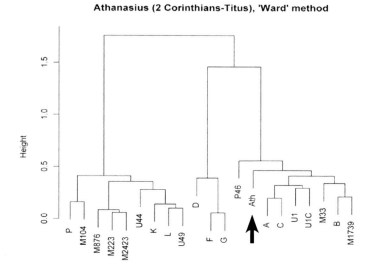

Figure 20: Dendrogram: Athanasius (Hebrews), 'Ward' method

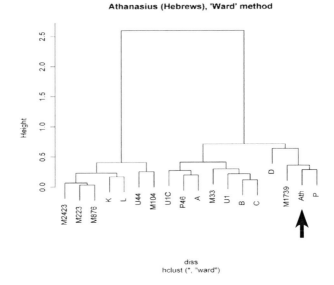

The Western cluster is consistently distinguished in all the maps for the sections of the Pauline Epistles except for Hebrews (Figure 20) where only D is extant. F and G pair first before joining D. The Byzantine and Alexandrian clusters are also easily identified. The alignment of P, Ψ and 104 with the Byzantine cluster is noted here. The corroborating evidence of these maps suggests the need for a re-evaluation of the textual alignments of these three manuscripts within the Pauline corpus. The one exception for P is in Hebrews (Figure 20) where this witness is aligned with the Alexandrian cluster.

Another notable aspect is the location of B in the dendrogram for Romans (Figure 17), which aligns here with K and 104 (after they have paired) in the Byzantine cluster. This is the only epistle where this is the case. Osburn's results for Epiphanius also show that B is a weak Alexandrian witness in Romans.[28] Athanasius' text is located in the Alexandrian cluster. No clear distinction between the Primary and Secondary sub-groups is observed here. Of the six witnesses that cluster together prior to Athanasius joining (C A ℵ ℵ^c 33 1739), two are Primary Alexandrian and four are Secondary Alexandrian. Athanasius' text joins prior to 𝔓⁴⁶ and B. Once the Alexandrian cluster is complete it joins with the Western witnesses before the final link with the Byzantine cluster.

---

[28] Osburn's results for the quantitative analysis in Romans shows MS B positioned just before the three Western witnesses (D F G) with a very low 38.5% agreement with Epiphanius. In 1 Corinthians this rises to 54.9%, in 2 Corinthians it raises again to 69.2% and is slightly lower in Hebrews at 62.5%. See Osburn, *Text of the Apostolos in Epiphanius*, 217.

Since the Ward method accentuates the height of the main stems (emphasizing distinctiveness) it is relatively easy to identify the main clusters in Figure 16. A line drawn horizontally at a height of 1.0 will cross through the three stems of the Byzantine, Western and Alexandrian clusters. One indication of how good an Alexandrian witness Athanasius' text is may be gauged by where he joins the Alexandrian cluster. In Romans, for example, already noted for having the weakest Alexandrian support in Athanasius' text of the Pauline Epistles, his text is the last to join the cluster (see Figure 17). In 1 Corinthians (Figure 18) Athanasius' text pairs with 33 and then together they are the final pair to join the Alexandrian cluster.

Optimal cluster maps also provide useful results if the intention is to specify a set number of distinct clusters, in order to observe how witnesses congregate under such a constraint. Since the dendrograms for the Pauline Epistles confirm three distinct clusters, maps consisting of three clusters will be constructed for the corpus and individual epistles. The maps are constructed with clusters identified by ellipses enclosing witnesses belonging to one distinct cluster. Symbols unique to each cluster identify the location of each witness and are useful in cases where clusters overlap (e.g. Figure 24, map for 2 Corinthians–Titus, and Figure 25, map for Hebrews). Figure 21 presents the map for the Pauline corpus.

Figure 21: Cluster Map: Athanasius (Pauline Epistles), 3 clusters

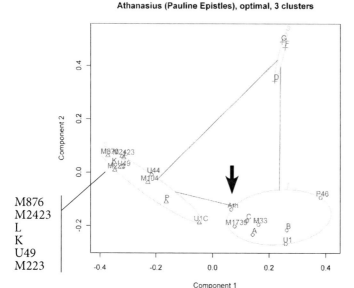

Athanasius (Pauline Epistles), optimal, 3 clusters

Component 1

These two components explain 53.98 % of the point variability.

The Western cluster is again clearly distinguished as are the Byzantine and Alexandrian clusters with most of the witnesses located according to indications derived from the MDS maps and dendrograms. However, there are some exceptions. Most notable is the location of אᶜ in the Byzantine rather than the Alexandrian cluster.[29] The phenomenon of a witness changing text type affinity in maps based on different techniques indicates that a clear partitioning tendency for this witness with one group or the other is not strong. אᶜ also changes affinity in different sections of the Pauline Epistles. In Romans and Hebrews (Figure 22, Figure 25) it is located in the Alexandrian cluster but in 1 Corinthians and 2 Corinthians–Titus (Figure 23, Figure 24) it is aligned with the Byzantine cluster.[30]

Figure 22: Cluster Map: Athanasius (Romans), 3 clusters

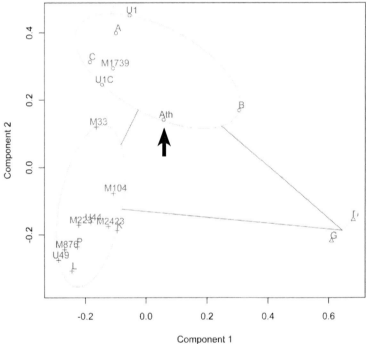

Component 1

These two components explain 49.99 % of the point variability.

---

[29] The dendrogram for 1 Corinthians (Figure 18) also notably locates אᶜ in the Byzantine cluster.

[30] In Romans, 1 Corinthians and Hebrews both the dendrogram and optimal cluster maps agree in the placement of אᶜ. Only in the Pauline corpus and in the section 2 Corinthians–Titus do the two types of maps differ in their location of אᶜ.

Figure 23: Cluster Map: Athanasius (1 Corinthians), 3 clusters

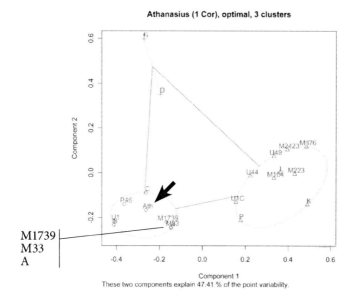

Figure 24: Cluster Map: Athanasius (2 Corinthians–Titus), 3 clusters

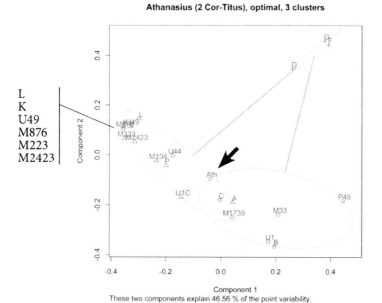

Figure 25: Cluster Map: Athanasius (Hebrews), 3 clusters[31]

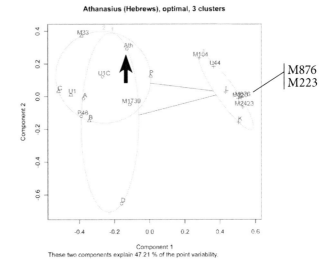

One way to test if ℵ[c] has a tendency to revert back into the Alexandrian cluster in this map is to increase the number of specified clusters and observe what movement of witnesses occurs. Figure 26 shows a map with four clusters specified.

Figure 26: Cluster Map: Athanasius (Pauline Epistles), 4 clusters

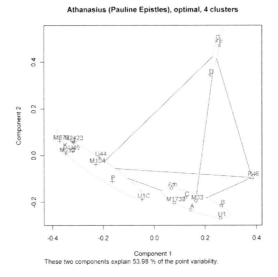

---

[31] Note that this map is inverted along the horizontal axis compared to the 2D MDS map.

It can be observed that ℵ^c maintains its location in the Byzantine cluster but 𝔓^{46} moves out from the Alexandrian cluster and forms a unique cluster. When the number of clusters is increased, it is notable that, though 𝔓^{46}, which is classified as a Primary Alexandrian, was the first to move away from the Alexandrian cluster, it does not attract other Primary Alexandrian witnesses to join it and form a Primary Alexandrian cluster as distinct from a Secondary Alexandrian cluster.[32] This tendency for the Primary and Secondary Alexandrian witnesses to remain intermingled and show no clear distinction appears to be a strikingly consistent outcome of these maps.[33]

This consistent demonstration of the Alexandrian witnesses showing no clear distinction between the Primary and Secondary sub-groups confirms the initial observations of Brogan. He addressed the question "as to what we mean when we speak of a 'Secondary Alexandrian' witness?" His response was to tentatively suggest that while there are some readings that are supported exclusively or primarily among these witnesses, "there are not enough of these shared readings to make the Secondary Alexandrian witnesses a distinct text-type."[34] When the number of clusters is increased to five, Athanasius' text is the next witness to leave the Alexandrian cluster (see Figure 27) confirming the characterisation of Athanasius' text as being a 'weak' Alexandrian.

---

[32] For a detailed description of the textual character of MS 𝔓^{46} see G. Zuntz, *The Text of the Epistles: A Disquisition upon the Corpus Paulinum* (London: Oxford University Press, 1953), 17ff. The generally acknowledged early date for 𝔓^{46} is an important factor in its importance as a Primary Alexandrian. See Young Kyu Kim, "Palaeographical Dating of 𝔓^{46} to the Later First Century," *Biblica* 69 (1988); also S. R. Pickering, "The Dating of the Chester Beatty-Michigan Codex of the Pauline Epistles (𝔓^{46})," in *Ancient History in a Modern University: Early Christianity, Late Antiquity and Beyond* (eds. T. W. Hillard, et al., Grand Rapids: Eerdmans, 1998).

[33] The one possible exception is in Hebrews (Figure 25) where the Alexandrian witnesses divide into two clusters since D joins one as the only Western representative. However even here the Primary and Secondary witnesses do not divide according to these classifications. One cluster is formed by Athanasius ℵ^c A 1739 𝔓^{46} D, while the other is formed by ℵ C 33 P B.

[34] Brogan, "Text of the Gospels," 301.

Figure 27: Cluster Map: Athanasius (Pauline Epistles), 5 clusters

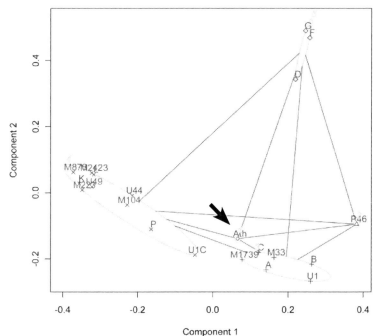

Athanasius (Pauline Epistles), optimal, 5 clusters

These two components explain 53.97 % of the point variability.

Summary: The critical values of dissimilarity indicate no statistically close relationship of Athanasius' text with any other witness except for C in 2 Corinthians–Titus. Athanasius' text is located at the periphery of the Alexandrian cluster which also shows no clear distinction between the Primary and Secondary Alexandrian witnesses. Both the dendrograms and optimal cluster maps confirm Athanasius' weak Alexandrian status as is especially indicated in the optimal cluster maps by his tendency to leave the Alexandrian cluster just after $\mathfrak{P}^{46}$.

ACTS

The critical values of dissimilarity for the Acts corpus (Table 58, Table 59) show that none of the selected witnesses demonstrate a significantly close relationship with Athanasius' text.

Table 58: Critical Values of Dissimilarity Using Simple Matching Distance with Each Respective Manuscript as the Witness of Interest Relative to Athanasius: Acts–Complete Corpus

Witness	Diss	LCV	UCV	<LCV	LCV≤ Diss≤UCV	>UCV
81	0.220	0.220	0.512		✓	
B	0.244	0.222	0.511		✓	
1891	0.244	0.222	0.511		✓	
A	0.267	0.222	0.489		✓	
Ψ	0.267	0.222	0.489		✓	
ℵ	0.289	0.222	0.489		✓	
630	0.289	0.222	0.489		✓	
1175	0.289	0.222	0.489		✓	
1704	0.289	0.222	0.489		✓	
945	0.311	0.222	0.511		✓	
1739	0.311	0.222	0.511		✓	
$\mathfrak{P}^{74}$	0.326	0.209	0.488		✓	
P	0.341	0.227	0.500		✓	
C	0.366	0.220	0.512		✓	
H	0.400	0.222	0.511		✓	
1073	0.400	0.222	0.489		✓	
L	0.406	0.188	0.500		✓	
049	0.422	0.222	0.489		✓	
1352	0.422	0.222	0.489		✓	
383	0.476	0.143	0.571		✓	
E	0.489	0.222	0.489		✓	
614	0.511	0.222	0.489			✓
D	0.611	0.222	0.528			✓

Table 59: Critical Values of Dissimilarity: Acts (complete)

Diss < LCV	LCV ≤ Diss ≤ UCV	Diss > UCV
	81 B 1891 A Ψ ℵ 630 1175 1704 9451739 $\mathfrak{P}^{74}$ P C H 1073 L 049 1352 383 E	614 D

Only two witnesses MSS 614 and D, which are both classified as Western, show significant dissimilarity. When Acts is divided into the two sections, chapters 1–12 (Table 60, Table 61) and 13–28 (Table 62, Table 63), it can be observed that in chapters 1–12 MS 1891 (which is classified as a Secondary Alexandrian) is significantly close to Athanasius' text. E is the only witness that is significantly dissimilar. In chapters 13–28 no witnesses show significant relationship except for D (Western) which is significantly dissimilar.

Table 60: Critical Values of Dissimilarity Using Simple Matching Distance with Each Respective Manuscript as the Witness of Interest Relative to Athanasius: Acts 1–12

Witness	Diss	LCV	UCV	<LCV	LCV≤ Diss≤UCV	>UCV
1891	0.158	0.211	0.579	✓		
B	0.211	0.158	0.579		✓	
81	0.211	0.158	0.579		✓	
ℵ	0.316	0.158	0.579		✓	
A	0.316	0.158	0.579		✓	
Ψ	0.316	0.158	0.579		✓	
1704	0.316	0.158	0.579		✓	
1739	0.316	0.158	0.579		✓	
630	0.368	0.211	0.579		✓	
945	0.368	0.211	0.579		✓	
$\mathfrak{P}^{74}$	0.412	0.176	0.588		✓	
C	0.421	0.158	0.579		✓	
H	0.421	0.158	0.579		✓	
1175	0.421	0.158	0.579		✓	
P	0.444	0.167	0.611		✓	
049	0.474	0.158	0.579		✓	
1073	0.474	0.158	0.579		✓	
1352	0.474	0.158	0.579		✓	
L	0.500	0.000	0.667		✓	
614	0.579	0.158	0.579		✓	
D	0.600	0.2	0.667		✓	
E	0.632	0.211	0.579			✓

Table 61: Critical Values of Dissimilarity: Acts 1–12

Diss < LCV	LCV ≤ Diss ≤ UCV	Diss > UCV
1891	B 81 ℵ A Ψ 1704 1739 630 945 $\mathfrak{P}^{74}$ C H 1175 P 049 1073 1352 L 614 D	E

Table 62: Critical Values of Dissimilarity Using Simple Matching Distance with Each Respective Manuscript as the Witness of Interest Relative to Athanasius: Acts 13–28

Witness	Diss	LCV	UCV	<LCV	LCV≤ Diss≤UCV	>UCV
1175	0.192	0.192	0.538		✓	
81	0.227	0.182	0.545		✓	
A	0.231	0.192	0.538		✓	
Ψ	0.231	0.192	0.538		✓	
630	0.231	0.192	0.538		✓	
𝔓⁷⁴	0.269	0.192	0.538		✓	
ℵ	0.269	0.192	0.538		✓	
B	0.269	0.192	0.538		✓	
P	0.269	0.192	0.538		✓	
945	0.269	0.192	0.538		✓	
1704	0.269	0.192	0.538		✓	
1739	0.308	0.192	0.538		✓	
1891	0.308	0.192	0.538		✓	
C	0.318	0.182	0.545		✓	
1073	0.346	0.192	0.538		✓	
E	0.385	0.192	0.538		✓	
H	0.385	0.192	0.538		✓	
L	0.385	0.192	0.538		✓	
049	0.385	0.192	0.538		✓	
1352	0.385	0.192	0.538		✓	
614	0.462	0.192	0.538		✓	
383	0.476	0.190	0.571		✓	
D	0.619	0.19	0.571			✓

Table 63: Critical Values of Dissimilarity: Acts 13–28

Diss < LCV	LCV ≤ Diss ≤ UCV	Diss > UCV
	1175 81 A Ψ 630 𝔓⁷⁴ ℵ B P 945 1704 1739 1891 C 1073 E H L 049 1352 614 383	D

The 2D and 3D maps for the Acts corpus (Figure 28–Figure 29) show that there are two main clusters for the Alexandrian and Byzantine witnesses.

Figure 28: Athanasius–Acts: 2D

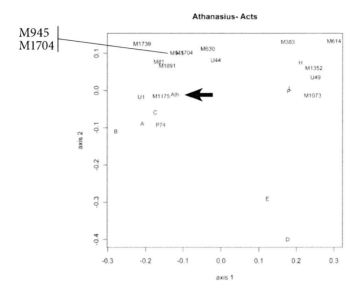

Figure 29: Athanasius–Acts: 3D View 1

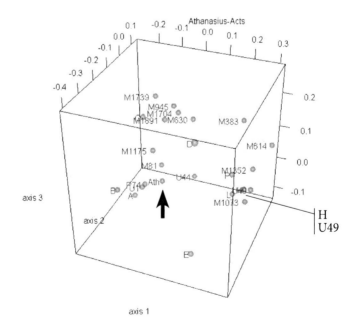

Athanasius is more integrated into the Alexandrian cluster than was the case in the Pauline Epistles. The Western witnesses, however, are dispersed in two locations. D and E are located away from other witnesses but also away from each other, as is seen more clearly in the 3D map. 383 and 614 are located closer together but much nearer to the Byzantine cluster. This tendency is also consistent in the two individual sections of Acts, though 383 is absent in chapters 1–12 so only 614 is located near the Byzantine witnesses.[35]

The dendrogram for the Acts corpus (Figure 30) shows 383 and 614 also aligned with the Byzantine group.

Figure 30: Dendrogram: Athanasius (Acts), 'Ward' method

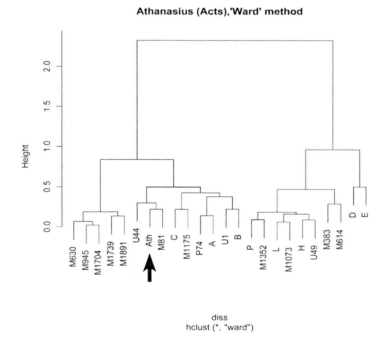

Ms 614 in chapters 1–12 is again aligned with the Byzantines (Figure 31).

---

[35] Ms 614 is classified as a Western witness by Metzger and Greenlee whereas only Metzger lists MS 383 as Western. See Metzger, *Text of the New Testament*, 214; also Greenlee, *New Testament Textual Criticism*, 117. Mullen included both as Western witnesses in his study on the text of Cyril of Jerusalem. See Mullen, *Text of Cyril*, 65.

Figure 31: Dendrogram: Athanasius (Acts 1–12), 'Ward' method

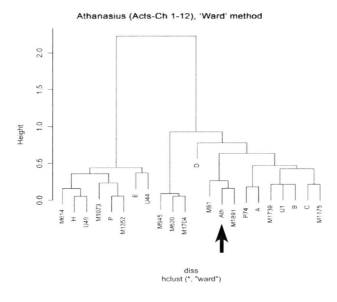

Figure 31: Dendrogram: Athanasius (Acts 1–12), 'Ward' method

In chapters 13–28 (Figure 32) both 383 and 614 pair with the Byzantine cluster before D and E join the same stem some distance later.

Figure 32: Dendrogram: Athanasius (Acts 13–28), 'Ward' method

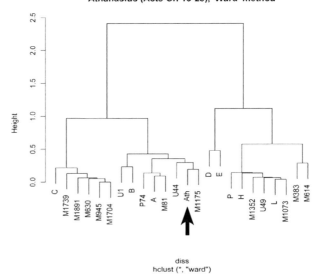

The optimal cluster map for the Acts corpus (Figure 33) with three clusters specified shows that all four witnesses classified as Western join the Byzantine cluster rather than form a unique Western cluster.

Figure 33: Cluster Map: Athanasius (Acts), 3 clusters

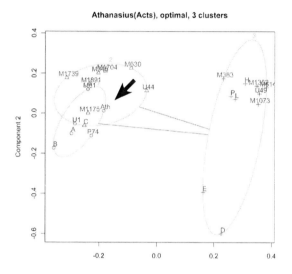

When four clusters are specified (Figure 34), D separates from the Byzantine cluster and becomes isolated.

Figure 34: Cluster Map: Athanasius (Acts), 4 clusters

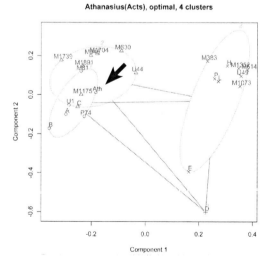

This pattern is repeated in 1–12 and 13–28 which indicates that these four witnesses cannot be said to constitute a clearly defined Western group in Acts.

The Byzantine cluster is well defined and remains reasonably consistent in all the maps. Its main members are MSS P 1352 L 1073 H and 049. Ψ (an Alexandrian witness) joins the Byzantine cluster in Acts 1–12 as noted in both the dendrogram for that section of Acts (Figure 31) as well as in the optimal cluster maps (both three and four clusters specified). Ψ is clearly in the Alexandrian cluster in Acts 13–28 which suggests a difference of text-type in that witness between the two sections.[36] It is notable that the dendrogram for the Acts corpus (Figure 30) preserves the Family 1739 witnesses (i.e. 630 945 1704 1739 1891) precisely as a unique cluster.[37] Athanasius' text pairs first with 81 before they link with Ψ and then join with the remaining Alexandrian witnesses. As in the results for the Pauline Epistles, there is again no clear distinction between the witnesses classified as Primary and Secondary Alexandrian. For example, while ℵ and B pair early (both Primary Alexandrian), 𝔓[74] (Primary Alexandrian) pairs with A (Secondary Alexandrian).

The optimal cluster map for the Acts corpus shows that the Alexandrian witnesses do produce two distinct groups when three clusters are specified, but they are not distinguished on the basis of a Primary/Secondary Alexandrian classification. Athanasius' text joins 𝔓[74] ℵ A B and 81 in one cluster with the remaining Alexandrian witnesses in the other which includes all the Family 1739 witnesses along with C Ψ and 1175. In the optimal cluster map for Acts 1–12 the Alexandrian cluster containing Family 1739 is weakened with only four witnesses (630 945 1704 1891) remaining in it. However in Acts 13–28 the five Family 1739 witnesses form an exclusive sub-cluster within the larger Alexandrian cluster. Athanasius' text is not associated with this cluster in any of the maps. His text does not therefore share the same affinity for Family 1739 that Epiphanius' text displayed in Acts 13–28 where his textual agreement with that group in the quantitative analysis was a high 74.7%.[38] In contrast to the lack of distinction between the Primary and Secondary Alexandrian witnesses displayed in these maps, the clear delineation of Family 1739 on the basis of a relatively small sample in Acts 13–28 is indeed striking and serves to demonstrate that where genuine text-type groups exist they will be observed in the maps.

Summary: In Acts, Athanasius' text is only significantly similar to 1891 in Acts 1–12. Both the 2D and 3D maps show that he is more integrated in the Alexandrian cluster than was the case in the Pauline epistles. This is confirmed by the dendrograms and optimal cluster maps. While the optimal cluster map shows the Alexandrian cluster divided into two smaller clusters they are not aligned on the basis of Primary and Secondary classifications.

---

[36] Since in Acts 1–12 L is extant in only six variation units and 383 is lacunose, they are both missing in the maps.

[37] see Thomas C. Geer Jr., *Family 1739 in Acts* (SBLMS 48; Atlanta: Scholars Press, 1994).

[38] See Osburn, *Text of the Apostolos in Epiphanius*, 199.

CATHOLIC EPISTLES

The results of a multivariate analysis of the Catholic Epistles in Athanasius provide surprising results when compared to the results from the quantitative and group profile analyses. The critical values of dissimilarity chart (Table 64 and Summary, Table 65) appear to corroborate the results from the earlier analyses, since it shows that the two witnesses, which are significantly dissimilar to Athanasius, are both Alexandrian ($\aleph$ B).

Table 64: Critical Values of Dissimilarity Using Simple Matching Distance with Each Respective Manuscript as the Witness of Interest Relative to Athanasius: Catholic Epistles

Witness	Diss	LCV	UCV	<LCV	LCV≤ Diss≤UCV	>UCV
L	0.500	0.167	0.667		✓	
105	0.500	0.167	0.667		✓	
201	0.500	0.167	0.667		✓	
1739	0.500	0.167	0.667		✓	
C	0.556	0.111	0.778		✓	
A	0.583	0.167	0.667		✓	
Ψ	0.583	0.167	0.667		✓	
1022	0.583	0.167	0.667		✓	
1424	0.583	0.167	0.667		✓	
2423	0.583	0.167	0.667		✓	
325	0.625	0.125	0.750		✓	
$\mathfrak{P}^{72}$	0.667	0.000	0.833		✓	
049	0.667	0.167	0.667		✓	
323	0.667	0.167	0.667		✓	
33	0.727	0.182	0.727		✓	
$\aleph$	0.750	0.167	0.667			✓
B	0.833	0.167	0.667			✓

Table 65: Critical Values of Dissimilarity: Catholic Epistles

Diss < LCV	LCV ≤ Diss ≤ UCV	Diss > UCV
	L 105 201 1739 C A Ψ 1022 1424 2423 325 $\mathfrak{P}^{72}$ 049 323 33	$\aleph$ B

However, it must be recognized that the order of witnesses in the critical values chart is based on the same uni-dimensional data as used in the two earlier

analytical methods. When the full range of data from the dissimilarity matrix is used, the picture portrayed in the MDS maps appears different.
The two text-type groups, Alexandrian and Byzantine, can be identified in the 2D and 3D maps (Figure 35–Figure 37).[39]

Figure 35: Athanasius–Catholic Epistles: 2D

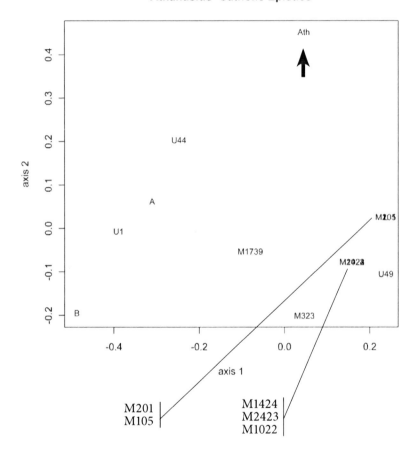

Athanasius- Catholic Epistles

M201
M105

M1424
M2423
M1022

[39] Some witnesses are excluded since the number of shared variation units they contain are less than the minimum required of 12 (i.e. 𝔓⁷² C 33 325).

Figure 36: Athanasius–Catholic Epistles: 3D View 1

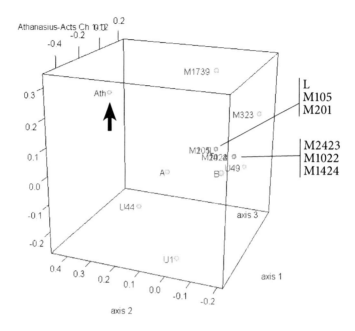

Figure 37: Athanasius–Catholic Epistles: 3D View 2

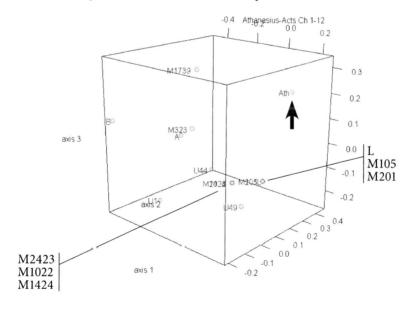

The Byzantine cluster is quite concentrated with multiple witnesses piled up on top of each other. This can be seen by referring to the axis coordinate tables associated with both the 2D and 3D maps (Table 66, Table 67 respectively).

Table 66: Axis Coordinates for 2D MDS map: Catholic Epistles

	axis 1	axis 2
Ath	0.045	0.452
U1	-0.389	-0.007
A	-0.31	0.062
B	-0.488	-0.195
L	0.237	0.026
U44	-0.248	0.203
U49	0.237	-0.105
M105	0.237	0.026
M201	0.237	0.026
M323	0.047	-0.202
M1022	0.158	-0.077
M1424	0.158	-0.077
M1739	-0.08	-0.053
M2423	0.158	-0.077

Table 67: Axis Coordinates for 3D MDS map: Catholic Epistles

	axis 1	axis 2	axis 3
Ath	0.045	0.452	0.176
U1	-0.389	-0.007	-0.26
A	-0.31	0.062	0.014
B	-0.488	-0.195	0.097
L	0.237	0.026	-0.045
U44	-0.248	0.203	-0.151
U49	0.237	-0.105	-0.102
M105	0.237	0.026	-0.045
M201	0.237	0.026	-0.045
M323	0.047	-0.202	0.161
M1022	0.158	-0.077	-0.042
M1424	0.158	-0.077	-0.042
M1739	-0.08	-0.053	0.325
M2423	0.158	-0.077	-0.042

In the 2D map three Byzantine witnesses, 1022 2423 and 1424 are located in exactly the same position and two other Byzantine witnesses, 105 and 201 are also located together. This is primarily due to the low (sample) number of varia-tion units used in the analysis of the Catholic Epistles. In these maps Athanasius' text is not closely associated with either cluster, though the more widely dis-persed Alexandrian cluster could incorporate Athanasius' text. A review of the dendrogram and optimal cluster maps clarifies the picture.

Figure 38: Dendrogram: Athanasius (Catholic Epistles), 'Ward' method

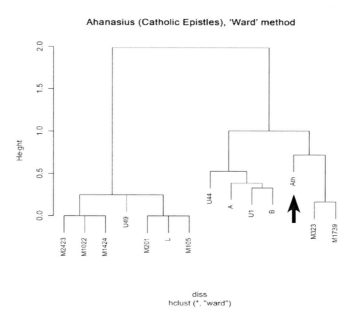

In the dendrogram and optimal cluster maps Athanasius' text is clearly associated with the Alexandrian cluster and not the Byzantine cluster. The dendrogram (Figure 38) locates the Byzantine witnesses in one cluster and the Alexandrian witnesses in the other with no swapping of representative witnesses either way. The optimal cluster map (Figure 39), where only two clusters are spec-ified, locates two Alexandrian witnesses, 1739 and 323 in the Byzantine cluster but Athanasius remains in the Alexandrian cluster.

Figure 39: Cluster Map: Athanasius (Catholic Epistles), 2 clusters

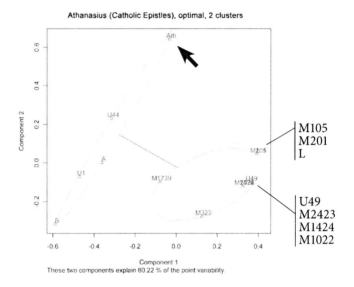

When the optimal cluster map is expanded to three clusters (Figure 40), 1739 and 323 are removed from the Byzantine cluster and form a unique cluster with Athanasius.

Figure 40: Cluster Map: Athanasius (Catholic Epistles), 3 clusters

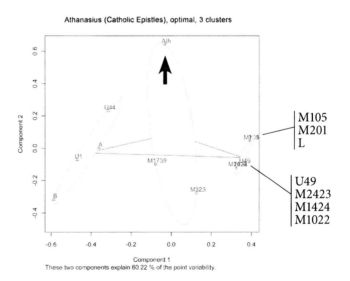

The results here are at odds with the conclusions of the quantitative and group profile analyses. It seems reasonable to conclude that the very low amount of usable sample data in the Catholic Epistles is responsible for this anomaly.

When analysing the data using a single dimension (i.e. proportional agreement of Athanasius' text with individual witnesses), the result appears to indicate his affinity (though only just and provisionally) with the Byzantine witnesses. However, as the MDS maps utilise the full dimensionality of the dissimilarity data and also depict a higher proportion of the variability of the data (70% in the 2D map, 86% in the 3D map, 60% in the optimal cluster maps), any statistical anomaly in the results from the earlier analyses is corrected and a more accurate picture emerges. The results of the multivariate analysis therefore provide an important correction to the quantitative and group profile analyses which concluded that Athanasius' text was primarily derived from a Byzantine text-type in the Catholic Epistles. To the contrary, what the multivariate analysis makes clear is that the priority of an Alexandrian text-type source for Athanasius' text remains consistent throughout the Apostolos.

Summary: In the Catholic Epistles Athanasius' text has no significantly similar relationship within any witness, but is seen to be significantly dissimilar to ℵ and B. The MDS maps however contradict this result by showing that Athanasius is more clearly aligned with the Alexandrian group than the Byzantine group. It appears that the very small amount of data variability used in the comparison of the critical values of dissimilarity (as is also the case in the quantitative and group profile analyses), has produced a statistical anomaly that is corrected in the MDS maps which use a greater proportion of the source data variability.

8

Conclusion

The primary aim of this study has been to determine the affinity of Athanasius' text of the Apostolos according to the major New Testament text-types. Due to the extremely low number of variation units in Revelation the data for this book could not be analyzed. The three remaining sections in the Apostolos—Acts, the Pauline epistles and Catholic Epistles—were analyzed separately. The two methods of a quantitative analysis and the Comprehensive Profile Method, as have been commonly adopted in previous studies on the texts of the Fathers, were utilised. A third method known as multivariate analysis was also utilized.

An important distinction between the previous methods and multivariate analysis is that whereas the quantitative and group profile analyses essentially utilise only one dimension of the source data (i.e. the proportional relationship between Athanasius' text and each representative witness), multivariate analysis utilizes the full dimensionality of the source data (i.e. the relationship of every witness to every other witness) to more accurately represent the location of witnesses relative to each other in a textual space. Another distinction is that the quantitative and group profile analyses utilise the range of witnesses classified within pre-defined manuscript text-types. While multivariate analysis utilizes the same set of witnesses, the *a priori* classifications are not applied as a constraint and hence any group or cluster affinity is derived from the data itself and not externally imposed. Therefore, while the results from these various analytical methods shared some similarities, differences were also noted as follows:

THE TEXT OF ACTS

The analyses are consistent in confirming Athanasius' text of Acts as Alexandrian with his support over 10% higher here than in the Pauline Epistles and the MDS maps show Athanasius' text located more centrally in the Alexandrian cluster. Athanasius' text does not show any significant relationship with Family 1739 (unlike Epiphanius of Salamis), though the multivariate analysis clearly demonstrates that this group forms a distinct cluster. The results of the quantitative analysis show Athanasius' text as Secondary Alexandrian. The multivariate analysis however, demonstrates that, though the Alexandrian witnesses do form two clusters, they are not divided into Primary and Secondary groups, but are mixed, sharing witnesses from both.

THE TEXT OF THE PAULINE EPISTLES

The quantitative and group profile analyses indicate that Athanasius' text has significant affinity with the Secondary Alexandrian text-type, though Romans is an exception since the results show that Athanasius' text is more mixed in this epistle, having no significant agreement with any text-type. Athanasius' text of the Pauline epistles shows generally less support for the Alexandrian group than in the Gospels. While the multivariate analysis confirms the basic affinity of Athanasius' text for the Alexandrian text-type, the results also conclusively demonstrate that there is no inherent distinction between Primary and Secondary Alexandrian witnesses. Athanasius' text is located at the periphery of the Alexandrian cluster and can therefore be considered a 'weak' Alexandrian witness.

THE TEXT OF THE CATHOLIC EPISTLES

A cause of concern for the results of the Catholic Epistles is the very low number of variation units (twelve) used as the source data, which suggests the results must be considered tentative. Nevertheless a difference is noted between the results from the quantitative and group profile analyses and those from the multivariate analysis. The results from the former methods indicate that Athanasius' text of the Catholic Epistles shifts to a Byzantine text-type affinity, though only just. However the multivariate analysis, in representing a greater proportion of the source data, is able to correct this anomaly and demonstrates that here also, Athanasius' text maintains its Alexandrian text-type affinity.

GENERAL CONCLUSIONS

Beyond these specific conclusions it is necessary to ask some further, more general, but nonetheless important questions. What insights do the results for Athanasius' text of the Apostolos give us for the history of the transmission of the NT text in Alexandria? Related to this, how do the results compare with previous studies of the text of other Alexandrian Fathers and particularly Brogan's results for the Gospels text of Athanasius? Finally in what ways do the results here suggest the direction further research should take?

THE TEXT IN ALEXANDRIA

As regards the first two related issues, this study serves to confirm the earlier conclusion of Brogan in which he suggested that the (Gospels) text of Athanasius does "not represent a concerted effort to revise or correct the Alexandrian text (contra Martini)."[1] Nor is Athanasius' text of the Apostolos (and the Gospels) an unambiguous witness to a Secondary Alexandrian text-type. Rather, his text is simply one representative of witnesses that have moved away from an earlier 'purer' form towards the periphery of the Alexandrian tradition while that text was still in a state of flux in the fourth century. In this regard the results for Athanasius' text of the Apostolos also graphically confirm one common conclusion from previous studies of the New Testament text of other Alexandrian Fathers; that the (so-called) Secondary Alexandrian witnesses should not be considered as belonging to a distinct text-type.[2] Rather what they possibly represent is a "movement towards" a distinct text-type that is ultimately rendered redundant due to the eventual ascendancy of the Byzantine text.[3] Indeed, as Brogan notes concerning the Gospels text and as is confirmed from this analysis of the Apostolos, Athanasius contributes both to the fluidity of the Alexandrian textual tradition when he sometimes introduces unique variants into that tradition and also contributes to the stabilization of that same text through the influence of his writings due to his position as an important ecclesiastical leader in Alexandria.[4] For these reasons, though Athanasius' text of the Apostolos does not lie at the center of the Alexandrian textual 'stream' it nonetheless serves as an important witness within that stream and as a convenient fixed point of reference with which to compare the 'location' of other witnesses within the New Testament textual tradition of Alexandria in the fourth century.

---

[1]   See Brogan, "Text of the Gospels," 299.

[2]   For example see Ehrman, *Didymus*, 265–266. Also note the earlier comment of Brogan regarding this matter on p. 295. Hannah also addressed this issue in his study on the text of 1 Corinthians in the writings of Origen. He states, "What are we to conclude from Origen's seeming lack of preference for either the primary or secondary Alexandrian sub-groups?... This raises a difficult question: how justified are we in distinguishing between the two sub-groups in the Pauline corpus (or at least in 1 Corinthians)?" Hannah, *Text of 1 Corinthians in Origen*, 292–293. While Hannah acknowleges there might be a difference in this respect between the Gospels text and the Pauline Epistles in the Alexandrian tradition he nonetheless concludes, "Either those manuscripts that are primary Alexandrians in the Gospels have been so compromised textually in 1 Corinthians that we can no longer speak of "primary" Alexandrians in 1 Corinthians or the "secondary" witnesses are of such textual purity in 1 Corinthians that they must be considered virtually equivalent with the "primary" witnesses." ibid. Even in the case of the Gospels text in Alexandria it appears uncertainty exists concerning how best to classify various witnesses. For example, Cosaert provides a (typically for this issue) ambiguous view when he concludes that, "it seems likely that Clement's text in John is best classified as Primary Alexandrian, although his lower than ideal rate of agreement suggests that he is not a very pure representative of the Alexandrian tradition." Cosaert, *Text of the Gospels in Clement*, 308. It appears therefore that also in the case of the Gospels text, the veracity of the designations Primary and Secondary Alexandrian are in need of re-evaluation.

[3]   See Brogan, "Text of the Gospels," 302.

[4]   ibid.

DIRECTIONS FOR FURTHER RESEARCH

Since the methodology of multivariate analysis as applied to New Testament text criticism may still be considered to be in its infancy, numerous promising avenues exist for further research. Primary is its use for future research on the New Testament text of (other) Greek Fathers, especially when it is considered that this methodology is ideal for situations where relatively minimal data exists (as is generally the case with the New Testament text of the Fathers), since it makes maximal use of the data and therefore produces more comprehensive and reliable results. Beyond this immediate application it would be advantageous for a wider comparative analysis of the text of the Fathers especially since the results can then be utilized as fixed points of reference in helping to elucidate the history of the development of the New Testament text. Finally, this methodology could potentially become an important tool in more general text-critical studies of the New Testament manuscript tradition as a means to produce graphical output data that may provide a convenient means for visualizing that tradition.

Table 68: Complete Corpus of Acts: Percentage Agreement

	Ath	𝔓74	ℵ	A	B	C	D	E	H	L	P	Ψ	049	81	383	614	630	945	1073	1175	1352	1704	1739	1891
Ath	-																							
𝔓74	67	·																						
ℵ	71	70	·																					
A	73	86	80	·																				
B	76	67	78	71	·																			
C	63	69	66	71	61	·																		
D	39	41	31	36	33	44	·																	
E	51	51	47	58	49	49	50	·																
H	60	56	51	53	44	51	39	56	·															
L	59	56	59	56	47	57	43	56	88	·														
P	66	58	55	59	52	55	51	64	86	84	·													
Ψ	73	65	60	67	53	56	33	56	67	56	66	·												
049	58	53	49	51	42	46	44	56	91	88	86	62	·											
81	78	74	71	76	71	66	31	44	59	61	65	71	56	·										
383	52	52	57	48	38	59	43	43	71	71	81	62	71	59	·									
614	49	40	38	38	33	41	36	49	71	63	73	62	73	41	60	·								
630	71	60	62	64	58	68	39	51	67	63	73	71	64	71	67	53	·							
945	69	65	64	67	64	76	39	44	60	59	68	69	58	76	62	67	93	·						
1073	60	56	51	53	44	54	47	58	89	94	89	64	89	59	76	49	62	56	·					
1175	71	70	73	76	69	78	39	51	58	59	59	64	58	68	52	73	71	78	51	·				
1352	58	53	47	51	42	46	44	56	87	88	91	58	87	56	76	56	69	62	89	53	·			
1704	71	65	62	69	62	73	39	47	62	59	68	71	60	76	62	47	96	98	58	76	64	·		
1739	69	70	69	71	69	78	33	38	53	53	59	64	49	76	67	51	82	89	47	78	53	87	·	
1891	76	67	64	76	64	73	39	47	58	59	64	67	56	78	57	51	87	89	53	71	60	91	87	·

Table 69: Acts 1–12: Percentage Agreement

	Ath	𝔭⁷⁴	ℵ	A	B	C	D	E	H	L	P	Ψ	049	81	614	630	945	1073	1175	1352	1704	1739	1891
Ath	-																						
𝔭⁷⁴	59	·																					
ℵ	68	71	·																				
A	68	82	79	·																			
B	79	65	79	58	·																		
C	58	71	79	79	58	·																	
D	40	62	33	47	40	53	·																
E	37	47	37	58	21	47	47	·															
H	58	59	47	58	42	47	47	74	·														
L	50	67	67	67	33	83	50	83	83	·													
P	56	59	39	56	44	50	57	72	89	67	·												
Ψ	68	59	58	58	53	47	47	63	79	67	67	·											
049	53	53	42	53	37	42	40	68	95	67	83	74	·										
81	79	59	68	58	68	58	40	37	58	67	61	58	53	·									
614	42	53	32	42	26	32	27	58	84	67	72	63	89	42	·								
630	63	47	53	53	53	53	33	47	74	67	72	63	68	58	68	·							
945	63	53	63	53	63	63	40	37	63	67	67	63	58	63	58	89	·						
1073	53	53	42	53	37	53	53	68	84	83	83	74	79	53	68	58	47	·					
1175	58	59	79	68	58	79	40	47	58	83	50	58	53	58	53	74	84	42	·				
1352	53	53	32	53	37	42	47	68	84	67	94	63	79	53	79	79	68	79	53	·			
1704	68	53	58	58	58	58	40	42	68	67	67	68	63	63	63	95	95	53	79	74	·		
1739	68	71	79	68	79	68	40	26	47	50	50	47	42	68	42	74	84	32	79	53	79	·	
1891	84	65	63	74	63	63	40	42	63	67	61	63	58	74	58	79	79	47	74	68	84	84	·

Table 70: Acts 1–12: Percentage ± Error Bound (95% Confidence Level)

	Ath	$\mathfrak{P}^{74}$	ℵ	A	B	C	D	E	H	L	P	Ψ	049	81	614	630	945	1073	1175	1352	1704	1739	1891
Ath	-																						
$\mathfrak{P}^{74}$	23	·																					
ℵ	21	22	·																				
A	21	18	18	·																			
B	18	23	18	22	·																		
C	22	22	18	18	22	·																	
D	25	26	24	25	25	25	·																
E	22	24	22	22	18	22	25	·															
H	22	23	22	22	22	22	25	20	·														
L	40	38	38	38	38	30	69	30	30	·													
P	23	23	23	23	23	23	26	21	15	38	·												
Ψ	21	23	22	22	22	22	25	22	18	38	22	·											
049	22	24	22	22	22	22	25	21	10	38	17	20	·										
81	18	23	21	22	21	22	25	22	22	38	23	22	22	·									
614	22	24	21	22	20	21	22	22	16	38	21	22	14	22	·								
630	22	24	22	22	22	22	24	22	20	38	21	22	21	22	21	·							
945	22	24	22	22	22	22	25	22	22	38	22	22	22	22	22	14	·						
1073	22	24	22	22	22	22	25	21	16	30	17	20	18	22	21	22	22	·					
1175	22	23	18	21	22	18	25	22	22	30	23	22	22	22	22	20	16	22	·				
1352	22	24	21	22	22	22	25	21	16	38	11	22	18	22	18	18	21	18	22	·			
1704	21	24	22	22	22	22	25	22	21	38	22	21	22	22	22	10	10	22	18	20	·		
1739	21	22	18	21	18	21	25	20	22	40	23	22	22	21	22	20	16	21	18	22	18	·	
1891	16	23	22	20	22	22	25	22	22	38	23	22	22	20	22	18	18	22	20	21	16	16	·

Table 71: Acts 13–28: Percentage Agreement

	Ath	𝔓74	ℵ	A	B	C	D	E	H	L	P	Ψ	049	81	383	614	630	945	1073	1175	1352	1704	1739	1891
Ath	-																							
𝔓74	73	-																						
ℵ	73	-	-																					
A	77	88	81	-																				
B	73	69	77	-	-																			
C	68	68	55	64	64	-																		
D	38	29	29	29	29	35	-																	
E	62	54	54	58	69	50	52	-																
H	62	54	54	50	46	55	33	42	-															
L	62	54	58	54	50	50	43	50	88	-														
P	73	58	65	62	58	59	48	58	85	88	-													
Ψ	77	69	62	73	54	64	24	50	58	54	65	-												
049	62	54	54	50	46	50	48	46	88	92	88	54	-											
81	77	86	73	91	73	73	24	50	59	59	68	82	59	-										
383	52	52	57	48	38	59	43	43	71	71	81	62	71	59	-									
614	54	31	42	35	38	50	43	42	62	62	73	62	62	41	71	-								
630	77	69	69	73	62	82	43	54	62	62	73	77	62	82	67	54	-							
945	73	73	65	77	65	86	38	50	58	58	69	73	58	86	62	50	96	-						
1073	65	58	58	54	50	55	43	50	92	96	92	58	96	64	76	65	65	62	-					
1175	81	77	69	81	77	77	38	54	58	54	65	69	62	77	52	46	69	73	58	-				
1352	62	54	58	50	46	50	43	46	88	92	88	54	92	59	76	69	62	58	58	54	-			
1704	73	73	65	77	65	86	38	50	58	58	69	73	58	86	62	50	96	100	96	73	58	-		
1739	69	69	62	73	62	86	29	46	58	54	65	77	54	82	67	50	88	92	58	77	54	92	-	
1891	69	69	65	77	65	82	38	50	54	58	65	69	54	82	57	46	92	96	58	69	54	96	88	-

Table 72: Acts 13–28: Percentage ± Error Bound (95% Confidence Level)

	Ath	𝔓74	ℵ	A	B	C	D	E	H	L	P	Ψ	049	81	383	614	630	945	1073	1175	1352	1704	1739	1891
Ath	-																							
𝔓74	17	-																						
ℵ	17	18	-																					
A	16	12	15	-																				
B	17	18	16	15	-																			
C	19	19	21	20	20	-																		
D	21	19	19	19	19	23	-																	
E	19	19	19	19	18	21	21	-																
H	19	19	19	19	19	21	20	19	-															
L	19	19	19	19	19	21	21	19	12	-														
P	17	19	18	19	19	21	21	19	14	12	-													
Ψ	16	18	19	17	19	20	18	19	19	19	18	-												
049	19	19	19	19	19	21	21	19	12	10	12	19	-											
81	18	14	19	12	19	19	20	21	21	21	19	16	21	-										
383	21	21	21	21	21	23	21	21	19	19	17	21	19	23	-									
614	19	18	19	18	19	21	21	19	19	19	17	19	19	21	19	-								
630	16	18	18	17	19	16	21	19	19	19	17	16	19	16	20	19	-							
945	17	17	18	16	18	14	21	19	19	19	18	17	19	14	21	19	7	-						
1073	18	19	19	19	19	21	21	19	10	7	10	19	7	20	18	18	18	19	-					
1175	15	16	18	15	16	18	21	19	19	19	18	18	19	18	21	19	18	17	19	-				
1352	19	19	19	19	19	21	21	19	12	10	12	19	10	21	18	18	19	19	7	19	-			
1704	17	17	18	16	18	14	21	19	19	19	18	17	19	14	21	19	7	0	19	17	19	-		
1739	18	18	19	17	19	14	19	19	19	19	18	16	19	16	20	19	12	10	19	16	19	10	-	
1891	18	18	18	16	18	16	21	19	19	19	18	18	19	16	21	19	10	7	19	18	19	7	12	-

Table 73: Percentage Agreement of Witnesses with Athanasius in Acts 1–12: By Text Type

a) Primary Alexandrian

Witness	Agreements	Comparisons
B	15	19
ℵ	13	19
$\mathfrak{P}^{74}$	10	<u>17</u>
Total	38	55
	Agreement=	**69.1% (±12%)**

b) Secondary Alexandrian

Witness	Agreements	Comparisons
1891	16	19
81	15	19
A	13	19
Ψ	13	19
1704	13	19
1739	13	19
630	12	19
945	12	19
1175	11	19
C	11	<u>19</u>
Total	129	190
	Agreement=	**67.9% (±6.6%)**

Total	167	245
All Alexandrian Agreement=		**68.2% (±5.8%)**

c) Byzantine

Witness	Agreements	Comparisons
H	11	19
P	10	18
1073	10	19
1352	10	19
049	10	19
L	3	<u>6</u>
Total	54	100
	Agreement=	**54.0% (±9.8%)**

d) Western

Witness	Agreements	Comparisons
614	8	19
D	6	15
E	7	<u>19</u>
383	Lac.	
Total	21	53
	Agreement=	**40% (±13%)**

Table 74: Percentage Agreement of Witnesses with Athanasius in Acts 13–28:
By Text Type

a) Primary Alexandrian

Witness	Agreements	Comparisons
B	19	26
ℵ	19	26
$\mathfrak{P}^{74}$	19	<u>26</u>
Total	57	78
	Agreement=	**73.1% (±9.8%)**

b) Secondary Alexandrian

Witness	Agreements	Comparisons
1175	21	26
81	17	22
A	20	26
Ψ	20	26
630	20	26
1704	19	26
945	19	26
1891	18	26
1739	18	26
C	15	<u>22</u>
Total	187	252
	Agreement=	**74.2% (±5.4%)**

Total	244	330
All Alexandrian Agreement=		**73.9% (4.7%)**

c) Byzantine

Witness	Agreements	Comparisons
P	19	26
1073	17	26
H	16	26
1352	16	26
049	16	26
L	16	26
Total	100	156
Agreement=	**64.1% (±7.5%)**	

d) Western

Witness	Agreements	Comparisons
E	16	26
614	14	26
383	11	21
D	8	21
Total	49	94
Agreement=	**52% (±10%)**	

Table 75: Athanasius' Attestation of Intra-Group Readings in Acts 1–12

	Uniform[1] Rdgs		**Predominant**[2] Rdgs		Agree Total	Total Rdgs	**%** **Agree**	**±%** **Error**
Alex	2	2	10	13	12	15	**80**	20
- Primary	9	12	5	7	14	19	**74**	20
- Secondary	3	4	9	12	12	16	**75**	21
Byz	6	12	4	7	10	19	**53**	22
West	2	7	7	10	9	17	**53**	24

---

[1] The Uniform (All) Alexandrian Readings in Acts 1–12 are: 8.20.1.1, 10.38.1.1; The Uniform Primary Alexandrian Readings in Acts 1–12 are: 1.8.1.2, 2.22.1.2, 2.22.2.1, 2.23.1.1, 2.23.2.1, 2.23.3.1, 2.36.1.1, 2.36.2.1, 8.20.1.1, 8.33.1.2, 8.34.2.1, 10.38.1.1; The Uniform Secondary Alexandrian Readings in Acts 1–12 are: 7.56.2.1, 8.20.1.1, 8.34.1.2, 10.38.1.1; The Uniform Byzantine Readings in Acts 1–12 are: 1.8.1.1, 2.22.1.1, 2.22.2.3, 2.23.1.2, 2.23.2.2, 2.36.2.2, 7.56.1.2, 7.56.2.1, 7.56.3.1, 8.33.1.1, 8.34.1.2, 8.34.2.1; The Uniform Western Readings in Acts 1–12 are: 2.23.1.2, 2.36.3.2, 2.36.4.1, 7.56.1.2, 8.32.1.2, 8.33.1.1, 8.34.1.2.

[2] The Predominant (All) Alexandrian Readings in Acts 1–12 are: 2.22.1.2, 2.22.2.1, 2.23.1.1 , 2.36.1.1, 2.36.2.1, 2.36.3.2, 7.50.1.1, 7.56.1.1, 7.56.2.1, 7.56.3.1, 8.33.1.1, 8.34.1.2, 8.34.2.1; The Predominant Primary Alexandrian Readings in Acts 1–12 are: 2.36.3.1, 7.50.1.1, 7.56.2.1, 7.56.3.1, 8.32.1.2, 8.34.1.2, 8.34.2.1; The Predominant Secondary Alexandrian Readings in Acts 1–12 are: 2.22.1.2, 2.22.2.1, 2.23.2.1, 2.23.3.2, 2.36.1.1, 2.36.2.1, 2.36.3.2, 7.50.1.1, 7.56.1.1, 7.56.3.1, 8.33.1.1, 8.34.2.1; The Predominant Byzantine Readings in Acts 1–12 are: 2.23.3.1, 2.36.1.1, 2.36.3.2, 7.50.1.2, 8.20.1.1, 8.32.1.2, 10.38.1.1; The Predominant Western Readings in Acts 1–12 are: 2.23.3.1, 2.36.1.1, 2.36.3.2, 7.50.1.2, 8.20.1.1, 8.32.1.2, 10.38.1.1.

Table 76: Complete Corpus of the Pauline Epistles: Percentage Agreement

	Ath	𝔓46	ℵ	ℵᶜ	A	B	C	D	F	G	K	L	P	Ψ	049	33	104	223	876	1739	2423
Ath	-																				
𝔓46	51.6	-																			
ℵ	59.5	65.9	-																		
ℵᶜ	60.1	57.9	71.4	-																	
A	61.3	62.3	73.5	72.3	-																
B	50.4	69.3	73.8	61.0	64.1	-															
C	67.8	59.3	75.4	71.2	76.4	70.7	-														
D	44.6	46.0	45.8	47.0	50.3	51.8	51.7	-													
F	39.5	49.4	41.2	42.9	41.5	39.4	49.4	70.6	-												
G	41.9	49.4	39.5	41.9	40.5	39.5	47.5	75.2	96.6	-											
K	51.4	55.5	42.5	61.6	46.7	47.1	53.5	43.8	38.4	38.5	-										
L	55.7	39.7	46.7	67.1	55.2	45.0	55.1	48.5	46.6	46.9	83.4	-									
P	62.2	51.2	55.5	70.1	67.5	54.7	68.1	48.2	43.5	43.2	71.8	77.9	-								
Ψ	54.8	46.8	51.2	64.9	58.7	52.5	59.3	48.2	45.4	47.3	74.0	79.6	72.6	-							
049	51.5	37.8	49.5	73.7	64.0	43.4	61.3	49.5	44.8	45.4	82.5	89.8	82.3	81.8	-						
33	61.3	57.1	69.6	66.7	70.3	65.2	69.5	45.8	45.4	44.2	44.5	52.1	67.7	59.5	53.5	-					
104	58.1	43.7	50.9	70.1	59.7	52.9	62.7	45.5	46.6	45.3	76.6	79.0	77.9	74.9	78.6	59.9	-				
223	55.2	39.7	44.8	66.3	49.3	45.6	55.9	44.8	39.5	41.1	83.0	84.6	72.3	77.3	84.8	51.5	76.5	-			
876	51.2	33.3	43.5	64.3	48.4	39.7	55.1	43.5	42.0	42.6	82.2	83.2	69.5	74.4	87.9	47.6	76.6	90.2	-		
1739	58.3	59.5	67.9	65.5	65.2	68.8	72.0	47.6	41.2	40.3	53.4	55.7	62.2	60.1	53.5	64.9	61.1	58.3	55.4	-	
2423	50.0	39.2	45.3	67.6	50.4	47.4	57.3	48.6	44.4	45.9	81.7	84.4	70.1	75.0	83.0	47.3	75.5	92.3	89.9	60.8	-

Table 77: Complete Corpus of the Pauline Epistles: Percentage ± Error Bound (95% Confidence Level)

	Ath	$\mathfrak{P}^{46}$	ℵ	ℵᶜ	A	B	C	D	F	G	K	L	P	Ψ	049	33	104	223	876	1739	2423
Ath	-																				
$\mathfrak{P}^{46}$	8.7	-																			
ℵ	7.4	8.3	-																		
ℵᶜ	7.4	8.6	6.8	-																	
A	7.7	8.9	6.9	7.0	-																
B	8.3	8.5	7.3	8.1	8.3	-															
C	8.4	10.4	7.8	8.2	8.1	9.0	-														
D	7.5	8.7	7.5	7.5	7.9	8.2	9.0	-													
F	8.8	10.5	8.8	8.9	9.4	9.4	10.4	8.2	-												
G	8.5	10.5	8.4	8.5	8.9	9.0	9.8	7.5	3.2	-											
K	8.1	9.1	8.0	7.9	8.4	9.0	9.8	8.0	9.6	9.1	-										
L	7.5	8.5	7.6	7.1	7.9	8.2	9.0	7.6	9.0	8.6	6.0	-									
P	7.4	8.8	7.6	7.0	7.5	8.3	8.5	7.6	9.1	8.7	7.4	6.4	-								
Ψ	7.5	8.7	7.6	7.2	7.8	8.2	8.9	7.6	8.9	8.6	7.1	6.1	6.8	-							
049	9.8	11.1	9.8	8.7	10.1	9.8	10.7	9.8	10.5	9.9	8.3	6.0	7.6	7.6	-						
33	7.4	8.6	7.0	7.1	7.2	7.9	8.3	7.5	8.9	8.6	8.1	7.6	7.2	7.4	9.8	-					
104	7.5	8.7	7.6	6.9	7.7	8.3	8.7	7.6	9.0	8.6	6.9	6.2	6.4	6.6	8.1	7.4	-				
223	7.6	8.7	7.6	7.3	8.0	8.4	9.0	7.6	8.8	8.5	6.2	5.6	7.0	6.4	7.1	7.7	6.5	-			
876	7.6	8.2	7.5	7.2	7.9	8.1	9.0	7.5	8.9	8.5	6.2	5.7	7.0	6.6	6.4	7.6	6.4	4.6	-		
1739	7.5	8.6	7.1	7.2	7.5	7.6	8.1	7.6	8.8	8.5	8.1	7.5	7.4	7.4	9.8	7.2	7.4	7.6	7.5	-	
2423	8.1	8.7	8.0	7.5	8.4	8.4	9.6	8.1	9.8	9.4	6.7	5.9	7.5	7.0	7.6	8.0	7.0	4.4	4.9	7.9	-

Table 78: Romans: Percentage Agreement

	Ath	𝔓46	ℵ	ℵᶜ	A	B	C	D	F	G	K	L	P	Ψ	049	33	104	223	876	1739	2423
Ath	-																				
𝔓46	50	-																			
ℵ	62	53	-																		
ℵᶜ	62	50	86	-																	
A	67	53	81	76	-																
B	38	75	52	57	52	-															
C	63	50	89	79	79	53	-														
D	43	53	33	38	33	52	32	-													
F	36	75	45	55	36	45	33	82	-												
G	43	75	33	38	33	43	32	90	100	-											
K	47	25	53	65	47	65	56	41	43	35	-										
L	57	13	48	62	48	38	53	33	36	38	76	-									
P	57	38	52	67	62	43	63	43	45	48	76	86	-								
Ψ	62	38	57	71	67	48	68	48	45	52	71	81	95	-							
049	57	25	48	62	52	38	63	33	36	38	71	90	90	86	-						
33	52	50	67	81	76	48	68	38	55	43	47	62	76	81	67	-					
104	48	50	52	67	62	62	63	43	55	43	76	67	81	76	71	76	-				
223	57	38	57	71	62	48	74	43	45	48	71	81	90	95	90	76	71	-			
876	52	38	52	67	57	43	68	38	45	43	76	86	95	90	95	71	76	95	-		
1739	52	38	76	81	86	57	79	38	36	38	53	52	67	71	57	81	67	67	62	-	
2423	52	38	57	71	57	57	63	48	45	52	71	81	86	90	81	71	67	90	86	71	-

Table 79: Romans: Percentage ± Error Bound (95% Confidence Level)

	Ath	𝔓46	ℵ	ℵc	A	B	C	D	F	G	K	L	P	Ψ	049	33	104	223	876	1739	2423
Ath	-																				
𝔓46	35	-																			
ℵ	21	34	-																		
ℵc	21	35	15	-																	
A	20	34	17	18	-																
B	21	30	21	21	21	-															
C	22	40	14	18	18	22	-														
D	21	34	20	21	20	21	21	-													
F	28	30	29	29	28	29	31	23	-												
G	21	30	20	21	20	21	21	13	0	-											
K	24	42	24	23	24	23	24	23	37	23	-										
L	21	23	21	21	21	21	22	20	28	21	20	-									
P	21	34	21	20	21	21	22	21	29	21	20	15	-								
Ψ	21	34	21	19	20	21	21	21	29	21	22	17	9	-							
049	21	30	21	21	21	21	22	20	28	21	22	13	13	15	-						
33	21	35	20	17	18	21	21	21	29	21	24	21	18	17	20	-					
104	21	35	21	20	21	21	22	21	29	21	20	20	17	18	19	18	-				
223	21	34	21	19	21	21	20	21	29	21	22	17	13	9	13	18	19	-			
876	21	34	21	20	21	21	21	21	29	21	20	15	9	13	9	19	18	9	-		
1739	21	34	18	17	15	21	18	21	28	21	24	21	20	19	21	17	20	20	21	-	
2423	21	34	21	19	21	21	22	21	29	21	22	17	15	13	17	19	20	13	15	19	-

Table 80: 1 Corinthians: Percentage Agreement

	Ath	𝔓46	ℵ	ℵc	A	B	C	D	F	G	K	L	P	Ψ	049	33	104	223	876	1739	2423
Ath	-																				
𝔓46	57	-																			
ℵ	58	66	-																		
ℵc	53	54	63	-																	
A	63	61	68	71	-																
B	45	54	83	55	66	-															
C	58	64	67	64	74	73	-														
D	43	43	55	60	50	58	58	-													
F	39	45	42	42	42	39	55	74	-												
G	39	45	42	42	42	39	55	74	100	-											
K	36	30	32	68	50	41	41	36	27	27	-										
L	48	46	43	80	61	40	55	55	45	45	82	-									
P	53	58	50	82	72	53	66	50	39	39	75	82	-								
Ψ	50	54	53	83	66	50	64	63	50	50	82	85	82	-							
049	43	39	50	82	62	43	57	61	48	48	77	89	74	82	-						
33	63	51	65	63	66	65	61	53	39	39	50	60	68	58	50	-					
104	45	43	45	83	58	43	61	53	45	45	91	88	79	88	82	58	-				
223	40	40	35	68	50	33	45	45	37	37	82	88	74	73	82	53	75	-			
876	35	29	33	65	45	25	39	40	39	39	82	80	61	70	86	45	78	83	-		
1739	53	66	65	50	58	65	73	48	39	39	55	50	58	58	50	63	55	53	45	-	
2423	40	40	38	70	50	35	52	53	45	45	82	85	66	80	86	45	78	88	85	55	-

Table 81: 1 Corinthians: Percentage ± Error Bound (95% Confidence Level)

	Ath	𝔓46	ℵ	ℵc	A	B	C	D	F	G	K	L	P	Ψ	049	33	104	223	876	1739	2423
Ath	-																				
𝔓46	16	-																			
ℵ	15	16	-																		
ℵc	15	17	15	-																	
A	15	17	15	14	-																
B	15	17	12	15	15	-															
C	17	18	16	16	15	15	-														
D	15	16	15	15	16	15	17	-													
F	16	17	16	16	16	16	18	14	-												
G	16	17	16	16	16	16	18	14	0	-											
K	20	20	19	19	21	21	23	20	19	19	-										
L	15	17	15	12	16	15	17	15	16	16	16	-									
P	16	17	16	12	15	16	16	16	16	16	19	12	-								
Ψ	15	17	15	12	15	15	16	15	16	16	16	11	12	-							
049	18	20	19	14	19	18	20	18	19	19	23	11	17	14	-						
33	15	17	15	15	15	15	17	15	16	16	21	15	15	15	19	-					
104	15	16	15	12	16	15	17	15	16	16	12	10	13	10	14	15	-				
223	15	16	15	15	16	15	17	15	15	15	16	10	14	14	14	15	13	-			
876	15	15	15	15	16	13	15	15	16	16	16	12	16	14	13	15	13	12	-		
1739	15	16	15	15	16	15	15	15	16	16	21	15	16	15	19	15	15	15	15	-	
2423	15	16	15	14	16	15	17	15	16	16	16	11	15	12	13	15	13	10	11	15	-

Table 82: 2 Corinthians–Titus: Percentage Agreement

	Ath	𝔓46	ℵ	ℵc	A	B	C	D	F	G	K	L	P	Ψ	049	33	104	223	876	1739	2423
Ath	-																				
𝔓46	40	-																			
ℵ	58	62	-																		
ℵc	61	49	70	-																	
A	55	46	70	70	-																
B	55	72	75	64	60	-															
C	78	50	72	74	80	74	-														
D	48	40	41	45	52	45	54	-													
F	40	48	40	41	42	38	49	67	-												
G	43	48	40	43	42	38	49	71	94	-											
K	61	34	46	68	50	48	64	46	41	43	-										
L	59	36	51	70	59	51	62	53	49	51	86	-									
P	64	43	57	71	71	57	71	49	46	44	75	78	-								
Ψ	56	47	55	62	57	59	60	46	43	44	75	77	65	-							
049	54	40	50	74	72	46	63	50	45	47	88	90	83	80	-						
33	59	50	70	65	68	73	70	49	47	47	49	51	68	58	50	-					
104	64	43	56	73	64	58	68	46	46	46	76	79	84	67	80	59	-				
223	63	38	49	72	48	52	64	46	40	41	85	83	70	73	84	49	77	-			
876	59	34	51	73	53	48	68	49	43	44	85	86	72	72	86	48	79	90	-		
1739	59	57	69	69	63	79	74	48	43	41	56	59	61	62	54	65	70	61	61	-	
2423	59	41	53	78	58	54	71	53	44	44	82	84	76	67	82	49	80	94	94	67	-

Table 83: 2 Corinthians–Titus: Percentage ± Error Bound (95% Confidence Level)

	Ath	𝔓46	ℵ	ℵc	A	B	C	D	F	G	K	L	P	Ψ	049	33	104	223	876	1739	2423
Ath	-																				
𝔓46	14	-																			
ℵ	11	·	-																		
ℵc	11	14	11	-																	
A	13	16	12	12	·																
B	13	13	11	13	14	·															
C	11	16	12	12	12	14	·														
D	12	14	11	12	13	13	14	·													
F	11	14	11	12	13	13	14	11	·												
G	12	14	11	12	13	13	14	11	5	·											
K	11	14	12	11	13	13	13	12	12	12	·										
L	12	14	12	11	13	13	13	12	12	12	8	·									
P	11	14	12	11	12	13	13	12	12	12	10	10	·								
Ψ	12	14	12	11	13	13	14	12	12	12	10	10	11	·							
049	14	15	14	12	14	14	15	14	14	14	9	8	11	11	·						
33	11	14	11	11	12	12	13	12	12	12	12	12	11	11	14	·					
104	11	14	12	10	12	13	13	12	12	12	10	10	9	11	11	12	·				
223	11	14	12	10	13	13	13	12	11	12	8	9	11	10	10	12	10	·			
876	11	14	12	10	13	13	13	12	12	12	8	8	11	10	10	12	10	7	·		
1739	11	14	11	11	12	11	12	12	12	12	12	12	12	11	14	11	11	11	11	·	
2423	14	15	14	11	15	14	15	14	14	14	10	10	12	13	11	14	11	6	6	13	·

Table 84: Hebrews: Percentage Agreement

	Ath	𝔓46	ℵ	ℵc	A	B	C	D	K	L	P	Ψ	33	104	223	876	1739	2423
Ath	-																	
𝔓46	61	-																
ℵ	64	72	-															
ℵc	67	75	75	-														
A	67	81	81	75	-													
B	58	83	75	67	79	-												
C	63	75	88	69	69	89	-											
D	42	53	53	42	58	58	56	-										
K	44	42	36	44	39	38	31	44	-									
L	58	44	42	50	47	46	38	42	83	-								
P	72	58	61	58	61	63	69	47	61	69	-							
Ψ	53	42	39	47	50	46	38	36	69	78	64	-						
33	69	61	75	67	75	63	88	36	31	39	61	53	-					
104	67	44	47	53	53	50	50	39	69	78	64	75	56	-				
223	55	42	39	48	42	53	31	42	87	87	65	81	39	81	-			
876	53	36	36	44	39	42	31	39	81	81	58	75	36	72	97	-		
1739	67	61	64	67	64	63	56	53	47	58	67	53	58	47	55	53	-	
2423	47	36	36	47	39	46	31	39	86	86	58	72	33	72	97	92	53	-

Table 85: Hebrews: Percentage ± Error Bound (95% Confidence Level)

	Ath	𝔓46	ℵ	ℵc	A	B	C	D	K	L	P	Ψ	33	104	223	876	1739	2423
Ath	-																	
𝔓46	16	-																
ℵ	16	15	-															
ℵc	15	14	14	-														
A	15	13	13	14	-													
B	20	15	17	19	16	-												
C	24	21	16	23	23	21	-											
D	16	16	16	16	16	20	24	-										
K	16	16	16	16	16	19	23	16	-									
L	16	16	16	16	16	20	24	16	12	-								
P	15	16	16	16	16	19	23	16	16	15	-							
Ψ	16	16	16	16	16	20	24	16	15	14	16	-						
33	15	16	14	15	14	19	16	16	15	16	16	16	-					
104	15	16	16	16	16	20	25	16	15	14	16	14	16	-				
223	18	17	17	18	17	22	23	17	12	12	17	14	17	14	-			
876	16	16	16	16	16	20	23	16	13	13	16	14	16	15	6	-		
1739	15	16	16	15	16	19	24	16	16	16	15	16	16	16	18	16	-	
2423	16	16	16	16	16	20	23	16	11	11	16	15	15	15	6	9	16	-

Table 86: Romans: Comparison Counts

	Ath	𝔓46	ℵ	ℵc	A	B	C	D	F	G	K	L	P	044	049	33	104	223	876	1739	2423
Ath	21	8	21	21	21	21	19	21	11	21	17	21	21	21	21	21	21	21	21	21	21
𝔓46	8	8	8	8	8	8	6	8	8	8	4	8	8	8	8	8	8	8	8	8	8
ℵ	21	8	21	21	21	21	19	21	11	21	17	21	21	21	21	21	21	21	21	21	21
ℵc	21	8	21	21	21	21	19	21	11	21	17	21	21	21	21	21	21	21	21	21	21
A	21	8	21	21	21	21	19	21	11	21	17	21	21	21	21	21	21	21	21	21	21
B	21	8	21	21	21	21	19	21	11	21	17	21	21	21	21	21	21	21	21	21	21
C	19	6	19	19	19	19	19	19	9	19	16	19	19	19	19	19	19	19	19	19	19
D	21	8	21	21	21	21	19	21	11	21	17	21	21	21	21	21	21	21	21	21	21
F	11	8	11	11	11	11	9	11	11	11	7	11	11	11	11	11	11	11	11	11	11
G	21	8	21	21	21	21	19	21	11	21	17	21	21	21	21	21	21	21	21	21	21
K	17	4	17	17	17	17	16	17	7	17	17	17	17	17	17	17	17	17	17	17	17
L	21	8	21	21	21	21	19	21	11	21	17	21	21	21	21	21	21	21	21	21	21
P	21	8	21	21	21	21	19	21	11	21	17	21	21	21	21	21	21	21	21	21	21
044	21	8	21	21	21	21	19	21	11	21	17	21	21	21	21	21	21	21	21	21	21
049	21	8	21	21	21	21	19	21	11	21	17	21	21	21	21	21	21	21	21	21	21
33	21	8	21	21	21	21	19	21	11	21	17	21	21	21	21	21	21	21	21	21	21
104	21	8	21	21	21	21	19	21	11	21	17	21	21	21	21	21	21	21	21	21	21
223	21	8	21	21	21	21	19	21	11	21	17	21	21	21	21	21	21	21	21	21	21
876	21	8	21	21	21	21	19	21	11	21	17	21	21	21	21	21	21	21	21	21	21
1739	21	8	21	21	21	21	19	21	11	21	17	21	21	21	21	21	21	21	21	21	21
2423	21	8	21	21	21	21	19	21	11	21	17	21	21	21	21	21	21	21	21	21	21

Table 87: Percentage Agreement of Witnesses with Athanasius in Romans

a) Primary Alexandrian

Witness	Agreements	Comparisons
ℵ	13	21
1739	11	21
B	8	21
𝔓⁴⁶	4	8
Total	36	71
	Agreement=	50.7% (±11.6%)

b) Secondary Alexandrian

Witness	Agreements	Comparisons	
A	14	21	
C	12	19	
P	12	21	
33	11	21	
104	10	21	
Total	59	103	(w/o Ψ & ℵᶜ)
	Agreement=	57.3% (±9.6%)	
ℵᶜ	13	21	
Ψ	13	21	
Total	85	145	(w/ Ψ & ℵᶜ)
	Agreement=	58.6% (±8.0%)	
Total	95	174	
All Alexandrian Agreement=	54.6% (±7.4%)	(w/o Ψ & ℵᶜ)	

c) Byzantine Witnesses

Witness	Agreements	Comparisons
049	12	21
L	12	21
223	12	21
2423	11	21
876	11	21
K	8	17
Total	66	122
	Agreement=	54.1% (±8.8%)

d) Western Uncials

Witness	Agreements	Comparisons
D	9	21
G	9	21
F	4	11
Total	22	53
	Agreement=	**41.5% (±13.3%)**

Table 88: Percentage Agreement of Witnesses with Athanasius in 1 Corinthians

a) Primary Alexandrian

Witness	Agreements	Comparisons
ℵ	23	40
1739	21	40
B	18	40
$\mathfrak{P}^{46}$	20	35
Total	82	155
	Agreement=	**52.9% (±7.9%)**

b) Secondary Alexandrian

Witness	Agreements	Comparisons	
C	19	33	
P	20	38	
A	24	38	
33	25	40	
104	18	40	
Total	106	189	(w/o Ψ & ℵ^{c})
	Agreement=	**56.1% (±7.1%)**	
ℵ^{c}	21	40	
Ψ	20	40	
Total	147	269	(w/ Ψ & ℵ^{c})
	Agreement=	**54.6% (±5.9%)**	
Total	188	344	
All Alexandrian Agreement=	**54.7% (±5.3%)**		(w/o Ψ & ℵ^{c})

c) Byzantine Witnesses

Witness	Agreements	Comparisons
049	12	28
L	19	40
223	16	40
2423	16	40
876	14	40
K	8	22
Total	85	210
	Agreement=	**40.5% (±6.6%)**

d) Western Uncials

Witness	Agreements	Comparisons
D	17	40
G	15	38
F	15	38
Total	47	116
	Agreement=	**40.5% (±8.9%)**

Table 89: Percentage Agreement of Witnesses with Athanasius in 2 Corinthians–Titus

a) Primary Alexandrian

Witness	Agreements	Comparisons
1739	42	71
ℵ	41	71
B	31	56
$\mathfrak{P}^{46}$	19	47
Total	133	245
	Agreement=	**54.3% (±6.2%)**

b) Secondary Alexandrian

Witness	Agreements	Comparisons	
104	45	70	
P	44	69	
33	42	71	
C	39	50	
A	33	60	
Total	203	320	(w/o Ψ & ℵᶜ)
	Agreement=	**63.4% (±5.3%)**	
ℵᶜ	43	71	
Ψ	40	71	
Total	286	462	(w/ Ψ & ℵᶜ)
	Agreement=	**61.9% (±4.4%)**	
Total	336	565	
All Alexandrian Agreement=		**59.5% (±4.0%)**	(w/o Ψ & ℵᶜ)

c) Byzantine Witnesses

Witness	Agreements	Comparisons
049	27	50
L	41	70
223	45	71
2423	30	51
876	42	71
K	43	71
Total	228	384
	Agreement=	**59.4% (±4.9%)**

d) Western Uncials

Witness	Agreements	Comparisons
D	34	71
G	30	70
F	28	70
Total	92	211
	Agreement=	**43.6% (±6.7%)**

Table 90: Percentage Agreement of Witnesses with Athanasius in Hebrews

a) Primary Alexandrian

Witness	Agreements	Comparisons
ℵ	23	36
1739	24	36
B	14	24
$\mathfrak{P}^{46}$	22	36
Total	83	132
	Agreement=	**62.9% (±8.2%)**

b) Secondary Alexandrian

Witness	Agreements	Comparisons	
C	10	16	
P	26	36	
A	24	36	
33	25	36	
104	24	36	
Total	109	160	(w/o Ψ & ℵ^c)
	Agreement=	**68.1% (±7.2%)**	
ℵ^c	24	36	
Ψ	19	36	
Total	152	232	(w/ Ψ & ℵ^c)
	Agreement=	**65.5% (±6.1%)**	
Total	192	292	
All Alexandrian Agreement=	**65.8% (±5.4%)**		(w/o Ψ & ℵ^c)

c) Byzantine Witnesses

Witness	Agreements	Comparisons
L	21	36
223	17	31
2423	17	36
876	19	36
K	16	36
049	Lac.	
Total	90	175
	Agreement=	**51.4% (±7.4%)**

d) Western Uncials

Witness	Agreements	Comparisons
D	<u>15</u>	<u>36</u>
G	Lac.	
F	Lac.	
Total	15	36
	Agreement=	**41.7% (±16.1%)**

Table 91: Complete Corpus of the Pauline Epistles: Dissimilarity (Simple Matching Distance)

	Ath	𝔓46	ℵ	ℵᶜ	A	B	C	D	F	G	K	L	P	Ψ	049	33	104	223	876	1739	2423
Ath	-																				
𝔓46	0.484	-																			
ℵ	0.405	0.341	-																		
ℵᶜ	0.399	0.421	0.286	-																	
A	0.387	0.377	0.265	0.277	-																
B	0.497	0.307	0.262	0.390	0.359	-															
C	0.322	0.407	0.246	0.288	0.236	0.293	-														
D	0.554	0.540	0.542	0.530	0.497	0.482	0.483	-													
F	0.505	0.506	0.588	0.571	0.585	0.606	0.506	0.294	-												
G	0.581	0.506	0.605	0.581	0.595	0.605	0.525	0.248	0.034	-											
K	0.486	0.645	0.575	0.384	0.533	0.529	0.465	0.562	0.616	0.615	-										
L	0.443	0.603	0.533	0.329	0.448	0.550	0.449	0.515	0.534	0.531	0.166	-									
P	0.378	0.488	0.445	0.299	0.325	0.453	0.319	0.518	0.565	0.568	0.282	0.221	-								
Ψ	0.452	0.532	0.488	0.351	0.413	0.475	0.407	0.518	0.546	0.527	0.260	0.204	0.274	-							
049	0.485	0.622	0.505	0.263	0.361	0.566	0.388	0.505	0.552	0.546	0.175	0.102	0.177	0.182	-						
33	0.387	0.429	0.304	0.333	0.297	0.348	0.305	0.542	0.546	0.558	0.555	0.479	0.323	0.405	0.465	-					
104	0.419	0.564	0.491	0.299	0.403	0.471	0.373	0.545	0.534	0.547	0.235	0.210	0.221	0.252	0.214	0.401	-				
223	0.448	0.603	0.552	0.337	0.507	0.544	0.441	0.552	0.605	0.589	0.170	0.154	0.277	0.227	0.152	0.485	0.235	-			
876	0.488	0.667	0.566	0.357	0.516	0.603	0.449	0.566	0.580	0.574	0.178	0.168	0.305	0.256	0.121	0.524	0.234	0.098	-		
1739	0.417	0.405	0.321	0.345	0.348	0.312	0.280	0.524	0.588	0.597	0.466	0.443	0.378	0.399	0.465	0.351	0.389	0.417	0.446	-	
2423	0.500	0.608	0.547	0.324	0.496	0.526	0.427	0.514	0.556	0.541	0.183	0.157	0.299	0.250	0.170	0.527	0.245	0.077	0.101	0.392	-

Table 92: Romans: Dissimilarity (Simple Matching Distance)

	Ath	𝔓46	ℵ	ℵc	A	B	C	D	F	G	K	L	P	Ψ	049	33	104	223	876	1739	2423
Ath	-																				
𝔓46	0.500	-																			
ℵ	0.381	0.375	-																		
ℵc	0.381	0.500	0.143	-																	
A	0.333	0.375	0.191	0.238	-																
B	0.619	0.250	0.476	0.429	0.476	-															
C	0.368	0.500	0.105	0.211	0.211	0.474	-														
D	0.571	0.375	0.667	0.619	0.667	0.476	0.684	-													
F	0.636	0.250	0.546	0.455	0.636	0.546	0.667	0.182	-												
G	0.571	0.250	0.667	0.619	0.667	0.571	0.684	0.095	0.000	-											
K	0.529	0.750	0.471	0.353	0.529	0.353	0.438	0.588	0.571	0.647	-										
L	0.429	0.875	0.524	0.381	0.524	0.619	0.474	0.667	0.636	0.619	0.235	-									
P	0.429	0.625	0.476	0.333	0.381	0.571	0.368	0.571	0.546	0.524	0.235	0.143	-								
Ψ	0.381	0.625	0.429	0.286	0.333	0.524	0.316	0.524	0.546	0.476	0.294	0.191	0.048	-							
049	0.429	0.750	0.524	0.381	0.476	0.619	0.368	0.667	0.636	0.619	0.294	0.095	0.095	0.143	-						
33	0.476	0.500	0.333	0.191	0.238	0.524	0.316	0.619	0.455	0.571	0.529	0.381	0.238	0.191	0.333	-					
104	0.524	0.500	0.476	0.333	0.381	0.381	0.368	0.571	0.455	0.571	0.235	0.333	0.191	0.238	0.286	0.238	-				
223	0.429	0.625	0.429	0.286	0.381	0.524	0.263	0.571	0.546	0.524	0.294	0.191	0.095	0.048	0.095	0.238	0.286	-			
876	0.476	0.625	0.476	0.333	0.429	0.571	0.316	0.619	0.546	0.571	0.235	0.143	0.048	0.095	0.048	0.286	0.238	0.048	-		
1739	0.476	0.625	0.238	0.191	0.143	0.429	0.211	0.619	0.636	0.619	0.471	0.476	0.333	0.286	0.429	0.191	0.333	0.333	0.381	-	
2423	0.476	0.625	0.429	0.286	0.429	0.429	0.368	0.524	0.546	0.476	0.294	0.191	0.143	0.095	0.191	0.286	0.333	0.095	0.143	0.286	-

Table 93: 1 Corinthians: Dissimilarity (Simple Matching Distance)

	Ath	𝔓46	ℵ	ℵc	A	B	C	D	F	G	K	L	P	Ψ	049	33	104	223	876	1739	2423
Ath	-																				
𝔓46	0.429	-																			
ℵ	0.425	0.343	-																		
ℵc	0.475	0.457	0.375	-																	
A	0.368	0.394	0.316	0.290	-																
B	0.550	0.457	0.175	0.450	0.342	-															
C	0.424	0.357	0.333	0.364	0.258	0.273	-														
D	0.575	0.571	0.450	0.400	0.500	0.425	0.424	-													
F	0.605	0.546	0.579	0.579	0.583	0.605	0.452	0.263	-												
G	0.605	0.546	0.579	0.579	0.583	0.605	0.452	0.263	0.000	-											
K	0.636	0.700	0.682	0.318	0.500	0.591	0.588	0.636	0.727	0.727	-										
L	0.525	0.543	0.575	0.200	0.395	0.600	0.455	0.450	0.553	0.553	0.182	-									
P	0.474	0.424	0.500	0.184	0.278	0.474	0.344	0.500	0.611	0.611	0.250	0.184	-								
Ψ	0.500	0.457	0.475	0.175	0.342	0.500	0.364	0.375	0.500	0.500	0.182	0.150	0.184	-							
049	0.571	0.609	0.500	0.179	0.385	0.571	0.435	0.393	0.519	0.519	0.231	0.107	0.259	0.179	-						
33	0.375	0.486	0.350	0.375	0.342	0.350	0.394	0.475	0.605	0.605	0.500	0.400	0.316	0.425	0.500	-					
104	0.550	0.571	0.550	0.175	0.421	0.575	0.394	0.475	0.553	0.553	0.091	0.125	0.211	0.125	0.179	0.425	-				
223	0.600	0.600	0.650	0.325	0.500	0.675	0.546	0.550	0.632	0.632	0.182	0.125	0.263	0.275	0.179	0.475	0.250	-			
876	0.650	0.714	0.675	0.350	0.553	0.750	0.606	0.600	0.605	0.605	0.182	0.200	0.395	0.300	0.143	0.550	0.225	0.175	-		
1739	0.475	0.343	0.350	0.500	0.421	0.350	0.273	0.525	0.605	0.605	0.455	0.500	0.421	0.425	0.500	0.375	0.450	0.475	0.550	-	
2423	0.600	0.625	0.300	0.500	0.500	0.650	0.485	0.475	0.553	0.553	0.182	0.150	0.342	0.200	0.143	0.550	0.225	0.125	0.150	0.450	-

Table 94: 2 Corinthians–Titus: Dissimilarity (Simple Matching Distance)

	Ath	𝔓46	ℵ	ℵc	A	B	C	D	F	G	K	L	P	Ψ	049	33	104	223	876	1739	2423
Ath	-																				
𝔓46	0.596	-																			
ℵ	0.423	0.383	-																		
ℵc	0.394	0.511	0.296	-																	
A	0.450	0.541	0.300	0.300	-																
B	0.446	0.277	0.250	0.357	0.400	-															
C	0.220	0.500	0.280	0.260	0.200	0.263	-														
D	0.521	0.596	0.592	0.549	0.483	0.554	0.460	-													
F	0.600	0.522	0.600	0.586	0.576	0.618	0.510	0.329	-												
G	0.571	0.522	0.600	0.571	0.576	0.618	0.510	0.286	0.057	-											
K	0.394	0.660	0.535	0.324	0.500	0.518	0.360	0.535	0.586	0.571	-										
L	0.414	0.638	0.486	0.300	0.407	0.491	0.380	0.471	0.507	0.493	0.143	-									
P	0.362	0.565	0.435	0.290	0.293	0.426	0.286	0.507	0.544	0.559	0.246	0.221	-								
Ψ	0.437	0.532	0.451	0.380	0.433	0.411	0.400	0.535	0.571	0.557	0.254	0.229	0.348	-							
049	0.460	0.605	0.500	0.260	0.282	0.540	0.368	0.500	0.551	0.531	0.120	0.102	0.167	0.200	-						
33	0.409	0.404	0.296	0.352	0.317	0.268	0.300	0.507	0.529	0.529	0.507	0.486	0.319	0.423	0.500	-					
104	0.357	0.575	0.443	0.271	0.356	0.418	0.320	0.543	0.536	0.536	0.243	0.214	0.162	0.329	0.204	0.414	-				
223	0.366	0.617	0.507	0.282	0.517	0.482	0.360	0.535	0.600	0.586	0.155	0.171	0.304	0.268	0.160	0.507	0.229	-			
876	0.409	0.660	0.493	0.268	0.467	0.518	0.320	0.507	0.571	0.557	0.155	0.143	0.275	0.282	0.140	0.521	0.214	0.099	-		
1739	0.409	0.426	0.310	0.310	0.367	0.214	0.260	0.521	0.571	0.586	0.437	0.414	0.391	0.380	0.460	0.352	0.300	0.394	0.394	-	
2423	0.412	0.585	0.471	0.216	0.425	0.460	0.286	0.471	0.560	0.560	0.177	0.160	0.245	0.333	0.178	0.510	0.200	0.059	0.059	0.333	-

Table 95: Hebrews: Dissimilarity (Simple Matching Distance)

	Ath	𝔭⁴⁶	ℵ	ℵᶜ	A	B	C	D	K	L	P	Ψ	33	104	223	876	1739	2423
Ath	-																	
𝔭⁴⁶	0.389	-																
ℵ	0.361	0.278	-															
ℵᶜ	0.333	0.250	0.250	-														
A	0.333	0.194	0.194	0.250	-													
B	0.417	0.167	0.250	0.333	0.208	-												
C	0.375	0.250	0.125	0.313	0.313	0.111	-											
D	0.583	0.472	0.472	0.583	0.417	0.417	0.438	-										
K	0.556	0.583	0.639	0.556	0.611	0.625	0.688	0.556	-									
L	0.417	0.556	0.583	0.500	0.528	0.542	0.625	0.583	0.167	-								
P	0.278	0.417	0.389	0.417	0.389	0.375	0.313	0.528	0.389	0.306	-							
Ψ	0.472	0.583	0.611	0.528	0.500	0.542	0.625	0.639	0.306	0.222	0.361	-						
33	0.306	0.389	0.250	0.333	0.250	0.375	0.125	0.639	0.694	0.611	0.389	0.472	-					
104	0.333	0.556	0.528	0.472	0.472	0.500	0.500	0.611	0.306	0.222	0.361	0.250	0.444	-				
223	0.452	0.581	0.613	0.516	0.581	0.474	0.688	0.581	0.129	0.129	0.355	0.194	0.613	0.194	-			
876	0.472	0.639	0.639	0.556	0.611	0.583	0.688	0.611	0.194	0.194	0.417	0.250	0.639	0.278	0.032	-		
1739	0.333	0.389	0.361	0.333	0.361	0.375	0.438	0.472	0.528	0.417	0.333	0.472	0.417	0.528	0.452	0.472	-	
2423	0.528	0.639	0.639	0.528	0.611	0.542	0.688	0.611	0.139	0.139	0.417	0.278	0.667	0.278	0.032	0.083	0.472	-

Table 96: Axis Coordinates for the Pauline Epistles (Complete) 2D MDS Map

Witness	Horiz. (x) axis	Vert. (y) axis
Ath	0.067	-0.101
P46	0.331	-0.041
U1	0.238	-0.178
U1C	-0.004	-0.127
A	0.145	-0.151
B	0.236	-0.142
C	0.127	-0.099
D	0.158	0.299
F	0.171	0.387
G	0.159	0.403
K	-0.272	-0.001
L	-0.223	0.04
P	-0.096	-0.075
U44	-0.144	-0.002
U49	-0.223	0.014
M33	0.158	-0.123
M104	-0.153	-0.025
M223	-0.249	-0.011
M876	-0.281	0.031
M1739	0.088	-0.139
M2423	-0.231	0.04

Table 97: Complete Corpus of the Catholic Epistles: Percentage Agreement

	Ath	𝔓72	ℵ	A	B	C	L	Ψ	049	33	105	201	323	325	1022	1424	1739	2423
Ath	-																	
𝔓72	33	-																
ℵ	25	33	-															
A	42	67	58	-														
B	17	50	67	67	-													
C	44	25	44	22	33	-												
L	50	33	33	42	25	67	-											
Ψ	42	67	58	58	42	67	42	-										
049	33	33	33	33	25	67	83	42	-									
33	27	50	27	55	36	38	55	27	45	-								
105	50	33	33	42	25	67	100	42	83	55	-							
201	50	33	33	42	25	67	100	42	83	55	100	-						
323	33	50	33	50	50	67	67	42	67	73	67	67	-					
325	38	33	63	63	50	60	88	38	75	63	88	38	75	-				
1022	42	33	42	50	33	67	92	42	83	64	92	92	75	100	-			
1424	42	33	42	50	33	67	92	42	83	64	92	92	75	100	100	-		
1739	50	50	33	50	58	67	50	42	50	64	50	50	83	50	58	58	-	
2423	42	33	42	50	33	67	92	42	83	64	92	92	75	100	100	100	58	-

Table 98: Complete Corpus of the Catholic Epistles: Percentage ±Error Bound (95% Confidence Level)

	Ath	𝔓72	ℵ	A	B	C	L	Ψ	049	33	105	201	323	325	1022	1424	1739	2423
Ath	-																	
𝔓72	33	-																
ℵ	25	33	-															
A	42	67	58	-														
B	17	50	67	67	-													
C	44	25	44	22	33	-												
L	50	33	33	42	25	67	-											
Ψ	42	67	58	58	42	67	42	-										
049	33	33	33	33	25	67	83	42	-									
33	27	50	27	55	36	38	55	27	45	-								
105	50	33	33	42	25	67	100	42	83	55	-							
201	50	33	33	42	25	67	100	42	83	55	100	-						
323	33	50	33	50	50	67	67	42	67	73	67	67	-					
325	38	33	63	63	50	60	88	38	75	63	88	88	75	-				
1022	42	33	42	50	33	67	92	42	83	64	92	92	75	100	-			
1424	42	33	42	50	33	67	92	42	83	64	92	92	75	100	100	-		
1739	50	50	33	50	58	67	50	42	50	64	50	50	83	50	58	58	-	
2423	42	33	42	50	33	67	92	42	83	64	92	92	75	100	100	100	58	-

APPENDIX B
FIGURES

Figure 41: Athanasius–Acts: 3D View 2

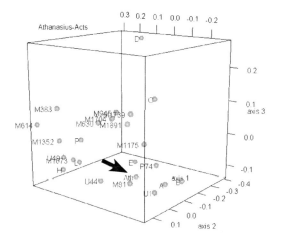

Figure 42: Athanasius–Acts 1–12: 2D

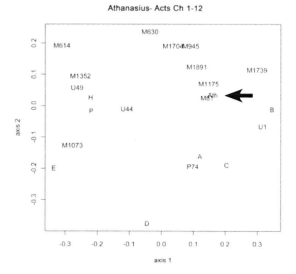

349

Figure 43: Athanasius–Acts 1–12: 3D View 1

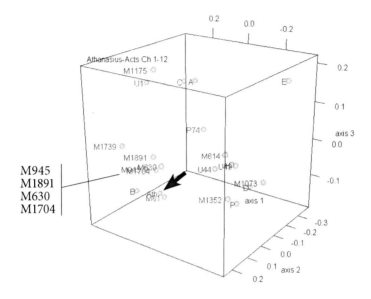

Figure 44: Athanasius–Acts 1–12: 3D View 2

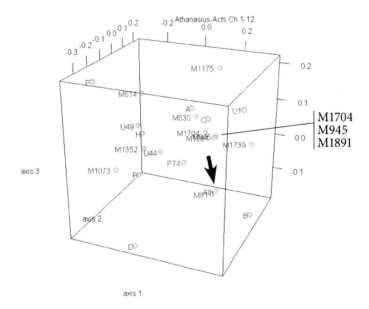

Figure 45: Athanasius–Acts 13–28: 2D

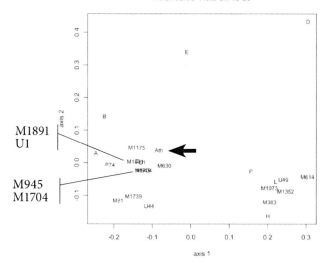

Figure 46: Athanasius–Acts 13–28: 3D View 1

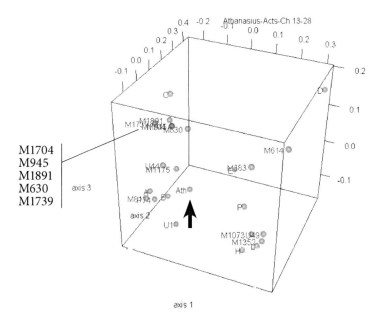

Figure 47: Athanasius–Acts 13–28: 3D View 2

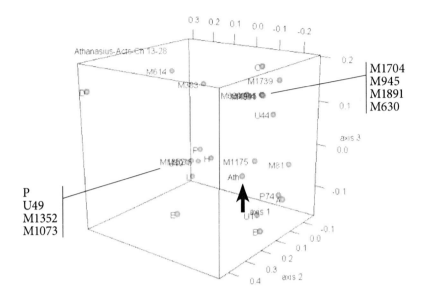

Figure 48: Cluster Map: Athanasius (Acts 1–12), 3 clusters

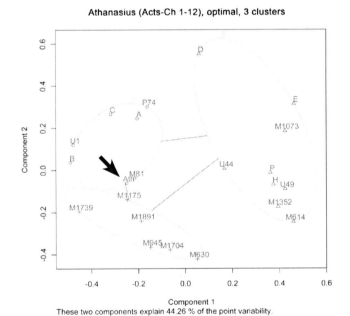

Figure 49: Cluster Map: Athanasius (Acts 1–12), 4 clusters

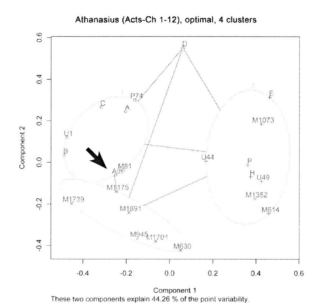

Figure 50: Cluster Map: Athanasius (Acts 13–28), 3 clusters

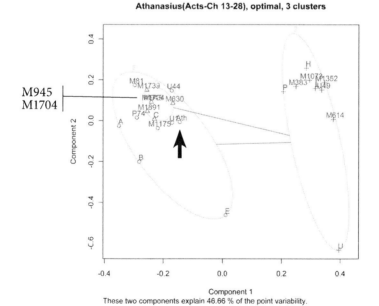

Figure 51: Cluster Map: Athanasius (Acts 13–28), 4 clusters

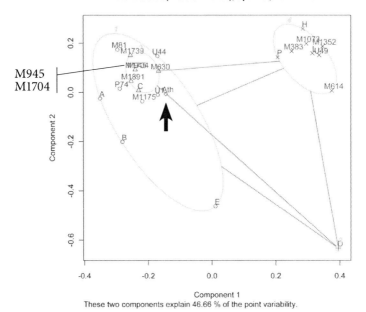

M945
M1704

Figure 52: Athanasius–2 Corinthians–Titus: 3D View

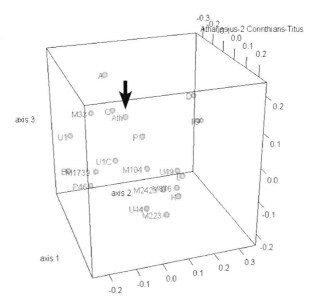

APPENDIX C
REFERENCES FOR THE BOOK OF ACTS: ERNEST–DONKER

Table 99: References for Quotations in the Book of Acts: Ernest–Donker

Ref in Acts	Reference in Athanasius' text	Classification	Ernest (no. Refs)	Donker (no. Refs)	Total	Difference
	Referencesfor quotations in the book of Acts: Athanasius					
1:1	Ep. Ad ep. Aeg. et Lib. 1	C	1	1	1	
1:2	Ep. Encycl. 1.9	A	1		1	1
1:7	Or. III C. Ar. 48	C	2	2	2	
	Or. III C. Ar. 1	C		1	1	1
	Or. III C. Ar. 49	Ad		1	1	1
1:7-8	Or. III C. Ar. 48	C	1	1	1	
1:9-11	Or. III C. Ar. 48	C	1		1	1
1:18	Ep. Ad ep. Aeg. Et Lib. 18	Q	1	1	1	
	Ep. Ad Ser.	C	1	1	1	
	Hist. Arian. 57.4	C	1	1	1	
2:14	Or. II C. Ar. 16	R	1*		1	1
2:16-17	Or. II C. Ar. 18	A	1		1	1
2:22	Or. II C. Ar. 12	C	1*2	1	3	2
	De Sent. Dion. 7	C		1	1	1
	Or. II C. Ar. 12	All		1	1	1
2:22-24	Or. I C. Ar. 44	A	1		1	1
2:23	Apol. De fuga 15	R	1*		1	1
	De Sent. Dion. 7	C		1	1	1
2:24	Or. I C. Ar. 44	C R	2	2	2	
	Or. I C. Ar. 44	All		1	1	1
	Or. de Inc. Verb. 27.3	All		1	1	1
	Or. II C. Ar. 16	All		1	1	1
2:27	Or. II C. Ar. 16	C	2		2	2
2:29	Or. II C. Ar. 16	R	2		2	2
2:36	Or. I C. Ar. 53	C	1	1	1	
	Or. II C. Ar. 1	C	1	1	1	
	Or. II C. Ar. 3	C	1*		1	1
	Or. II C. Ar. 11	C	1	1	1	
	Or. II C. Ar. 12	C	2*2	3	4	1
	Or. II C. Ar. 13	C	1*		1	1
	Or. II C. Ar. 14	C	1	1	1	
	Or. II C. Ar. 16	Q	1	1	1	
	Or. II C. Ar. 16	R	2		2	2
	Or. II C. Ar. 17	C	1	1	1	
3:12	Or. III C. Ar. 2	Q	1	1	1	
3:15	Or. II C. Ar. 16	All		1	1	1
	De Sent. Dion. 8	All		1	1	1
4:4	Or. III C. Ar. 20	All	1*	1	1	
4:10	Or. II C. Ar. 16	C All		2	2	2
	De Sent. Dion. 7	C		1	1	1
	Or. I C. Ar. 53	Ad		1	1	1
4:13	Vita. Ant. 85.5	R	1*		1	1
4:18	Apol. de fuga 21	A	1		1	1
4:32	Or. III C. Ar. 20	All		1	1	1
4:34-35	Vita. Ant. 2.2	A	1		1	1
	Vita. Ant. 2.2	C		1	1	1
5:29	Apol. c. Ar. 3.57	C	1	1	1	
5:39	Ep. Ad ep. Aeg. et Lib. 16	R	1		1	1
7:10	Hist. Arian. 79.4	A	1*		1	1
7:50	Or. II C. Ar. 71	C	1	1	1	
7:54	De decretis 40.3	R	1		1	1
7:56	De Sent. Dion. 7	C		1	1	1
8:10	Vita Ant. 40.1	R	1	1	1	

355

References for quotations in the book of Acts: Athanasius						
Ref in Acts	Reference in Athanasius' text	Classification	Ernest (no. Refs)	Donker (no. Refs)	Total	Difference
8:20	Or. III C. Ar. 65	C	1	1	1	
	Vita Ant. 11.4	Q	1	1	1	
8:27-38	Hist. Arian. 38.4	A	1	1	1	
8:32	Ep. ad ep. Aeg. et Lib. 17	C	1*		1	1
	Or. de Inc. Verb. 34.2	C		1	1	1
	Or. I C. Ar. 54	C		1	1	1
8:33	Or. de Inc. Verb. 34.2	C		1	1	1
8:34	Or. I C. Ar. 54	C	1	1	1	
9:4	Or. II C. Ar. 80	C	1	1	1	
9:14	Hist. Arian. 31.1	R	1		1	1
10:12	Vita Ant. 51.5	All		1	1	1
10:25-26	Or. II C. Ar. 23	A C	2	1	2	1
10:26	Vita Ant. 48.2	R	1	1	1	
10:38	Or. I C. Ar. 47	C	1	1	1	
12:2-11	Apol. De fuga 25	A	1		1	1
13:22	De Sent. Dion. 7	C		1	1	1
13:23	De Sent. Dion. 7	C		1	1	1
13:32	De decretis 2	Ad		1	1	1
13:36	Ep. ad ep. Aeg. et Lib. 21.1	C		1	1	1
14:15-17	Or. c. Gentes 35	C	1	1	1	
15:36	Vita Ant. 15.1	All		1	1	1
17:5	Hist. Arian. 10.1	R	3*		3	3
17:24	Or. III C. Ar. 42	Q	1		1	1
17:26	Or. III C. Ar. 18	All		1	1	1
17:27	Or. de Inc. Verb. 8.1	R	1	1	1	
17:28	Or. III C. Ar. 1	C	2	1	2	1
	De decretis 2	C		1	1	1
	De Syn. 39	C		1	1	1
	Or. de Inc. Verb. 1.1	All		1	1	1
	Or. de Inc. Verb. 42.4	Q	1		1	1
17:28-29	Ep. ad Amun 65	Q	1	1	1	
17:30	De Sent. Dion. 7	C		1	1	1
17:31	De Sent. Dion. 7	C		1	1	1
20:28-29	Apol. ad Const. 1	A	1		1	1
20:29	Apol. c. Ar. 47.2	R	1*		1	1
21:27-24:17	Hist. Arian. 66.5	A	1		1	1
23:11	Apol. de fuga 18	C	1	1	1	
24:10	Ap. ad Const. 1	C	1		1	1
24:19	Apol. c. Ar. 82.2	C	1	1	1	
25:11	Ap. ad Const. 12	A	1	1	1	
	Apol. de fuga 17.9	R	1	1	1	
25:16	Apol. c. Ar. 82.2	C	1	1	1	
26:1	Ap. ad Const. 3	Q	1		1	1
26:14	Hist. Arian. 39.3	C	1		1	1
	De decretis 1	Ad		1	1	1
26:25	Ap. ad Const. 3	R	1		1	1
26:25-26	Ap. ad Const. 25	R	1		1	1
26:26	Or. de Inc. Verb.	Q	1	1	1	
				Totals=	116	75
				Difference=		65%

Note: * = 1 word only   Ad= Adaptation

C=Citation   Q= Quotation

A/All= Allusion   R= Reminisence

APPENDIX D
THE APOSTOLOS OF ATHANASIUS IN THE CRITICAL
APPARATUS OF NA²⁷ AND UBS⁴

The following list indicates places in the Apparatus of NA²⁷ and UBS⁴ in which Athanasius' witness to the text of the Apostolos may be included. No references will be noted where Athanasius' witness is already cited correctly and only those places where the editions already provide an apparatus will be listed. Athanasius' reading is indicated, followed by either the designation *txt* (which indicates agreement with the reading given in the text of the edition) or *v.l.* (which indicates agreement with one of the variant readings). Instances where the apparatus incorrectly cites Athanasius' witness will be indicated.

THE APOSTOLOS OF ATHANASIUS IN THE APPARATUS OF NA²⁷

Acts 2:36	εποιησεν ο θεος (txt)
Acts 7:50	ταυτα παντα (txt)
Acts 7:56	διηνοιγμενους (txt)
Acts 8:32	κειροντος (v.l.)
Acts 8:33	ταπεινωσει αυτου (txt)
Acts 8:34	λεγει περι (v.l.)
Acts 14:17	εαυτον αφηκεν (v.l.); υετους διδους (txt)
Acts 25:16	ανθρωπον πριν (txt)
Rom 1:24	διο και παρεδωκεν (v.l.)
Rom 1:27	δε (v.l.)
Rom 3:30	επειπερ (v.l.)
Rom 8:28	συνεργει ο θεος (v.l.); το αγαθον (v.l.)
Rom 10:20	εγενομην τοις (txt)
1 Cor 2:9	α (txt)
1 Cor 3:16	οικει εν υμιν (txt)
1 Cor 3:20	ανθρωπων (v.l.)
1 Cor 4:6	α (txt); γεγραπται φυσιουσθαι (txt)
1 Cor 5:7	το πασχα ημων (txt)
1 Cor 5:13	εξαρατε (txt)
1 Cor 6:10	θεου κληρονομησουσιν (txt)
1 Cor 8:8	παραστησει (txt)
1 Cor 9:16	ευαγγελιζωμαι (v.l.)
1 Cor 11.2	υμας οτι παντα (txt)
1 Cor 15:47	ανθρωπος εξ ουρανου (txt)
1 Cor 15:54	οταν δε το θνητον τουτο ενδυσηται αθανασιαν (v.l.)
1 Cor 15:55	που σου θανατε το νικος που σου αδη το κεντρον (v.l.)
1 Cor 16:23	Χριστου (v.l.)

2 Cor 1:10	και ρυσεται (txt)
2 Cor 5:10	του σωματος επραξεν (v.l.)
2 Cor 5:14	οτι ει (v.l.)
2 Cor 5:17	τα παντα καινα (v.l.)
2Cor 11:3	και της αγνοτητος (txt)
Eph 2:15	εαυτω (v.l.)
Eph 3:18	υψος και βαθος (txt)
Eph 3:19	πληρωθητε εις (txt)
Eph 6:12	σκοτους τουτου (txt)
Phil 2:5	τοῦτο φρον- (txt); φρονεισθω (v.l.)
Phil 2:9	αυτω ονομα (v.l.)
Phil 2:11	εξομολογησηται (txt)
Phil 3:14	εις (txt)
Col 1:12	τω θεω και πατρι (v.l.); ικανωσαντι (txt)
Col 1:16	τα παντα τα τε (v.l.); ουρανοις και τα (v.l.)
2 Tim 1:10	Ιησου Χριστου (v.l.)
2 Tim 2:14	επ ουδεν (txt)
2 Tim 2:18	την (txt)
Heb 1:3	δι εαυτου (v.l.); των αμαρτιων ημων ποιησαμενος (v.l.)
Heb 7:22	τοσουτον (v.l.); κρειττονος (v.l.)
Heb 8:6	νυνι (txt); τετυχηκε (v.l.)
Heb 11:32	Βαρακ Σαμψων (txt)
Heb 12:18	ορει (v.l.); και ζοφω (txt)
Heb 12:23	απογεγραμμενων εν ουρανοις (txt)
Jam 1:17	αποσκιασμα (txt)
Jam 1:20	ου κατεργαζεται (v.l.)
1 Peter 4:1	παθοντος υπερ ημων σαρκι (v.l.)
1 Peter 4:19	εαυτων ψυχας (v.l.)
1 John 3:5	ημων (v.l.)
1 John 5:20	η ζωη η αιωνιος (v.l.)

THE APOSTOLOS OF ATHANASIUS IN THE APPARATUS OF UBS[4]

Acts 13:23	Apparatus correct
Acts 17:31	Apparatus correct
Rom 8:28	συνεργει ο θεος (v.l.)
1 Cor 2:4	πειθοι σοφιας λογοις (txt)
1 Cor 5:4	ημων Ιησου Χριστου (v.l.)
1 Cor 15:47	Apparatus correct
1 Cor 15:54	οταν δε το θνητον τουτο ενδυσηται αθανασιαν[1] (v.l.)
1 Cor 15:55	Apparatus correct

---

[1] UBS[4] incorrectly lists Athanasius as supporting the reading of the text: οταν δε το φθαρτον τουτο ενδυσηται αφθαρσιαν και το θνητον τουτο ενδυσηται αθανασιαν.

2 Cor 1:10	Apparatus correct
2 Cor 5:17	Apparatus correct
2 Cor 11:3	και της αγνοτητος (txt)
Gal 1:8	ευαγγελισηται υμᾶς (v.l.)
Gal 4:6	Apparatus correct
Eph 3:19	Apparatus correct
Phil 2:5	τοῦτο φρον- (txt)
Phil 2:9	Apparatus correct
Phil 2:11	Apparatus correct
Col 1:12	Apparatus correct
Col 1:14	Apparatus correct
2 Tim 2:18	την (txt)
Heb 1:12	ελιξεις[2] (txt); αυτους και Apparatus correct
James 1:8	Apparatus correct
James 1:17	Apparatus correct
1 Peter 4:1	Apparatus correct
1 John 3:5	Apparatus correct

---

[2] UBS[4] incorrectly lists Athanasius as supporting the variant reading αλλαξεις

BIBLIOGRAPHY

CRITICAL EDITIONS OF ATHANASIUS' WRITINGS

Bartelink, G. J. M., ed. *Athanase d'Alexandrie: Vie d'Antoine–Introduction, texte critique, traduction, notes et Index.* Sources chrétiennes 400. Paris: Editions du Cerf, 1994.

Brennecke, Hans Christof, Uta Heil, and Annette von Stockhausen, eds. *Athanasius Werke: Die "Apologien"–Apologia ad Constantium, Epistula ad Joannem et Antiochum, Epistula ad Palladium, Epistula ad Dracontium, Epistula ad Afros, Tomus ad Antiochenos, Epistula ad Jovianum, Epistula Joviani ad Athanasium, Petitiones Arianorum.* Vol. (Band) 2, Lieferung 8. Berlin: de Gruyter, 2006.

Halkin, Francisci, ed. *Sancti Pachomii Vitae Graecae. Subsidia Hagiographica.* Bruxelles: Société des Bollandistes, 1932.

Hall, Stuart George. Review of Karin Metzler, ed. *Athanasius Werke.* I/i. *Die dogmatischen Schriften. 2. Lieferung. Orationes I et II Contra Arianos. Journal of Theological Studies* 51, no. 1 (2000): 329-336.

―――. Review of Karin Metzler, ed. *Athanasius Werke.* I/i. *Die dogmatischen Schriften. 3. Lieferung. Oratio III Contra Arianos. Journal of Theological Studies* 53, no. 1 (2002): 333-337.

Joannou, P.-P., ed. *Fonti. Fasciolo ix. Discipline générale antique (ii-ix s.). Les canon des pères grecs.* Rome: Tipographia Italo-Orientale "S.Nilo", 1963.

Kannengiesser, Charles, ed. *Athanase d'Alexandrie: Sur l' incarnation du Verbe: Introduction, Texte Critique, Traduction Notes et Index.* Sources chrétiennes 199. Paris: Editions du Cerf, 1973.

Leone, Luigi, ed. *Sancti Athanasii, Archiepiscopi Alexandriae: Contra Gentes–Introduzione, Testo Critico, Traduzione.* Collana di Studi Greci 43. Napoli: Libreria Scientifica Editrice, 1965.

Ludwig, Georgius, ed. *Athanasii Epistula ad Epictetum.* Jenae: Typis H. Pohle, 1911.

Metzler, Karin, Dirk U. Hansen, and Kyriakos Savvidis, eds. *Athanasius Werke: Die Dogmatischen Schriften - Epistula ad Episcopos, Aegypti et Libyae.* Vol. (Band) 1, Teil 1, Lieferung 1. Berlin: de Gruyter, 1996.

Metzler, Karin and Kyriakos Savvidis, eds. *Athanasius Werke: Die Dogmatischen Schriften - Orationes I et II Contra Arianos.* Vol. (Band) 1, Teil 1, Lieferung 2. Berlin: de Gruyter, 1998.

―――, eds. *Athanasius Werke: Die Dogmatischen Schriften - Oratio III Contra Arianos.* Vol. (Band) 1, Teil 1, Lieferung 3. Berlin: de Gruyter, 2000.

Orlandi, Tito, ed. *Testi Copti: 1) Encomio de Atanasio. 2) Vita di Atanasio; Edizione critica, Traduzione e commento di Tito Orlandi. Testi e documenti per lo studio dell'antichità.* Milano: Istituto Editoriale Cisilpano, 1968.

Szymusiak, Jan M., ed. *Athanase d'Alexandrie: deux apologies, à l'empereur Constance et apologie pour sa fuite–Introduction, texte critique, traduction et notes.* Sources chrétiennes 56. Paris: Editions du Cerf, 1987.

Thomson, Robert W., ed. *Athanasius: Contra Gentes and De Incarnatione.* Oxford: Clarendon, 1971.

Winstedt, E. O., ed. *The Christian Topography of Cosmas Indicopleustes*. Cambridge: Cambridge University Press, 1909.

Wolska-Conus, Wanda, ed. *Cosmas Indicopleustes: Topographie chrétienne*. Sources chrétiennes 197. Paris: Editions du Cerf, 1973.

BIBLICAL TEXT: MANUSCRIPTS, EDITIONS AND COLLATIONS

Aland, Kurt, Matthew Black, Carlo M. Martini, Bruce M. Metzger, and Allen P. Wikgren, eds. *The Greek New Testament*. 4th ed. Stuttgart: United Bible Societies, 1993. (UBS⁴).

———, eds. *Nestle-Aland Novum Testamentum Graece*. 27th ed. Stuttgart: Deutsche Bibelgesellschaft, 1994.

Athos, Dionysiu, 124 (37). (Gregory-Aland 945). Microfilm from Ancient Biblical Manuscript Centre (ABMC). Claremont, California.

Athos, Kutlumusiu, 356. (Gregory-Aland 1704). Microfilm at Institut für Neutestamentliche Textforschung (INTF). Münster, Germany.

Athos, Lavra, A' 51. (Gregory-Aland 1073). Microfilm at Institut für Neutestamentliche Textforschung (INTF). Münster, Germany.

Athos, Lavra, A' 88. (Gregory-Aland 049). Microfilm from Ancient Biblical Manuscript Centre (ABMC). Claremont, California.

Athos, Lavra, B' 52. (Gregory-Aland Ψ 044). Microfilm from Ancient Biblical Manuscript Centre (ABMC). Claremont, California.

Brogan, John Jay. "The Text of the Gospels in the Writings of Athanasius." PhD. diss., Department of Religion, Duke University, 1997.

Brooks, James A. *The New Testament Text of Gregory of Nyssa*. Society of Biblical Literature The New Testament in the Greek Fathers 2. Atlanta: Scholars Press, 1991.

Chicago/Ill., *Jesuit-Krauss-McCormick Libr., Gruber Ms. 152*. (Gregory-Aland 1424). Microfilm from Ancient Biblical Manuscript Centre (ABMC). Claremont, California.

Clark, Kenneth Willis. *Eight American Praxapostoloi*. Chicago: University of Chicago Press, 1941.

Codex Bezae Cantabrigiensis Quattor Evangelia et Actus Apostolorum complectens Graece et Latine Sumptibus Academiae phototypice repraesentatus. Cambridge: Cambridge University Press, 1899.

Comfort, Philip W. and David P. Barrett. *The Text of the Earliest New Testament Greek Manuscripts: A Corrected, Enlarged Edition of The Earliest New Testament Manuscripts*. Wheaton: Tyndale House, 2001.

Cosaert, Carl P. *The Text of the Gospels in Clement of Alexandria*. Society of Biblical Literature The New Testament in the Greek Fathers 9. Atlanta: Society of Biblical Literature, 2008.

Ehrman, Bart D. *Didymus the Blind and the Text of the Gospels*. Society of Biblical Literature The New Testament in the Greek Fathers 1. Atlanta: Scholars Press, 1986.

Ehrman, Bart D., Gordon D. Fee, and Michael W. Holmes. *The Text of the Fourth Gospel in the Writings of Origen*. Society of Biblical Literature The New Testament in the Greek Fathers 3. Atlanta: Scholars Press, 1992.

Elliott, W. J. "The Relationship between MSS 322 and 323 of the Greek New Testament." *Journal of Theological Studies* 18 (1967): 423-425.

———. "An Examination of Von Soden's IB² Group of Manuscripts." MA thesis, University of Birmingham, Dept. of Theology, 1969.

Hannah, Darrell D. *The Text of 1 Corinthians in the Writings of Origen.* Society of Biblical Literature The New Testament in the Greek Fathers 4. Atlanta: Scholars Press, 1997.

Hansell, Eduardus H., ed. *Novum Testamentum Graece: Antiquissimorum codicum textus in ordine parallelo dispositi, accedit collatio codicis Sinaitici.* 3 vols. Oxford: Oxford University, 1864.

Hatch, William Henry Paine. *The Principal Uncial Manuscripts of the New Testament.* Chicago: The University of Chicago Press, 1939.

———. "On the Relationship of Codex Augiensis and Codex Boernerianus of the Pauline Epistles." *Harvard Studies in Classical Philology* 60 (1951): 187-199.

Herren, Luc. "New Testament Transcripts Prototype." No pages. Online: http://nttranscripts.uni-muenster.de/AnaServer?NTtranscripts+0+start.anv

Jerusalem, Orthod. Patriarchat, Saba, 107; St. Petersburg, Ross. Nac. Bibl., Gr. 317. (Gregory-Aland 1891). Microfilm from Ancient Biblical Manuscript Centre (ABMC). Claremont, California.

Jerusalem, Orthod. Patriarchat, Stavru 94. (Gregory-Aland 1352). Microfilm from Ancient Biblical Manuscript Centre (ABMC). Claremont, California.

Junack, K., E. Güting, U. Nimtz, and K. Witte, eds. *Das Neue Testament Auf Papyrus: Die Paulinischen Briefe. Teil 1: Röm., 1 Kor., 2 Kor.* ANTF 12. Berlin: de Gruyter, 1989.

Kasser, Rudolf. *Papyrus Bodmer XVII: Actes des Apôtres, Epîtres de Jacques, Pierre, Jean et Jude.* Cologny, 1961.

Kenyon, Frederic George, ed. *The Codex Alexandrinus in Reduced Photographic Fascimile: New Testament and the Clementine Epistles.* London: British Museum, 1909.

———. *The Chester Beatty Biblical Papyri, fasc. 3, supp. 3.1, Pauline Epistles, Text.* London: Emery Walker, 1936.

———. *The Chester Beatty Biblical Papyri, fasc. 3, supp. 3.2, Pauline Epistles, Plates.* London: Emery Walker, 1937.

Lake, Kirsopp and Helen Lake. *Codex Sinaiticus Petropolitanus.* Oxford: Clarendon Press, 1911.

London, Brit. Lib., m Butler 2, Ms 11,387. (Gregory-Aland 201). Microfilm from Ancient Biblical Manuscript Centre (ABMC). Claremont, California.

London, Brit. Libr., Add. 20003; Alexandria, Bibl. Patriarch., 59. (Gregory-Aland 81). Microfilm from Ancient Biblical Manuscript Centre (ABMC). Claremont, California.

London, Brit. Libr., Harley 5537. (Gregory-Aland 104). Microfilm from Ancient Biblical Manuscript Centre (ABMC). Claremont, California.

Modena, Bibl. Estense, α. V. 6.3 (G. 196). (Gregory-Aland H 014). Microfilm from Ancient Biblical Manuscript Centre (ABMC). Claremont, California.

Mullen, Roderic L. *The New Testament Text of Cyril of Jerusalem.* Society of Biblical Literature The New Testament in the Greek Fathers 7. Atlanta: Scholars Press, 1997.

Osburn, Carroll D. *The Text of the Apostolos in Epiphanius of Salamis.* Society of Biblical Literature The New Testament in the Greek Fathers 6. Atlanta: Society of Biblical Literature, 2004.

Oxford, Bodl. Libr., Auct E. 5.9. (Gregory-Aland 325). Microfilm at Institut für Neutestamentliche Textforschung (INTF). Münster, Germany.

Oxford, Bodl. Libr., Auct. T. inf 1.10. (Gregory-Aland 105). Microfilm at Institut für Neutestamentliche Textforschung (INTF). Münster, Germany.

Paris, Bibl. Nat. Gr. 14. (Gregory-Aland 33). Microfilm from Ancient Biblical Manuscript Centre (ABMC). Claremont, California.

Patmos, Joannu, 16. (Gregory-Aland 1175). Microfilm at Institut für Neutestamentliche Textforschung (INTF). Münster, Germany.

Racine, Jean-François. *The Text of Matthew in the Writings of Basil of Caesarea.* Society of Biblical Literature The New Testament in the Greek Fathers 5. Atlanta: Society of Biblical Literature, 2004.

Reichardt, Alexander, ed. *Der Codex Boernerianus: Der Briefe Des Apostels Paulus.* Leipzig: Karl W. Hiersemann, 1909.

Roma, Bibl. Angelica, 39. (Gregory-Aland L 020). Microfilm from Ancient Biblical Manuscript Centre (ABMC). Claremont, California.

Roma, Bibl. Vatic., Ottob. Gr. 298. (Gregory-Aland 630). Microfilm at Institut für Neutestamentliche Textforschung (INTF). Münster, Germany.

Schmid, Josef. *Studien zur Geschichte des griechischen Apokalypse-Textes.* 3 vols. Munich: Karl Zink Verlag, 1955-1956.

Scrivener, Frederick Henry A. *A Full and Exact Collation of About Twenty Greek Manuscripts of The Holy Gospels, (Hitherto Unexamined), Deposited in the British Museum, The Archiepiscopal Library at Lambeth, &c. with a Critical Introduction.* Cambridge: John W. Parker & Son, 1853.

———. *An Exact Transcript of the Codex Augiensis.* Cambridge: Deighton, Bell & Co., 1859.

———, ed. *Bezae Codex Cantabrigiensis.* Cambridge: Deighton, Bell and Co., 1864.

Smith, William Benjamin. "The Pauline Manuscripts F and G: A Text-Critical Study. Part 1." *The American Journal of Theology* 7, no. 3 (1903): 452-485.

———. "The Pauline Manuscripts F and G: A Text-Critical Study. Part 2." *The American Journal of Theology* 7, no. 4 (1903): 662-688.

Swanson, Reuben Joseph, ed. *New Testament Greek Manuscripts: Acts. Variant Readings Arranged in Horizontal Lines Against Codex Vaticanus.* Wheaton: Tyndale House, 1998.

———, ed. *New Testament Greek Manuscripts: Galatians. Variant Readings Arranged in Horizontal Lines Against Codex Vaticanus.* Wheaton: Tyndale House, 1999.

———, ed. *New Testament Greek Manuscripts: 2 Corinthians. Variant Readings Arranged in Horizontal Lines Against Codex Vaticanus.* Wheaton: Tyndale House, 2005.

Testuz, Michael, ed. *Papyrus Bodmer VII-IX.* Cologny: Bibliotheca Bodmeriana, 1959.

Tischendorf, Constantinus, ed. *Epistulae Pauli Omnes: Ex Codice Parisiensi Celeberrimo Nomine Claromontani Plerumque Dicto.* Leipzig: F. A. Brockhaus, 1852.

———, ed. *Epistulae Pauli et Catholicae: fere integrae ex Libro Porphryii Episcopi Palimpsesto. Monumenta Sacra Inedita (Nova collectio).* Leipzig: J. C. Hindrichs, 1865.

———, ed. *Apocalypsis et Actus Apostolorum: Duobus Codicibus Palimpsestis, Altero Porphryii Episcopi. Monumenta Sacra Inedita (Nova collectio).* Leipzig: J. C. Hindrichs, 1869.

————, ed. *Novum Testamentum Graece*. Octava Critica Maior ed. 2 vols. Leipzig: Giesecke & Devrient, 1869-1872.

Valentine-Richards, A.V., ed. *The Text of Acts in Codex 614 (Tisch. 137) and its Allies*. Cambridge: Cambridge University Press, 1934.

Westcott, Brooke Foss and Fenton John Anthony Hort. *The New Testament in the Original Greek*. 2 vols. London: Macmillan & Co., 1881, 1882.

βιβλια, τα ἱερα. *Novum Testamentum e Codice Vaticano Graeco 1209 (Codex B): tertia vice phototypice expressum*., Biblioteca apostolica vaticana. Codices e Vaticanus selecti quam simillime expressi. ser. maior. In Civitate Vaticana: Ex Bibliotheca Apostolica Vaticana, 1968.

MULTIVARIATE ANALYSIS

Afifi, Abdelmonem, Virginnia A. Clark, and Susanne May. *Computer-Aided Multivariate Analysis*. 4th ed. Texts in Statistical Science. Boca Raton, Fla.: Chapman & Hall, 2004.

Bergmann, Reinhard, John Ludbrook, and Will P. J. M. Spooren. "Different Outcomes of the Wilcoxon-Mann-Whitney Test from Different Statistics Packages." *The American Statistician* 54, no. 1 (2000): 72-77.

Chatfield, Christopher and Alexander J. Collins. *Introduction to Multivariate Analysis*. London: Chapman & Hall, 1980.

Cleveland, William S. *The Elements of Graphing Data*. Rev. ed. New Jersey: Hobart Press, 1994.

Cox, Trevor F. and Michael A. A. Cox. *Multidimensional Scaling*. 2d ed. Monographs on Statistics and Applied Probability 88. Boca Raton, Fla.: Chapman & Hall, 2001.

Everitt, Brian. *An R and S-Plus Companion to Multivariate Analysis*. Springer Texts in Statistics. London: Springer, 2005.

Finney, Timothy J. "The Ancient Witnesses of the Epistle to the Hebrews: A computer-assisted analysis of the papyrus and uncial manuscripts of προς εβραιους." PhD diss., Murdoch University, 1999.

————. "Analysis of Textual Variation." No pages. Cited 17 April 2009. Online: http://purl.org/tfinney/ATV/book/.

Floud, Roderick. *An Introduction to Quantitative Methods for Historians*. London: Methuen & Co., 1973.

Groenen, Patrick J.F. and Michael van de Velden. "Multidimensional scaling." *Econometric Institute Report EI 2004-15 (2004)*: 1-14.

Libby, James A. "An Introduction to the Use of Advanced Data Reduction Approaches to Address Longstanding Issues in Biblical Studies." Paper presented at the Annual Conference of the SBL. San Diego, November 19, 2007.

Lutz, Mark and David Ascher. *Learning Python*. Sebastopol, Calif.: O'Reilly, 1999.

Maindonald, John and John Braun. *Data Analysis and Graphics using R–An Example Based Approach*. 2d ed., Cambridge Series in Statistical and Probabilistic Mathematics. Cambridge: Cambridge University Press, 2007.

Manly, Bryan F. J. *Multivariate Statistical Methods: A Primer*. 2d ed. London: Chapman & Hall, 1994.

Metropolis, Nicholas and Stanislaw Ulam. "The Monte Carlo Method." *Journal of the American Statistical Association* 44, no. 247 (1949): 335-341.

Murrell, Paul. *R Graphics.* Boca Raton, Fla.: Chapman & Hall, 2006.

R Development Core Team. "R: A language and environment for statistical computing." (2007): No pages. Online: http://www.R-project.org

Thorpe, J. C. "Multivariate Statistical Analysis for Manuscript Classification." No pages. Cited 1 December 2008. Online: http://rosetta.reltech.org/TC/vol07/Thorpe2002.html

Tufte, Edward R. *The Visual Display of Quantitative Information.* Cheshire, Conn.: Graphics Press, 1983.

Venables, W. N. and B. D. Ripley. *Modern Applied Statistics with S.* 4th ed., Statistics and Computing. New York: Springer, 2002.

Willker, Wieland. "Principal Component Analysis of Manuscripts of the Gospel of John." No pages. Cited 1 December 2008. Online: http://www-user.uni-bremen.de/~wie/pub/Analysis-PCA.html

GENERAL BIBLIOGRAPHY

Abramowski, Luise. "Die dritte Arianerrede des Athanasius: Eusebianer und Arianer und das westliche Serdicense." *Zeitschrift für Kirchengeschichte* 102, no. 3 (1991): 389–413.

Aland, Kurt. *Kurzgefasste Liste der griechischen Handschriften des Neuen Testaments.* Arbeiten zur neutestamentlichen Textforschung 1. Berlin: de Gruyter, 1994.

Aland, Kurt and Barbara Aland. *The Text of the New Testament: An Introduction to the Critical Editions and to the Theory and Practice of Modern Textual Criticism.* Translated by Erroll F. Rhodes. 2d ed. Grand Rapids: Eerdmans, 1989.

Altaner, Berthold. *Patrology.* Translated by Hilda C. Graef. Freiburg: Herder, 1960.

Anatolios, Khaled. *Athanasius.* The Early Church Fathers. London: Routledge, 2004.

Arnold, Duane W. H. *The Early Episcopal Career of Athanasius of Alexandria.* Christianity and Judaism in Antiquity 6. Notre Dame, Ind.: University of Notre Dame Press, 1991.

Barnard, L. W. "The Date of S. Athanasius' 'Vita Antonii'." *Vigiliae Christianae* 28 (1974): 169–175.

Barnes, Timothy D. *Athanasius and Constantius: Theology and Politics in the Constantinian Empire.* Cambridge, Mass.: Harvard University Press, 1993.

Bauer, Walter. *A Greek-English Lexicon of the New Testament and Other Early Christian Literature.* 2d ed. Chicago: University of Chicago Press, 1979.

Bell, Harold Idris, ed. *Jews and Christians in Egypt: The Jewish Troubles in Alexandria and the Athanasian Controversy.* London: Oxford University Press, 1924.

Brakke, David. *Athanasius and the Politics of Asceticism.* Baltimore: John Hopkins University, 1998.

Brennan, B. R. "Dating Athanasius' 'Vita Antonii'." *Vigiliae Christianae* 30 (1976): 52–54.

Bright, William. *The Orations of Saint Athanasius against the Arians according to the Benedictine Text, with an account of His Life.* Translated by William Bright. Oxford: Clarendon Press, 1873.

Brogan, John Jay. "Another Look at Codex Sinaiticus." Pages 17–32 in *The Bible as Book: The Transmission of the Greek Text*. Edited by Scot McKendrick and Orlaith A. O'Sullivan. London: The British Library, 2003.

Broman, Vincent. Review of Roderic L. Mullen, *The New Testament Text of Cyril of Jerusalem*. *TC: A Journal of Biblical Textual Criticism* 2 (1997): No pages. Cited 12 April 2007. Online: http://rosetta.reltech.org/TC/vol02/Mullen1997rev.html

Brown, Charles Gordon and James Edward Swallow, eds. *Select Orations of Saint Gregory Nazianzen*. In vol. 7 of *The Nicene and Post-Nicene Fathers*, Series 2. Edited by Philip Schaff and Henry Wace. 1894. Peabody, Mass.: Hendrickson, 1994.

Butterweck, Christel. *Athanasius von Alexandrien: Bibliographie*. Abhandlungen der Nordhein-Westfälischen Akademie der Wissenschaften 90. Opladen: Westdeutscher Verlag, 1995.

Carlson, Stephen C. "The Origin(s) of the 'Caesarean' Text." Paper presented at the Annual Conference of the SBL. San Antonio, Tex., November 20, 2004.

Casey, Robert Pierce. "Greek Manuscripts of Athanasian Corpora." *Zeitschrift für die neutestamentliche Wissenschaft und die Kunde der älteren Kirche* 30 (1931): 49-70.

———. "The Patristic Evidence for the Text of the New Testament." Pages 69–80 in *New Testament Manuscript Studies*. Edited by Merrill M. Parvis and Allen P. Wikgren. Chicago: University of Chicago Press, 1950.

———. "Armenian Manuscripts of St. Athanasius of Alexandria." *The Harvard Theological Review* 24, no. 1 (Jan., 1931): 43–59.

Colwell, Ernest C. "Method in Evaluating Scribal Habits: A Study of P^{45}, P^{66}, P^{75}." Pages 106–24 in *Studies in Methodology in Textual Criticism of the New Testament*. New Testament Tools and Studies 9. Leiden: Brill, 1969.

Colwell, Ernest C. and Ernest W. Tune. "The Quantitative Relationships Between Ms Text-Types." Pages 25–32 in *Biblical and Patristic Studies in Memory of Robert Pierce Casey*. Edited by J. Neville Birdsall and Robert W. Thompson. Frieburg im Breisgau: Herder, 1963. Repr., as pages 56–62 in *Studies in Methodology in Textual Criticism of the New Testament*. Leiden: Brill, 1969.

———. "Method in Classifying and Evaluating Variant Readings." Pages 96–105 in *Studies in Methodology in Textual Criticism of the New Testament*. New Testament Tools and Studies 9. Leiden: E. J. Brill, 1969. Repr., from *Journal of Biblical Literature* 83 (1964): 253–61.

Conybeare, Fred C. "On the Sources of the Text of S. Athanasius." *Journal of Philology* 24, no. 48 (1896): 284–299.

Drake, H. A. "Athanasius' First Exile." *Greek, Roman and Byzantine Studies* 27, no. 2 (1986: Summer): 193–204.

Ehrman, Bart D. "The Use of Group Profiles for the Classification of New Testament Documentary Evidence." *Journal of Biblical Literature* 106, no. 3 (1987): 465–486.

———. "Methodological Developments in the Analysis and Classification of New Testament Documentary Evidence." *Novum Testamentum* 29, no. 1 (1987): 22–45.

———. *The Orthodox Corruption of Scripture: The Effect of Early Christological Controversies on the Text of the New Testament*. New York: Oxford University Press, 1993.

———. "The Use of the Church Fathers in New Testament Textual Criticism." Pages 155–165 in *The Bible as Book: The Transmission of the Greek Text*. Edited by Scot McKendrick and Orlaith A. O'Sullivan. London: The British Library, 2003.

Elliott, J. K. *A Bibliography of Greek New Testament Manuscripts*. 2d ed. Society for New Testament Studies Monograph Series 109. Cambridge: Cambridge University Press, 2000.

Epp, Eldon Jay. "Toward the Clarification of the Term 'Textual Variant.'" Pages 47–61 in *Studies in the Theory and Method of New Testament Textual Criticism*. Studies and Documents 45. Grand Rapids: Eerdmans, 1993.

———. "The Claremont Profile Method for Grouping New Testament Miniscule Manuscripts." Pages 211–220 in *Studies in the Theory and Method of New Testament Textual Criticism*. Studies and Documents 45. Grand Rapids: Eerdmans, 1993.

———. "The Multivalence of the Term 'Original Text' in New Testament Textual Criticism." *Harvard Theological Review* 92, no. 3 (1999): 245–281.

———. "It's All about Variants: A Variant Conscious Approach to New Testament Textual Criticism." *Harvard Theological Review* 100, no. 3 (2007): 275–308.

Ernest, James D. "Athanasius of Alexandria: The Scope of Scripture in Polemical and Pastoral Context." *Vigiliae Christianae* 47 (1993): 341–362.

———. *The Bible in Athanasius of Alexandria*. The Bible in Ancient Christianity 2. Boston: Brill, 2004.

Fee, Gordon D. "Codex Sinaiticus in the Gospel of John: A Contribution to Methodology in Establishing Textual Relationships," Pages 221–44 in *Studies in the Theory and Method of New Testament Textual Criticism*. Studies and Documents 45. Grand Rapids: Eerdmans, 1993. Repr., from New Testament Studies 15 (1968/69): 23–44.

———. "P^{75}, P^{66}, and Origen: The Myth of Early Textual Recension in Alexandria," Pages 247–73 in *Studies in the Theory and Method of New Testament Textual Criticism*. Studies and Documents 45. Grand Rapids: Eerdmans, 1993. Repr., from Pages 19–45 in *New Dimensions in New Testament Study* Edited by Richard N. Longenecker and Merrill C. Tenney. Grand Rapids: Zondervan, 1974.

———. "The Text of John in Origen and Cyril of Alexandria: A Contribution to Methodology in the Recovery and Analysis of Patristic Citations," Pages 301–34 in *Studies in the Theory and Method of New Testament Textual Criticism*. Studies and Documents 45. Grand Rapids: Eerdmans, 1993. Repr., from *Biblica* 52 (1971): 357–394.

———. "The Text of John in *The Jerusalem Bible*: A Critique of the Use of Patristic Citations in New Testament Textual Criticism," Pages 335–43 in *Studies in the Theory and Method of New Testament Textual Criticism*. Studies and Documents 45. Grand Rapids: Eerdmans, 1993. Repr., from *Journal of Biblical Literature* 90 (1971): 163–173.

———. "The Use of Greek Patristic Citations in New Testament Textual Criticism: The State of the Question," Pages 344–359 in *Studies in the Theory and Method of New Testament of New Testament Textual Criticism*. Studies and Documents 45. Grand Rapids: Eerdmans, 1993.

———. "The Use of the Greek Fathers for New Testament Textual Criticism," Pages 191–207 in *The Text of the New Testament in Contemporary Research: Essays on the Status Quaestionis*. Studies and Documents 46. Grand Rapids: Eerdmans, 1995.

Geer, Thomas C., Jr. "The Two Faces of Codex 33 in Acts." *Novum Testamentum* 31, no. 1 (1989): 39–47.

———. *Family 1739 in Acts*. Society of Biblical Literature Monograph Series 48. Atlanta: Scholars Press, 1994.

Geerard, Maurice, ed., *Clavis patrum graecorum* 5 vols. Turnhout: Brepols, 1974–1987.

Gonzalez, Justo L. *A History of Christian Thought.* 3 vols. Rev. ed. Nashville: Abingdon Press, 1970.

Grant, Robert M. "Theological Education at Alexandria," Pages 178–189 in *The Roots of Egyptian Christianity.* Edited by Birger A. Pearson and James E. Goehring. Philadelphia: Fortress, 1986.

Greenlee, J Harold. *Introduction to New Testament Textual Criticism.* Grand Rapids: Eerdmans, 1964.

Gregg, Robert C., ed. *Arianism: Historical and Theological Reassesments.* Patristic Monograph Series 11. Cambridge, Mass.: The Philadelphia Patristic Foundation, 1985.

Gwatkin, Henry Melvill. *Studies of Arianism.* 2d ed. Cambridge: Deighton, Bell & Co., 1900.

Gwynn, David M. *The Eusebians: The polemic of Athanasius of Alexandria and the construction of the 'Arian controversy'.* Oxford Theological Monographs. Oxford: Oxford University Press, 2007.

Hanson, R. P. C. "The Source and Significance of the Fourth 'Oratio contra Arianos' attributed to Athanasius." *Vigiliae Christianae* 42 (1988): 257–266.

Hollerich, Michael J. "The Alexandrian Bishops and the Grain Trade: Ecclesiastical Commerce in Late Roman Egypt." *Journal of the Economic and Social History of the Orient* 25, no. 2 (1982): 187–207.

Holmes, Michael W. "The Case for Reasoned Eclecticism," Pages 77–100 in *Rethinking New Testament Textual Criticism.* Edited by David A. Black. Grand Rapids: Baker Academic, 2002.

Hurtado, Larry W. *Text-Critical Methodology and the pre-Caesarean Text: Codex W in the Gospel of Mark.* Studies and Documents 43. Grand Rapids: Eerdmans, 1981.

Jones, A. H. M. "The Date of the 'Apologia Contra Arianos' of Athanasius." *Journal of Theological Studies* 5 (1954): 224–227.

Jongkind, Dirk. *Scribal Habits of Codex Sinaiticus.* Texts and Studies: Third Series 5. Piscataway, N.J.: Gorgias Press, 2007.

Kannengiesser, Charles, "Athanasius of Alexandria, *Three Orations Against the Arians*: A Reappraisal." *Studia Patristica* 18, no. 3 (1982): 981–995. Repr., as Chapter IX in *Arius and Athanasius.* Hampshire: Variorum, 1991.

———. "The Athanasian decade 1974–84: A Bibliographical Report." *Theological Studies* 46 (1985): 524–541.

———. "Athanasius of Alexandria vs. Arius: The Alexandrian Crisis," Pages 204–15 in *The Roots of Egyptian Christianity.* Edited by Birger A. Pearson and James E. Goehring. Philadelphia: Fortress, 1986.

———. *Arius and Athanasius: Two Alexandrian Theologians.* Collected Studies Series CS353. Hampshire: Variorum, 1991.

———. "The Dating of Athanasius' Double Apology and Three Treatises Against the Arians." *Zeitschrift für Antikes Christentum* 10, no. 1 (2006): 19–33.

———, ed. *Handbook of Patristic Exegesis.* The Bible in Ancient Christianity. Edited by D. Jeffrey Bingham. Leiden: Brill, 2006.

Kilpatrick, George D. "Atticism and the Text of the Greek New Testament," Pages 125–137 in *Neutestamentliche Aufsatze.* Edited by J. Blinzler, O. Kuss, and F. Mussner. Regensburg, 1963. Repr., as pages 15–32 in *The Principles and Practice of New*

Testament Textual Criticism: Collected Essays of G. D. Kilpatrick. Leuven: University Press, 1990.

Kim, Young Kyu. "Palaeographical Dating of $\mathfrak{P}^{46}$ to the Later First Century." *Biblica* 69 (1988): 248–257.

Lake, K. "Some Further Notes on the Mss of the Writings of St Athanasius." *Journal of Theological Studies* 5 (1904): 108–114.

Lake, Kirsopp and Robert Pierce Casey. "The Text of the De Virginitate of Athanasius." *The Harvard Theological Review* 19, no. 2 (1926): 173–190.

Lampe, G. W. H., ed. *A Patristic Greek Lexicon.* Oxford: Clarendon Press, 1961.

Leemans, Johan. "Thirteen Years of Athanasius Research (1985–1998): A Survey and Bibliography." *Sacris Erudiri* 39 (2000): 105–217.

Lorimer, W. L. "Critical notes on Athanasius." *Journal of Theological Studies* 40 (1939): 37–46.

Louth, A. "St. Athanasius and the Greek 'Life of Antony'." *Journal of Theological Studies* 39 (1988): 504–509.

Margerie, Bertrand de, *An Introduction to the History of Exegesis.* 3 vols. Petersham, Mass.: Saint Bede's Publications, 1993.

Martin, Annick. *Athanase d'Alexandrie et l'Eglise d'Egypte au IVe siècle : (328–373).* Collection de l'Ecole française de Rome 216. Rome: Ecole Française de Rome, 1996.

Martini, Carlo M. "Is There a Late Alexandrian Text of the Gospels?". *New Testament Studies* 24 (1977–78): 285–296.

Meijering, E. P. *Orthodoxy and Platonism in Athanasius: Synthesis or Antithesis?* Leiden: E. J. Brill, 1974.

Metzger, Bruce Manning. *The Text of the New Testament: Its Transmission, Corruption and Restoration.* 2d ed. Oxford: Clarendon Press, 1968.

Metzger, Bruce Manning and Bart D. Ehrman. *The Text of the New Testament: Its Transmission, Corruption and Restoration.* 4th ed. New York: Oxford University Press, 2005.

Metzler, Karin. *Welchen Bibeltexte Benutzte Athanasius im Exil?* Opladen: Westdeutscher Verlag, 1997.

Meyer, John R. "Athanasius' use of Paul in his Doctrine of Salvation." *Vigiliae Christianae* 52, no. 2 (May, 1998): 146–171.

Milne, H. J. M., T. C. Skeat, and Douglas Cockerell. *Scribes and Correctors of the Codex Sinaiticus.* London: British Museum, 1938.

Mink, Gerd. "Eine umfassende Genealogie der neutestamentlichen Überlieferung." *New Testament Studies* 39 (1993): 481–499.

———. "Editing and Genealogical Studies: The New Testament." *Literary and Linguistic Computing* 15 (2000): 51–56.

Morrill, Bruce. "The Classification of the Greek Manuscripts of First Corinthians." M.A. thesis, Harding Graduate School of Religion, 1981.

Nordberg, Henric. *Athanasius' Tractates Contra Gentes and De Incarnatione; An attempt at Redating.* Societas Scientiarum Fennica: Commentationes Humanorum Litterarum 28.3. Helsinki: Helsingfors, 1961.

———. "A Reconsideration of the Date of St. Athanasius' *Contra Gentes* and *De Incarnatione*," Pages 262–266. Studia Patristica 3. Berlin: Akademie Verlag, 1961.

———. "On the Bible Text of St. Athanasius." *Arctos* 3 (1962): 119–141.

————. *Athanasius and the Emperor.* Societas Scientarium Fennica: Commentationes Humanarum Litterarum 30.3. Helsinki: Helsingfors, 1963.

Opitz, Hans Georg, ed. *Athanasius Werke: Die "Apologien"-De decretis Nicaenae synodi, De sententia Dionysii, Apologia de fuga sua, Apologia contra Arianos, Epistula encyclica, Epistula ad Serapionem de morte Arii, Epistula ad monachos, Historia Arianorum, De syodis Arimini in Italia et Seleucia in Isauria.* Vol. (Band) 2, Lieferung 1–7. Berlin: de Gruyter, 1934–35.

Parker, D. C. *Codex Bezae: An Early Christian Manuscript and its Text.* Cambridge: Cambridge University Press, 1992.

Patrologia graeca. Edited by J.-P. Migne. 162 vols. Paris, 1857–1886.

Pettersen, Alvyn. *Athanasius.* London: Geoffrey Chapman, 1995.

Pickering, S. R. "The Dating of the Chester Beatty–Michigan Codex of the Pauline Epistles ($\mathfrak{P}^{46}$)," Pages 216–227 in *Ancient History in a Modern University: Early Christianity, Late Antiquity and Beyond.* Edited by T. W. Hillard, R. A. Kearsley, C. E. V. Nixon, and A. M. Nobbs. Grand Rapids: Eerdmans, 1998.

Pollard, T. E. "The Exegesis of Scripture and the Arian Controversy." *Bulletin of the John Rylands Library* 41 (1959): 414–429.

Quasten, Johannes. *Patrology.* 4 vols. Utrecht: Spectrum Publishers, 1960.

Richards, W. Larry. *The Classification of the Greek Manuscripts of the Johannine Epistles.* Society of Biblical Literature Dissertation Series 35. Missoula: Scholars Press, 1977.

Robertson, Archibald, ed. *Select Writings and Letters of Athanasius, Bishop of Alexandria.* In vol. 4 of *The Nicene and Post-Nicene Fathers,* Series 2. Edited by Philip Schaff and Henry Wace. 1894. 14 vols. Repr. Peabody, Mass.: Hendrickson, 1994.

Royce, James R. "Scribal Tendencies in the Transmission of the Text of the New Testament," Pages 239–52 in *The Text of the New Testament in Contemporary Research: Essays on the Status Questionis.* Studies and Documents 46. Grand Rapids: Eerdmans, 1995.

Ryan, George Jeremiah and Robert Pierce Casey, eds. *De incarnatione verbi Dei: Part 1. The Long Recension Manuscripts by George Jeremiah Ryan; Part 2. The Short Recension by Robert Pierce Casey.* Studies and Documents 14. London: Christophers, 1945–46.

Sanders, Henry A. "New Manuscripts of the Bible from Egypt." *American Journal of Archaeology* 12, no. 1 (Jan.–Mar., 1908): 49–55.

Sawirus ibn 'al-Muqaffa'. *History of the Patriarchs of the Coptic Church of Alexandria.* Patrologia Orientalis 2. Paris: Firmin-Didot, 1904.

Schwartz, Eduard. *Zur Geschichte des Athanasius.* Vol. 3 of *Gesammelte Schriften.* Berlin: de Gruyter, 1959.

Sieben, Hermann Josef. "Studien zur Psalterbenutzung des Athanasius von Alexandrien im Rahmen seiner Schriftauffassung und Schriftlesung." PhD diss., Institut Catholique zu Paris, 1968.

Simonetti, Manlio. *Biblical Interpretation in the Early Church: An Historical Introduction to Patristic Exegesis.* Translated by John A. Hughes. Edinburgh: T & T Clark, 1994.

Stead, George Christopher. "Rhetorical Method in Athanasius." *Vigiliae Christianae* 30 (1976): 121–137.

————. "The 'Thalia' of Arius and the Testimony of Athanasius." *Journal of Theological Studies* 29 (1978): 20–52.

————. Review of C. Kannengiesser, *"Athanase d'Alexandrie, évêque et écrivain." Journal of Theological Studies* 36 (1985): 220–29.

——. "Athanasius' Earliest Written Work." *Journal of Theological Studies* 39 (1988): 76–91.

——. "Athanasius als Exeget." Pages 174–184 in *Christliche Exegese zwischen Nicaea und Chalcedon*. Edited by J. van Oort and U. Wickert. Kampen: Kok Pharos, 1992.

Suggs, M. Jack. "The Use of Patristic Evidence in the Search for a Primitive New Testament Text." *New Testament Studies* 4 (1957–8): 139–147.

Thompson, Edward Maunde. *An Introduction to Greek and Latin Palaeography*. New York: Lenox Hill, 1912.

Trigg, Joseph W. *Biblical Interpretation*. Message of the Fathers of the Church 9. Wilmington, Del.: Michael Glazier, 1988.

von Lemm, O. *Koptische Fragmente zur Patriarchengeschichte Alexandriens*. Mémoires de l'Académie Impériale des sciences de St.-Pétersbourg. VIIe série; tome 36, no. 11. St.-Pétersbourg: Académie Impériale des sciences, 1888.

Wallis, F. "On Some Mss of the Writings of St. Athanasius: Part 1." *Journal of Theological Studies* 3 (1902): 97–109.

——. "On Some Mss of the Writings of St. Athanasius: Part 2." *Journal of Theological Studies* 3 (1902): 245–255.

Wasserman, Tommy. review of Carroll D. Osburn, *The Text of the Apostolos in Epiphanius of Salamis*. *Review of Biblical Literature* [http://www.bookreviews.org] (2005).

Weinandy, Thomas G. *Athanasius: A Theological Introduction*. Great Theologians Series. Aldershot, England: Ashgate, 2007.

Williams, Rowan. *Arius: Heresy and Tradition*. 2d ed. Grand Rapids: Eerdmans, 2002.

Winden, J. C. M. van. "On the Date of Athanasius' Apologetical Treatises." *Vigiliae Christianae* 29 (1975): 291–295.

Winstedt, E. O. "Notes from Cosmas Indicopleustes." *Journal of Theological Studies* 6 (1905): 282–285.

——. "A further note on Cosmas." *Journal of Theological Studies* 7 (1906): 626–629.

Wisse, Frederik. *The Profile Method for the Classification and Evaluation of Manuscript Evidence, as Applied to the Continuous Text of the Gospel of Luke*. Studies and Documents 44. Grand Rapids: Eerdmans, 1982.

Zamagni, Claudio. Review of James D. Ernest, *The Bible in Athanasius of Alexandria*. *Review of Biblical Literature* 8 (2006): 569–573.

Zervopoulos, Gerassimos. "The Gospels-Text of Athanasius." PhD diss., Boston University, 1955.

Zuntz, G. *The Text of the Epistles: A Disquisition upon the Corpus Paulinum*. London: Oxford University Press, 1953.

STATISTICS

Bauer, David F. "Constructing Confidence Sets Using Rank Statistics." *Journal of the American Statistical Association* 67 (1972): 687–690.

Hollander, Myles and Douglas A. Wolfe. *Nonparametric Statistical Methods*. New York: John Wiley & Sons, 1973.

Kaufman, Leonard and Peter J. Rousseeuw. *Finding Groups in Data: An Introduction to Cluster analysis*. New York: Wiley, 1989.

Metropolis, Nicholas. "The Beginning of the Monte Carlo Method." *Los Alamos Science* Special Issue (1987): 125–130.

Moore, David S. and George P. McCabe. *Introduction to the Practice of Statistics*. 4th ed. New York: Freeman, 2003.

Rowntree, Derek. *Statistics Without Tears: A Primer for Non-mathematicians*. London: Penguin Books, 1981.

Spatz, Chris and James O. Johnstone. *Basic Statistics: Tables of Distributions*. 2d ed. Belmont, Calif.: Wadsworth Inc., 1981.

Sprent, Peter. *Quick Statistics: An Introduction to Non-Parametric Methods*. Harmondsworth: Penguin Books, 1981.

van der Laan, Mark J., Katherine S. Pollard, and Jennifer Bryan. "A New Partitioning Around Medoids Algorithm." No pages. Cited 18 October 2008. Online: http://www.bepress.com/ucbbiostat/paper105.

CPSIA information can be obtained at www.ICGtesting.com
264225BV00003B/1/P

9 781589 835504